———————————————

"Trasumanar significar *per verba*
non si poria; pero l'esemplo basti
a cui esperienza grazia serba."

Paradiso I, 70–72.

Transhumanizing—its meaning to convey in words cannot
be done; but let the example suffice to whom grace grants
experience.

———————————————

Light from Light

AN ANTHOLOGY OF CHRISTIAN MYSTICISM

EDITED BY
LOUIS DUPRÉ &
JAMES A. WISEMAN, O.S.B.

PAULIST PRESS
New York ◊ Mahwah

Library of Congress Cataloging-in-Publication Data

Light from light : an anthology of Christian mysticism / edited by Louis Dupré and James A. Wiseman.
    p.   cm.
    Includes bibliographies and index.
    ISBN 0-8091-2943-4 (pbk.) : $12.95 (est.)   0-8091-0415-6 (cloth) : $24.95
    1. Mysticism.   I. Dupré, Louis K., 1925–   . II. Wiseman, James A., 1942–   .
BV5072.L54 1988
248.2'2—dc19
87-32915
CIP

Published by Paulist Press
997 Macarthur Boulevard
Mahwah, N.J. 07430

Printed and bound in the United States of America

CONTENTS

ACKNOWLEDGMENTS

The publisher is grateful to the Abhishiktananda Society for permission to reprint extracts from *Saccidananda,* copyright 1974 by Sw. Abhishik; to William Collins Sons & Co. for permission to reprint one of Catherine of Siena's letters, from *I, Catherine. Selected Writings of Catherine of Siena,* copyright 1980; to the Centrum Ignatianum Spiritualitatis, Rome, for permission to reprint selections from St. Ignatius Loyola's *Spiritual Journey;* to Loyola University Press, Chicago, Illinois, for permission to reprint selections from the following works: *The Spiritual Exercises of St. Ignatius,* by Louis Puhl, *St. Ignatius's Own Story As Told to Luis Gonzales de Camara,* and *The Life of Marie of the Incarnation;* to ICS Publications for permission to reprint selections from *Story of a Soul: The Autobiography of St. Therese of Lisieux,* copyright © 1975, 1976, Washington Province of Discalced Carmelites ICS Publications, 2131 Lincoln Road, N.E., Washington, D.C. 20002; to Anthony Clarke Books, Hertfordshire, England, for permission to reprint selections from *Seeds of Contemplation,* by Thomas Merton; to New Directions Publishing Corporation, New York, N.Y., for permission to reprint selections from the following works: *Seeds of Contemplation,* by Thomas Merton, copyright 1949 by Our Lady of Gethsemani Monastery, and *New Seeds of Contemplation,* by Thomas Merton, Copyright © 1961 by the Abbey of Gethsemani, Inc.; to Cistercian Publications, Kalamazoo, MI, for permission to reprint selections from William of St. Thierry, *The Golden Epistle,* translated by Theodore Berkeley, O.C.S.O., Copyright Cistercian Publications, 1976; to ICS Publications for permission to reprint selections from *The Collected Works of St. Teresa of Avila,* Vol. II, copyright © 1980, Washington Province of Discalced Carmelites, ICS Publications, 2131 Lincoln Road, N.E., Washington, D.C. 20002.

PREFACE

To publish a selection of other people's writings requires a justification. Ours may be brief: an anthology of Christian mystical texts is needed and none is available. All existing collections feature texts from more than one religion. This forces the excerpts taken from Christian mystics to be exceedingly short. In addition, such an approach all too often reflects the idea that all forms of mysticism are basically identical, a position which we reject.

The editors of this work believe that for a reader to enter into the spirit of a mystic's thought and to acquire an adequate idea of the particular tradition to which that mystic belongs requires exposure to texts of some length as well as a concentration on one faith. Even with such a focus, our own attempts fall lamentably short of doing justice to their proposed subject. Selecting twenty-five mystics out of a possible one hundred and culling approximately four hundred pages out of a possible 400,000 has proven to be a frustrating task. The editors know that the result here presented remains a compromise that will not satisfy all readers, nor even any single reader entirely. In our defense we can stress only that this book offers no substitute for reading the works from which the selections were taken and many other works which are not represented here at all. We hope that what we offer may entice the reader to turn to these works, especially now that texts are becoming generally available in The Classics of Western Spirituality.

A critical problem we had to solve was which passages to select. Here again we cannot claim total success. In works of great writers, such as Gregory of Nyssa, Augustine, Eckhart, Ruusbroec, and Teresa, the whole looks quite different from even the most carefully chosen parts. To select here is to misrepresent. In other cases, a successful choice may raise expectations which the reading of the entire work or works will never fulfill. A short selection taken from Madame Guyon leaves a more favorable impression than the reading of hundreds of pages of her rather tepid prose. Here, too, the editors may mislead their readers, albeit in a different direction. *Caveat lector!*

The format of our anthology is meant to be both simple and sound. Following the General Introduction are twenty-five chapters, each containing selections from one of the most significant Christian mystics. Each chapter begins with a short introduction to the life and writings of that mystic, with special attention regularly given to points that will help elucidate the texts presented. In a few cases, English translations of the texts have been modernized and the punctuation slightly modified. Footnotes have been kept to a minimum. A selected bibliography concludes each chapter and provides, as far as possible, information about British as well as American editions of these works.

As we bring this project to its conclusion after almost exactly two years of work, it is our pleasure to express our thanks to those who have helped us along the way. Of these, the Paulist Press ranks first. Not only were its editors eager to sponsor this venture, but they also gave us free access to their considerable resources: The Classics of Western Spirituality and the collection of Ancient Christian Writers. Other publishers and institutions which generously permitted us to reprint material from their works were the Abhishiktananda Society, Delhi; the Centrum Ignatianum Spiritualitatis, Rome; Cistercian Publications, Kalamazoo, Michigan; Anthony Clarke Books, Wheathamstead, Hertfordshire; Collins Publishers, London; the Institute of Carmelite Studies, Washington, D.C.; Loyola University Press, Chicago; New Directions Publishing Corporation, New York; and Yale University Press. It was most gratifying to experience in them some of the selflessness which motivated the mystics whose works they had published. That our work is able to appear at an affordable price is something for which they all deserve thanks.

Of individual persons, our greatest debt is to John Farina, the most supportive of editors, and to his assistant, Patricia Egan. We also owe special thanks to Brian Davies, O.P., who wrote the introduction to Catherine of Siena and assisted in the selection of her writings, as well as to Paul Mommaers, S.J., Joseph Alaerts, S.J., and Simon Tugwell, O.P., for their critical reading of the General Introduction. Finally, without the clerical assistance of the ever-faithful Susan Lucibelli this book might never have appeared.

GENERAL INTRODUCTION

Reading mystical writers—even if they are mediocre stylists, poorly educated, and separated from us by antiquated theologies and questionable methods of exegesis—may be an illuminating experience. It allows a rare glimpse of that mystery that surrounds our entire existence. For a Christian the translation of doctrine into experience or even into theory about experience may also mean a homecoming into his or her faith, a feeling of "So that's what it was all about." I shall never forget the impression of awe when at age nineteen I started reading the life of the sixteenth century Jesuit mystic Balthasar Alvarez by Luis de la Puente, S.J. Passages quoted from Alvarez's spiritual diary in this obsolete hagiography, replete with improbable miracle stories, suddenly seemed to open up a wholly new, heretofore hidden perspective on life. I understood then and there that the deepest insights in human existence might well lie buried in these and similar writings. Even those who feel less inclined to credit mystics with such a momentous significance will have to admit that they have pioneered in the life of the spirit as much as prominent philosophers and great scientists have. There have been times when they, more than others, determined the culture of their age. Such was clearly the case with the early Cistercian movement, and, perhaps even more, with Francis of Assisi. Less conspicuous with respect to civilization as a whole, but religiously no less significant, was their contribution after faith had ceased to feed into the bloodstream of culture. We obtain a very warped picture of the novelty of the modern age if we fail to account for the strong spiritual movements that link it to an earlier tradition. Even marginal figures far removed from the main current of culture succeeded in inserting a powerful dialectical opposition to the secularizing tendencies of their times. Jeanne Guyon and Fénelon, though clearly losers in the battle fought in the already narrowly restricted arena of late seventeenth-century Church politics in France, nevertheless reached a stature surpassing not only that of their victorious antagonists, but even that of some of the leaders of that Enlightenment movement which was to dominate the epoch.

I. THE READING OF MYSTICAL TEXTS

Yet our task here is not to define the cultural import of spiritual life, but rather to present the mystical writings as they themselves define that life—from within, so to speak—independently of external circumstances. This chosen point of view should account for a selection which reflects no historical "balance." The great majority of the texts here offered were written before the eighteenth century, the century when, in Troeltsch's words, European civilization ceased to be Christian. If the quantity and perhaps even the literary quality of "spiritual writings" had been our principle of selection, the modern epoch would have been more amply represented than any previous one, for no time has witnessed a flood of religious literature of all kinds comparable to the one that started in the eighteenth century. Nevertheless most of the *mystics* in the sense here given to the term did write before the eighteenth century. This, of course, immediately leads us to the delicate question: What counts as a mystical text?

The answers have varied from being almost undefinably comprehensive to being almost inapplicably restrictive. No definitive answer has presided over our choice. The history of the term itself has proven to be too slippery to provide hard and fast answers. It is well known how the adjective *mystikos*, derived from Greek mystery cults, through the Alexandrian writers Clement and Origen, hesitantly found its way into the Christian vocabulary.[1] The objective quality of the original concept, so different from our own emphasis upon private experience, persists through the sixth century. "Mystical" applies to the hidden (Christian) meaning of the Old Testament, to the hidden presence of Christ in the Eucharist, and, eventually, to the universally Christian experience of God's presence in Scripture. All these meanings convey the idea of a reality concealed by surface appearances but at least potentially manifest to all Christians. Indeed, I doubt whether before the late Middle Ages the word ever referred to a purely private, inner experience. The meaning continues to shift through the Middle Ages so much that few authors here presented would have agreed on a common definition before the end of the Middle Ages, and that none would have used the one common today of a secret knowledge communicated in an extraordinary, personal experience. Even the emphasis on contemplation which to us ap-

pears such a distinct characteristic of the mystical could not have served as a specific difference, for the active life of good works counted as equally "mystical." The literary genres themselves of the older texts featured in this collection would, in most cases, be judged inappropriate for communicating a strictly private experience. Sermons and theological and pastoral treatises hardly seem indicated media for personal confessions.

Only toward the end of the Middle Ages, when spiritual life itself became marginal to a (still publicly religious) society, did the term move toward the highly individual, subjective meaning we tend to regard as its very essence. Thus Chancellor Gerson, somewhat ahead of his time, defined it as "cognitio experimentalis de Deo." The last two centuries (at least in Western Christendom) have narrowed that meaning further down to an *extraordinary* grace granted to those who directly experience the divine presence. However questionable we may find those restrictions, the editors writing for a modern public had to take them into account. This decision, in turn, created further complications. For who, by the subjective norms now prevailing, deserves to be included? Clearly, compromises are inevitable, and we had to include much, indeed most, of what was written according to very different definitions of the term "mystical" and which yet had some relation to the modern, private, contemplative conception. This strategy forced us to forego any judgment concerning a writer's private experience and, even more, concerning the "natural" or "supernatural" quality of what he or she describes.

The adopted policy leaves us no choice but to abide strictly by the written text. The

---

1. We may refer the interested reader to Louis Bouyer, *The Spirituality of the New Testament and the Fathers*, Vol. I of *A History of Christian Spirituality* (New York: Desclée, 1963).

pre-verbal experience, such as it may be, lies beyond our reach. Even to the writer's intentions we have no direct access. Nothing in the text ever entitles us to assert without a doubt that the author was actually privileged with extraordinary experiences induced by "supernatural" grace. To assume that he or she was must remain a matter of pious speculation made on the basis of an expression which, however unusual, does not necessarily reflect the presence of an extraordinary experience. Doubts about the nature of their experience continue to surround such "mystical" luminaries as Augustine, Pseudo-Dionysius, and Eckhart. Few of the writers here presented ever appeal to personal experience. Instead, they articulate various theories of God's presence to the soul which we have come to describe as "mystical," but which in most cases *they* themselves never even considered in the light of the private, subjective, or extraordinary experience which we attach to the meaning of the term. By the same token, if we deny a text any definitive information about its author's state of mind, it may grant us a securer basis for interpretation. A text possesses an intentionality of its own which enables later generations to read it in accordance with their method of understanding.

Literary hermeneutics relates to experience in two directions—indirectly to the author's, directly to the reader's. Though we may never know with certainty what the author's experience was like, the very quality of the text impels us today, on the basis of *our own* experience, to surmise the presence of an unusual, or unusually strong, religious impression. In that capacity a "mystical" text differs from a purely scientific treatise in systematic theology, or from a pastoral, or even an ascetical tract. Merton once wrote in a preface: "Remember that in this book the author is talking about spiritual things from the point of view of experience rather than in the concise terms of dogmatic theology or of metaphysics. In religions, as in the natural life, the language of experience and the language of dogma or science may find themselves opposed."[2] Merton here speaks the subjective language of modern spirituality. Nevertheless, his remark contains a valuable principle of interpretation. The *appearance* of a spiritual text differs from that of one in systematic theology or philosophy, even though it may appear in a *treatise* on these or other such subjects. It differs by its reference to "experience," Merton claims. As mentioned before, if the term *experience* refers exclusively to the private sphere, his principle would not apply to most of our texts. But it need not be so restrictive, and it remains generally true that mystical texts place a greater emphasis upon the communally or individually *experienced* presence of God than related systematic or pastoral ones do. This provides the reader with no pretext for discarding the theoretical husk in favor of some alleged core of pure experience. We can refer to experience only as it is reflected *in the text*, that is, as the hidden factor to which in some manner (not necessarily private!) the expression itself appeals and which grants it its specific character.

But a text carries a second intentionality by which it refers to the *reader's* experience. Through the centuries we have come to consider certain texts as mystical more for the unique insight—at once cognitive

2. *Seeds of Contemplation*, Preface, rev. ed. (New York: Dell Books, 1953), 7.

and affective—in the spiritual nature of reality they convey to the reader than for the assumed (but totally hidden) experience that led to their writing. Ideally they evoke a response related to the one described by the disciples of Emmaus after their mysterious encounter with the risen Lord: "Did we not feel our hearts on fire at his words?" In this respect the study of a mystical text may be compared to Luther's reading of Scripture. Not so much the words as what the Spirit awakens in the hearer or reader through these words—*was Christum treibt*— leads him or her to consider a text inspired. In mystical reading the principle of personal interpretation prevailed long before the Reformation applied it to Scripture—with this difference, however: that the authority of the text, rather than preceding the inspirational "experience," becomes established *in* and *through* it. To consider a text "mystical," then, often amounts to regarding it as conducive to that special religious perception of reality in which the various functions of the mind, the affective as well as the cognitive, become united in a uniquely harmonious and often intensively experienced manner. To "grasp" it as such implies not, to be sure, that the reader must share the religious convictions expressed in the text, even less that the reader profess the same religious faith as the writer, or, for that matter, any religious faith at all. It *does* imply though that the reader must recognize the properly religious quality of the message (rather than, for instance, reducing it to a mere expression of psycho-pathology), and, in order to grasp the specifics, that at some time, however indirectly, the reader has been exposed to the faith expressed in that message.

The texts collected here have, across the centuries, generally been thought to display qualities that distinguish them from other religious texts as well as move religious-minded readers to insights and attitudes cognate to the ones they perceive in the message itself. If our reflections possess any claim to truth, the reasons for considering confessional writings to be essentially different from theoretical ones vanish altogether. All mystical texts are confessional in the minimal sense that all place a greater stake in the *sapere* (experiential "tasting" of truth) than in *cognoscere* (purely intellectual knowledge). None of them is entirely confessional to the extent that pure experience as such (especially the extraordinary one) remains beyond the realm of communication.

II. THE MYSTICAL ELEMENT IN CHRISTIAN FAITH

A more fundamental question may present itself to the Christian reader: How essential is the mystical element to the Christian faith? One need not share the fierce opposition of extreme "transcendentists" (Catholics as well as Protestants) to any kind of experiential partaking of the divine, to question the oft-heard statement "Mysticism is the essence of religion." Unqualifiedly thus to describe religion is seriously to distort its nature. Christianity for one has never equated its religious ideal with the attainment of a particular state of mind, though some traditions (e.g., Vedantic Hinduism) may have done so. The significance of the mystical factor varies, in quality as well as in weight, from one faith to another. Nevertheless, we believe that the mystical *belongs* to the very essence of every religion, even though that essence usually contains other elements as well. Not only does it occasionally take a complete hold of some, but, more importantly, it shapes and informs, inspires and renews, all religious activity, whether it be ritual, moral, or theoretical. Without some share of spiritual experience religion withers away in sterile ritualism, arid moralism, or theological intellectualism. Nor is that experience entirely reserved to the few. The same power which overwhelms some exerts an active, though often barely conscious momentum on all genuine religious endeavor. Each religious man and woman at times feels the gentle urge to visit, or, more correctly, to allow himself or herself to be visited by, a spiritual power that allures him or her with strange fascination. True enough, few follow this road to the mystical end of the journey. But that is no reason to sever the beginning from the end. The mysterious peace, the inexplicable joy, the compassionate sorrow we experience in rare moments of recollection remain fully continuous with the privileged states of the chosen ones.

To evaluate the mystical quality of the Christian faith would require a full spiritual history of it. Over the centuries the significance of the mystical has varied, without ever having dominated the entire faith or having lost its impact on that faith altogether. Already the Gospels strongly stress the continuous, intimate presence of God to Jesus. The mystical quality of a life so thoroughly penetrated by God's own life receives a unique emphasis in the Fourth Gospel. The presence of Jesus' Spirit turns that quality into a promise to all true believers. It entitles his followers to the very love with which God loves his own Son. St.

Paul articulated the *Mysterium Christi* from a different perspective. The famous passage of 2 Corinthians 3:18 has become a traditional starting point of mystical speculation: "We all reflect as in a mirror the splendor of the Lord; thus we are transfigured into his likeness, from glory to glory." In the center of faith stands the "mystery of Christ"—not a secret, but a revelation to be assimilated by the Christian ever more intimately until his or her personal life coincides with the divine life. In that respect we may safely assert the presence of a mystical element at the heart of the Christian faith. What has been questioned is the extent to which the various types of "Christian mysticism," developed at least in part under non-Christian influences, have remained faithful to that original vision. Once again, our book provides no definitive answer to that question. We have attempted to steer a middle course. Religion, like any living organism, must be allowed to develop—often in wholly unexpected ways, occasionally undergoing the impact of extrinsic sources—as long as it continues to hold the original message (expressed in canonical Scripture) as primary and remains faithful to its primitive symbols. From that viewpoint we think that Pseudo-Dionysius, despite his ambiguous religious identity, qualifies for inclusion, while the profoundly religious, but theosophical, Jacob Boehme does not.

The specific quality of Christian mysticism renders it, of course, distinct from other mystical forms of religion. But it does not separate it from them. Indeed, some mystics have been known to maintain a dialogue with one another across confessional boundaries which exceeded that of officially accepted theoretical exchange.

Muslim mystics have been influenced by Christians, and some medieval Jewish mystics betray the impact of Muslim doctrines, while Christians have persistently derived mystical inspiration from pagan writings of the classical age and their religious interpretations by Jews and Muslims. Today more than ever, spiritual men and women of different faiths tend to form an invisible brotherhood which often allows them to communicate as easily with mystics of another faith as with believers in their own confession—not surprisingly, for mystical texts, however distinct in quality, tend to have a universal appeal. This fact has led some to conclude that, from a mystical point of view, all religions are alike, or even that there is only one, universal mystical religion which only subsequent interpretations distinguish according to theologies or schools. Both these positions are, of course, erroneously simplistic and, as our awareness of the specific quality of each religion has increased, the number of advocates of a universal mystical religion is rapidly dwindling. Today most students of the subject would, indeed, deny the existence of any mysticism-in-general.

What remains true, however, is that the various mystical traditions show a certain independence vis-à-vis the doctrinal bodies within which they originated. Also, they often display surprising family resemblances with similar trends in other traditions. Thus Muslim mystical love poems may be almost indistinguishable from their Christian counterparts, while the idea of the image of God that dominates Patristic and Cistercian mysticism has clearly borrowed from Jewish and Hellenistic sources. We may carry the analogy even further and, at some risk of either vagueness or arbitrariness, attempt a general phenomenology of the mystical experience as such. In doing so, however, we must take particular care to keep the common characteristics of the mystical *state* distinct from the intentionality which gives that state its specific content. To admit that distinction seriously qualifies the import of the term "common." If we posit *passivity* as a universal quality of the *state*, we must immediately add that the passivity of a Christian mystic with respect to the Father differs from a Buddhist state of Nirvana or a Samkhya state of concentrated self-awareness.

William James' efforts to construe a mystical typology led to four well-known characteristics. They all bear the mark of the modern emphasis on private experience of an extraordinary nature. The subjective slant of James' typology is especially notable in what he calls the "transient" quality of the mystical awareness. Even if we were to adopt private experience as a valid basis for description, we would have to question the aptness of a characteristic which fails to account for permanent or prolonged states of enhanced consciousness (such as the spiritual marriage which Teresa and Marie of the Incarnation describe). That the mystical life displays a certain rhythmic quality, however, seems undeniable: moments of great intensity are usually followed by periods of quiet. James captures a more universal trait of the mystical consciousness in declaring it to be essentially passive. Those who have described experiences to which we now tend to attribute the predicate "mystical" are unanimous in asserting their gratuitous, undeserved quality. Here the Scholastic definition of the mystical state as a supernatural "grace" finds its strongest support. The other two characteristics may be acceptable without restriction, since they apply to *all* mystical writings, not only to the ones that describe subjective, individual states: ineffability of its object and a certain noetic quality, though they appear to exclude each other in ordinary knowledge, are simultaneously present in the mystical.

We may well wonder why so little of the great mystical writings has found its way into the body of established theological doctrine. To be sure, its writers themselves insist that the subject of their discourse remains ultimately inexpressible, and that they are only paraphrasing, mostly in negative terms, what allows no positive description. Nevertheless, their expressed intentions as well as the effective results of their efforts bear an unmistakably noetic quality. In reading them we soon become aware of the intention to convey a message—one which we are never able to decode completely, but which nonetheless clearly points in one particular direction rather than another. Especially at this point the theory that all mysticism is identical and that the differences must be entirely accounted for by post-mystical interpretations breaks down. Nowhere has the subjectivist individualism of the modern mind left its footprints more heavily than in this sweeping dismissal of any and all attributes that surpass the level of feeling or emotional exaltation. What the mystics themselves believe is clearly right: noetic distinctions form an inherent part of the entire mystical act. *They*, not post-mystical interpretations, justify at least the major distinctions among mystical traditions, not only, and not primarily, along doctrinal lines, but even within one or several confessional groups. To these divisions we now turn.

III. IMAGE MYSTICISM AND NEGATIVE THEOLOGY

Incontrovertible as the existence of different noetic characteristics in different mystics or "schools" of mysticism may appear, any attempt to capture a number of them under a single heading results in highly contestable emphases of some traits at the expense of others. To speak of "image mysticism," "apophatic mysticism," "Trinitarian mysticism," "love mysticism," is to conceal more than one reveals. Indeed, only one or two of the writers here presented would fall entirely under one or another of these headings, and then mostly for the simple reason that their writings were the ones to give rise to the concept. Even so, problems remain. If we rank Gregory of Nyssa among the image mystics of whom some consider him the prototype, we must still remember that he was also one of the first apophatic theologians as well as one of the earlier writers on mystical love. Nor is there any simple way of categorizing such modern spiritual writers as Marie of the Incarnation, Merton, or Abhishiktananda. But, if so much overlapping occurs, why attempt any categorization at all? Because our task consists in interpreting, we cannot dispense with categories, however much undue generalization may distort the particular picture. Hence we have adopted, with others before us, those concepts that initially guided some of the writers in their quest of the Absolute and subsequently directed those who followed them or who, often across the ages, shared a similar religious outlook.

So to begin our typology with a mysticism of the image is not altogether an arbitrary decision. We may regard it a proven fact of history, I believe, that theoretical writing on the elevation of the mind to ecstatic levels (not necessarily as a strictly personal privilege, but as a privilege divinely granted to the members of the Christian community) focused on the soul as image of God and, by the same token, as residence of God's own eternal Image, the Word. In Alexandria of the third century three currents met and merged in the concept of the Image: (1) the Johannine theology of the Logos combined with the Pauline doctrine of the Spirit's transfiguration into God's likeness; (2) Hellenistic interpretations of Old Testament texts, especially by Philo; (3) a selective reading of Plato's dialogues which Plotinus, possibly under Christian influence, developed into the doctrine we now call Neoplatonism.

The three currents became so intertwined that it is nearly impossible to determine what each one contributed individually. Saint Paul already speaks of *gnosis*, the principal gift of the Spirit, which enables the believer to attain insight into the hidden meaning of the Scripture. Yet the term *gnosis* was also very much part of Philo's philosophy and, of course, it was the key concept that united the multitude of esoteric movements, of uncertain origin and pluriform expression, which we amalgamate in the one term "Gnosticism." Of the latter Alexandria was a hotbed: it pervaded its entire culture in the third century. Though Origen developed his mystical theology of the image before Plotinus (whose co-disciple he may have been of the mysterious Ammonius Saccas, the half-legendary father of Neoplatonism), nevertheless Plotinus' theory would provide much of the conceptual framework of all later ecstatic mysticism, including the theologies

of the image. This is not the proper place to expose the complex thought of this most mystical of the pagan philosophers. Yet one thesis demands our attention. According to the *Enneads*, the nine treatises in which Plotinus in an unsystematic way wrote down his basic insights, reality consists in a process that emanates from an Absolute that stands beyond all determination (the *One*), that next renders itself intelligible as *Mind* (the *Nous*), and that reaches its lowest *hypostasis* in the *Soul* (the *Psyche*, or world soul in which all individual souls partake). The mystical import of Plotinus' schema lies in two principles: (1) The Absolute remains present in the lower hypostases as its immanent core. (2) It induces the soul to return to that core within itself. Now Plotinus develops his theory of immanent presence by conceiving each stage as an *image* of the higher one which it reflects. Crucial thereby is the idea that in the image the higher hypostasis remains *present* (re-presented) in the lower one. Thus the *Nous* contemplates the One and this constitutes its return to its source, while the soul returns to the One through the image of the *Nous*.

The idea of *return* receives particular emphasis in Proclus (fifth century), who systematized the mystical elements in Plotinus' theory. The idea of the *ontological* presence of the symbolized in the symbol survives in the Eastern Church's cult of the icons as well as in the entire Christian doctrine of the sacraments. But it strongly conflicts with the modern tendency to consider the image as wholly external to what it represents—to the point where the root meaning of *presence* has almost entirely vanished from our understanding of "representation." The Christian theology of the image, implicit in the New Testament, and first speculatively developed by Origen, survived uninterruptedly in the East. It reemerged in the twelfth century Cistercian schools of the West. After the mystical schools of the Rhineland and Flanders it faded away in the fifteenth century, only to reappear with renewed vigor in the twentieth century (Merton, Teilhard de Chardin). In the same way in which the divine Image holds God's presence in itself, the soul holds the Word's presence by being its image. The mystical ascent then consists in being converted *entirely* to that Image with which its inner core already coincides. Hence the soul becomes deified by becoming what, in its innermost nature, it is. The movement toward its Image may be described as *ec-static* insofar as the soul surpasses its given nature, but the movement consists more in an inward turn than in an "ascent."

There is no doubt, however, that the *ec-static* metaphor clearly dominates a mystical trend born in the same Neoplatonic school of thought and frequently combined with that of the image, namely, negative theology. We mentioned the pioneering role Gregory of Nyssa played in the development of both. Yet the definitive model was provided by a mysterious sixth century writer, probably a Syrian monk, who, by presenting his work as the creation of the Dionysius whom St. Paul converted on the Areopagus, added the weight of apostolic authority to words that already carried a powerful message of their own. He incorporated the entire Neoplatonic theology of descent and ascent into the Christian idea of the soul's spiritual journey. In his *Mystical Theology* he daringly declared God to be beyond all names, even beyond Being.

Spiritual life consists in moving beyond all attachments and attributions toward the dark abyss of the Godhead—the nameless One. Few followed Dionysius' radical denying—"beyond the Trinity"—to the end, but the later Greek Fathers and a number of Latin writers, either directly or indirectly, underwent his influence. Among the few "radicals" stand out the ninth century Scottus Eriugena, who translated his work into Latin, and the fourteenth century Dominican friar Johannes Eckhart. Both paid for it by prolonged difficulties with the ecclesiastical authorities. But none of the Latin writers can be understood without reference to that equally towering figure of the Western Church, Augustine.

Augustine also had been schooled in the Neoplatonic tradition and advocated a theology of "ascent." But with him there is no question of moving *beyond* the God revealed in his Eternal Word. His theology remains "within the light," so to speak. He also set the doctrine of the image, which dominates his spiritual outlook, on a different course. Whether Augustine ever read Gregory of Nyssa, with whom he had a great deal in common, has not been proven. But with him the image comes to be an external analogy, rather than an immanent presence, a similarity of the effect to the Cause. His greatest theological work, *De Trinitate*, seeks everywhere for "vestiges" of the divine Trinity, most of all in the soul. Superficially, at least, these traces appear to be nothing more than external resemblances, though, as we shall see, they also possess a deeper spiritual meaning, for they enable the mind to turn to its archetype and thus to become united with God. But the hidden riches of the Augustinian way to union would not be fully explored

until the Cistercians started combining it
with the ontological image of the Greeks.

IV. TRINITARIAN MYSTICISM

Generally speaking, spiritual writers of
the Latin West were less daring in their
thinking than their Greek counterparts.
Had it not been for Augustine the spiritual
theology of the first millennium would
have belonged entirely to the Greeks. Eventually Augustine's theology of the Trinity
would inspire Western mystics to unprecedented flights of speculation. Until the
twelfth century, however, Latin spirituality
retained a more moral, ascetical quality.
Comparing it with the Greek we may often
find it somewhat pedestrian, or at least
overly cautious. Meanwhile, it also avoided
the extremes of negative theology, and
gradually prepared the soil for a positive
theology of the image. The Augustinian
theology finally bore spiritual fruit in what
we have, somewhat freely, called trinitarian
mysticism. In a sense, all Christian mysticism has been trinitarian. God's self-
expression forms the center of the mystery
that holds the mystic's mind. Even a negative theologian like Eckhart views the spiritual life of the soul with God as a birth of
the Word in the soul. Yet while for negative
theologians the image, even the divine
Image, belongs to the level of manifestation, for trinitarian mystics that manifestation itself constitutes the very essence of
God's Being. The rediscovery of the Greek
Fathers as well as a more profound understanding of St. Augustine in the twelfth century played a crucial role in the development of the new spirituality.

I believe it is not exaggerated to claim
that most of the writings of the Greek Fathers between the third and the fifth centuries centered around the Trinity. Not only
was it the main subject of theological speculation, but it was also the source of spiritual inspiration. Already Origen describes
the presence of God in the soul as the presence of the Word. The Cappadocian theology of the Image daringly begins to link creation to the generation of the Son. To grow
toward the Image, then, for the creature,
means to return to its uncreated presence in
the divine Word. In early Western theology
treatises on the Trinity abound, but the
trinitarian mystery played no major role in
spiritual doctrine. God's operation in the
soul appears as a single effect that does not
reflect distinctions in which he reveals himself. In one sense, at least, Augustine
changed that. If the trinitarian God had
created the world, he must have left traces
of his internal life in that world and, even
more so, in the soul. God's presence to the
soul must in some way manifest his own
nature. Characteristic for Augustine (and
his followers), however, is that he conceives that manifestation in psychological
terms, thus apparently restricting it to the
order of creation. There the matter rested
for centuries. But underneath Augustine's
arbitrary and often shifting analogies lay a
deeper insight that initially escaped his
readers. Beyond being an external analogy,
the trinitarian quality of the soul referred,
in a much higher degree, to the soul's relation to its divine origin. In the act of directing its powers to God, then, the mind
transforms its external image of the Trinity
into an internal one. By turning remembrance, understanding, and love to God the
mind becomes *intrinsically* trinitarian, so
to speak, since each function links it to a
different hypostasis in the Deity. Early in

the twelfth century this deeper level of Augustine's theology finally received due attention. When the Cistercians rediscovered the Greek Fathers, the superficial, psychological analogies of the past interpretation made room for a deeper understanding of Augustine's text in which the real image is the *presence of the Word* in the soul—a presence which leads beyond all analogies. William of Saint Thierry may be credited with having been one of the first writers to acquaint the West with a spirituality that had continued to exist in the East.[3] Once reintroduced, trinitarian spirituality rapidly spread. One of its main centers became the Abbey of Saint Victor and its most influential writer was Richard of St. Victor. Image mysticism more and more turned into full-fledged trinitarian mysticism. Even mystics such as Eckhart, who, strongly leaning toward the negative theology of Dionysius, placed the Absolute beyond the Trinity, begin their spiritual ascent with the birth of the Word in the soul.

For the blessed Jan van Ruusbroec, a Flemish priest, the Trinity became the very essence of spiritual life. He fully shared the insight of the negative theologians that God resides beyond light and beyond words. But darkness and silence are no more the ultimate goal of the spiritual quest than they are the terminus of God's own life. Precisely the mystery of the Trinity transforms negative theology into a mysticism of light and charitable communication. Instead of considering the divine darkness as a final point of rest beyond the Trinity, as Eckhart had done, Ruusbroec identified it with the fertile hypostasis of the Father. The Father is darkness ready to break out in Light, silence about to speak the Word. Having reunited itself with the Word, the soul returns with that Word in the Spirit to the divine darkness. But it does not remain there. For in that point of origin the dynamic cycle recommences: "For in this darkness an incomprehensible light is born and shines forth—this is the Son of God in whom a person becomes able to see and to contemplate eternal life" (*Spiritual Espousals* III/1). The principle here formulated by Ruusbroec not only leads out of the impasse of a consistently negative theology; it also initiates a spiritual theology of action. The human person is called to partake in the *outgoing* movement of the Trinity itself and while sharing the common life of the triune God to move outward into creation.

Once this doctrine had fully entered the West it profoundly affected most spiritual writing of the later ages: the entire Flemish school, the Spanish mystics, especially Ignatius of Loyola and Teresa of Avila, the so-called "French School," as well as Marie of the Incarnation and Elizabeth of the Trinity. In the Quietist movement, it must be admitted, its impact was minimal. Coming at a time when the devotional life had been marginalized from the mainstream of culture and even of religion, the doctrinal

3. Though William may not have used any Greek sources in the original language. Cf. John Anderson, *The Works of William of St. Thierry*, Vol. 3, *The Enigma of Faith*, Introduction (Washington, D.C.: Cistercian Publications, 1974), 17–19. His friend, Bernard, also began to use expressions rarely heard since the West became spiritually separated from the East. In *De diligendo Deo*, Chapter X, appears the famous comparison of the drop of water blended with a large quantity of wine and then assuming all the qualities of wine. In the same manner the identity of the soul that truly loves God becomes entirely transformed. Bernard does not hesitate to use the Greek *theosis*, the expression that, by then, had become universally accepted in the East: "To experience this state is to be *deified*."

lassitude which generally characterizes it may be, on a practical level, compared to the more *speculative*, negative theology of the past. Once again we confront the inadequacy of such distinctions as trinitarian spirituality, mysticism of the image, negative theology, etc. All those so-called movements overlap, and the most we may claim for them is a degree of emphasis. Nowhere is this more true than in what we have described as "love mysticism."

V. LOVE MYSTICISM

In a very real sense all Christian mysticism has been love mysticism. The role of love already distinguishes Origen and Gregory of Nyssa from their Platonic sources. Love is what links Eckhart to Bernard, and love is the moving power of Ruusbroec's dynamic theology. Love relates twelfth century French Cistercian mysticism to thirteenth century Italian Franciscans, sixteenth century Spanish Carmelites and Jesuits, seventeenth century "devout humanism," and eighteenth century French Quietism. Despite this universal presence there came a moment in the spiritual life of the West when love became equated with the very essence of it, when *contemplatio* came to be defined as *amor*. If we had to assign the beginning of that movement to one man, that man would have to be Bernard of Clairvaux. With him the words of St. Gregory, *amor ipse notitia est*, became the guiding principle of the contemplative life. What Bernard taught in his treatise *De diligendo Deo* and what he preached in his *Sermons on the Song of Songs* must have impressed his contemporaries as a powerful new sound. Ever since Origen, the Song of Songs had

served as the favorite biblical vehicle for mystical commentary. But what the Greeks had cautiously spiritualized Bernard applied in its full erotic power to the relation between God and the soul: "No sweeter names can be found to embody that sweet interflow of affections between the Word and the soul than bridegroom and bride." With this singularly austere Cistercian monk, intolerant of any indulgence to human frailty, a new spiritual humanism emerged that would continue to bloom in a variety of flowers up to the present day. Henceforth, earthly love stands in a direct relation to, and may be wholly consecrated by, the mystical union with God. It is difficult to overestimate the significance of this spiritual revolution—the first dawn of what a century later would expand into an overall Christian humanism (by no means always "mystical" and sometimes of dubious Christian parentage). But not more than the dawn, for, while emphasizing a human element in the relation between God and the creature (erotic love), Bernard and the early Cistercians remain far from a universal love of creation.

Nor should the humanist quality of love mysticism mislead one into considering it the easy way to heaven. Nothing could be further from the truth. Its real quality appears in what Bernard ranks as the fourth and highest degree in loving God, whereby a person "no longer even loves himself except for God."[4] Nor does such a love come "naturally" to human beings. It requires a conversion to bring the will (in which resides the power of loving for Bernard) into conformity with the divine will.

The moral demands of love mysticism

---

4. *De diligendo Deo* 10.27.

exceed those of negative theology. While the latter requires detachment, the former implies a return to the creature—not for its own sake or for the pleasure I am to derive from it, but for the sake of God who expresses himself in it. To love the creature without becoming "attached" to it, however, is exceedingly difficult, as the masters of spiritual life insist. Though we may no longer realize it, Francis of Assisi's love for all creatures required infinitely more than the spontaneous impulse of a friendly disposition. The grace of perfection here hides the pain of abnegation. Not surprisingly, precisely among love mystics we find the strongest emphasis on ascetic discipline. John of the Cross, one of its most articulate spokesmen, formulated its demands in his famous principles at the beginning of the *Ascent of Mount Carmel*:

> In order to arrive at possessing everything, desire to possess nothing.
> In order to arrive at being everything, desire to be nothing.
> In order to arrive at knowing everything, desire to know nothing. (I, 13, 11)

The mystical love for the creature has passed through several stages. St. Bernard still remains a transitional figure. However "human" the quality of his love was, its object was more the divine Word than the human nature of Christ, as it would be for later writers. That human nature remains a means which, by its attractiveness, draws our carnal love in order to raise it to spiritual love. Still, that mediating nature begins to assume a certain independence which comes close to being sought for its own sake. "Notice," he writes, "that the love of the heart is, in a certain sense, carnal, because our hearts are attracted most toward the humanity of Christ and what he did or commanded while in the flesh."

The religious dawn of twelfth century humanism was to reshape the civilization of Western Europe. Love suddenly appeared everywhere: it was the sole subject of the new poetry that began in Provence, and it became the topic of monastic treatises such as Aelred's letter on friendship. Forms of spiritual life more and more came to concentrate on the humanity of Christ. The Crusades functioned probably no less as cause than as effect of the new devotion: in liberating the Holy Land Christians would be able to see the places and earthly circumstances of Jesus' life and death. The new devotion came to rest in Francis of Assisi. With him the humanity of Christ stands in the very center of mystical love. In that humanity the entire world, in which the incarnation took place, has become sanctified. Francis looked upon nature with eyes different from those of his spiritual predecessors. All of creation came to partake in the incarnational union of the divine and the human. More than before, God's presence came to be sought within nature, rather than beyond it. This, of course, is not to say that a sense of God's immanence within the creature had been absent from earlier mysticism. The preceding part of this Introduction shows how little this was the case. Still an unmistakable change in attitude has obviously taken place. Love for the infinite in the finite had constantly characterized Christian mysticism. Yet now the creature more and more appears divinely lovable not only in its core, where, as Eckhart would say, it touches God's own nature, but also in its finitude, even in its imperfection. Owing its existence to a divine act of creation, that very finitude has become endowed with a sacred quality. The mystic is now allowed to love the creature *for its own sake*—since that is the mode in which it exists for God. In presenting this attitude as a love of the creature *for God's sake*, one undervalues the mystic's emphasis upon the finite *as such*.

What Francis initiated, others completed. Being a man of little theological learning, Francis never attempted to unite his spiritual humanism with traditional Christian theology. The Trinity plays no major role in his thinking. The task of synthesizing the new with the old fell upon his disciple, St. Bonaventure. In *The Tree of Life* Bonaventure would develop the first "meditations" on the life of Christ within a theological framework. In the *Itinerarium Mentis* he would assign to the new spirituality of creation its place in a traditional mystical theology.

In most forms of modern spirituality, among them those of the Carmelites, the Capuchins, the Jesuits, the Quietists, love occupies a central position. Yet there remain a number of differences. John of the Cross, Teresa of Avila, and their followers in the Carmel emphasize the need for total detachment from all creatures except the humanity of Christ. Ignatius of Loyola and the masters of the Society of Jesus set as their ideal the love of God in *all* things and all things in God. The two may appear opposites. But the Jesuits, no less than the Carmelites, stress the necessity of total abnegation, while the Carmelites down to St. Thérèse of Lisieux display remarkably human, even erotic, qualities in their love of Christ. For the so-called Quietists, the

love of God consists mainly in a passive acceptance of the dispositions of divine Providence and a selfless abandon to his will. The continuous difficulties of their school with ecclesiastical authorities and with rival factions in the Church have unduly eclipsed the traditional and very solid quality of their piety. Much in Molinos, Madame Guyon, or Fénelon could have been written by any master of the modern age. If it were not for a certain self-consciousness, characteristic of a group that, removed from the mainstream of religious life, excessively asserted its identity, one might hardly notice any difference between it and the solidly orthodox "devout humanism" of Francis de Sales. The notion of "quiet" itself appears as much in Teresa of Avila as in Jeanne Guyon. Eventually the entire controversy settled around the rather subtle distinction between actively acquired contemplation and infused quiet. To the layman the disproportion between the vehemence of the polemics and the delicacy of the distinction cannot fail to arouse suspicion about both sides in the controversy. To a large extent those suspicions are legitimate. We clearly find ourselves in the final part of a spiritual movement that not only has run its course but that announces the end of an age. The ever more subtle distinctions, the striving for absolute "purity" of love, detract attention from the God to be loved to the love itself. Nevertheless, even in this autumnal flowering of the mysticism of love, today's devout reader will find much that is beautiful and even sublime. Quietism must be seen as an attempt to uphold the mystical love tradition in an age that had become detached from its spiritual moorings. A new, introspective interest in religious feelings threatened to replace the interest in the object of those feelings.

VI. PSYCHOLOGICAL, SOCIAL, AND CULTURAL DETERMINANTS

Spiritual movements create a lore of their own which then in a remarkable way determines their future development. One of the most basic ideas in Western mysticism is that spiritual life moves through stages in an ascending order. The classical division into a purgative, illuminative and unitive stage established since the Greek Fathers survived all transitional differences and school polemics. Variations and subdivisions multiplied, but the core of the doctrine remained the same. At the end of the Middle Ages it became an unquestioned assumption that such were the ways of divine Providence in granting spiritual favors. As all conceptual schemata devised to introduce logical order in the organic development of life, this one had to be fitted and adjusted to such a variety of cases that often little more than the *idea* of a teleological succession survived the attribution of identical names to altogether different realities. Some spiritual writers stressed the relativity of the succession. Thus Ruusbroec does not hesitate to emphasize the cyclic character of the stages, while others, such as Catherine of Genoa or Hadewych, describe their own experiences as starting with what would appear to be a state of union which is then followed by stages of purgation and illumination. Yet the schema itself survived all such qualifications and exceptions.

Saint John of the Cross presents the entire mystical "ascent" as a *night*. The image conveys the idea both of ever deeper purification (both "active" and "passive") and of "dark" illumination. In neither one of his systematic treatises, *The Ascent of Mount Carmel* and *The Dark Night of the Soul*, does he explicitly discuss the *via unitiva*. Yet the entire spiritual process for him consists in a growing union of the soul with God. The love poem that introduces both works leaves no doubt about the ultimate intention of the text in this respect. Turning to the description of the stages in St. Teresa's *Interior Castle*, we are confronted with a language of bridal mysticism leading up to spiritual betrothal and marriage, with scant discussion of illumination *as such*. Yet few works provide more classical examples of the "visions" commonly assigned to the *via illuminativa* than Teresa's writings. A rigorous application of the three stages actually occurs mostly in systematic treatises composed by authors who write about the experience of others. Thus while Marie of the Incarnation reports her conversion, her visions, and her gradual unification in the order in which they occurred, her son, Dom Claude Martin, O.S.B., in the spiritual biography of his mother, has arranged her narrative in systematically ordered stages of purgation, illumination, and union. In the modern epoch where "mystical theology" became a separate branch of theology—a typical "marginalization" phenomenon—the triple division became frozen into a rigid principle that was forced upon all spiritual writers to render their reports acceptable or, at least, intelligible.

Such adjustments to prevailing rules—theological or social—raise the question to what extent descriptions of the mystical life, perhaps even the experience itself, may be conditioned by psychic, social, or generally cultural factors. Though the issue of psychic disposition has received considerable attention, it is not, I believe, the one that poses the most delicate problems. No one doubts that experience is conditioned by the personal disposition and psychic capacity of the experiencing subject. To interpret this fact, however, as justifying a neglect of the transcendent factor in our interpretation of mystical life is naively simplistic. Subjectivist reductionism has, of course, for a long time beset the discussion of religion. It finds some support in the fact that mental states, regardless of their "meaning," possess a psychic quality which is clearly determined by the person's aptitude and development. Some mystical authors, such as Ignatius of Loyola, write in an emotionally low-key, dry style, while others, such as Jeanne Guyon, are prolific and sentimental. Some display an orientation toward the mother, while others are clearly father-oriented. Some have been diagnosed as being pathological types. If the term "hysterical" retains any definable meaning at all, it is difficult to avoid applying it to Margaret Mary Alacoque. And which other term would better describe the prolonged period of Father Surin's possession by the devil than "insanity"? But what does the link between the subject's psychic condition and the nature of the experience amount to? Does it mean that mystical states are *nothing more than* projections of psychic dispositions? At least one great psychologist, William James, knew better and, instead of reducing the unknown to the known, assumed that a full knowledge of the self would demand the inclusion of

those states which we are unable to explain by common categories of knowledge. A true psychology of the mystical experience should not "apply" what we know about ordinary states of consciousness, but rather attempt to expand the ordinary. Having been based on this principle, the classical treatises on the subject, both written by psychologists, William James' *The Varieties of Religious Experience* (Chapters 18–19) and Joseph Maréchal's *Studies in the Psychology of Mystics,*[5] contain little ordinary psychology. Because mystics write not only and not primarily about God—and in this they differ from theologians—but about the soul's exposure to the divine mystery, they reveal aspects of the self which few psychologists have ever explored. In this deeper layer of the mind the laws ruling ordinary consciousness appear to be suspended. Space and time recede or are transformed into rhythms and successions of an inner reality. The ordinary consciousness, James wrote, is only one kind of consciousness that is separated from, and surrounded by, completely different forms. Of these the mystical must certainly rank as the most extraordinary. Why, then, does what appears so remote appeal so much to the ordinary? Does this paradoxical fact itself not support the principle that transcendence belongs to the very essence of human existence? Is not the concept of the *soul* itself a religious one? That, at least, is how it started upon its variegated career, and that still remains its main content in some traditions. In the Upanishads the Self

---

5. For a more substantial discussion of some of the problems involved, cf. Louis Dupré, *Transcendent Selfhood*, especially Ch. 8 (New York: Seabury [now owned by Harper], 1976).

coincides with the Absolute—Atman is Brahman—and the Absolute is conceived as *Selfhood.* Yet even in those most "psychic" interpretations, that deeper "soul" is carefully distinguished from ordinary consciousness.[6] Christian writers have, of course, been even more cautious in distinguishing ordinary, or even extraordinary but acquired, states from what they invariably have interpreted as a gratuitously *given* state, a grace. But this raises all the more the question of what the mind must be to be capable of such transformation. In his theory of the *potentia obedientialis* Karl Rahner attempts to provide an anthropological foundation for what the Greek Fathers so expressively called the process of deification.

The mystics themselves have drawn the conclusion that the soul in its innermost self *is* in the direct presence of that ultimate mystery which totally transcends it. In St. John of the Cross' words, "His majesty dwells *substantially* in the soul" and makes his presence felt through "*substantial* touches of a divine union between the soul and God" (*Dark Night* II, 23, 11). Many have objected to Eckhart's bold assertion: "There is something in the soul that is so near akin to God that it is one with Him and need never be united to Him.... If man were wholly this, he would be wholly uncreated and uncreatable" (Sermon 13 [Quint 1955]: "Qui Audit Me"). The language may indeed require qualification, but

the meaning converges with what Ruusbroec referred to as the soul's "uncreated nature," the *superessence* through which the soul abides within the Godhead.

No philosophers or psychologists have sounded the depths of the soul as thoroughly as the mystics. Often through theoretically inadequate and theologically hazardous language they have succeeded in opening a wholly new vista upon the self.

The social status of mystical states and descriptions has received far less attention than the psychological.[7] Yet the matter deserves some attention. Is it coincidental that until recent times, especially in Latin countries, all mystical writers belonged to the higher classes of society? The language itself, particularly in sixteenth century Spain and seventeenth century France, is the language of late feudalism. The status of female mystics raises a number of social questions. It appears unlikely that fewer mystics in the past were women than men: the facts argue rather overwhelmingly in the opposite direction. Yet their writings about mystical life were eyed with suspicion if not with condescension. Even St. Teresa of Avila, one of the two canonized female *Doctores Ecclesiae*, feels obliged constantly to defer to such male authorities as her "confessor," or "the theologians," and to adopt for herself (perhaps somewhat disingenuously) the part of the ignorant

6. The Katha Upanishad teaches: "Atman is not to be obtained by instruction, nor by intellect, nor by much learning. He is to be obtained only by the one whom he chooses; to such a one Atman reveals his own essence." R. E. Hume, *Thirteen Principal Upanishads* (New York: Oxford University Press, 1931), 230 (*Katha* 2, 23).

7. Lucien Goldman's classical work, *"Le Dieu caché,"* on the Jansenist literature of Pascal and Racine, remains more memorable for its intention and its valuable description of the historical conditions that made Jansenism possible than for its depth in understanding an essentially spiritual phenomenon. Ernst Bloch, though an atheist himself, showed far greater sensitivity in evaluating the proper nature of spiritual movements by seeing them as inspirational and often decisive forces in social revolutions.

woman who speaks out of order if she speaks at all. The case of Jeanne Guyon is worse. Whatever one may think of her doctrine, the treatment she received at the hands of bishops and priests shows all the marks of contempt reserved for an "uneducated" woman presuming to intrude upon a male clergy's hereditary turf. The charge of "hysteria" is never far away—a term which Françoise Mallet-Joris in her beautiful biography of Jeanne Guyon aptly describes as "that commodious and ill-defined vocable which allows us to classify all one wants to discredit in woman."[8]

Yet there is another side to the coin. Precisely *because* of these deeply ingrained prejudices, the exceptionally important part which women nevertheless succeeded in playing shows how mystical movements transcend the accepted role patterns of society in the very area where they appear to be most solidly entrenched. During the twelfth and early thirteenth centuries women enjoyed an unprecedented prestige in spiritual life. Their ascent coincides with the cult of courtly love which granted them a status superior to that of men. Thus an abbess would rule both the male and the female monasteries of the followers of the Breton priest Robert d'Abrissel.[9] For a while women in Brabant, Flanders, northern France, and some of the German lands dominated the scene, and known female mystics outnumbered males. The time of Bernard of Clairvaux, William of Saint-Thierry, and Richard of Saint Victor was,

even more, the period of Mechthild of Magdeburg, Hildegard of Bingen, Lutgard of Aywières, Hadewych of Brabant, Marie d'Oignies, Beatrijs of Nazareth, Christina of Sint Truiden, Margaret of Ieper. Their names are less known today, because they left us fewer writings. Some, though by no means all, were ignorant of Latin and uneducated in theology; a few were illiterate. But their impact upon contemporaries, according to learned and not always sympathetic witnesses, must have been considerable. Part of their success they may well have owed to a relative scarcity of canonically organized religious communities for women before the Cistercians started theirs. This allowed women greater freedom in choosing their own religious structures unencumbered by constrictive traditions and uncongenial companionships. Thus emerged those loose communities of women, derogatively called *beghines*, living without public vows, in separate little dwellings clustered around a church in a relatively open compound. Those and similar spiritual sororities preceded the activity of the mendicant orders in bringing an intensive religious life to the laity through non-hierarchical channels. In northern Europe the democratization of piety and even the use of the vernacular in religious matters owes much to these impressive women. Many had to pay a high price for their independence. Some were imprisoned and several beghines died at the stake (among them, the well-known spiritual writer Margaret Porete). Despite repression and the prerogative of a male clergy to teach and to test theological doctrine, spiritual women in subsequent centuries continued to impose their spiritual authority upon their contemporaries. Catherine of

---

8. *Jeanne Guyon* (Paris, 1978), 140.
9. R. Bezzola, *Les origines et la formation de la littérature courtoise en Occident*, Part 2: *La société féodale et la transformation de la littérature de cour*, 2 vols. (Paris, 1966), 2:275–92.

Siena, Teresa of Avila, Jeanne de Chantal, and Jeanne Guyon were able to exercise their undisputed leadership over spiritual movements. In this area at least we notice a discrepancy between hierarchy and mystical impulse.

Finally, and most importantly, a word must be said about the relation between culture and mystical movements. Here, above all, we encounter difficulties in evaluating the import of mystical writings not only for their own time, but even more for future generations. What in a mystic's message derives from the theology of his time and what is original? I have already touched on this issue in discussing the relation between mysticism and the particular theology in which it is couched. If we are right in assuming that that relation may not be conceived as merely extrinsic, then all the hermeneutic problems surrounding a particular theology of the past affect the mystical writings it helped to structure. Even if the reader belongs to the same confessional and theological tradition as a mystic of the past, he or she will not be able to take the text at face value. This problem remains manageable, however, as long as no *total* break with the theological tradition has occurred. The very transcendence of the mystical text with respect to the theological discourse it employs secures it an intelligibility that often far surpasses that of the theological concepts in which it was conceived and expressed. The gap widens to problematic dimensions, however, when an entire culture becomes estranged from the religious worldview within which such texts were written. This may well be the case of our own age with respect to most of the excerpts presented in this collection. The spiritual mutation which our culture

underwent between the sixteenth and the eighteenth century and which has since changed our entire way of thinking and feeling poses an unprecedented difficulty to our very capacity for properly *understanding* the mystical literature of an earlier epoch. While we assume the primary source of meaning and value to lie in the mind, our ancestors before the modern age traced it back to a deeper ground, *transcendent* with respect to the thinking, acting subject. Everything in the intellectual climate of our age leads us to abandon this view with as much resolution as we have abandoned the theory of a geocentric universe. Most of our educated contemporaries have by now done so. But this causes them to read mystical texts from a perspective opposite to the one from which they were written. Their focus remains entirely on the experience—which is ours—while the mystic was exclusively interested in the *God* experienced. Paradoxically, our spiritual "geocentrism" began at the time when scientists started abandoning their astronomical one. Since then, it has become so deeply rooted in the modern mind that we must almost despair of our capacity even temporarily to overcome it. Once meaning is thought to originate exclusively in the mind, a relation to God soon comes to mean "a religious experience." No mental attitude could remove us farther from the ability to understand the message of the mystics than that one.

I write this not to discourage modern readers, but to caution them that, while reading the mystics, they should remain aware of their own inadequacy in fully understanding their message. Indeed, to understand, in this case, would require nothing less than some sort of mental "conversion" which would render us clearly conscious of our own loss and poverty. To approach the mystics on an equal footing, so to speak, as if they were teachers of spiritual "techniques" that any educated person is able to master, is merely to extend the secular, self-centered attitude of modern culture to religion itself. If there is anything this book does not want to be, it is a manual with technical instructions.

VII. MYSTICISM AND THE MODERN AGE

Spiritual decline, to be sure, is not exclusively a modern phenomenon. But it becomes particularly corruptive when, as in the present climate, it is confused with spiritual progress. This perversion, I am afraid, has corroded religious faith in the West to an alarming degree. Not only the practice but often the teaching itself has shifted its center from God to man, from message to experience. Given the surreptitious and all-pervasive nature of the process, we may even wonder whether it has not affected the mystics of the later age themselves. At least in one respect this appears to have been the case. Since the final part of the seventeenth century mystical currents have become ever more marginal, not only with respect to culture as a whole but even with respect to the institutions and doctrines of organized religion. It is not so much that mystics "withdrew" from society, as monks, nuns, and anchorites had done in the past, but that they tended to set up some kind of spiritual counterculture separate from (and, in their own eyes, by no means equal to) the mass of believers.

Still, one might object, has any previous age ever seen a flood of spiritual writings comparable to the one that began in the seventeenth century? Indeed, but here precisely we confront perhaps the most subtle perversion of the modern age. Spiritual men and women who refused to accept in themselves the religious loss that had become all too plain in their more worldly contemporaries began to compensate for it by construing a spiritual universe of their own, consisting, to a great extent, of an elaborate and highly articulate vocabulary.[10] Typical of the entire trend is what happened to the word *mystique* in France—the major producer of spiritual literature in the seventeenth and eighteenth centuries. What previously had been an adjective now became an independent *noun*. Mystical language refined to worldly perfection served as a refuge from an increasingly secular culture. Being charged, so to speak, with constituting its own object, it became a *performative* language: *to be* more and more came to consist in being able *to say*, a *modus loquendi*. Language became its own goal.[11]

This situation, still so different from our own today, nevertheless announces and partly explains the one in which we find ourselves. We also, and in a far more conscious way, have become dissatisfied with the emptiness of a secular culture. Many have turned for spiritual nurture toward the richer expressions of an earlier, religious worldview. Our position differs from the one just described in one major respect: the language of the seventeenth and eighteenth centuries, though no longer reflective of the culture at large, remained never-

---

10. Michel de Certeau, *La fable mystique*, Vol. I (Paris: Gallimard, 1982).

11. *Ibid.*, 108.

theless rooted in a faith which that culture had not rejected. Today that common confessional basis has largely vanished and our contemporary mystagogues—modern men and women themselves—tend to seek their religious language largely outside the circle of a faith (that of their own tradition) with which they no longer identify. Often the mystical quest has moved outside the language of religion altogether. Many of our contemporaries searching the deeper dimension of the real are more likely to turn to the music of Mahler or Scriabin, or the literature of Musil, Hesse, Proust, or Virginia Woolf, than to the writings of Catherine of Siena or of Ruusbroec.

Yet even if we remain within religious discourse proper we see, instead of the coherent language of one faith, patches of unassimilated, foreign faiths being woven into motley quilts. It would be naive to regard this new syncretism as an ecumenical extension of traditional faith. The words, both the old and the new, merely serve as signposts in the search of a religious *experience without faith.* Here we find the quintessential expression of that typically modern phenomenon—a religion of *pure experience.* What started as a refuge from modern culture into religious language has come full turn, subordinating the ancient cult of God to the modern cult of subjective experience. By sheer *fiat* poor Lazarus has transformed himself into Dives, without either divine assistance or human conversion.

Fortunately, there is another, more promising, aspect to the modern interest in the mystics of the past. It is on this positive note that I prefer to conclude this Introduction. What, often unconsciously, attracts the modern reader to the masters of spiri-

tual life is, I suspect, a surprising similarity between their demands and our situation. Anyone today who feels the need to escape the flat, secular quality of public life must turn inward—not that she or he is forced to become a recluse in order to find meaning in existence, but in the sense that *no* transcendent meaning is simply *given* with the structures of contemporary society or culture (despite the abundance of hollow, often meretricious, references to God in public parlance). Since religion has ceased to integrate society and culture, as it once did, it has become transferred to the individual decision. The religious person embraces only those doctrines which cast light upon his inner awareness and joins only those institutions to which she or he feels inwardly drawn. Any quest for spiritual meaning today requires an inward turn, however much the ultimate goal may be communal. Yet here a new problem arises. For what the believing, or even the searching, person encounters within himself is the same spiritual emptiness that pervades our entire culture. Painful as such a confrontation with one's inner silence is for most of our contemporaries, it constitutes a basic condition for establishing any spiritual life by liberating us from the illusion of having one and by throwing us back upon our own inner poverty. But how do we convey a positive sense to religious emptiness? Precisely at this point the faithful seeker may turn to the spiritual masters of the past. For they also, in very different circumstances, felt this sense of absence, yet converted the night of absence into the very meeting place between God and the soul.

Christian mystics have invariably commenced their journey by becoming aware of the abyss that separates God from the creature. However, a sense of absence, sometimes felt to be overwhelming, has often marked particular stages of that journey. Nowhere in the past has the atheism of contemporary culture found a clearer *spiritual* echo than in the negative moment—whether defined as *via purgativa* or, more intellectually, as *via negativa*—that forms an *essential* part of the spiritual process. In some religious movements the attainment of total emptiness is the very goal of the process. Christianity, being the religion of the Word, has always moved beyond silence. Nonetheless, the mystical journey begins also with silence and, in some mystical theologians, such as Dionysius and Eckhart, even ends with it. The "language" of silence may in many cases be the only one the modern seeker understands at the start of his journey. Sharing, however unwillingly, the practical "atheism" of his entire culture, he is left no choice but to take his departure from that negative awareness which dominates his own mind as well as the mentality of his entire culture. Yet precisely there he finds himself taking the same road as spiritual pilgrims in religiously more propitious times. Women and men grown up in a secular environment have at least one advantage on the way to a spiritual life: they have learned to distinguish more critically between the Absolute and its relative images. Having seen one argument after another, one spiritual model after another, one sacred image after another debunked, they are more readily disposed to accept that God dwells beyond *all* representations. This in itself counts as no mean lesson for one called to the contemplative life, for it enables her or him to avoid many illusions right from the start. What was once the route traveled by a spiritual elite has now, in many instances, become the only one still open to us. The desert of an atheistic culture provides the only available space for the encounter with the Absolute. Under the guidance of spiritual masters, that desert may still be converted into a solitude of contemplation. The spiritual emptiness of our age may yet, for the God-seeking person, attain a unique religious significance. All mysticism begins with negation and must constantly return to it. That negation may provide us with a model for spiritual survival, perhaps the only one available.

Yet another factor, more specifically Christian, has forced the spiritual masters of the past into the focus of today's attention. Though hard to define, it is directly related to the "worldliness" of our present outlook. Christian mystics, especially after the twelfth century, have strongly stressed the intrinsic value of creation. (The attribution to Christianity here is specific, but by no means exclusive: we find it also in Jewish mysticism and, to some extent, in Muslim.) However determined to surpass the finite in their search for the absolute, Christian mystics have usually ended up by religiously reintegrating the creation they had initially abandoned. They have increasingly done so in recent times. As we may learn already in Saint John of the Cross, merely to "negate" creation is not yet to adopt God's attitude (who created it), but one that still remains determined by human finitude. A further step demanded in the spiritual ascent consists in overcoming the opposition between God and his creation, and to accept creation as it exists *within God*, so to speak. The mystic begins by asserting the "otherness" of God with respect to the creature, but the final vision must be one of identity. Ignatius of Loyola and the many who followed in his steps have powerfully expressed this. After having led the exercitant through the austere demands of renunciation, the *Spiritual Exercises* teach him, in the "Contemplation to Attain Divine Love," how God dwells in all creatures and all creatures in God. Such a contemplation, if still possible, may convey to the worldliness of the modern mind a new spiritual depth. The basis of this position is not only that in its core each creature touches, and indeed, coincides with God, but, more directly, that also in its finitude and imperfection its "otherness" is endowed with divine significance. Not only the spark in which God's creative act *touches* the creature, but also the fragile result of that act is worthy of religious respect. If one thing characterizes the modern mind, it is its world-orientedness. In itself this does not particularly predispose it to become "spiritual" in the sense here employed. Quite the contrary! Yet the emergence of a new respect for nature may make our contemporaries more open to a mysticism of creation. Having learned to take the finite on its own terms, spiritual men and women of our time may be disposed to explore aspects of creation that spiritual writers of the past had inadequately emphasized, even though they did provide the principles for doing so. (Teilhard de Chardin applies the spiritual principles of Saint Ignatius to the conclusions of modern science, while the worldly vision of Merton's later years traces its origins to early Christian sources.) More explicitly than earlier mystics, our contemporaries appear anxious to find the divine presence in *createdness itself*, not merely and not primarily in its inherence in God. In their search, however

ever new, they are bound to draw meanings from the mystery of the incarnation that had previously remained unrecognized. In a well-known passage, Teresa of Avila accuses herself of having neglected the *humanity* of Christ in the early stages of her conversion. She felt that, in doing so, she had failed to grant creation the central place it rightfully holds in the Christian spiritual vision. In fact, the prominent position of Christ in Christian mysticism becomes meaningless unless one grants the creature a divine significance in its own right.

In Christian piety Jesus plays not merely the role of a teacher of divine Enlightenment (as the Buddha did), or even of a prophet (as Muhammad or Elijah did), but he himself becomes the object of mystical love. Precisely this incarnational quality has given Christian mysticism in the last seven centuries a marvelously earthy and humane quality. Not merely the particular individuality of the person of Jesus becomes an object of reverence, but the entire creation (in all its finite aspects) is virtually included in the incarnated Christ. From this perspective the love of all creatures in Christ implies more than loving them *as if they were Christ*. What Christians are really invited to love is creaturehood *for its own sake*. Saints have always understood that the incarnation has united the Christian's love of God to the love of the creature. Many, especially modern ones, have balanced the vertical ascent to God by a horizontal communion with creation. Today more and more men and women in their quest for spiritual meaning are ready to accept, both in theory and in practice, the principle that God is the ultimate dimension of *all* reality, rather than a transcen-

dent reality opposed to the worldly one.
The new vision, however, requires a new
sort of conversion. As long as our attitude
remains one of conquest and possession
which reduces creation to an "object" of
human power, we shall remain blind to the
divine presence in it. Unless we abandon
the conquering posture we have come to
adopt toward our fellow creatures (human
and other), we shall not be able to recognize
the profoundly symbolic quality of their
entire being. In emphasizing the symbolic
quality of all created being, mystics of the
past may, in their own way, assist us in re-
versing the baneful principle of modern
culture, that meaning originates through
man alone. No function could be more useful to the present age.

Louis Dupré

Unlike the other introductions and the
selections of this anthology, I must bear
sole responsibility for this General Introduction. My gratitude for the criticisms of
my friend and co-editor, Dom James
Wiseman, in no way places on him the burden of theories here defended or attacked.

Origen

(c.185–c.253)

Christianity's first systematic theologian, its first practitioner of the textual criticism of the Bible, and the first to give an orderly description of the principal stages of the Christian's journey toward union with God—such was the man with whom we begin our anthology. Born in Egypt toward the end of the second century, Origen grew up in its major city, Alexandria, at a time when the Roman persecutions of Christianity were at their height. His own father was martyred when Origen was still in his teens, and the early Church historian Eusebius writes that Origen would at that time have joined his father in suffering a martyr's death if his mother had not constrained him to remain at home.

Suddenly entrusted with the responsibility of supporting his mother and six younger brothers, Origen first became a teacher of grammar, but since all the Christian catechists had left Alexandria because of the persecution, he, aged only eighteen, was named head of the catechetical school there. He thereby became entrusted with the duty of instructing those who wished to become Christians and of preparing *them* for the possibility of martyrdom. Those coming to him for instruction soon became so numerous that, in Eusebius' words, "they left him no time even to breathe," so

he appointed another man to give beginners their first instruction while he retained the more advanced students for himself. These early years of catechetical instruction coincided with Origen's adoption of a severely ascetical way of life, marked by regular fasting, the possession of only one cloak, and a literalistic interpretation of Matthew 19:12 ("and there are eunuchs who have made themselves such for the sake of the kingdom of heaven") that, according to Eusebius, led Origen to emasculate himself—an act which his later enemies would hold against him.

As Origen's reputation as a teacher grew, he was at times called abroad by important personages such as the governor of the Roman province of Arabia or the mother of the emperor Alexander Severus to share his learning with them. He also began writing and publishing his works, principally commentaries on various books of Scripture. A decisive turning point in his life occurred in the year 230 when, during a visit to Palestine, he allowed himself to be ordained a priest by local bishops without the permission of his own bishop at Alexandria. A synod convened by the latter declared Origen unfit for catechizing and expelled him from the Church of Alexandria. He thereupon settled at Caesarea in Palestine, where he founded another school, continued his writing, and gave homilies almost daily, many of which have been preserved.

In 249–250, while Origen was living in Caesarea, the newly enthroned emperor Decius began a persecution of Christians throughout the empire. Origen was arrested and underwent severe torture upon the rack, but did not die before the persecution ceased with the death of the emperor in battle in 251. There is nothing further written about Origen after his release from prison, but it is commonly thought that he died several years later, at least in part because of the torture he had endured.

Within two centuries of his death, Origen's work had become the focus of several controversies. Shortly after the Council of Constantinople in 381, the Cypriot bishop Epiphanius scathingly denounced Origen as the principal source of the recently defeated Arian heresy. Two decades later, Egyptian monks whose anthropomorphic concepts of God ran directly counter to Origen's understanding of God as spirit prevailed upon the Patriarch of Alexandria to expel from their midst those monks who championed the Origenist position. Finally, at the Second Council of Constantinople in 553, the Emperor Justinian I secured the condemnation of Origen as a heretic together with Arius, Nestorius, Eutyches, and others. It was not until the Renaissance that there arose a lasting revival of interest in his writings, a revival that has been carried forward in our own century by the work of such major theologians as Henri de Lubac, Jean Daniélou, and Hans Urs von Balthasar.

Our selections from Origen come from two of his most important spiritual works,

his *Commentary on the Song of Songs* and his twenty-seventh homily on the Book of Numbers. Hippolytus of Rome had previously given a Christian interpretation to the Song of Songs by depicting it as a dialogue between Christ and the Church. Origen, while retaining this interpretation, became the first Christian writer to see the text as referring also to the love between Christ and the individual soul. As he writes in his Prologue to his commentary, "The present book of Scripture, then, speaks of this love with which the blessed soul burns and is on fire in regard to the Word of God." With this, Origen became the first in a long line of Christian mystical writers to approach the Song of Songs in this way: Gregory of Nyssa, Bernard of Clairvaux, Teresa of Avila, and John of the Cross, to name only some of the best known.

Another important part of Origen's Prologue to the *Commentary on the Song of Songs* is his treatment of the way this book of Scripture deals with what he calls "contemplation." Origen's frequently noted intellectualism is at times evident here, as when he defines the contemplative discipline as that by which we "contemplate something of divine and heavenly things and gaze at them with the mind alone." Other parts of the Prologue, however, make it abundantly clear that for Origen contemplation was not simply a matter of intellectual insight but also of love, as when he writes that Solomon, in passing on to us the contemplative discipline in the Song of Songs, was "teaching us that we must attain fellowship with God by the paths of loving affection and of love." What Origen means by this is spelled out in greater detail in his commentary on the verse "I have been wounded by love" (Sg 2:5), where he writes:

If there is ever anyone who at any time has burned with this faithful love for the Word of God; if there is anyone who, as the Prophet says, has received the sweet wound of him who is the "chosen dart"; if there is anyone who has been pierced with the lovable spear of his knowledge, so that he sighs and longs for him day and night, is able to speak of nothing else, wishes to hear of nothing else, can think of nothing else, and is not disposed to desire, seek, or hope for anything other than him; then such a soul truly says, "I have been wounded by love."

In the light of such a passage, it is easy to understand how Jean Daniélou could conclude his long study of Origen's thought with the claim that his "mystical theology centered around the Incarnate Word" and that the source of unity in his entire theological enterprise lay not in logical coherence but, "deeper than that, in Origen's intimate knowledge and eager love of the Lord Jesus."[1]

---

1. Jean Daniélou, *Origen,* trans. Walter Mitchell (London and New York: Sheed and Ward, 1955), 314.

Our second selection, from the twenty-seventh homily on Numbers, embodies several other distinctive aspects of Origen's spiritual doctrine. His interpretations of the Hebrew names of the various stopping places of the Israelites in their exodus from Egypt to the promised land may strike many readers today as fanciful, but they were an integral part of his overall understanding of Scripture, according to which a hidden or "mystical" sense was to be found beneath or alongside the "narrative" sense. Equally significant is the fact that in the forty-two stages by which one's journey to God is here traced, the overcoming of temptation is not confined simply to the earlier stages. As late as the thirty-ninth, the traveler comes upon a "beehive of temptations," an indication of the realism with which Origen viewed the spiritual journey and a warning to those who might be ignorant of the truth that the way to full union with God is beset with dangers of one kind or another all along the route. Perseverance is needed at all times, not just at the beginning. That Origen did not succumb to apostasy under torture near the end of his life is an indication that he himself lived the doctrine which he taught.

Selections

THE PROLOGUE TO THE COMMENTARY
ON THE SONG OF SONGS*

This book seems to me an epithalamium, that is, a wedding song, written by Solomon in the form of a play, which he recited in the character of a bride who was being married and burned with a heavenly love for her bridegroom, who is the Word of God. For whether she is the soul made after His image or the Church, she has fallen deeply in love with Him. Moreover, this book of Scripture instructs us in the words this marvelous and perfect bridegroom uses toward the soul or the Church that has been united with Him. As well, from the same book, which is entitled Song of Songs, we come to know what the young girls appointed as the bride's companions said, and also what the friends and companions of the bridegroom said. And the friends of the bridegroom were given the ability of saying some things, so far as they could, that they had heard from the bridegroom Himself, since they were rejoicing at His union with the bride. Moreover, the bride addresses not only the bridegroom but also the young girls, and further the bridegroom not only addresses the bride but also turns to the friends of the bridegroom. And this is what we meant a moment ago by saying that it is a wedding song written in the form of a play. For a play is defined as a story, usually acted on the stage, where different characters are introduced, and where with some characters entering and others making their exits the structure of the narrative is completed by different speeches addressed to different characters. Each of these elements the book of Scripture includes by its own order, and its whole body is fashioned together through fine and mysterious words.

But first we must understand that just as children are not moved to the passion of love, so neither is the age of the inner man, if it is that of a little one and an infant, allowed to grasp these words. I am referring to those who are nourished in Christ by milk and not by solid food (cf. Heb. 5:12) and who now for the first time long for the milk that is spiritual and without deceit (cf. 1 Pet. 2:2). Indeed, in the words of Song of Songs may be found that food of which the Apostle says, "But solid food is for the perfect" and requires such people as listeners who "have their faculties trained by practice to distinguish good from evil" (Heb. 5:14). Thus, if those we have called "little ones" come to these places in Scripture, it can happen that they receive no profit at all from this book or even that they are badly injured either by reading what has been written or by examining what has been said to interpret it. But if any one approaches who is a grown man according to the flesh, no

*All selections in this chapter are taken from *Origen: An Exhortation to Martyrdom, Prayer and Selected Works*, trans. Rowan A. Greer, The Classics of Western Spirituality (New York: Paulist, 1979), 217–20, 223–24, 230–32, 235–36, 245–49, 257–58, 267–69. Reprinted with permission of the publisher.

little risk and danger arises for such a person from this book of Scripture. For if he does not know how to listen to the names of love purely and with chaste ears, he may twist everything he has heard from the inner man to the outer and fleshly man and be turned away from the Spirit to the flesh. Then he will nourish in himself fleshly desires, and it will seem because of the divine Scriptures that he is impelled and moved to the lusts of the flesh. For this reason I give warning and advice to everyone who is not yet free of the vexations of flesh and blood and who has not withdrawn from the desire for corporeal nature that he completely abstain from reading this book and what is said about it. Indeed, they say that the Hebrews observe the rule that unless some one has attained a perfect and mature age, he is not even permitted to hold this book in his hands. Moreover, we also accept the observance of the following rule from them—it is their custom that all the Scriptures should be given to children by the teachers and the wise, and that at the same time those passages which they call *deuterōseis* should be held back to the last. There are four of them: the beginning of Genesis in which the creation of the world is described, the first chapters of Ezekiel the prophet in which mention is made of the cherubim, the end of Ezekiel, which includes the building of the Temple, and this book, Song of Songs.

With all this in mind it seems to me necessary before we begin our discussion of what is written in this book to discuss briefly, first, love itself, which is the chief subject of the book and, next, the order of Solomon's books, among which this book is apparently put in third place. Then we shall also discuss the title of the book itself and why it is called "Song of Songs." . . .

Among the Greeks a good many learned men, wishing to inquire into the investigation of truth, have published many different books about the nature of love, some of them even written in a dialogue style. They have tried to show that the power of love is no other than the power that leads the soul from earth to the lofty heights of heaven and that we cannot arrive at the highest blessedness unless the ardent desire of love impels us. Moreover, questions about love are brought up for discussion, as it were, in banquets among those, I think, who were holding a banquet not of food but of words. Others, as well, have left us certain books of "arts" by which this love is apparently capable of being born or increased in the soul. But fleshly people have carried off these arts to vicious desires and to the mysteries of a faulty love. It is, therefore, no wonder if also with us, where the simple and, consequently, the ignorant seem to be in the majority, we have called the consideration of the nature of love difficult and dangerous. For among the Greeks who were reputed wise and learned there were nevertheless some who did not take these books in the sense in which they were written; but pleading the authority of what had been written about love, they fell headlong into the sins of the flesh and the precipitous paths of lewdness, either by taking suggestions and inducements from the writings we have already mentioned or by presenting the writings of those of old as a veil for their incontinence.

Therefore, lest we also should in any way offend against what was written well and spiritually by those of old through twisting it in a vicious or fleshly sense, let us stretch forth the hands of our soul as of our body to God, that the Lord, who gave His Word to the preachers with great power (Ps. 67:12 LXX–Ps. 68:11), may also give us the Word with His power, by whom we may be enabled to make clear from our treatise a sound understanding of the name and nature of love and one suitable for building up chastity.

At the beginning of Moses' words, where he describes the creation of the world, we find reference to two men that were created, the first made after the image and likeness of God (cf. Gen. 1:26) and the second formed from the dust of the ground (cf. Gen. 2:7). Paul the Apostle well knew this and possessed a clear understanding of these matters. In his letters he wrote more openly and clearly that every person is two different men. This is what he said, "Though our outer man is wasting away, our inner man is being renewed every day" (2 Cor. 4:16) and further, "For I delight in the law of God in my inner man" (Rom. 7:22). And he wrote a good many passages like these. On this basis I think that no one ought now to doubt that Moses at the beginning of Genesis wrote about the making or forming of two men, when he sees Paul, who understood better than we do what was written by Moses, saying that every person is two different men. He mentions that one of them, that is, the inner man, is renewed every day; but he asserts that the other, the outer man, in the saints and in people like Paul, is wasting away and growing weak. But if there will appear to be any doubt in the matter, it will be better explained in the proper places. Now, however, that we have made mention of the inner and the outer man, we shall go on. . . .

. . . Just as there is said to be a fleshly love, which the poets also call Love, according to which the person who loves sows in the flesh, so also there is a spiritual love according to which the inner man when he loves sows in the Spirit (cf. Gal. 6:8). And to speak more plainly, if there is someone who still bears the image of the earthly according to the outer man, he is led by an earthly desire and love. But the person who bears the image of the heavenly according to the inner man is led by a heavenly desire and love (cf. 1 Cor. 15:49). Indeed, the soul is led by a heavenly love and desire when once the beauty and glory of the Word of God has been perceived, he falls in love with His splendor and by this receives from Him some dart and wound of love. For this Word is the image and brightness of the invisible God, the First Born of all creation, in whom all things were created, in heaven and on earth, visible and invisible (cf. Col. 1:15f; Heb. 1:3). Therefore, if anyone has been able to hold in the breadth of his mind and to consider the glory and splendor of all those things created in Him, he will be struck by their very beauty and transfixed by the magnificence of their brilliance or, as the prophet says, "by the chosen arrow" (Is. 49:2). And he will receive from Him the saving wound and will burn with the blessed fire of His love.

We should also realize that just as illicit and unlawful love can come upon the outer man, for example, that he should love not his bride or wife but a harlot or adulteress, so also there can come upon the inner man, that is, the soul, a love not for its legitimate bridegroom, who we have said is the Word of God, but for some adulterer and seducer. Ezekiel the prophet makes this quite clear, using the same figure, when he brings forward "Oholah" and "Oholibah" to appear for Samaria and Jerusalem depraved by adulterous love (cf. Ezek. 23:4ff.). The Scriptural passage in the prophet clearly shows this to those who wish to know more about it. And so the spiritual love of the soul blazes up, as we have taught, sometimes toward certain spirits of wickedness, but sometimes toward the Holy Spirit and the Word of God, who is called the faithful bridegroom and husband of the well-trained soul. And the soul, especially in this book of Scripture we have in hand, is called the Word's bride, as we shall show more fully with the Lord's help when we begin to explain the words of the book itself. . . .

. . . The present book of Scripture, then, speaks of this love with which the blessed soul burns and is on fire in regard to the Word of God. And she sings this wedding song through the Spirit, by which the Church is joined and united with its heavenly bridegroom Christ, desiring to be mingled with Him through the Word so that she may conceive from Him and be enabled to be saved through this chaste bearing of children (cf. 1 Tim. 2:15). And this will happen when the children continue in faith and holiness with modesty as they were conceived of the seed of the Word of God and brought forth and born either by the spotless Church or by the soul that seeks nothing corporeal, nothing material, but is on fire with love only for the Word of God.

For the time being these are the thoughts that have been able to come our way concerning love or loving affection, which is the theme of this epithalamium, the Song of Songs. . . . Now let us turn to the other subjects for discussion.

First, let us examine why it is, since the churches of God acknowledge three books written by Solomon, that of them the book of Proverbs is put first, the one called Ecclesiastes second, and the book Song of Songs has third place. The following ideas have been able to come our way about this subject. There are three general disciplines by which one attains knowledge of the universe. The Greeks call them ethics, physics, and enoptics; and we can give them the terms moral, natural, and contemplative. . . . The moral discipline is defined as the one by which an honorable manner of life is equipped and habits conducive to virtue are prepared. The natural discipline is defined as the consideration of the nature of each individual thing, according to which nothing in life happens contrary to nature, but each individual thing is assigned those uses for which it has been brought forth by the Creator. The contemplative discipline is defined as that by which we transcend visible things and contemplate something of divine and heavenly things and gaze at them with the mind alone, since they transcend corporeal appearance.

Now it seems to me that certain wise men of the Greeks took these ideas from Solomon, since it was long before them in age and time that he first gave these teachings through the Spirit of God. The Greeks have brought them forth as their own discoveries, and they have also included them in their books of instructions and left them to be handed down to their successors. But, as we have said, Solomon discovered them before all the rest and taught them through the wisdom he received from God, as it is written, "And God gave Solomon understanding and wisdom beyond measure, and largeness of heart like the sand on the seashore. And his wisdom was made greater than that of all the ancient sons of men and all the wise men of Egypt" (1 Kings 4:29–30). Thus, Solomon, since he wished to distinguish from one another and to separate what we have called earlier the three general disciplines, that is, moral, natural, and contemplative, set them forth in three books, each one in its own logical order.

Thus, he first taught in Proverbs the subject of morals, setting regulations for life together, as was fitting, in concise and brief maxims. And he included the second subject, which is called the natural discipline, in Ecclesiastes, in which he discusses many natural things. And by distinguishing them as empty and vain from what is useful and necessary, he warns that vanity must be abandoned and what is useful and right must be pursued. He also handed down the subject of contemplation in the book we have in hand, that is, Song of Songs, in which he urges upon the soul the love of the heavenly and the divine under the figure of the bride and the bridegroom, teaching us that we must attain fellowship with God by the paths of loving affection and of love. . . .

Therefore, if a person completes the first subject by freeing his habits from faults and keeping the commandments—which is indicated by Proverbs—and if after this, when the vanity of the world has been discovered and the weakness of its perishable things seen clearly, he comes to the point of renouncing the world and everything in the world, then he will come quite suitably also to contemplate and to long for the things that are unseen and are eternal (2 Cor. 4:18). But in order to be able to attain them we shall need the divine mercy, if we are indeed to be strong enough, when we have gazed upon the beauty of the Word of God, to be kindled with a saving love for Him, so that He too may think it right to love affectionately a soul that He has seen longing for Him.

Next, the order of our discussion obliges us to speak also about the title of Song of Songs. Indeed, it resembles what is called in the tent of testimony the "Holy of Holies" (cf. Ex. 30:29), what is mentioned in the book of Numbers as the "works of works" (cf. Num. 4:47), and what in Paul is called the "ages of ages" (cf., e.g., Rom. 16:27). But we have discussed, so far as we were able, in our commentaries what the difference is between holies and holy of holies in Exodus and between works and works of works in the book of Numbers (cf. *Hom. Num.* 5:2). Moreover, we have not passed over ages of ages in the places where it occurs; and lest we say the same thing again, let this be enough (cf. *In Ep. ad Rom. comm.* 10:23). But now let us ask first what the songs are of which this is said to be the Song of Songs. I think, then, that they are those that were sung of old by the prophets or by the angels. For the Law is said to have been "ordained by angels by the hand of an intermediary" (Gal. 3:19). Thus, all the proclamations made by them were songs that went before, sung by the friends of the bridegroom; but this is the one song that was to be sung in the form of an epithalamium to the bridegroom when He is about to take His bride. In it the bride does not want the song sung to her by the friends of the bridegroom right away, but she longs to hear the words of the bridegroom now present. She says, "Let Him kiss me with the kisses of His mouth" (Song 1:2). This is why it deserves to be placed before all the other songs. For apparently the other songs, which the Law and the prophets sang, were recited for the bride when she was still a little girl and had not yet crossed the threshold of a mature age; but this song is recited for her when she is grown up, quite strong, and now able to receive manly power and perfect mystery. In accord with this it is said of her that "one is perfect, the dove" (cf. Song 6:8). Thus, as the perfect bride of the perfect husband she received the words of the perfect teaching.

HOMILY TWENTY-SEVEN ON THE BOOK OF NUMBERS

1. When God established the world, He created numberless different kinds of foods in accordance, of course, with the differences of human desire or of the nature of animals. That is why when a person sees the food of animals, he knows it was created not for him but for the animals. Not only is this the case, but even the animals themselves know their own food; and, for example, the lion uses some; the

deer, others; the cow, others; birds, others. Moreover, among men there are some differences in the food that is sought. One person who is quite healthy and has a strong bodily constitution needs strong food and has the conviction and confidence he can eat everything, like the strongest of athletes (cf. Rom. 14:2). But if someone perceives he is weaker and feeble, he is pleased with vegetables and does not accept strong food because of the weakness of his body. And if someone is a child, although he cannot put what he wants into words, still he seeks no other nourishment than that of milk. So it is that each individual, whether in accordance with his age or his strength or the health of his body, looks for food suitable for himself and fit for his strength.

If you have considered sufficiently this illustration from corporeal things, let us now turn from them to an understanding of spiritual things. Every rational nature needs to be nourished by foods of its own and suitable for it. Now the true food of a rational nature is the Word of God. But just as in the nourishment of the body we have a moment ago granted many differences, so also in the case of a rational nature, which feeds, as we have said, on reason and the Word of God, not every one is nourished by one and the same Word. That is why, as in the corporeal example, the food some have in the Word of God is milk, that is, the more obvious and simpler teachings, as may usually be found in moral instructions and which is customarily given to those who are taking their first steps in divine studies and receiving the abc's of rational instruction. Thus, when they are read some passage from the divine books in which there is nothing apparently obscure, they gladly receive it, for example, the book of Esther or of Judith, or even of Tobit, or the precepts of Wisdom. But if they are read the book of Leviticus, their mind is constantly offended and refuses it as not its own food. For since such a mind comes to learn how to worship God and to accept His commandments of righteousness and true religion, if he hears instead orders given about sacrifices and rites of immolation taught, how could he avoid constantly being inattentive and refusing the food as not suitable for him?

Moreover, when the Gospels or the Apostle or the Psalms are read, another person joyfully receives them, gladly embraces them, and rejoices in assembling from them, as it were, remedies for his weakness. But if the book of Numbers is read to him, and especially those passages we have now in hand, he will judge that there is nothing helpful, nothing as a remedy for his weakness or a benefit for the salvation of his soul. He will constantly reject and spit them out as heavy and burdensome food, because they do not agree with his sick and weak soul. But, for example—to come back to examples from corporeal things—if understanding were given to a lion, he would not constantly blame the abundance of grasses that has been created simply because he feeds himself on raw meat, nor would he say that they have been produced by the Creator unnecessarily because he does not use them as food. Neither should a human being, because he uses bread and other food suitable for him as nourishment, blame God for making snakes, which apparently supply food for deer. Nor should the sheep or the cow, for example, find fault with the fact it has been given to other animals to feed on meat, while grasses alone are enough for them to eat. Now it is just the same way in the case of rational food, I mean the divine books. You should not constantly either blame or reject Scripture when it appears too difficult or too obscure to understand or when it contains what either the beginner and child or the weaker and feebler in his general understanding cannot use and does not think will bring him anything useful or saving. Rather, you should bear in mind that the snake and the sheep, the cow and the human being, and straw are all creatures of God; and their very diversity points to the praise and glory of their Creator, because they either supply or take food suitably and timely for each of those for whom they were created. In just the same way each individual insofar as he perceives himself healthy or weak takes all the passages that are words of God and in which there is different food according to the capacity of the souls.

Moreover, if we examine as carefully as possible, for example, the reading of the Gospel or the apostolic teaching in which you apparently delight and in which you reckon to find the food most suitable and agreeable to you, how many are the points that have escaped your notice, if you investigate and inquire carefully into the commandments of the Lord? But if what seems obscure and difficult is constantly shunned and avoided, you will find even in the passages about which you are confident so many obscure and difficult points that if you persist in your opinion, you will be forced to give it up. Nevertheless, there are a great many passages in them that are spoken openly and simply enough to edify the hearer of limited understanding.

Now we have made all these points first by way of a preface so as to stir up your minds, since the passage we have in hand is one that is hard to understand and seems unnecessary to read. But we cannot say of the Holy Spirit's writings that there is anything useless or unnecessary in them, however much they appear obscure to some. What we ought rather to do is to turn the eyes of our mind toward Him who ordered this to be written and to ask of Him their meaning. We must do this so that if there is weakness in our soul, He who heals all its infirmities (Ps. 103:3) may heal us, or so that if we are children in understanding, the Lord may be with us guarding His children and may nourish us and add to the measure of our age (cf. Eph. 4:13). For it is in our power to be able to attain both health from weakness and manhood from childhood. It is, then, our part to ask this of God. And it is God's to give to those who ask and to open to those who knock (cf. Mt. 7:7). Let this be enough by way of introduction.

2. Now let us turn to the beginning of the passage that has been read so that with

God's help we may be able to summarize the main points and explain their mean-ing, even though we may not expect total clarity. This is what it says, "These are the stages of the children of Israel, when they went forth out of the land of Egypt with their power by the hand of Moses and Aaron. And Moses wrote down their starting places and stages by the Word of the Lord, and so forth" (Num. 33:1–2). You have heard that Moses wrote this down by the Word of the Lord. Why did the Lord want him to write it down? Was it so that this passage in Scripture about the stages the children of Israel made might benefit us in some way or that it should bring us no benefit? Who would dare to say that what is written "by the Word of God" is of no use and makes no contribution to salvation, but is merely a narrative of what hap-pened and was over and done a long time ago, but pertains in no way to us when it is told? These opinions are irreligious and foreign to the Catholic faith; they belong only to those who deny that the God and Father of our Lord Jesus Christ (cf. Rom. 15:6) is the one and only wise God of the Law and the Gospels. We shall try, then, in a summary fashion so far as time allows, to investigate what a faithful under-standing ought to think about these stages.

Now the previous homily gave us the opportunity of speaking about the departure of the children of Israel from Egypt, and we said that in a spiritual sense there can be seen a double exodus from Egypt, either when we leave our life as Gentiles and come to the knowledge of the divine Law or when the soul leaves its dwelling place in the body. Therefore, these stages, which Moses now writes down "by the Word of the Lord," point toward both. Indeed, it is concerning those stages in which souls divested of their bodies or again clothed with bodies will dwell that the Lord made His proclamation in the Gospel by saying, "With my Father are many stages; if it were not so, would I have told you that I go to prepare a stage for you?" (Jn. 14:2). Thus, there are many stages that lead to the Father. And in the case of each of them what purpose, what sojourn of use to the soul, or what instruction or enlightenment a person may receive is something only the Father of the age to come knows (cf. Is. 9:6). He says of Himself, "I am the door . . . no one comes to the Father but by me" (Jn. 10:9, 14:6). He will probably become in each of the different stages the door for each soul, so that it may go in through Him and go out through Him and find pas-ture (cf. Jn. 10:9), and again so that it may go into another and from there to another stage until it attains to the Father Himself.

But we have nearly forgotten our preface and have suddenly raised your hearing to lofty heights. Let us then, by all means, return to what happens among us and in us. When the children of Israel were in Egypt, they were afflicted with mortar and brick (Ex. 1:14) for the works of Pharaoh the king until they cried out in their groan-ing to the Lord (cf. Ex. 2:23). And He heard their cry and sent His Word to them by Moses and led them out of Egypt. . . .

9. So, the children of Israel went forth from Egypt, and setting out from Ramesse, they came to Sochoth. The order of setting out and the distinction of the stages are quite necessary and must be observed by those who follow God and set their minds on progress in the virtues. With respect to this order I remember that already in other places where we have spoken for edification we have pursued the points that the Lord thought right to give us. But we shall now remind you of them again briefly, since you ask it.

Now the first starting place was from Ramesse; and whether the soul starts out from this world and comes to the future age or is converted from the errors of life to the way of virtue and knowledge, it starts out from Ramesse. For in our language Ramesse means "confused agitation" or "agitation of the worm." By this it is made clear that everything in this world is set in agitation and disorder, and also in corruption; for this is what the worm means. The soul should not remain in them, but should set out and come to Sochoth.

Sochoth is interpreted "tents." Thus, the first progress of the soul is to be taken away from earthly agitation and to learn that it must dwell in tents like a wanderer, so that it can be, as it were, ready for battle and meet those who lie in wait for it unhindered and free.

Then when the soul thinks it is ready, it sets out from Sochoth and camps at Buthan (Num. 33:6, Etham). Buthan means "valley." Now we have said that the stages refer to progress in the virtues. And a virtue is not acquired without training and hard work, nor is it tested as much in prosperity as in adversity. So the soul comes to a valley. For in valleys and in low places the struggle against the devil and the opposing powers takes place. Thus, in the valley the battle must be fought. Then, too, Abraham fought against the barbarian kings in the Valley of Siddim (Gen. 14:8), and there he gained the victory. Therefore, this wanderer of ours descends to those who are in deep and low places, not to linger there, but to gain the victory there. . . .

12. . . . From there [Gai, the thirty-eighth stage], they come in turn to Dibongad, which bears the meaning "beehive of temptations" (Num. 33:45). How marvelous is the caution of divine providence! For look, this wanderer on his heavenly journey comes right up to the highest perfection by a succession of virtues; and nevertheless, temptations do not leave him, though I hear temptations of a new kind. It means "beehive of temptations." Scripture considers the bee a praiseworthy insect, and kings and commoners use what it produces for their health. This may rightly be taken of the words of the prophets and the apostles and all who wrote the sacred books. And I think this can be understood most appropriately as the beehive, that is the entire body of divine Scriptures. Thus, for those who strive for perfection, even in this beehive, that is in the prophetic and apostolic words, there is some temptation. Do you wish to see that the temptation in them is no small one? I find

written in the beehive, "Beware lest . . . when you see the sun and the moon . . . you worship . . . things which the Lord your God has allotted to the Gentiles" (Deut. 4:19). Do you see what a temptation comes from that beehive? And again when it says, "You shall not revile God" (Ex. 22:28). And again in the beehive of the New Testament, where we read, "Why do you wish to kill me, a man who has told you the truth?" (Jn. 8:40). And again the Lord Himself says in another place, "This is why I speak to them in parables so that seeing they may not see and hearing they may not understand, lest they should turn and I heal them" (cf. Mt. 13:13, 15). Moreover, when the Apostle says, "In their case the god of this world has blinded the minds of the unbelievers" (2 Cor. 4:4). And you will find many temptations of this kind in this divine beehive. Each of the saints must come to them, so that also by them it may be known how perfect and religious his beliefs about God are.

Next, then, they come to Gelmon Deblathaim, which means "scorn of figs," that is, where earthly things are completely scorned and despised (Num. 33:46; Almondiblathaim). For unless what seems to delight us on earth is rejected and scorned, we cannot pass through to heavenly things.

There follows next the stage at Abarim opposite Nabau, which is "passage" (Num. 33:47; Abarim, Nebo). But Nabau means "separation." For when the soul has made its journey through all these virtues and has climbed to the height of perfection, it then "passes" from the world and "separates" from it, as it is written of Enoch, "And he was not found, because God had taken him across" (Gen. 5:24). Someone like this, even if he seems to be still in the world and to dwell in flesh, nonetheless will not "be found." Where will he not be found? In no worldly deed, in no fleshly thing, in no vain conversation is he found. For God has taken him across from these pursuits and placed him in the realm of the virtues.

The last stage is east of Moab by the Jordan (Num. 33:48). For the whole journey takes place, the whole course is run for the purpose of arriving at the river of God, so that we may be made neighbors of the flowing Wisdom and may be watered by the waves of divine knowledge, and so that purified by them all we may be made worthy to enter the promised land. And so, this is what we have been able to touch upon in passing and to expound in public concerning the Israelites' stages according to one method of interpretation.

13. But lest an interpretation of this kind, which depends upon the Hebrews' language and the meaning of their words, should seem to those who do not know the conventions of that language contrived and forced, we shall give a comparison in our language by which the meaning of this logic may be clarified. In the literary game by which children receive elementary instruction, some children are called "abcd's"; others, "syllabarians"; others, "namers"; and others, "counters." And when we hear these names, we know from them how far the children have progressed. Likewise in

the liberal arts, when we hear a passage recited or a consolation or an encomium or any other topics in order, we notice by the name of the topic how much progress the youth has made. Why, then, should we not believe that by these names of places as by the names of topics there can be indicated points of progress for those who are learning by divine instructions? In our analogy the students appear to linger in each different topic for public speaking and to make, as it were, stages in them; and they set out from one to the next, and again from it to another. In the same way why should not the names of the stages and the setting out from one to the next and from it to another be believed to indicate the progress of the mind and to signify the acquisition of virtues?

But I leave the rest of the interpretation to be discussed and contemplated on this basis by any who are wise. For it is enough for the wise to give them the opportunity (cf. Prov. 9:9 LXX), because it does not help to let the understanding of the hearers remain completely idle and lazy. Therefore, on the basis of this discussion let him meditate upon the rest; indeed, let him contemplate something more perceptive and more divine. "For it is not by measure that God gives the Spirit" (Jn. 3:34). But because the Lord is Spirit (2 Cor. 3:17), He blows where He wills (cf. Jn. 3:8). And we pray that He may blow upon you, so that you may perceive better and higher things than these in the words of the Lord. May you make your journey through the places we have described in our weakness, so that in that better and higher life we may be able, as well, to walk with you. Our Lord Jesus Christ, who is the way and the truth and the life (Jn. 14:6), will lead us until we attain to the Father, when Christ hands over the kingdom to God the Father (cf. 1 Cor. 15:24) and subjects every principality and power to Him. To Him be glory and power forever and ever. Amen (cf. 1 Pet. 5:11).

SELECTED BIBLIOGRAPHY

TEXTS AND TRANSLATIONS

Opera. Migne, Patrologia Graeca, Vols. 11–17. Many of Origen's works have been critically reedited in *Die griechischen christlichen Schriftsteller der ersten drei Jahrhunderte* (Leipzig).

Commentary on the Song of Songs. Translated by R. P. Lawson. Ancient Christian Writers. Westminster, Md.: Newman; London: Longmans Green, 1957. Reprint. New York: Newman, n. d.

On First Principles. Translated by G. W. Butterworth. London: SPCK, 1936; New York: Harper and Row, Harper Torchbooks, 1966.

Origen: An Exhortation to Martyrdom, Prayer and Selected Works. Translated by Rowan A. Greer. The Classics of Western Spirituality. New York: Paulist; London: SPCK, 1979.

STUDIES

Balthasar, Hans Urs von. "Le mysterion d'Origène." *Recherches de science religieuse.* Parts 1, 2. 26 (1936): 513–62; 27 (1937): 38–64.

Crouzel, H. *Bibliographie critique d'Origène.* The Hague, 1971.

———. *Bibliographie critique d'Origène.* Supplement I. The Hague, 1982.

———. *Origène.* Paris, 1985.

———. *Origène et la "connaissance mystique."* Paris, 1961.

Daniélou, Jean. *Origen.* Translated by Walter Mitchell. London and New York: Sheed and Ward, 1955.

Lieske, A. *Die Theologie der Logosmystik bei Origenes.* Münster, 1938.

Lubac, Henri de. *Histoire et esprit: L'intelligence de l'Ecriture d'après Origène.* Paris, 1950.

Nautin, Pierre. *Origène: Sa vie et son oeuvre.* Paris, 1977.

Trigg, Joseph Wilson. *Origen: The Bible and Philosophy in the Third-Century Church.* Atlanta: John Knox, 1983.

Völker, Walther. *Das Vollkommenheitsideal des Origenes.* Tübingen, 1930.

Gregory of Nyssa

(c.335–c.395)

If the holiness of a family could be determined by the number of its members officially recognized as saints, then Gregory of Nyssa could perhaps be said to have belonged to the holiest family in the history of the Church: his paternal grandmother, both parents, two brothers, a sister, and Gregory himself all bear the title "Saint"! More important for our purposes is the fact that he was one of the most creative and influential spiritual thinkers of the patristic era; some patrologists have even called him the founder of mystical theology.

Gregory was born in Cappadocia about the year 335. Unlike his elder brother, St. Basil the Great, he did not pursue higher studies at the great centers of learning, Constantinople and Athens, but he was nevertheless very well educated: he had Basil himself as his teacher and gives clear evidence in his writings of a penetrating grasp of Scripture, the Platonic corpus, and the works of such theologians as Origen and Clement of Alexandria. After marrying and earning his living for some years as a professional rhetorician, he was persuaded to become a priest by Basil and by their mutual friend Gregory Nazianzen (the three of whom were later to become known as the Cappadocian Fathers). In the au-

tumn of 371, Basil, by then archbishop of Caesarea, had Gregory made bishop of the town of Nyssa in the same metropolitan district so that he might be of greater assistance to Basil in the struggle against the Arian heresy. As a bishop, Gregory was several times reproached by his brother for a lack of firmness in dealing with people and a lack of prudence in matters of Church politics and finance, and as a theologian Gregory's efforts were overshadowed by those of Basil during the latter's lifetime. But upon his brother's death in 379, Gregory came into his own as one of the leading theologians of the Christian East. He played a prominent role in defending the orthodox faith at the Council of Constantinople in 381, and from then until his death around the year 395 he remained very active as a preacher and as the author of important doctrinal treatises (especially his *Catechetical Oration*, the first attempt after Origen's *On First Principles* to create a systematic theology) as well as works of spiritual theology (such as *The Life of Moses*, the *Commentary on the Song of Songs*, and *De instituto Christiano*, his final statement on Christian asceticism).

As a mystical theologian, Gregory is perhaps most significant for being one of the first major proponents of the apophatic way, and our selections from his works— from his sixth sermon on the Beatitudes and from *The Life of Moses*—have been chosen primarily to illustrate this aspect of his thought. Whereas for Origen the soul pursues a path of increasing light on its way to God (notwithstanding the presence of temptations all along the way), for Gregory the journey is described instead as one from light to darkness. This is treated most explicitly in *The Life of Moses*, where Moses' entrance into the cloud on Mount Sinai is seen as symbolizing the truth that God is so utterly incomprehensible that true knowledge of God is in fact a "seeing that consists in not seeing" (*Life of Moses*, n. 163). Gregory makes essentially the same point in the sermon on the sixth Beatitude ("Blessed are the clean of heart, for they shall see God") when he writes that this promised sight is not a direct vision of God but rather a matter of having God present within oneself. Moreover, the way to attain this "vision" is not through intellectual abstraction from all sensible reality (as in the extreme Origenism of Evagrius of Pontus) but rather through living in accordance with Christ's teaching that we must refrain not merely from certain outward acts ("Thou shalt not kill") but even from the interior attitudes that lie at the root of such acts. This way of life, says Gregory, will restore in us those divine attributes which were imprinted on our nature at the beginning but were then covered over with the evil of sin. In words taken from that same sermon, "If you but return to the grace of the Image with which you were informed from the beginning, you will have all you seek in yourselves. For the Godhead is purity, freedom from passion, and separation

from all evil. If therefore these things be in you, God is indeed in you. . . . You are able to perceive what is invisible to those who are not purified."

For this reason, it could scarcely be emphasized too much that for Gregory the utter incomprehensibility of God's nature does not mean that God is absent or inaccessible. Not only is God present to a faithful soul; this presence can be experienced. If at times this experience is described as one of vision, the "spiritual senses" in which Gregory seems even more interested are those of taste, touch, and smell, ones which more clearly imply that God's presence in the divine darkness can in some way be felt even if not directly seen. As he writes in his *Commentary on the Song of Songs*: "How can that which is invisible reveal itself in the night? By the fact that He gives the soul some sense of His presence *(aisthēsin tina . . . tēs parousias),* even while he eludes her clear apprehension, concealed as He is by the invisibility of His nature" (*In Cant.*, XI). This mysticism of knowing God beyond knowing, of experiencing God's presence in the darkness of the cloud, was something new in the history of Christian spirituality. Through Pseudo-Dionysius in the early sixth century it would later pass to the West and there lie at the basis of the apophatic formulations of Meister Eckhart, the author of *The Cloud of Unknowing*, John of the Cross, and countless lesser figures.

The final point to be made here concerns a corollary of Gregory's emphasis on God's ultimate incomprehensibility, namely, the fact that the soul's experience of the divine presence can never be fully satisfying and its desire for God never fully satisfied. This—Gregory's doctrine of *epektasis*, of always striving for those things which still lie ahead—is symbolized by Moses' never ceasing to rise higher, but always finding "a step higher than the one he had attained." According to Gregory, "such an experience seems to me to belong to the soul which loves *(erōtikē)* what is beautiful. Hope always draws the soul from the beauty which is seen to what is beyond" (*Life of Moses*, n. 231). The reference to *erōs* in this passage is significant, for Gregory holds that *erōs* is the ecstatic form of *agapē*, as he writes in his *Commentary on the Song of Songs*: The bride "is wounded by a spiritual and fiery dart of *erōs*, for *agapē* that is strained to intensity is called *erōs*. And no one should be ashamed of this whenever the arrow comes from God and not from the flesh" (*In Cant.*, XIII). If, as we have seen, contemplation for Origen was not exclusively a matter of intellectual insight but also of love, for Gregory this is much more emphatically the case, so much so that for this Cappadocian Father the highest level of the spiritual life is not primarily one of knowledge or contemplation *(theōria)*, but rather the way of union through love.[1]

---

1. On this point, see Jean Daniélou, *Platonisme et théologie mystique. Essai sur la doctrine spirituelle de Saint Grégoire de Nysse,* 2nd ed. (Paris, 1954), 199–208.

Selections

SERMON SIX ON THE BEATITUDES*

When from the sublime words of the Lord resembling the summit of a mountain I looked down into the ineffable depths of His thoughts, my mind had the experience of a man who gazes from a high ridge into the immense sea below him. On the coast one can often see some mountain whose front, facing the sea, is cut off straight from top to bottom, while its projecting upper part forms a peak overhanging the depth. Now if a man looked down from such a high peak into the sea below, he would feel giddy. So also my soul does now, as it is raised from the ground by this great word of the Lord, "Blessed are the clean of heart, for they shall see God" (Mt 5:8). God is promised to the vision of those whose heart has been purified. But "No one has seen God at any time" (Jn 1:18), as says the great John. And the sublime mind of Paul confirms this verdict when he says, "Whom no one has seen or can see" (1 Tim 6:16).

This is the slippery, steep rock that affords no basis for our thoughts, which the teaching of Moses, too, declared to be so inaccessible that our mind can nowhere approach Him. For all possibility of apprehension is taken away by this explicit denial, "No one can see the Lord and live" (cf. Ex 33:20). Yet to see the Lord is eternal life. On the other hand, those pillars of the faith, John and Paul and Moses, declare it to be impossible. Do you realize the vertigo of the soul that is drawn to the depths contemplated in these words? If God is life, then the man who does not see Him does not see life. On the other hand, the Divinely inspired prophets and apostles testify that God cannot be seen. Is not the hope of man annihilated? Yet the Lord supports this faltering hope, as He did with Peter whom He put back on the water He had made solid, when he was in danger of sinking. If, therefore, the Hand of the Word is stretched out also to us and confirms in a different view those who have lost their balance in the depths of their speculations, we may be without fear, as we are firmly held by the guiding Hand of the Word. For He says, "Blessed are the clean of heart, for they shall see God." . . .

. . . How is it then that the voice of the Lord, which promises that God may be seen if we are pure, should not contradict those who, according to St. Paul, evidently speak the truth if they contend that the contemplation of God is beyond our power?

I think it will be best first to say a few words relevant to this subject by way of digression, so that our consideration of the present question may become more methodical. The Divine Nature, whatever It may be in Itself, surpasses every mental

*From St. Gregory of Nyssa, *The Lord's Prayer; The Beatitudes,* trans. Hilda C. Graef, Ancient Christian Writers (Westminster, Md.: Newman, 1954), 143–44, 146–53. Reprinted with permission of Newman/Paulist Press.

concept. For It is altogether inaccessible to reasoning and conjecture, nor has there been found any human faculty capable of perceiving the incomprehensible; for we cannot devise a means of understanding inconceivable things. Therefore the great Apostle calls His ways "unsearchable" (Rom 11:33), meaning by this that the way that leads to the knowledge of the Divine Essence is inaccessible to thought. That is to say, none of those who have passed through life before us has made known to the intelligence so much as a trace by which might be known what is above knowledge.

Since such is He whose nature is above every nature, the Invisible and Incomprehensible is seen and apprehended in another manner. Many are the modes of such perception. For it is possible to see Him who has "made all things in wisdom" (Ps 103:24) by way of inference through the wisdom that appears in the universe. It is the same as with human works of art where, in a way, the mind can perceive the maker of the product that is before it, because he has left on his work the stamp of his art. In this, however, is seen not the nature of the artist, but only his artistic skill which he has left impressed on his handiwork. Thus also, when we look at the order of creation, we form in our mind an image not of the essence, but of the wisdom of Him who has made all things wisely. And if we consider the cause of our life, that He came to create man not from necessity, but from the free decision of His Goodness, we say that we have contemplated God by this way, that we have apprehended his Goodness—though again not His Essence, but His Goodness. It is the same with all other things that raise the mind to transcendent Goodness, all these we can term apprehensions of God, since each one of these sublime meditations places God within our sight. For power, purity, constancy, freedom from contrariety—all these engrave on the soul the impress of a Divine and transcendent Mind. Hence it is clear through what has just been said that the Lord speaks the truth when He promises that God will be seen by those who have a pure heart; nor does Paul deceive when he asserts in his letters that no one has seen God nor can see Him. For He is invisible by nature, but becomes visible in His energies, for He may be contemplated in the things that are referred to Him.

But the meaning of the Beatitude is not only restricted to this, that He who operates can be known by analogy through His operations; for perhaps the wise of this world, too, might gain some knowledge of the transcendent Wisdom and Power from the harmony of the universe. No; I think this magnificent Beatitude proffers another counsel to those able to receive and contemplate what they desire. I make clear by examples what I have in mind.

Bodily health is one of the desirable things in human life; but it is blessed not only to know the principle of health, but to be healthy. For supposing someone had sung the praises of health, yet took some unwholesome food that generated bad juices— what use is it to him to have praised health, seeing he is afflicted with diseases? In the same way, therefore, we should understand the words we are considering. The Lord does not say it is blessed to know something about God, but to have God present within oneself. "Blessed are the clean of heart, for they shall see God." I do not think that if the eye of one's soul has been purified, he is promised a direct vision of God; but perhaps this marvellous saying may suggest what the Word expresses more clearly when He says to others, "The Kingdom of God is within you" (Lk 17:21). By this we should learn that if a man's heart has been purified from every creature and all unruly affections, he will see the Image of the Divine Nature in his own beauty. I think that in this short saying the Word expresses some such counsel as this: There is in you, human beings, a desire to contemplate the true good. But when you hear that the Divine Majesty is exalted above the heavens, that Its glory is inexpressible, Its beauty ineffable, and Its Nature inaccessible, do not despair of ever beholding what you desire. It is indeed within your reach; you have within yourselves the standard by which to apprehend the Divine. For He who made you did at the same time endow your nature with this wonderful quality. For God imprinted on it the likeness of the glories of His own Nature, as if moulding the form of a carving into wax. But the evil that has been poured all around the nature bearing the Divine Image has rendered useless to you this wonderful thing, that lies hidden under vile coverings. If, therefore, you wash off by a good life the filth that has been stuck on your heart like plaster, the Divine Beauty will again shine forth in you.

It is the same as happens in the case of iron. If freed from rust by a whetstone, that which but a moment ago was black will shine and glisten brightly in the sun. So it is also with the inner man, which the Lord calls the heart. When he has scraped off the rustlike dirt which dank decay has caused to appear on his form, he will once more recover the likeness of the archetype and be good. For what is like to the Good is certainly itself good. Hence, if a man who is pure of heart sees himself, he sees in himself what he desires; and thus he becomes blessed, because when he looks at his own purity, he sees the archetype in the image.

To give an example. Though men who see the sun in a mirror do not gaze at the sky itself, yet they see the sun in the reflexion of the mirror no less than those who look at its very orb. So, He says, it is also with you. Even though you are too weak to perceive the Light Itself, yet, if you but return to the grace of the Image with which you were informed from the beginning, you will have all you seek in yourselves. For the Godhead is purity, freedom from passion, and separation from all evil. If therefore these things be in you, God is indeed in you. Hence, if your thought is without any alloy of evil, free from passion, and alien from all stain, you are blessed because you are clear of sight. You are able to perceive what is invisible to those who are not purified, because you have been cleansed; the darkness caused by material entanglements has been removed from the eyes of your soul, and so you see the blessed vision radiant in the pure heaven of your heart. But what is this vision? It is purity, sanctity, simplicity, and other such luminous reflections of the Divine Nature, in which God is contemplated.

Now after what has been said, we do not doubt that such is the case. Yet our sermon is still left with the same impasse which has disconcerted us in the beginning. It is this, that admittedly if someone is in Heaven he shares in the Heavenly marvels; but that the manner of ascent is impossible; and none of the things upon which we have agreed leads us any further. For no one doubts that a man becomes blessed if his heart is purified; but how anyone should cleanse it from its stains, this is what seems to oppose itself to the ascent to Heaven. What then is this Jacob's ladder? How can we find such a fiery chariot by which the prophet Elias was carried up to Heaven, and by which our heart, too, could be lifted up towards the marvels that are above, and shake off this earthly heaviness? . . .

Now how you can become pure, you may learn through almost the whole teaching of the Gospel. You need only peruse the precepts one by one to find clearly what it is that purifies the heart. For one can divide wickedness under two headings, the one connected with works, the other with thoughts. The former, that is to say, the iniquity that shows itself in works, He has punished through the Old Law. Now, however, He has given the Law regarding the other form of sin, which punishes not so much the evil deed itself, as guards against even the beginning of it. For to remove evil from the very choice of the will is to free life perfectly from bad works. Since evil has many parts and forms, He has opposed by His precepts its own remedy to each of the forbidden things. The disease of wrath is present everywhere all through life, so He begins the cure from what is most prominent, and first lays down the law to refrain from anger. "You have learned," He says, from the Old Law, "You shall not kill" (Mt 5:21). Learn now to keep your soul from wrath against your neighbor. . . .

He then passes on to the healing of the sins committed for the sake of pleasure, and, by His commandment, frees the heart from the vile desire of adultery. Thus you will find in what follows how the Lord corrects them all one by one, opposing by His Law each one of the forms of evil. He prevents the beginning of unjust violence by not even permitting self-defence. He banishes the passion of avarice by ordering a man who has been robbed and stripped to give up also what is left to him. He heals cowardice by commanding to scorn death. And, in general, you will find that by means of each of these commandments the Word digs up the evil roots from the depths of our hearts as if by a plough, and so through them we are purged from bringing forth thorns. . . .

. . . Hence, as we have learned what is an evil life and what is a good one—for we have it in the power of our free will to choose either of these—let us flee from the form of the devil, let us lay aside the evil mask and put on again the Divine Image. Let us become clean of heart, so that we may become blessed when the Divine Image is formed in us through purity of life, in Christ Jesus Our Lord, to whom be glory for ever and ever. Amen.

THE LIFE OF MOSES*

BOOK TWO
CONTEMPLATION ON THE LIFE OF MOSES

The Burning Bush

19. It is upon us who continue in this quiet and peaceful course of life that the truth will shine, illuminating the eyes of our soul with its own rays. This truth, which was then manifested by the ineffable and mysterious illumination which came to Moses, is God.

20. And if the flame by which the soul of the prophet was illuminated was kindled from a thorny bush, even this fact will not be useless for our inquiry. For if truth is God and truth is light—the Gospel testifies by these sublime and divine names to the God who made himself visible to us in the flesh—such guidance of virtue leads us to know that light which has reached down even to human nature. Lest one think that the radiance did not come from a material substance, this light did not shine from some luminary among the stars but came from an earthly bush and surpassed the heavenly luminaries in brilliance.

21. From this we learn also the mystery of the Virgin: The light of divinity which through birth shone from her into human life did not consume the burning bush, even as the flower of her virginity was not withered by giving birth.

22. That light teaches us what we must do to stand within the rays of the true light: Sandaled feet cannot ascend that height where the light of truth is seen, but the dead and earthly covering of skins, which was placed around our nature at the beginning when we were found naked because of disobedience to the divine will, must be removed from the feet of the soul. When we do this, the knowledge of the truth will result and manifest itself. The full knowledge of being comes about by purifying our opinion concerning nonbeing.

23. In my view the definition of truth is this: not to have a mistaken apprehension of Being. Falsehood is a kind of impression which arises in the understanding about

---

*From *Gregory of Nyssa: The Life of Moses,* trans. Abraham J. Malherbe and Everett Ferguson, The Classics of Western Spirituality (New York: Paulist, 1978), 59–61, 94–95, 113–16. Reprinted with permission of the publisher.

nonbeing: as though what does not exist does, in fact, exist. But truth is the sure apprehension of real Being. So, whoever applies himself in quietness to higher philosophical matters over a long period of time will barely apprehend what true Being is, that is, what possesses existence in its own nature, and what nonbeing is, that is, what is existence only in appearance, with no self-subsisting nature.

24. It seems to me that at the time the great Moses was instructed in the theophany he came to know that none of those things which are apprehended by sense perception and contemplated by the understanding really subsists, but that the transcendent essence and cause of the universe, on which everything depends, alone subsists.

25. For even if the understanding looks upon any other existing things, reason observes in absolutely none of them the self-sufficiency by which they could exist without participating in true Being. On the other hand, that which is always the same, neither increasing nor diminishing, immutable to all change whether to better or to worse (for it is far removed from the inferior and it has no superior), standing in need of nothing else, alone desirable, participated in by all but not lessened by their participation—this is truly real Being. And the apprehension of it is the knowledge of truth.

26. In the same way that Moses on that occasion attained to this knowledge, so now does everyone who, like him, divests himself of the earthly covering and looks to the light shining from the bramble bush, that is, to the Radiance which shines upon us through this thorny flesh and which is (as the Gospel says) the true light and the truth itself. A person like this becomes able to help others to salvation, to destroy the tyranny which holds power wickedly, and to deliver to freedom everyone held in evil servitude.

The Darkness

162. What does it mean that Moses entered the darkness and then saw God in it? What is now recounted seems somehow to be contradictory to the first theophany, for then the Divine was beheld in light but now he is seen in darkness. Let us not think that this is at variance with the sequence of things we have contemplated spiritually. Scripture teaches by this that religious knowledge comes at first to those who receive it as light. Therefore what is perceived to be contrary to religion is darkness, and the escape from darkness comes about when one participates in light. But as the mind progresses and, through an ever greater and more perfect diligence, comes to apprehend reality, as it approaches more nearly to contemplation, it sees more clearly what of the divine nature is uncontemplated.

163. For leaving behind everything that is observed, not only what sense com-

prehends but also what the intelligence thinks it sees, it keeps on penetrating deeper until by the intelligence's yearning for understanding it gains access to the invisible and the incomprehensible, and there it sees God. This is the true knowledge of what is sought; this is the seeing that consists in not seeing, because that which is sought transcends all knowledge, being separated on all sides by incomprehensibility as by a kind of darkness. Wherefore John the sublime, who penetrated into the luminous darkness, says, "No one has ever seen God" (Jn 1:18), thus asserting that knowledge of the divine essence is unattainable not only by men but also by every intelligent creature.

164. When, therefore, Moses grew in knowledge, he declared that he had seen God in the darkness, that is, that he had then come to know that what is divine is beyond all knowledge and comprehension, for the text says, "Moses approached the dark cloud where God was" (Ex 20:21). What God? He who "made darkness his hiding place" (Ps 17:12), as David says, who also was initiated into the mysteries in the same inner sanctuary.

Eternal Progress

225. If nothing comes from above to hinder its upward thrust (for the nature of the Good attracts to itself those who look to it), the soul rises ever higher and will always make its flight yet higher—by its desire of the heavenly things "straining ahead for what is still to come" (Phil 3:13), as the Apostle says.

226. Made to desire and not to abandon the transcendent height by the things already attained, it makes its way upward without ceasing, ever through its prior accomplishments renewing its intensity for the flight. Activity directed toward virtue causes its capacity to grow through exertion; this kind of activity alone does not slacken its intensity by the effort, but increases it.

227. For this reason we also say that the great Moses, as he was becoming ever greater, at no time stopped in his ascent, nor did he set a limit for himself in his upward course. Once having set foot on the ladder which God set up (as Jacob says), he continually climbed to the step above and never ceased to rise higher, because he always found a step higher than the one he had attained.

228. He denied the specious kinship with the Egyptian queen. He avenged the Hebrew. He chose the desert way of life where there was no human being to disturb him. In himself he shepherded a flock of tame animals. He saw the brilliance of the light. Unencumbered, having taken off his sandals, he made his approach to the light. He brought his kinsmen and countrymen out to freedom. He saw the enemy drowning in the sea.

229. He made camps under the cloud. He quenched thirst with the rock. He produced bread from heaven. By stretching out his hands, he overcame the foreigner. He heard the trumpet. He entered the darkness. He slipped into the inner sanctuary of the tabernacle not made with hands. He learned the secrets of the divine priesthood. He destroyed the idol. He supplicated the divine Being. He restored the Law destroyed by the evil of the Jews.

230. He shone with glory. And although lifted up through such lofty experiences, he is still unsatisfied in his desire for more. He still thirsts for that with which he constantly filled himself to capacity, and he asks to attain as if he had never partaken, beseeching God to appear to him, not according to his capacity to partake, but according to God's true being.

231. Such an experience seems to me to belong to the soul which loves what is beautiful. Hope always draws the soul from the beauty which is seen to what is beyond, always kindles the desire for the hidden through what is constantly perceived. Therefore, the ardent lover of beauty, although receiving what is always visible as an image of what he desires, yet longs to be filled with the very stamp of the archetype.

232. And the bold request which goes up the mountains of desire asks this: to enjoy the Beauty not in mirrors and reflections, but face to face. The divine voice granted what was requested in what was denied, showing in a few words an immeasurable depth of thought. The munificence of God assented to the fulfillment of his desire, but did not promise any cessation or satiety of the desire.

233. He would not have shown himself to his servant if the sight were such as to bring the desire of the beholder to an end, since the true sight of God consists in this, that the one who looks up to God never ceases in that desire. For he says: "You cannot see my face, for man cannot see me and live" (Ex 33:20).

234. Scripture does not indicate that this causes the death of those who look, for how would the face of life ever be the cause of death to those who approach it? On the contrary, the Divine is by its nature life-giving. Yet the characteristic of the divine nature is to transcend all characteristics. Therefore, he who thinks God is something to be known does not have life, because he has turned from true Being to what he considers by sense perception to have being.

235. True Being is true life. This Being is inaccessible to knowledge. If then the life-giving nature transcends knowledge, that which is perceived certainly is not life. It is not in the nature of what is not life to be the cause of life. Thus, what Moses yearned for is satisfied by the very things which leave his desire unsatisfied. . . .

239. This truly is the vision of God: never to be satisfied in the desire to see him. But one must always, by looking at what he can see, rekindle his desire to see more.

Thus, no limit would interrupt growth in the ascent to God, since no limit to the Good can be found nor is the increasing of desire for the Good brought to an end because it is satisfied.

SELECTED BIBLIOGRAPHY

TEXTS AND TRANSLATIONS

Gregorii Nysseni Opera. Edited by Werner Jaeger, H. Langerbeck, *et al.* 11 vols. to date. Berlin, 1921, 1925; Leiden, 1952-.

From Glory to Glory: Texts from Gregory of Nyssa's Mystical Writings. Translated by Herbert Musurillo, S.J. New York: Charles Scribner's Sons, 1961; London: J. Murray, 1962. Reprint. Crestwood, N.Y.: St. Vladimir's Seminary Press, 1979.

Gregory of Nyssa: The Life of Moses. Translated by Abraham Malherbe and Everett Ferguson. The Classics of Western Spirituality. New York: Paulist; London, SPCK, 1978.

The Lord's Prayer; The Beatitudes. Translated by Hilda C. Graef. Ancient Christian Writers. Westminster, Md.: Newman; London: Longmans Green, 1954. Reprint. New York: Newman, n. d.

STUDIES

Balthasar, Hans Urs von. *Présence et pensée: Essai sur la philosophie religieuse de Grégoire de Nysse.* Paris, 1942.

Bebis, George S. "Gregory of Nyssa's 'De Vita Moysis': A Philosophical and Theological Analysis." *Greek Orthodox Theological Review* 12 (1967): 369–93.

Daniélou, Jean. *Platonisme et théologie mystique: Essai sur la doctrine spirituelle de saint Grégoire de Nysse.* 2nd ed. Paris, 1954.

Leys, R. *L'image de Dieu chez saint Grégoire de Nysse: Esquisse d'une doctrine.* Paris, 1951.

Völker, Walther. *Gregor von Nyssa als Mystiker.* Wiesbaden, 1955.

Augustine of Hippo

(354–430)

The person who was to become the most influential of all Christian writers after St. Paul was born in the obscure Numidian town of Thagaste in what is today northeastern Algeria. Although Augustine was enrolled in his infancy as a candidate for baptism, according to the custom of that time the baptism itself was indefinitely postponed to avoid the risk of post-baptismal sin—a postponement which he later sorely regretted. After receiving his early schooling in Thagaste and nearby Madaura, he went on to Carthage for further training and to begin practice as a professional rhetorician. In 383 he left Africa for Rome in the hope of furthering his career, but the following year, in what was to occasion a fundamental reorientation of his life, he moved to Milan to accept a position there.

Throughout these years of youth and early adulthood, Augustine had been avidly seeking the truth about God and the strength to live in accordance with God's will, free from those shackles of selfishness and sensuality which he so exhaustively describes in his *Confessions*. For a time he turned to the dualistic religion of the Manichees, later to the Platonic philosophy of Plotinus and Porphyry; finally, in Milan he came into contact with its great bishop, Ambrose, from whose sermons he learned how one could interpret the Judeo-Christian Scriptures without the sacrifice of one's intelligence. Not long thereafter he underwent his sudden, but long-prepared-for, conversion in the garden of his villa. Having earlier dismissed his concubine of many years (not for religious reasons, but because at that time he wished to be free to enter into a lawful marriage with someone of his own standing), he now retired to Cassiciacum, north of Milan, together with his mother Monica, his son, and several friends. There he prepared for baptism and began writing a group of philosophical dialogues, the earliest of his works that have come down to us.

After being baptized by Ambrose at Easter of 387, Augustine set off for his native Africa with his mother and friends. On the way, at the Roman port of Ostia, he and Monica held that religious conversation which, as he later wrote, led them to transcend the realm of matter and even their own minds and so—for a fleeting moment and "with the full impulse of the heart"— touch "the Eternal Wisdom abiding over all." That experience, described in our anthology's first selection from Augustine, was followed by his mother's death at Ostia and Augustine's return to Thagaste, where he lived for several happy and peaceful years in a monastic community that he had founded.

This contemplative way of life changed abruptly when, during a visit to Hippo in 391, he was persuaded by Bishop Valerius to accept ordination to the priesthood. Four years later he was made Valerius' coadjutor and succeeded him as bishop when Valerius died shortly thereafter. During his thirty-five years as bishop of Hippo, Augustine not only showed himself to be thoroughly devoted to the pastoral needs of the people of his diocese but also produced most of the works for which he is best known: the *Confessions, On the Trinity, The City of God*, and his great commentaries on books of the Old and New Testaments. He died on August 28, 430, at the age of 76, while the invading Vandals were beseiging his episcopal city.

It is sometimes suggested that the really new element in Augustine's spirituality was "the move within." To be sure, interiority is a pervasive theme in his works. God, he tells us, "is in the most secret place of the heart, yet the heart has strayed from him" (*Conf.* 4.12), while in the course of his reflections on memory in book ten of the *Confessions* he breaks forth in the poignant cry: "Late have I loved you, O Beauty, so ancient and so new, late have I loved you! And behold, you were within me and I was outside, and there I sought for you. . . . You were with me, and I was not with you" (*Conf.* 10.27). But this alone did not set Augustine apart from many of his contemporaries, nor is it this alone which makes him so akin to us today. As Augustine's modern biographer Peter Brown observes, it was

largely from Plotinus that Augustine inherited a sense of the dynamism of the inner world and a belief that God could be discovered in the memory of this world. But there the similarity ends. For Plotinus, "the inner world was a reassuring continuum. The 'real self' of man lay in its depths; and this real self was divine, it had never lost touch with the world of Ideas. . . . For Augustine, by contrast, the sheer size of the inner world was a source of anxiety quite as much as of strength."[1] In the Neoplatonist, there was accordingly a sense of tranquillity which was as foreign to Augustine after his conversion as before:

Here also is a lamentable darkness in which the capacities within me are hidden from myself, so that when my mind questions itself about its own powers it cannot be assured that its answers are to be believed. For what is in it is often hidden unless manifested by experience, and in this life, described as a continuous trial, no one ought to be overassured that, though he is capable of becoming better instead of worse, he is not actually becoming worse instead of better. Our one hope, our one confidence, our one firm promise is in your mercy. (*Conf.* 10.32)

This sense of the precariousness of our life with God necessarily affected Augustine's mystical theology. In our selection from the fourteenth book of *On the Trinity*, one does indeed see Augustine as a clear representative of what we have called a "mysticism of the image," specifically, the

1. Peter Brown, *Augustine of Hippo: A Biography* (Berkeley and Los Angeles: Univ. of California Press, 1967), 178.

image of the Trinity which he finds in the mind's power to remember, to understand, and to love its God. In doing this, writes Augustine, the mind attains wisdom and participates in the supreme Light that is God. But he is equally insistent that such participation is never complete in this life, that the possibility of a complete forgetfulness of God must never be presumptuously dismissed, and that "the likeness of God will be perfect in this image only in the perfect vision of God: of which vision the Apostle Paul says: 'Now we see through a glass darkly, but then face-to-face'" (*De Trin.* 14.17).

Our final selection is from *The Literal Meaning of Genesis,* an exhaustive commentary on the first three chapters of Genesis which Augustine worked on between the years 401-415 (approximately the same period of time as that needed for the composition of *On the Trinity*). The passages we have chosen for this anthology, all from the twelfth and final book of the treatise, were especially influential on later mystical theology in the West, both because of their description of the nature of an "intellectual vision" and because of Augustine's concomitant reflections on the possibility of enjoying a vision of the divine essence in this life. As one would expect, he allows for this possibility only in a very limited sense: such a vision can be granted "only to him who in some way dies to this life," since we are exiled from God "as long as we walk by faith and not by vision, even when we live justly in this world" (*De Gen ad litt.* 12.28). Sixteen years earlier he had made essentially the same point in the famous opening paragraphs of the *Confessions*, addressed to the God whom he had been seeking all his life: "You have made us for yourself, and our hearts are restless until they rest in you."

Selections

THE CONFESSIONS*

BOOK NINE

The day was now approaching on which she [Augustine's mother Monica] was to depart this life—the day you knew though we did not. It came about, as I believe, by your secret arrangement that she and I stood alone leaning in a window which looked onto the garden inside the house where we were staying, at Ostia on the Tiber where, apart from the group, we were resting for the sea voyage after the weariness of our long journey by land. There we conversed, she and I alone, very sweetly, and "forgetting the things that were behind and straining forward to those ahead" (Phil 3:13), we were discussing in the presence of Truth, which you are, what the eternal life of the saints would be like, "which eye has not seen nor ear heard, nor has it entered into the heart of man" (1 Cor 2:9). But with the mouth of our heart we also panted for the supernal streams from your fountain, the fountain of life which is with you (Ps 35:10), so that if some drops of that fountain, according to our capacity, were to be sprinkled over us, we might somehow be able to think of such high matters.

And our discourse arrived at this point, that the greatest pleasure of the bodily senses, in the brightest corporeal light whatsoever, seemed to us not worthy of comparison with the joy of that eternal life, unworthy of being even mentioned. Then with our affections burning still more strongly toward the Selfsame we advanced step by step through the various levels of bodily things, up to the sky itself from which the sun and moon and stars shine upon this earth. And higher still we ascended, by thinking inwardly and speaking and marveling at your works, and we came to our own minds and transcended them to reach that region of unfailing abundance where you feed Israel forever on the food of truth (Ez 34:13). There, life is wisdom by whom all these things come into being, both those which have been and those which will be. And wisdom itself is not made; it is as it has ever been, and so it shall be forever. Indeed, "has ever been" and "shall be forever" do not pertain to it, but it simply is, for it is eternal; whereas "to have been" and "to be going to be" are not eternal. And while we were speaking and panting for wisdom, we did with the whole impulse of the heart slightly touch it. We sighed and left behind "the first fruits of the Spirit" (Rom 8:23) which were bound there, and returned to the sound of our own tongue where the spoken word has both beginning

*The selections from the *Confessions* and *On the Trinity* are from *Augustine of Hippo: Selected Writings,* trans. Mary T. Clark, The Classics of Western Spirituality (New York: Paulist, 1984), 114–15, 136–37, 143–44, 342, 346–48, 354, 356–58. Reprinted with permission of the publisher.

and ending. How is it like your word, our Lord, "remaining ageless in Itself and renewing all things" (Wis 7:27)? We said therefore: If to any man the uproar of the flesh grew silent, silent the images of earth and sea and air; and if the heavens also grew silent and the very soul grew silent to itself, and by not thinking of self ascended beyond self; if all dreams and imagined revelations grew silent, and every tongue and every sign and if everything created to pass away were completely silent—since if one hears them, they all say this: We did not make ourselves, but He who abides made us. Suppose that, having said this and directed our attention to Him who made them, they also were to become hushed and He Himself alone were to speak, not by their voice but in His own, and we were to hear His Word, not through any tongue of flesh or voice of an angel or sound of thunder or involved allegory, but that we might hear Him whom in all these things we love, might hear Him in Himself without them, just as a moment ago we two, as it were, rose beyond ourselves and in a flash of thought touched the Eternal Wisdom abiding over all. If this were to continue and other quite different visions disappear, leaving only this one to ravish and absorb and enclose its beholder in inward joys so that life might forever be such as that one moment of understanding for which we had been sighing, would not this surely be: "Enter into the joy of your Lord" (Mt 25:21)? But when shall it be? Perhaps when "we shall all rise again" and "shall not all be changed" (1 Cor 15)?

BOOK TEN

17. Great is the power of memory! It is something terrifying, my God, a profound and infinite multiplicity; and this is the mind, and I am this myself. What therefore am I, my God? What is my nature? A life various, manifold, and utterly immeasurable.

Behold the plains, caverns and abysses of my memory; they are filled beyond number with innumerable kinds of things, present either in their images as in the case of all bodies or by means of their own presence, as with the arts, or in the form of some kind of notions or impressions, as with the affections of the mind which, even when the mind is not experiencing them, the memory still retains, although whatever is in the memory is also in the mind! Through all this I range in all directions and flit here and there. I dive down as deeply as I can, yet there is no limit. So great is the power of memory, so great is the power of life in man who lives mortally.

What, then, shall I do, my true Life, my God? I shall pass even beyond this power of mine, called memory, I shall pass beyond it that I may draw near to you, sweet Light. What are you saying to me? I am now ascending through my mind to you who dwell above me. I shall pass beyond this power of mine called memory in the desire to touch you at the point where you may be touched, to cleave to you where it is possible to be in contact with you. For even beasts and birds have memory; otherwise, they could never find their lairs and nests, or the many other things to which they become accustomed. In fact, without memory they could not become accustomed to anything. I shall pass beyond memory to find you—oh, where, where shall I find you, my truly good and serene delight? If I find you without memory, I shall not remember you. And how shall I find you if I do not remember you? . . .

25. But where do you dwell in my memory, O Lord, where do you dwell? What resting place have you fashioned for yourself? What sanctuary have you built for yourself? You have honored my memory by dwelling within it: but in what part of it do you dwell? This I am now considering. For I transcended those parts of it which the beasts also have when I was recalling you (because I did not find you there among the images of material things), and I came to those parts of it where I had stored up the affections of my mind, nor did I find you there. And I entered into the seat of my mind itself (which the mind has in my memory, since the mind remembers itself) and you were not there. For just as you are not a bodily image nor an affection of any living being, such as we feel when we rejoice, sorrow, desire, fear, remember, forget, or whatever else like this we do, no, you are not the mind itself, because you are the Lord God of the mind, and all these things change, but you remain changeless over all things, and you deigned to dwell in my memory ever since I first learned of you, and I find you there when I recall you to mind.

26. Where, then, did I find you so that I might learn of you? For you were not already in my memory before I learned of you. Where, then, did I find you so that I might learn of you, unless in yourself above me? There is no place; we go "backward and forward" (Jb 23:8) yet there is no place. Everywhere, O Truth, you preside over all asking counsel of you and you simultaneously respond to all the diverse requests for counsel. You respond clearly, but not all hear clearly. All ask what they wish, but they do not always hear what they wish. He is your best servant who is not so eager to hear from you what he himself wills as to will what he hears from you.

27. Late have I loved you, O Beauty, so ancient and so new, late have I loved you! And behold, you were within me and I was outside, and there I sought for you, and in my deformity I rushed headlong into the well-formed things that you have made. You were with me, and I was not with you. Those outer beauties held me far from you, yet if they had not been in you, they would not have existed at all. You called, and cried out to me and broke open my deafness; you shone forth upon me and you scattered my blindness: You breathed fragrance, and I drew in my breath and I now pant for you: I tasted and I hunger and thirst; you touched me, and I burned for your peace.

ON THE TRINITY

BOOK FOURTEEN

Chapter Eight

We have now arrived at that point in our discussion where we begin to consider that highest point of the human mind by which it knows or can know God, in order to discover therein an image of God. Although the human mind is not of God's own nature, yet the image of that nature which transcends in excellence every other nature is to be sought and discovered in the most excellent part of our own nature.

But primarily we have to consider the mind in itself, before it participates in God, and there discover His image. We have asserted that it still remains the image of God, although an image obscured and defaced by the loss of its participation in God. This is His image because it has a capacity for God and can participate in God: It has this high destiny only because it is His image.

Here, therefore, is the mind remembering itself, understanding itself, loving itself. Perceiving this, we perceive a trinity—a trinity far less than God, but now finally an image of God. In this trinity the memory has not brought in from outside what it is to retain, nor has the understanding found in the outer world the object for its contemplating, as with the bodily eye. In this case the will has not made an outer union of these two, as of the material form and its derivative in the eye of the beholder. An image of the observed external object, taken up, so to speak, and stored in the memory, has not been found by thought directed toward it, with form having been given to the recollecting attention, while the two are linked by an additional activity of will. This was the arrangement manifest in those trinities which we found present in material processes, or somehow passing into our inner experience from the external body through the bodily sense. . . .

Chapter Ten

. . . But this is not the case with the mind itself. The mind cannot come from outside to itself, as if to a self already in existence there should be added an identical self previously nonexistent, or as if, rather than coming from outside, there should be born in the existing self an identical self which did not previously exist, just as faith arises from nonexistence in the existing mind. Nor does the mind when it knows itself see itself by recollection as constituted in its own memory, as if it had not been there before it became the object of its own knowledge. From the time of its origin the mind has certainly never stopped remembering itself, understanding itself, and loving itself, as already indicated. Consequently, in its act of conversion upon itself in thought, a trinity is manifested in which we can recognize a "word"—formed from the act of thinking and united to its origin by will. This is where we may recognize more clearly than before the image we seek. . . .

Chapter Twelve

Now this trinity of the mind is the image of God, not because the mind remembers, understands, and loves itself, but because it also has the power to remember, understand, and love its Maker. And in doing this it attains wisdom. If it does not do this, the memory, understanding, and love of itself is no more than an act of folly. Therefore, let the mind remember its God, to whose image it was made, let it understand and love Him.

In brief, let it worship the uncreated God who created it with the capacity for Himself, and in whom it can be made partaker. Hence it is written: "Behold, the worship of God is wisdom" (Jb 28:28). By participating in that supreme Light, wisdom will belong to the mind not by its own light, and it will reign in bliss only where the eternal Light is. The wisdom is so called the wisdom of man as to be also that of God. If wisdom were only human it would be vain, for only God's wisdom is true wisdom. Yet when we call it God's wisdom, we do not mean the wisdom by which God is wise: He is not wise by partaking in Himself as the mind is wise by partaking in God. It is more like speaking of the justice of God not only to mean that God is just but to mean the justice He gives to man when He "justifies the ungodly": to which the Apostle alludes when speaking to those who "being ignorant of God's justice, and wanting to establish their own justice, were not subject to the justice of God" (Rom 4:5, 10:3). In this way we might speak of those who, ignorant of the wisdom of God and wanting to establish their own, were not subject to the wisdom of God.

There is an uncreated Being who has made all other beings great and small, certainly more excellent than everything He made, and thus also more excellent than the rational and intellectual being which we have been discussing, namely, the mind of man, made to the image of its Creator. And the Being more excellent than all others is God. Indeed, He is "not far from any one of us," as the Apostle says, adding, "for in him we live and move and have our being" (Acts 17:27f). Were this said in a material sense we could understand it of our material world: for in it also, in respect to our body, we live and move and are. The text should be taken, however, in a more excellent and also invisible and intelligible way, namely, with respect to the mind that has been made to His image.

In fact, what is there that is not in Him of whom Holy Scripture says: "For from Him and through Him and in Him are all things" (Rom 11:36)? If all things are in

Him, in whom except in Him in whom they are can the living live or the moving move? Yet all men are not with Him in the sense in which He says "I am always with you" (Ps 73:23). Nor is He with all things in the sense in which we say, "The Lord be with you." The great misery of man, therefore, is not to be with Him without whom he cannot exist. Unquestionably, man is never without Him in whom man is; but if a man does not remember Him, does not understand Him or love Him, he is not with Him. But complete forgetfulness makes it impossible even to be reminded of what we have forgotten. . . .

Chapter Sixteen

Those moved by the reminder to convert again to the Lord from that state of deformity wherein worldly desires conformed them to this world have to receive from the Lord their re-formation, as the Apostle says, "Be not conformed to this world, but be reformed in newness of your mind" (Rom 12:2); the beginning of the image's reforming must come from him who first formed it. It cannot of itself re-form the self which it could de-form. The Apostle says in another place: "Be renewed in the spirit of your mind, and put on the new man, which has been created according to God in justice and holiness of truth" (Eph 4:23). The words "according to God" agree with what we read elsewhere: "to the image of God" (Gn 1:27). Justice and holiness of truth were lost through sin; hence this image became deformed and discolored. When the image is re-formed and renewed the mind receives what it once had. . . .

Chapter Seventeen

Certainly the renewal we are discussing is not accomplished in one moment of conversion, like the renewal occurring in the moment of baptism by the forgiveness of all sins, none remaining unforgiven. But it is one thing to recover from a fever, and another to regain one's health after weakness resulting from fever. It is one thing to remove the spear from the body, and another to heal the inflicted wound with treatment that follows. So to begin the cure is to remove the cause of sickness: and this occurs through the forgiveness of sins. There is in addition the healing of the sickness itself accomplished gradually by progressive renewal of the image. Both are manifest in one text of the Psalm where we read: "Who shows mercy upon all your iniquities," which occurs in baptism; and then: "Who heals all your sicknesses" (Ps 103:3), which refers to daily advances whereby the image is renewed. The Apostle spoke of this in clear words: "If our outer man decays, yet is our inner man renewed from day to day" (2 Cor 4:16)—but he is "renewed" as he said in the previously quoted texts, "in the knowledge of God," that is, "in justice and holiness of truth."

He who is thus renewed by daily progressing in the knowledge of God, in justice and holiness of truth, is converting the direction of his love from the temporal to the eternal, from visible to intelligible things, from carnal to spiritual things, trying assiduously to control and reduce all desire for the former and to bind himself by love to the latter. All his success in this depends on divine assistance, for it is God's word that "without me you can do nothing" (Jn 15:5).

When the final day of life reveals a man, in the midst of this progress and growth, holding steadfast to the faith of the Mediator, the holy angels will await him to bring him home to the God whom he has served and by whom he must be perfected; and at the end of the world he will receive an incorruptible body, not for punishment but for glory. For the likeness of God will be perfect in this image only in the perfect vision of God: of which vision the Apostle Paul says: "Now we see through a glass darkly, but then face to face" (1 Cor 13:12). And again: "But we with unveiled face beholding the glory of the Lord are transformed into the same image from glory to glory, as from the spirit of the Lord" (2 Cor 3:18). This describes the daily process in those progressing as they should.

Chapter Eighteen

This statement is from the Apostle John: "Beloved, we are now the children of God, and it has not yet appeared what we shall be: but we know that when He appears we shall be like Him, for we shall see Him as He is" (1 Jn 3:2). This indicates that the full likeness of God is attained in His image only when it has attained the full vision of Him. John's words may indeed be considered as referring to the body's immortality; for also in that we shall be like God, but only like the Son, since He alone in the Trinity took a body in which He died, rose again, and which He bore with Him into heaven. We may also speak here of an image of the Son of God in which we, like Him, shall have an immortal body, conformed in that respect to the image of the Son only, not of the Father nor of the Holy Spirit. For of Him alone do we read and receive with very sound faith that "the Word was made flesh" (Jn 1:14). So the Apostle says: "Whom He foreknew, them He also predestined to be conformed to the image of His Son, that He might be firstborn among many brethren" (Rom 8:29). "Firstborn," in fact, "of the dead," in the words of the same Apostle (Col 1:18)—that death whereby His flesh was sown in dishonor and rose again in glory (1 Cor 15:43). According to this image of the Son, to which we are conformed through immortality in the body, we likewise do that which the same Paul says elsewhere: "As we have borne the image of the earthly, let us also bear the image of Him who is from heaven" (1 Cor 15:49). This means: Let us who were mortal according to Adam believe with true faith and sure and steadfast hope that we shall be immortal according to Christ. For thus we can bear the same image now, not yet in vision but through faith, not yet in reality but in hope. Indeed, in this context the Apostle was speaking of the resurrection of the body.

Chapter Nineteen

But if we consider that image of which it is written: "Let us make man in our image and likeness" (Gn 1:26), not "in my image" or "in your image," we must believe that man was made in the image of the Trinity; and we have devoted our best efforts to discover and understand this. Therefore in respect to this image we may better interpret John's words: "We shall be like Him, for we shall see Him as He is!" Here the Apostle is speaking of Him of whom he has said: "We are the children of God!"

The immortality of the flesh, moreover, will be made perfect in the moment of resurrection which, as Paul says, will be "in the twinkling of an eye, at the last trumpet: and the dead shall be raised uncorrupted, and we shall be changed" (1 Cor 15:52). For in the twinkling of an eye there shall rise again before the judgment that spiritual body in strength, incorruption, and glory which now as a natural body is being sown in weakness, corruption, and dishonor. But the image that is being renewed day by day in the spirit of the mind, and in the knowledge of God, not outwardly but inwardly, will be perfected by that vision which shall exist after the judgment as face-to-face—the vision which now is only developing, through a glass darkly.

THE LITERAL MEANING OF GENESIS*

BOOK TWELVE

15. To see an object not in an image but in itself, yet not through the body, is to see with a vision surpassing all other visions. There are various ways of seeing, and with God's help I shall try to explain them and show how they differ. When we read this one commandment, "You shall love your neighbor as yourself," we experience three kinds of vision: one through the eyes, by which we see the letters; a second through the spirit, by which we think of our neighbor even when he is absent; and a third through an intuition of the mind, by which we see and understand love itself.

*From St. Augustine, *The Literal Meaning of Genesis,* trans. John Hammond Taylor, S.J., 2 vols. (New York: Newman, 1982), 2:186–85, 193–94, 216–17, 219, 228–30. Reprinted with permission of the publisher.

Of these three kinds of vision the first is clear to everyone: through it we see heaven and earth and in them everything that meets the eye. The second, by which we think of corporeal things that are absent, is not difficult to explain, for we think of heaven and earth and the visible things in them even when we are in the dark. In this case we see nothing with the eyes of the body but in the soul behold corporeal images: whether true images, representing the bodies that we have seen and still hold in memory, or fictitious images, fashioned by the power of thought. My manner of thinking about Carthage, which I know, is different from my manner of thinking about Alexandria, which I do not know. The third kind of vision, by which we see and understand love, embraces those objects which have no images resembling them which are not identical with them. A man, a tree, the sun, or any other bodies in heaven or on earth are seen in their own proper form when present, and are thought of, when absent, in images impressed upon the soul. There are two ways of seeing them: one through the bodily senses, the other through the spirit, in which images are contained. But in the case of love, is it seen in one manner when present, in the form in which it exists, and in another manner when absent, in an image resembling it? Certainly not. But in proportion to the clarity of our intellectual vision, love itself is seen by one more clearly, by another less so. If, however, we think of some corporeal image, it is not love that we behold.

16. These are the three kinds of visions about which we had something to say in the preceding books as occasion arose, though we did not there specify their number. Now that we have briefly explained them, since the question under consideration demands a somewhat fuller explanation of them, we must give them definite and appropriate names, in order to avoid the encumbrance of constant circumlocution. Hence let us call the first kind of vision corporeal, because it is perceived through the body and presented to the senses of the body. The second will be spiritual, for whatever is not a body, and yet is something, is rightly called spirit; and certainly the image of an absent body, though it resembles a body, is not itself a body any more than is the act of vision by which it is perceived. The third kind will be intellectual, from the word "intellect." . . .

25. . . . When, during our waking hours, in full possession of our bodily senses, we experience a corporeal vision, we distinguish between this vision and the spiritual vision by which we think of absent bodies in imagination—whether recalling in memory objects that we know, or somehow forming unknown objects which are in the power of thought possessed by the spirit, or arbitrarily and fancifully fashioning objects which have no real existence. From all such objects we distinguish the bodies which we see and which are present to our senses, so that we have no doubt that these are bodies and that the others are images of bodies. But it may sometimes be that by an excessive application of thought, or by the influence of some disorder

(as happens to those who are delirious with fever), or by the agency of some other spirit, whether good or evil, the images of bodies are produced in the spirit just as if bodies were present to the senses of the body, though the attention of the soul may meanwhile remain alert even in the bodily senses. In this case images of bodies are seen appearing in the spirit, and real bodies are perceived through the eyes. The result is that at the same time one man who is present will be seen with the eyes and another who is absent will be seen in the spirit as if with the eyes. I have known people affected thus, who conversed not only with those truly present but also with others who were absent, addressing them as if they were present. Returning to their normal state, some related what they saw but others were unable to do so. In the same way also some people forget their dreams while others remember theirs.

But when the attention of the mind is completely carried off and turned away from the senses of the body, then there is rather the state called ecstasy. Then any bodies that are present are not seen at all, though the eyes may be wide open; and no sounds at all are heard. The whole soul is intent upon images of bodies present to spiritual vision or upon incorporeal realities present to intellectual vision without benefit of bodily images. . . .

53. There are occasions, then, when the soul is carried off to objects of vision that are similar to corporeal things and are seen by the spirit in such a way that the soul is quite removed from the senses of the body, more than in sleep but less than in death. In such cases it is by virtue of divine guidance and assistance that it realizes it is seeing in a spiritual way not bodies but the likenesses of bodies. Similarly, it sometimes happens that a man in his sleep is aware that he is dreaming even before he awakes. And in spiritual vision it may also be that future events, represented under images present to the soul, are clearly recognized as future because of the fact that divine assistance is given to the human mind or that someone in the vision explains the meaning of it, as happened to John in the Apocalypse. Now the revelation given in such a case must be important, even though it may happen that the man who receives it does not know whether he went out of the body during the vision or was still in the body but with his spirit withdrawn from the bodily senses. If this information is not revealed to a man who experiences such an ecstasy, it is possible for him to remain in ignorance on this point.

54. Moreover, if a man has not only been carried out of the bodily senses to be among the likenesses of bodies seen by the spirit, but is also carried out of these latter to be conveyed, as it were, to the region of the intellectual or intelligible, where transparent truth is seen without any bodily likenesses, his vision is darkened by no cloud of false opinion, and there the virtues of the soul are not tedious and burdensome. For then there is no restraining of lust by the effort of temperance, no bearing of adversity by fortitude, no punishing of wicked deeds by justice, no avoiding of

evil by prudence. The one virtue and the whole of virtue there is to love what you see, and the supreme happiness is to possess what you love. For there beatitude is imbibed at its source, whence some few drops are sprinkled upon this life of ours, that amid the trials of this world we may spend our days with temperance, fortitude, justice, and prudence.

It is surely in pursuit of this end, where there will be secure peace and the unutterable vision of truth, that man undertakes the labor of restraining his desires, of bearing adversities, of relieving the poor, of opposing deceivers. There the brightness of the Lord is seen, not through a symbolic or corporeal vision, as it was seen on Mount Sinai, nor through a spiritual vision such as Isaiah saw and John in the Apocalypse, but through a direct vision and not through a dark image, as far as the human mind elevated by the grace of God can receive it. In such a vision God speaks face to face to him whom he has made worthy of this communion. And here we are speaking not of the face of the body but of that of the mind. . . .

55. . . . This vision is granted only to him who in some way dies to this life, whether he quits the body entirely or is turned away and carried out of the bodily sense, so that he really knows not (to use the words of St. Paul) whether he is "in the body or out of the body" (2 Cor 12:2) when he is carried off to this vision.

56. If, then, the Apostle has given the name "third heaven" (2 Cor 12:3) to this third type of vision, which is superior to every corporeal vision by which bodies are perceived through the senses of the body, and superior also to all spiritual vision by which the likenesses of bodies are beheld not by the mind but by the spirit, in this vision the brightness of God is seen by those whose hearts are purified for the vision. Hence it is said, "Blessed are the pure of heart, for they shall see God" (Mt 5:8), not through any symbol fashioned in a corporeal or spiritual manner, as if through a mirror in a riddle, but face to face or "mouth to mouth" (Num 12:8), as it is said of Moses, through a vision, that is, of God's own essence, according to the limited measure that it can be comprehended by a mind distinct from God Himself, even after it has been cleansed from all earthly stain and carried away from all body and likeness of body. From Him we are exiled, laden with a mortal and corruptible burden, as long as we walk by faith and not by vision, even when we live justly in this world. . . .

67. It seems that we are right, then, in understanding the first heaven in general as this whole corporeal heaven (to use a general term), namely, all that is above the waters and the earth, and the second heaven as the object of spiritual vision seen in bodily likenesses (as, for instance, the vision seen by Peter in ecstasy when he saw the dish let down from above full of living creatures), and the third heaven as the objects seen by the mind after it has been so separated and removed and completely

carried out of the senses and purified that it is able through the love of the Holy Spirit in a mysterious way to see and hear the objects in that heaven, even the essence of God and the Divine Word through whom all things have been made. If all this is true, then I believe that Paul was carried off to that third heaven and that there is a paradise which is more excellent than all others and is, if we may use the term, the paradise of paradises. For if a good soul finds joy in the good that is in every creature, what is more excellent than that joy which is found in the Word of God through whom all things have been made?

68. But why must the spirits of the departed be reunited with their bodies in the resurrection, if they can be admitted to the supreme beatitude without their bodies? This is a problem that may trouble some, but it is too difficult to be answered with complete satisfaction in this essay. There should, however, be no doubt that a man's mind, when it is carried out of the senses of the flesh in ecstasy, or when after death it has departed from the flesh, is unable to see the immutable essence of God just as the holy angels see it, even though it has passed beyond the likenesses of corporeal things. This may be because of some mysterious reason or simply because of the fact that it possesses a kind of natural appetite for managing the body. By reason of this appetite it is somehow hindered from going on with all its force to the highest heaven, so long as it is not joined with the body, for it is in managing the body that this appetite is satisfied.

Moreover, if the body is such that the management of it is difficult and burdensome, as is the case with this corruptible flesh, which is a load upon the soul (coming as it does from a fallen race), the mind is much more readily turned away from the vision of the highest heaven. Hence it must necessarily be carried out of the senses of the flesh in order to be granted this vision as far as it is able. Accordingly, when the soul is made equal to the angels and receives again this body, no longer a natural body but a spiritual one because of the transformation that is to be, it will have the perfect measure of its being, obeying and commanding, vivified and vivifying with such a wonderful ease that what was once its burden will be its glory.

69. . . . Finally, although St. Paul was carried out of the senses of the body into the third heaven and Paradise, he was wanting in one point the full and perfect knowledge of things that the angels have: he did not know whether he was in the body or out of the body. But this knowledge will not be wanting to us when we shall be reunited to our bodies at the resurrection of the dead and when this corruptible body will put on incorruption and this mortal body will put on immortality. For everything will be clear without any error and without any ignorance, all things occupying their proper place, the corporeal, the spiritual, and the intellectual, in untainted nature and perfect beatitude.

SELECTED BIBLIOGRAPHY

TEXTS AND TRANSLATIONS

Opera. Migne, Patrologia Latina, Vols. 32–47. Many of Augustine's works have been critically reedited in the *Corpus Scriptorum Ecclesiasticorum Latinorum* (Vienna) and the *Corpus Christianorum. Series Latina* (Turnhout).

Augustine of Hippo: Selected Writings. Translated by Mary T. Clark. The Classics of Western Spirituality. New York: Paulist; London: SPCK, 1984.

The Literal Meaning of Genesis. Translated by John Hammond Taylor, S.J. 2 vols. Ancient Christian Writers. New York: Newman, 1982.

STUDIES

Andresen, C. *Bibliographia Augustiniana.* Darmstadt, 1962. 2nd ed., 1973.

Brown, Peter. *Augustine of Hippo: A Biography.* Berkeley and Los Angeles: University of California Press; London: Faber, 1967.

Burnaby, John. *Amor Dei: A Study of the Religion of St. Augustine.* London: Hodder and Stoughton, 1938.

Cayré, F. *La contemplation augustinienne.* Paris, 1927.

Henry, Paul. *La vision d'Ostie: Sa place dans la vie et l'oeuvre de saint Augustin.* Paris, 1933.

Pope, Hugh. *The Teaching of St. Augustine on Prayer and the Contemplative Life.* London: Burns, Oates and Washbourne, 1935.

Pseudo-Dionysius

(early sixth century)

No writer presented in this anthology is likely to have exercised a greater influence upon Christian mysticism—East and West. Yet of none do we know less. Was he a Greek, an Egyptian, or a Syrian? A monk or a lay philosopher? Was he even a Christian? In what century did he live? None of these questions are we able to answer with absolute certainty, though we may safely conjecture him to have been a Syrian monk of the sixth century. He himself must bear the main responsibility for the confusion surrounding his identity, since all that he writes about himself has proven to be false. Textual evidence shows that he was not a contemporary of the apostles, a witness at the crucifixion and at the death of the Virgin. Nor was he the Dionysius whom St. Paul converted in the Areopagus, nor the third century martyr believed to have been the first bishop of Paris.

His writings show a clear dependence on Proclus, the Neoplatonic philosopher of the fifth century, who systematized Plotinus' philosophy. Through Dionysius' fake apostolic pedigree, philosophy gained such a firm foothold in the Christian spiritual tradition that it became, together with Scripture, its primary source of inspiration. Dionysius' writings once and for all defined the nature of what we now call negative theology. To be sure, negative theology had existed before Dionysius, specifically in Gregory of Nyssa. But it had been a dynamic movement, fully integrated with a theology of the Image. The apophatic extremes attained by Dionysius would probably not have been tolerated had it not been for the respect due to a venerable, apostolic figure. The "Areopagite" applies the ascetic concepts of purification and self-emptying in the most radical way to the discourse about God. The mind must exercise the same continuing self-denial which the desert fathers had applied to the moral order. Beyond all names, even beyond Being itself lies the dark reality of the divine "superessence." "Super-essential" means that God's "nature" remains beyond definition. Even the character of personhood does not apply. Dionysius calls this Absolute "One," as Plotinus had done. But the unity stands not opposed to plurality or number—God is neither one nor many. It indicates that the Absolute contains in an undifferentiated mode what exists separately in the created world. The Trinity itself, for Dionysius, belongs to the Godhead only insofar as the latter manifests itself. What Western theology calls the

"Persons" of the Trinity are, for Dionysius, super-essential and, hence, *super-personal* manifestations of the one Godhead.

In creation, God, in an ec-static move of love, reaches beyond His own essence. Creation does not lie "outside" God—all that is exists within this one super-essence—yet it belongs neither to the divine superessence nor to its trinitarian manifestation. In the contemplative life the creature reverses this process, moving beyond all created manifestations and even beyond the internal manifestation of the Trinity, into the darkness of the Godhead. In doing so the human mind surpasses its own created being and, in the ecstatic ascent, loses itself in the divine superessence. It thereby becomes deified. As one commentator puts it: "As the Super-Essence creates the world and our human souls by a species of divine 'ecstasy,' so the human soul must return by an answering 'ecstasy' to the Super-Essence. On both sides there is the same principle of Self-Transcendence."[1] The deepest mode of "knowing" God, then, consists in a continuous overcoming of all cognitive categories. The *ecstatic movement* itself, rather than any cognitive content, directs the mind to its union with God. From the preceding it should appear that this ascent of the mind is primarily an "intellectual" mysticism. Authorities doubt whether Dionysius would deserve the title "mystic" in the modern sense of extraordinary, private (and strongly affective) experience at all.[2]

Not all of Dionysius' theology, however, is "negative," though he reserves the title "mystical" exclusively to the negative one. Dionysius himself cautions that the "mystical theology" must be preceded by a theology which affirms the Trinity and all the traditional mysteries of the Catholic faith. The *Outline of Theology* in which Dionysius claims to have done this has not been preserved. But the *Divine Names* has. Here he explains the relativity of all attributes predicated of God and thus prepares the way to the final, "dark" theology of negation. This appears clearly in the last chapter (here presented) where Dionysius discusses the ultimate attribute of unity.

Since few scholars in the West read Greek, it took some time for Dionysius' work to influence the Latin Church. The ninth-century Irish theologian, John Scottus Eriugena, translated him into Latin. But not until the eleventh century did his authority become firmly established. From then on it ever increased in Scholastic theology (St. Thomas wrote a celebrated commentary on *The Divine Names* and constantly invokes the authority of "St. Denys") and, even more, in spiritual writings. Among the mystics featured in this anthology we can clearly trace his impact not only upon the ones we have called negative theologians (such as the author of *The Cloud of Unknowing* and Eckhart), but also upon trinitarian mystics (such as Ruusbroec), and even upon the Carmelites John of the Cross and Teresa of Avila. Even after he lost his arrogated apostolic reputation, his influence did not wane. We still find it effectively present in Merton. The atmosphere of doubt and dogmatic skepticism created by modern secularism has secured his "divine ignorance" a revived and renewed interest.

---

1. C. E. Rolt, Introduction to *Dionysius the Areopagite: The Divine Names and The Mystical Theology* (London: SPCK, 1940), 29.

2. Thus Jan Vanneste, S.J.: *Le mystère de Dieu: Essai sur la structure rationnelle de la doctrine mystique du Pseudo-Denys l'Aréopagite* (Paris, 1959). In the opposite direction: Walther Völker: *Kontemplation und Ekstase bei Pseudo-Dionysius Areopagita* (Wiesbaden, 1958).

Selections

THE DIVINE NAMES*

CHAPTER THIRTEEN
CONCERNING "PERFECT" AND "ONE"

. . . Let us proceed now to the most enduring [name] of them all. Theology, attributing every quality to the Cause of everything, calls him "Perfect" and "One." He is perfect not only insofar as he is absolute perfection, defining perfection in himself and from his singular existence and total perfection, but also because he is far beyond being so. He sets a boundary to the boundless and in his total unity he rises above all limitation. He is neither contained nor comprehended by anything. He reaches out to everything and beyond everything and does so with unfailing generosity and unstinted activity.

To speak of perfection is to proclaim that it cannot be increased or diminished, for it is eternally perfect, that it contains all things beforehand in itself, that it overflows in one unceasing, identical, overflowing, and undiminished supply, thereby perfecting the perfect and filling all things with its own perfection.

2. The name "One" means that God is uniquely all things through the transcendence of one unity and that he is the cause of all without ever departing from that oneness. Nothing in the world lacks its share of the One. Just as every number participates in unity—for we refer to one couple, one dozen, one-half, one-third, one-tenth—so everything, and every part of everything, participates in the One. By being the One, it is all things. The One Cause of all things is not one of the many things in the world but actually precedes oneness and multiplicity and indeed defines oneness and multiplicity. For multiplicity cannot exist without some participation in the One. That which is many in its parts is one in its entirety. That which is many in its accidental qualities is one in its subject. That which is many in number or capabilities is one in species. That which is numerous in species is one in genus. That which is numerous in its processions is one in its source. For there is nothing at all lacking a share in that One which in its utterly comprehensive unity uniquely contains all and everything beforehand, even opposites. Without the One there is no multiplicity, but there can still be the One when there is no multiplicity, just as one precedes all multiplied numbers. And, then, if one thinks of all things as united in all things, the totality of things must be presumed to be one.

3. There is something else to remember also. When things are said to be unified,

*All selections in this chapter are from *Pseudo-Dionysius: The Complete Works,* trans. Colm Luibheid with the collaboration of Paul Rorem, The Classics of Western Spirituality (New York: Paulist, 1987), 127–41. Reprinted with permission of the publisher.

this is in accordance with the preconceived form of the one proper to each. In this way the One may be called the underlying element of all things. And if you take away the One, there will survive neither whole nor part nor anything else in creation. The reality is that all things are contained beforehand in and are embraced by the One in its capacity as an inherent unity. Hence scripture describes the entire thearchy, the Cause of everything, as the One. Furthermore, "there is one God the Father and one Lord Jesus Christ" (1 Cor 8:6) and "one and the same Spirit" (1 Cor 12:11) and this is so in the overwhelming indivisibility of that oneness of God within which all things are banded together as one in the possession of a transcendent unity and in the transcendence of their preexistence. So all things are rightly ascribed to God since it is by him and in him and for him that all things exist, are co-ordered, remain, hold together, are completed, and are returned. You will find nothing in the world which is not in the One, by which the transcendent Godhead is named. Everything owes to the One its individual existence and the process whereby it is perfected and preserved. Given this power of God's unity, we must be returned from the many to the One and our unique song of praise must be for the single complete deity which is the one cause of all things and which is there before every oneness amid multiplicity, before every part and whole, before the definite and indefinite, before the limited and the unlimited. It is there defining all things that have being, defining Being itself. It is the Cause of things and of the sum total of things. It is simultaneously there with them and before them and beyond them. It is there beyond the one itself, defining this one. Unity among creatures is a unity of number, and number has its own share of being.

But the transcendent unity defines the one itself and every number. For it is the source, and the cause, the number and the order of the one, of number, and of all being. And the fact that the transcendent Godhead is one and triune must not be understood in any of our own typical senses. No. There is the transcendent unity of God and the fruitfulness of God, and as we prepare to sing this truth we use the names Trinity and Unity for that which is in fact beyond every name, calling it the transcendent being above every being. But no unity or trinity, no number or oneness, no fruitfulness, indeed, nothing that is or is known can proclaim that hiddenness beyond every mind and reason of the transcendent Godhead which transcends every being. There is no name for it nor expression. We cannot follow it into its inaccessible dwelling place so far above us and we cannot even call it by the name of goodness. In our urge to find some notion and some language appropriate to that ineffable nature, we reserve for it first the name which is most revered. Here, of course, I am in agreement with the scripture writers. But the real truth of these matters is in fact far beyond us. That is why their preference is for the way up through negations, since this stands the soul outside everything which is correlative with its own finite nature. Such a way guides the soul through all the divine notions, notions which are themselves transcended by that which is far beyond every name, all reason and all knowledge. Beyond the outermost boundaries of the world, the soul is brought into union with God himself to the extent that every one of us is capable of it.

4. These, then, are the divine names. They are conceptual names, and I have explained them as well as I can. But of course I have fallen well short of what they actually mean. Even the angels would have to admit such a failure and I could scarcely speak praises as they do. Even the greatest of our theologians are inferior to the least of the angels. But in this I have fallen wretchedly short not only of the theologians, their hearers and their followers but even of my own peers. So if what I have said is right and if, somehow, I have correctly understood and explicated something of the names of God, the work must be ascribed to the Cause of all good things for having given me the words to speak and the power to use them well. It may be that I have omitted some [name] of similar power, and if so this should be explained using the same methods. And perhaps there is something incorrect or imperfect about what I have done. Perhaps I have completely or partly strayed from the truth. If so I ask you to be charitable, to correct my unwished-for ignorance, to offer an argument to one needing to be taught, to help my faltering strength and to heal my unwanted frailty. I beg that you pass on to me whatever you have discovered by yourself or from others, all received from the Good. Please, let not this kindness to a friend be a burden to you. I have not kept to myself any of the hierarchical words which were handed down to me. I have passed them on unchanged to you and to other sacred men, and I will continue to do so as long as I have the power of words and you have the power to listen. I do an injustice to the tradition only when the strength to conceive and to utter these truths leaves me. May what I do and what I speak be pleasing to God.

So here I finish my treatise on the conceptual names of God, and, with God's guidance, I will move on to *The Symbolic Theology*.[1]

---

1. The lost or fictitious *Symbolic Theology* concerned those biblical symbols for God taken from the realm of sense perception. As such, it follows the presentation of names taken from the realm of concepts *(The Divine Names)* as part of the descent or procession from lofty simplicity to lowly plurality.

THE MYSTICAL THEOLOGY

CHAPTER ONE
What is the divine darkness?

1. Trinity!! Higher than any being,
                   any divinity, any goodness!
           Guide of Christians
           Higher in the wisdom of heaven!
    Lead us up beyond unknowing and light,
         up to the farthest, highest peak
              of mystic scripture.
         where the mysteries of God's Word
              lie simple, absolute and unchangeable
              in the brilliant darkness of a hidden silence.
         Amid the deepest shadow
              they pour overwhelming light
              on what is most manifest.
         Amid the wholly unsensed and unseen
              they completely fill our sightless minds
              with treasures beyond all beauty.

For this I pray; and, Timothy, my friend, my advice to you as you look for a sight of the mysterious things, is to leave behind you everything perceived and understood, everything perceptible and understandable, all that is not and all that is, and, with your understanding laid aside, to strive upward as much as you can toward union with him who is beyond all being and knowledge. By an undivided and absolute abandonment of yourself and everything, shedding all and freed from all, you will be uplifted to the ray of the divine shadow which is above everything that is.

2. But see to it that none of this comes to the hearing of the uninformed, that is to say, to those caught up with the things of the world, who imagine that there is nothing beyond instances of individual being and who think that by their own intellectual resources they can have a direct knowledge of him who has made the shadows his hiding place. And if initiation into the divine is beyond such people, what is to be said of those others, still more uninformed, who describe the transcendent Cause of all things in terms derived from the lowest orders of being, and who claim that it is in no way superior to the godless, multiformed shapes they themselves have made? What has actually to be said about the Cause of everything is this. Since it is the Cause of all beings, we should posit and ascribe to it all the affirmations we make

in regard to beings, and, more appropriately, we should negate all these affirmations, since it surpasses all being. Now we should not conclude that the negations are simply the opposites of the affirmations, but rather that the cause of all is considerably prior to this, beyond privations, beyond every denial, beyond every assertion.

3. This, at least, is what was taught by the blessed Bartholomew.[1] He says that the Word of God is vast and minuscule, that the Gospel is wide-ranging and yet restricted. To me it seems that in this he is extraordinarily shrewd, for he has grasped that the good cause of all is both eloquent and taciturn, indeed wordless. It has neither word nor act of understanding, since it is on a plane above all this, and it is made manifest only to those who travel through foul and fair, who pass beyond the summit of every holy ascent, who leave behind them every divine light, every voice, every word from heaven, and who plunge into the darkness where, as scripture proclaims, there dwells the One who is beyond all things. It is not for nothing that the blessed Moses is commanded to submit first to purification and then to depart from those who have not undergone this. When every purification is complete, he hears the many-voiced trumpets. He sees the many lights, pure and with rays streaming abundantly. Then, standing apart from the crowds and accompanied by chosen priests, he pushes ahead to the summit of the divine ascents. And yet he does not meet God himself, but contemplates, not him who is invisible, but rather where he dwells. This means, I presume, that the holiest and highest of the things perceived with the eye of the body or the mind are but the rationale which presupposes all that lies below the Transcendent One. Through them, however, his unimaginable presence is shown, walking the heights of those holy places to which the mind at least can rise. But then he [Moses] breaks free of them, away from what sees and is seen, and he plunges into the truly mysterious darkness of unknowing. Here, renouncing all that the mind may conceive, wrapped entirely in the intangible and the invisible, he belongs completely to him who is beyond everything. Here, being neither oneself nor someone else, one is supremely united by a completely unknowing inactivity of all knowledge, and knows beyond the mind by knowing nothing.

CHAPTER TWO
How one should be united, and attribute praises, to the Cause of all things who is beyond all things.

I pray we could come to this darkness so far above light! If only we lacked sight and knowledge so as to see, so as to know, unseeing and unknowing, that which lies

---

1. Like the other apostles, the Bartholomew of the New Testament was later credited with several apocryphal works.

beyond all vision and knowledge. For this would be really to see and to know: to praise the Transcendent One in a transcending way, namely through the denial of all beings. We would be like sculptors who set out to carve a statue. They remove every obstacle to the pure view of the hidden image, and simply by this act of clearing aside they show up the beauty which is hidden.

Now it seems to me that we should praise the denials quite differently than we do the assertions. When we made assertions we began with the first things, moved down through intermediate terms until we reached the last things. But now as we climb from the last things up to the most primary we deny all things so that we may unhiddenly know that unknowing which itself is hidden from all those possessed of knowing amid all beings, so that we may see above being that darkness concealed from all the light among beings.

<h2 style="text-align:center">CHAPTER THREE</h2>
What are the affirmative theologies and what are the negative?

In my *Theological Representations,*[2] I have praised the notions which are most appropriate to affirmative theology. I have shown the sense in which the divine and good nature is said to be one and then triune, how Fatherhood and Sonship are predicated of it, the meaning of the theology of the Spirit, how these core lights of goodness grew from the incorporeal and indivisible good, and how in this sprouting they have remained inseparable from their co-eternal foundation in it, in themselves, and in each other. I have spoken of how Jesus, who is above individual being, became a being with a true human nature. Other revelations of scripture were also praised in *The Theological Representations*.

In *The Divine Names* I have shown the sense in which God is described as good, existent, life, wisdom, power, and whatever other things pertain to the conceptual names for God. In my *Symbolic Theology* I have discussed analogies of God drawn from what we perceive. I have spoken of the images we have of him, of the forms, figures, and instruments proper to him, of the places in which he lives and of the ornaments he wears. I have spoken of his anger, grief, and rage, of how he is said to be drunk and hungover, of his oaths and curses, of his sleeping and waking, and indeed of all those images we have of him, images shaped by the workings of the symbolic representations of God. And I feel sure that you have noticed how these latter come much more abundantly than what went before, since *The Theological Representations* and a discussion of the names appropriate to God are inevitably briefer than what can be said in *The Symbolic Theology*. The fact is that the more

2. This lost or fictitious treatise is mentioned and perhaps summarized in the first chapter of *The Divine Names*.

we take flight upward, the more our words are confined to the ideas we are capable of forming; so that now as we plunge into that darkness which is beyond intellect, we shall find ourselves not simply running short of words but actually speechless and unknowing. In the earlier books my argument traveled downward from the most exalted to the humblest categories, taking in on this downward path an ever-increasing number of ideas which multiplied with every stage of the descent. But my argument now rises from what is below up to the transcendent, and the more it climbs, the more language falters, and when it has passed up and beyond the ascent, it will turn silent completely, since it will finally be at one with him who is indescribable.

Now you may wonder why it is that, after starting out from the highest category when our method involved assertions, we begin now from the lowest category when it involves a denial. The reason is this. When we assert what is beyond every assertion, we must then proceed from what is most akin to it, and as we do so we make the affirmation on which everything else depends. But when we deny that which is beyond every denial, we have to start by denying those qualities which differ most from the goal we hope to attain. Is it not closer to reality to say that God is life and goodness rather than that he is air or stone? Is it not more accurate to deny that drunkenness and rage can be attributed to him than to deny that we can apply to him the terms of speech and thought?[3]

CHAPTER FOUR
That the supreme Cause of every perceptible thing is not itself perceptible.

So this is what we say. The Cause of all is above all and is not inexistent, lifeless, speechless, mindless. It is not a material body, and hence has neither shape nor

---

3. "Life," "goodness," "air," etc., are all biblical examples and are discussed elsewhere in the Dionysian corpus. The point here is that not all affirmations concerning God are equally inappropriate; they are arranged in a descending order of descending congruity. Affirmative theology begins with the loftier, more congruous comparisons and then proceeds "down" to the less appropriate ones. Thus, as the author reminds us, *The Theological Representations* began with God's oneness and proceeded down into the multiplicity of affirming the Trinity and the incarnation. *The Divine Names* then affirmed the more numerous designations for God which come from mental concepts, while *The Symbolic Theology* "descended" into the still more pluralized realm of sense perception and its plethora of symbols for the deity. This pattern of descending affirmations and ascending negations can be interpreted in terms of late Neoplatonism's "procession" from the One down into plurality and the "return" of all back to the One.

In this return, not all negations concerning God are equally appropriate; the attributes to be negated are arranged in an ascending order of decreasing incongruity. Thus the first to be denied are the perceptible attributes, starting with *The Mystical Theology*, chapter 4, which therefore previews the two subsequent treatises on perceptible symbols, *The Celestial Hierarchy* and *The Ecclesiastical Hierarchy*. "As we climb higher" in the ascent from the perceptible to the intelligible, chapter 5 of *The Mystical Theology* denies and moves beyond all our concepts or "conceptual" attributes of God and concludes by abandoning all speech and thought, even negations.

On this sequence of treatises, see Paul Rorem, "The Place of *The Mystical Theology* in the Pseudo-Dionysian Corpus," *Dionysius* 4 (1980): 87–98.

form, quality, quantity, or weight. It is not in any place and can neither be seen nor be touched. It is neither perceived nor is it perceptible. It suffers neither disorder nor disturbance and is overwhelmed by no earthly passion. It is not powerless and subject to the disturbances caused by sense perception. It endures no deprivation of light. It passes through no change, decay, division, loss, no ebb and flow, nothing of which the senses may be aware. None of all this can either be identified with it nor attributed to it.

CHAPTER FIVE
That the supreme Cause of every conceptual thing is not itself conceptual.

Again, as we climb higher we say this. It is not soul or mind, nor does it possess imagination, conviction, speech, or understanding. Nor is it speech per se, under-standing per se. It cannot be spoken of and it cannot be grasped by understanding. It is not number or order, greatness or smallness, equality or inequality, similarity or dissimilarity. It is not immovable, moving, or at rest. It has no power, it is not power, nor is it light. It does not live nor is it life. It is not a substance, nor is it eternity or time. It cannot be grasped by the understanding since it is neither knowl-edge nor truth. It is not kingship. It is not wisdom. It is neither one nor oneness, divinity nor goodness. Nor is it a spirit, in the sense in which we understand that term. It is not sonship or fatherhood and it is nothing known to us or to any other being. It falls neither within the predicate of nonbeing nor of being. Existing beings do not know it as it actually is and it does not know them as they are. There is no speaking of it, nor name nor knowledge of it. Darkness and light, error and truth—it is none of these. It is beyond assertion and denial. We make assertions and denials of what is next to it, but never of it, for it is both beyond every assertion, being the perfect and unique cause of all things, and, by virtue of its preeminently simple and absolute nature, free of every limitation, beyond every limitation; it is also beyond every denial.

SELECTED BIBLIOGRAPHY

TEXTS AND TRANSLATIONS

Opera. Migne, Patrologia Graeca, vol. 3. A critical edition of the works of Pseudo-Dionysius, under the editorship of A. M. Ritter, G. Heil, and B. Suchla, is forthcoming from the Patristische Kommission der Westdeutschen Akademie der Wissenschaften (Göttingen).

The Divine Names and Mystical Theology. Translated by John D. Jones. Milwaukee: Marquette University Press, 1980.

Pseudo-Dionysius: The Complete Works. Translated by Colm Luibheid. The Classics of Western Spirituality. New York: Paulist; London: SPCK, 1987.

STUDIES

Balthasar, Hans Urs von. "Denys." In *The Glory of the Lord: A Theological Aesthetics.* Vol. 2, *Studies in Theological Style: Clerical Styles,* translated by Andrew Louth *et al.,* 144–210. San Francisco: Ignatius Press; New York: Crossroad; Edinburgh: T. & T. Clark, 1984.

Gersh, Stephen. *From Iamblichus to Eriugena: An Investigation of the Prehistory and Evolution of the Pseudo-Dionysian Tradition.* Leiden, 1978.

Lossky, Vladimir. "La théologie négative dans la doctrine de Denys l'Aréopagite." *Revue des sciences philosophiques et théologiques* 28 (1939): 204–21.

Puech, H. C. "La ténèbre mystique chez le Ps.-Denys et dans la tradition patristique." *Etudes Carmélitaines* 23 (1938): 33–53.

Roques, René. "De l'implication des méthodes théologiques chez le Pseudo-Denys." *Revue d'ascétique et de mystique* 30 (1954):268–74.

————. *L'univers dionysien: Structure hiérarchique du monde selon le pseudo-Denys.* Paris, 1954.

Rorem, Paul. *Biblical and Liturgical Symbols within the Pseudo-Dionysian Synthesis.* Toronto: Pontifical Institute of Mediaeval Studies, 1984.

Vanneste, Jan. *Le mystère de Dieu: Essai sur la structure rationnelle de la doctrine mystique du pseudo-Denys l'Aréopagite.* Brussels, 1959.

Völker, Walther. *Kontemplation und Ekstase bei Pseudo-Dionysius Areopagita.* Wiesbaden, 1958.

Maximus the Confessor

(580–662)

Considered by historians of spirituality to be one of the most profound mystics the Greek Church ever produced and "the most philosophical mind in the Christian East after Origen" (V. Soloviev), Maximus was also like Origen in suffering cruel physical punishment toward the end of his life for his adherence to the faith. It is for this reason that he is known as "the Confessor," one who remained faithful even to the confession of martyrdom.

For long it was believed, on the basis of a tenth century *vita,* that Maximus was born and educated in Constantinople, even serving as protosecretary of the emperor Heraclius before entering monastic life at Chrysopolis on the Asiatic side of the Bosphorus. More recently it has been argued by I.-H. Dalmais that he was more likely born in Palestine and that he perhaps lived there as a monk for a decade or more before seeking refuge in Constantinople at the time of the Persian invasion of Palestine in 614.[1] In any case, when the Persians in turn threatened Constantinople some twelve years later, he fled to North Africa and entered a monastery near Carthage under the abbatial leadership of Sophronius, the future patriarch of Jerusalem. It was here that Max-

imus likely gave final form to the majority of his spiritual writings, including the *Chapters on Knowledge* from which we have chosen excerpts for this anthology. It was also during these years that he became more and more involved in the controversies of Monenergism and Monothelitism, that is, the dogmatic disputes over whether Christ had one "activity" and "will" or two. If such questions seem far removed from the concerns of most Christians today, Maximus nevertheless recognized that something truly important for Christian faith and spirituality was at stake: Since "will" pertains to a nature rather than to a person, then Christ—one person in two natures, according to the formula of the Council of Chalcedon—must have had both a human will and a divine will. Otherwise, as Maximus' modern translator George Berthold has written, "on the basis of the ancient patristic principle that whatever was not assumed in the Incarnation was not healed in the Redemption, the absence of a truly human will in Jesus Christ would have meant that . . . the human will of sinful humanity would not have been saved."[2]

Because of his opposition to the Mono-

---

1. I.-H. Dalmais, "Maxime le Confesseur," *Dictionnaire de Spiritualité* 10:836–37.

2. George Berthold, ed., *Maximus Confessor. Selected Writings* (New York: Paulist; London: SPCK, 1985), 4.

thelite teaching, Maximus was arrested in 653 by order of the emperor Constans II, found guilty of treason, and banished to exile in Thrace in 655. Seven years later, at the age of eighty-two, he was brought back to Constantinople to undergo a second trial, where he was again condemned by the Monothelite party and suffered the punishment of having his tongue ripped out and his right hand amputated. After a few further months of exile, he died on August 13, 662. Eighteen years after his death, the sixth ecumenical council at Constantinople vindicated his teaching on the two wills of Christ and he has ever since been revered as a saint and doctor of the Church.

Although Maximus was profoundly influenced by a number of earlier Christian writers—above all by Origen, Evagrius, Gregory Nazianzen, Gregory of Nyssa, and Pseudo-Dionysius—it would be altogether wrong to regard him as a mere compiler of their teachings. For example, he took definite exception to the Origenist teaching on the preexistence of souls and of their being joined to bodies as punishment for a sin committed in that earlier existence. His rejection of that position was based largely on his fear that we would otherwise be led to affirm that "this unique masterpiece of creation which is the visible world, in which God is made known through a silent revelation, would have no other cause than sin" (*Ambiguorum Liber;* Migne, PG 91, 1328A). Such a passage led Hans Urs von Balthasar, in his seminal study of Maximus' theology, to conclude that in some respects he was more open to the world, more disposed to see a positive value in creation, than any of the other Fathers.[3]

The real heart of Maximus' mysticism, however, lies not in his teaching about this "silent revelation" of the world around us but in what we might call the "Word revelation" of the incarnation and redemption. While retaining much of the language of Pseudo-Dionysius, he gives it a far more explicitly trinitarian and Christocentric orientation, as even the most cursory comparison of the two authors will indicate. Many of the short passages or "chapters" from Maximus in our anthology deal with precisely this theme; he writes, for example: "Just as our human word which proceeds naturally from the mind is messenger of the secret movements of the mind, so does the Word of God, who knows the Father by essence as Word knows the Mind which has begotten it (since no created being can approach the Father without him), reveal the Father whom he knows" (*Chapters on Knowledge* 2.22; henceforth abbreviated *CK*). Furthermore, the acceptance of this revelation on our part is not primarily a matter of understanding but of doing; more exactly, in the words of another Maximus scholar, "knowledge is the *effect,* the *sign* of union with God brought about by love, but an effect which reacts in turn on the cause, intensifying love."[4] The efficacy of praxis is particularly clear in another of our excerpts from Maximus, where he argues that because the Word of God is mystically present in each of his commandments, and because both the Father and the Holy Spirit are in the Word by nature, anyone "who has accepted a commandment and performed it has received in mystical possession the Holy Trinity" (*CK* 2.71).

3. Hans Urs von Balthasar, *Liturgie cosmique. Maxime le Confesseur* (Paris, 1947), 18.

4. J. Pegon, S.J., Intro. to *Maxime le Confesseur. Centuries sur la charité.* Sources chrétiennes 9 (Paris, 1945), 55.

A final theme that is very prominent in our selections is reminiscent of Gregory of Nyssa: the dynamic, progressive nature of the Christian life. Again and again Maximus uses such phrases as "from strength to strength" and "from glory to glory," all with reference to our continual movement toward that final state of perfect rest "which reveals face to face to those who are worthy the truth as it is in itself. Then one will possess not just a part of the fullness but rather acquire through participation the entire fullness of grace" (*CK* 2.87). This is what he and others of the Greek Fathers elsewhere call deification, *theosis,* and this is the ultimate goal of the Christian life as Maximus the Confessor understands it: "The Word of God and God the Son of the Father became son of man and man himself for this reason, to make men gods and sons of God" (*CK* 2.25).

Selections

CHAPTERS ON KNOWLEDGE*

Second Century[1]

18. The one who prays ought never to halt his movement of sublime ascent toward God. For just as we should understand the ascents "from strength to strength" as the progress in the practice of the virtues, [and] "from glory to glory" (2 Cor 3:18) as the advance in the spiritual knowledge of contemplation . . . so in the same way the one who is settled in the place of prayer should lift his mind from human matters and the attention of the soul to more divine realities. This will enable him to follow the one who has "passed through the heavens, Jesus the Son of God" (Heb 4:14), who is everywhere and who in his incarnation passes through all things on our account. If we follow him, we also pass through all things with him and come beside him if we know him not in the limited condition of his descent in the incarnation but in the majestic splendor of his natural infinitude.

19. It is always a good thing to devote ourselves to seeking God, as we have been commanded. For although in the present life we are unable to arrive at the limit of God's depth, yet at least by reaching in some small way his depth we would see the holier among holy things and the more spiritual among spiritual things. This is clearly indicated in the figure of the high priest who, from the holy place which is more sacred than the courtyard, enters into the Holy of Holies, which is more sacred than the holy place.

20. Each word of God is neither multiple nor wordy but rather is one, though made up of different parts of speech, of which each is a part of the meaning. Thus if one is speaking about truth, even if he could speak about it in such a way that nothing is left out, he has spoken about the one Word of God.

21. In Christ who is God and the Word of the Father there dwells in bodily form the complete fullness of deity by essence; in us the fullness of deity dwells by grace whenever we have formed in ourselves every virtue and wisdom, lacking in no way what is possible to man in the faithful reproduction of the archetype. For it is not unnatural . . . that the fullness of deity dwell also in us by adoption, expressed in the various spiritual ideas.

22. Just as our human word which proceeds naturally from the mind is messenger of the secret movements of the mind, so does the Word of God, who knows the Father by essence as Word knows the Mind which has begotten it (since no created

---

*From *Maximus Confessor: Selected Writings,* trans. George C. Berthold, The Classics of Western Spirituality (New York: Paulist, 1985), 151–54, 163–67. Reprinted with permission of the publisher.

1. "Century" here refers to a collection of one hundred chapters. Maximus wrote two centuries *On Knowledge* and four centuries *On Love.*

94

being can approach the Father without him), reveal the Father whom he knows. As the Word of God by nature, he is spoken of as the "messenger of the great counsel" (Is 9:6).

23. The great plan of God the Father is the secret and unknown mystery of the dispensation which the only-begotten Son revealed by fulfilling in the incarnation, thus becoming a messenger of the great plan of God the eternal Father. The one who knows the meaning of the mystery and who is so incessantly lifted up both in work and in word through all things until he acquires what is sent down to him is likewise a messenger of the great plan of God.

24. If it was for us that the Word of God in his incarnation descended into the lower parts of the earth and ascended above all the heavens, while being himself perfectly unmoved, he underwent in himself through his incarnation as man our future destiny. Let the one who is moved by a love of knowledge mystically rejoice in learning of the great destiny which he has promised to those who love the Lord.

25. If the Word of God and God the Son of the Father became son of man and man himself for this reason, to make men gods and sons of God, then we must believe that we shall be where Christ is now as head of the whole body, having become in his human nature a forerunner to the Father on our behalf. For God will be in the "assembly of the gods" (Ps 82:1), that is, of those who are saved, standing in their midst and apportioning there the ranks of blessedness without any spatial distance separating him from the elect.

26. The one who is still satisfying the passionate appetites of the flesh dwells as a maker and worshiper of idols in the land of the Chaldeans. But after some reflection on this matter he becomes aware of behavior which is more proper to nature, leaves the land of the Chaldeans, and goes to Haran in Mesopotamia, that is, the frontier state between virtue and vice which is not yet purified of the deception of the senses. This is what the word Haran means. But if one looks even beyond the understanding of the good which is suitable to the senses, he will press on to the good land, that is, to the state which is free from all vice and ignorance, which a faithful God points out and professes to give as a reward of virtue to those who love him.

27. If the Word of God was crucified for us out of weakness and was raised up by the power of God, it is evident that he is always doing and suffering this for us in a spiritual way, because he became all things to all men in order to save all. Well, then, did the holy Apostle while among the weak Corinthians determine that he would know nothing except Jesus Christ, and him crucified. But to the Ephesians, who were perfect, he writes that God "raised us up with Christ Jesus and seated us with him in the heavens" (Eph 2:6). He speaks of the reality of the Word of God in a manner which corresponds to each one's strength. Thus he is crucified for those who are still beginners in the practice of virtue and who crucify their passionate

drives with reverential fear. But he rises and ascends into heaven for those who have completely put off the old self which is corrupted through deceitful desires, who have completely put on the new self which is created in God's image through the Spirit, and who have become the Father's by virtue of the grace which is in them: "high above every principality and power, virtue and domination, and every name that can be given either in this age or in the one to come" (Eph 1:21). For everything which is less than God, things and names and dignities, will be subject to the one who has come to be in God through grace.

28. Just as before his visible and fleshly appearance the Word of God dwelt spiritually with the patriarchs and prophets, prefiguring the mysteries of his coming, so after this presence he comes not only to those who are still infants, spiritually supporting them and bringing them to the age of perfection in God, but he comes also to the perfect and in a hidden way he delineates in advance in them as in a picture the features of his future coming.

29. Just as the understanding of the Law and the Prophets as precursors of the coming of the Word in the flesh instructed souls about Christ, so has this same glorified Word of God incarnate become a precursor of his spiritual coming, and he instructs souls by his words about the acceptance of his visible divine coming. This coming he always effects by changing those who are worthy from the flesh to the spirit through the virtues. And he will do this also at the end of time, clearly revealing to all what is still secret.

30. So long as I am imperfect and insubordinate in not obeying God through the keeping of the commandments, and have not reached the interior perfection of knowledge, then Christ also must be considered imperfect and insubordinate as related to me and in me. In this case I diminish him and cut him down and fail to grow up with him spiritually, since we are Christ's body, each one a member of it.

31. "The sun rises and the sun goes down," says Scripture (Eccl 1:5). Thus it is also with the Word, who is sometimes regarded as up and sometimes as down, obviously depending on the dignity and nature and character of those who practice virtue and who are moved toward divine knowledge. Then blessed is he who like Joshua, the son of Nun, can keep the sun of justice from falling in himself, and the complete duration of whose day in the present life is not limited by the evening of sin and ignorance in order to enable him to rout in a lawful way the wicked spirits who are attacking him.

32. When the Word of God is exalted in us through asceticism and contemplation, he draws everyone to himself, sanctifying our thoughts and ideas about the flesh and the soul and the nature of things, as well as these members and senses of the body by virtue and knowledge, and bringing them under his yoke. Therefore the one who is a witness of divine things should quickly ascend and follow the Word

until he arrives at the place where he is. For there he draws him, as Ecclesiastes says (1:5 [LXX]): "he draws toward his place" those, that is, who follow him as a great High Priest who leads them into the Holy of Holies, where "he entered on our behalf as a forerunner" (Heb 6:20). . . .

73. So long as we see the Word of God take flesh in the letter of Holy Writ in a variety of figures we have not yet spiritually seen the incorporeal and simple and singular and only Father as in the incorporeal and simple and singular and only Son. As the Scripture says, "The one who has seen me has seen the Father," and also, "I am in the Father and the Father is in me" (Jn 14:9, 10). It is, therefore, very necessary for a deep knowledge that we first study the veils of the statements regarding the Word and so behold with the naked mind the pure Word as he exists in himself, who clearly shows the Father in himself, as far as it is possible for men to grasp. Thus it is necessary that the one who seeks after God in a religious way never hold fast to the letter lest he mistakenly understand things said about God for God himself. In this case we unwisely are satisfied with the words of Scripture in place of the Word, and the Word slips out of the mind while we thought by holding on to his garments we could possess the incorporeal Word. In a similar way did the Egyptian woman lay hold not of Joseph but of his clothing, and the men of old who remained permanently in the beauty of visible things and mistakenly worshiped the creature instead of the Creator.

74. The meaning of Holy Writ reveals itself gradually to the more discerning mind in loftier senses when it has put off the complex whole of the words formed in it bodily, as in the sound of a gentle breeze. Through a supreme abandonment of natural activities, such a mind has been able to perceive sense only in a simplicity which reveals the Word, the way that the great Elijah was granted the vision in the cave at Horeb. For Horeb means "newness," which is the virtuous condition in the new spirit of grace. The cave is the hiddenness of spiritual wisdom in which one who enters will mystically experience the knowledge which goes beyond the senses and in which God is found. Therefore, anyone who truly seeks God as did the great Elijah will come upon him not only on Horeb, that is, as an ascetic in the practice of the virtues, but also in the cave of Horeb, that is, as a contemplative in the hidden place of wisdom, which can exist only in the habit of the virtues.

75. When the mind shakes off the many distractions about things which are pressing on it, then the clear meaning of truth appears on it and gives it pledges of genuine knowledge after it has driven off the preoccupations bothering it of late as scales on its power of seeing, as with the great and holy apostle Paul. For notions about the mere letter of Scripture and considerations of visible things prejudicial to sense are indeed scales which cling to the clear-sighted part of the soul and hinder the passage to the pure meaning of truth.

76. The divine apostle Paul said he knew in part the knowledge of the Word. But the great evangelist John said that he saw his glory: "We have seen his glory, the glory as the only-begotten of the Father, full of grace and truth" (Jn 1:14). And why did St. Paul say that he knew in part the knowledge of the divine Word? For he is known only to a certain extent through his activities. The knowledge of himself in his essence and personhood remains inaccessible to all angels and men alike and he can in no way be known by anyone. But St. John, initiated as perfectly as humanly possible into the meaning of the Word's incarnation, claims that he has seen the glory of the Word as flesh, that is, he saw the reason or the plan for which God became man, full of grace and truth. For it was not as God by essence, consubstantial to God the Father, that the only-begotten Son gave this grace, but as having in the incarnation become man by nature, and consubstantial to us, that he bestows grace on us who have need of it. This grace we receive from his fullness always in proportion to our progress. Therefore, the one who keeps sacred the whole meaning of the Word of God's becoming incarnate for our sake will acquire the glory full of grace and truth of the one who for our sake glorifies and consecrates himself in us by his coming: "When he appears we shall be like him" (1 Jn 3:2).

77. So long as the soul makes the passage from strength to strength and "from glory to glory" (2 Cor 3:18), progress from virtue to greater virtue, and makes the ascent from knowledge to higher knowledge, it does not cease being a sojourner, as it is stated: "My soul has long been a sojourner" (Ps 120:5). For great is the distance and the multitude of steps of knowledge to be passed until it "comes to the place of your wondrous tabernacle, up to the house of God, in a voice of exultation and thanksgiving, and of those keeping festival" (Ps 42:5), ever adding a voice to voices, a spiritual one to spiritual ones, as it progresses in divine contemplations with rejoicing over the spiritual contemplations, that is, with joy and proper thanksgiving. These festivals are celebrated by all those who have received the Spirit of grace, who cry out in their hearts, "Abba, Father" (Gal 4:6).

78. The place of the wondrous tabernacle is the virtuous condition which is free of passion and harm in which the Word of God comes and adorns the soul like a tabernacle with various beauties of virtues. The house of God is a knowledge composed of many and varied contemplations, according to which God goes out to the soul and fills it with the chalice of wisdom. The voice of exultation is the joy of the soul over the wealth of virtues. The voice of thanksgiving is gratitude for the glory of the feasting in wisdom. The sound is the continuous mystical doxology which comes about from both exultation and thanksgiving.

79. The one who has genuinely overcome the bodily passions and has done sufficient battle against unclean spirits and has banished their devices from the region of his soul should pray to be given a clean heart and that an upright heart be renewed deep within him, that is, that he be completely purged of evil imaginings and

through grace be filled with divine thoughts. In this way there will come about God's world both great and spiritually luminous, brought together by moral, natural, and theological insights.

80. The one who has rendered his heart clean not only understands the meanings of things which are inferior to God but also, after passing through all of them, can look in some way on God himself, who is the ultimate good. On this heart God comes and deigns to engrave his own words through the Spirit as on the tablets of Moses, to the extent that it has devoted itself through ascetical practice and contemplation according to the mystically given commandment: "Increase" (Gen 35:11).

81. A clean heart might be said to be one which has not at all any natural movement in any way whatever. The Lord comes to it in perfect simplicity and as on a beautifully clean tablet writes his own laws on it.

82. A heart is clean if it presents its memory of God in a condition completely devoid of shape and form and is prepared to be imprinted only by his characters by means of which it becomes visible.

83. The mind of Christ which the saints receive according to the saying, "We have the mind of Christ" (1 Cor 2:16), comes along not by any loss of our mental power, nor as a supplementary mind to ours, nor as essentially and personally passing over into our mind, but rather as illuminating the power of our mind with its own quality and bringing the same energy to it. For to have the mind of Christ is, in my opinion, to think in his way and of him in all situations.

84. We are said to be the body of Christ according to the Scripture. "We are the body of Christ, each one a member of it" (1 Cor 12:27), not by losing our own bodies and becoming his, nor because he passes into us in his person or is divided up in our members. Rather it is because the corruption of sin is shaken off in a likeness to the Lord's flesh. For as Christ is by nature sinless in both body and soul by which he is known as man, so can we who believe in him and who are clothed with him in the Spirit be in him without sin by the use of our free will. . . .

86. We know from Scripture that there is a realm above time which gives evidence of its existence, but to what it is we can give no name; as Scripture says, "The Lord reigns forever and ever and ever" (Ex 15:18). Thus there is something beyond time: the pure reign of God. For it is not correct to say that the reign of God had a beginning or falls under ages and times. Rather we believe that it is the inheritance and the abode and the place of those who are saved, as the genuine word of Scripture tells us. It is the fulfillment of those who are moved by a longing for the ultimate object of desire. When they reach it they receive a special kind of repose from all movement, because they will require no further time or period to go through, since at the completion of these they arrive at God who is before all ages and whom the very nature of time cannot even approach.

87. So long as one is in the present time of this life, even if he be perfect in his

earthly state both in action and in contemplation, he still has knowledge, prophecy, and the pledge of the Holy Spirit only in part, but not in their fullness. He has yet to come at the end of the ages to the perfect rest which reveals face to face to those who are worthy the truth as it is in itself. Then one will possess not just a part of the fullness but rather acquire through participation the entire fullness of grace. For the Apostle says, "All of us (that is, those who are saved) will be that perfect man in the measure of the age of Christ's fullness" (Eph 4:13), in whom "are hidden the treasures of wisdom and knowledge" (Col 2:3); "and when he appears, what is in part shall pass away" (1 Cor 13:10).

SELECTED BIBLIOGRAPHY

TEXTS AND TRANSLATIONS

Opera. Migne, Patrologia Graeca, Vols. 90–91.

The Ascetic Life; The Four Centuries on Charity. Translated by Polycarp Sherwood, O.S.B. Ancient Christian Writers. Westminster, Md.: Newman; London: Longmans Green, 1955. Reprint. New York: Newman, n.d.

Maximus Confessor: Selected Writings. Translated by George C. Berthold. The Classics of Western Spirituality. New York: Paulist; London: SPCK, 1985.

STUDIES

Balthasar, Hans Urs von. *Kosmische Liturgie: Das Weltbild Maximus des Bekenners.* 2nd ed. Einsiedeln, 1961.

Dalmais, I.-H. "Maxime le Confesseur." *Dictionnaire de Spiritualité* 10:836–42.

Garrigues, J.-M. *Maxime le Confesseur: La charité, avenir divin de l'homme.* Paris, 1976.

Riou, A. *Le monde et l'église selon Maxime le Confesseur.* Paris, 1973.

Sherwood, Polycarp, O.S.B. *The Earlier Ambigua of St. Maximus the Confessor and His Refutation of Origenism.* Rome, 1955.

Thunberg, Lars. *Microcosm and Mediator: The Theological Anthropology of Maximus the Confessor.* Lund, 1965.

Völker, Walther. *Maximus Confessor als Meister des geistlichen Lebens.* Wiesbaden, 1965.

William of St. Thierry

(c.1080–c.1148)

The five centuries between Maximus the Confessor and William of St. Thierry represent by far the longest period from which no writings were selected for this anthology. While this certainly does not imply that there were no important mystical writers during these centuries (the omission of Symeon the New Theologian [945–1022], for example, will be regretted by some of our readers), it is nevertheless true that, at least as regards mystical literature in the Christian West, these five centuries were primarily ones of preparation or gestation. Indeed, one of the most influential writers of this period, John Scottus Eriugena (c.810–c.877), is remembered almost as much for his Latin translations of treatises by the Greek Fathers (including Gregory of Nyssa, Maximus the Confessor, and Pseudo-Dionysius) as for his own writings. It was, in fact, Dom Jean-Marie Déchanet's discovery in the late 1930s that William of St. Thierry had used Eriugena's translation of one of Gregory of Nyssa's treatises in the construction of his own *De natura corporis et animae* that led Déchanet to concentrate in his further research on the larger question of the influence of the Greek Fathers on William's thought as a whole. More recent scholarship has argued forcefully that

Déchanet, overlooking the still greater influence of Augustine on William, exaggerated the impact of the Greeks,[1] but it is nevertheless true that we have in William a genial interpenetration of Eastern and Western themes leading to an impressive synthesis that is still uniquely his own. In him and in his close friend, Bernard of Clairvaux, we see a rich flowering of mystical expression after those centuries of preparation.

William was born in Liège sometime in the final quarter of the eleventh century. After studies at Rheims (or perhaps at Laon), he entered the Benedictine monastery of St. Nicaise at Rheims around the year 1115 and about five years later was elected abbot of the nearby monastery of St. Thierry. The anonymous *Vita antiqua* praises his abbacy as a time of exemplary discipline and leadership but also says that during his years as abbot William was drawn more and more to the Cistercian way of life out of a desire for solitude and spiritual growth. At first, William was dissuaded from making such a change by Ber-

---

1. See, e.g., David N. Bell, *The Image and Likeness. The Augustinian Spirituality of William of St. Thierry* (Kalamazoo, Mich.: Cistercian Pubs., 1984), esp. 13–19.

nard of Clairvaux, who argued that he was needed at St. Thierry, but after more than fourteen years as abbot he left that monastery to enter the Cistercian house at Signy, also in the diocese of Rheims. Of sickly disposition, he was unable to share fully in the strenuous manual labor and devoted himself instead to writing. He died on September 8, 1147 or 1148.

During his thirteen or fourteen years at Signy, William apparently traveled outside the monastery very little, but a visit to the Carthusian monks at their new foundation of Mont-Dieu was significant in that it provided the occasion for his later composing the celebrated *Epistola ad Fratres de Monte-Dei.* More commonly known as *The Golden Epistle,* its final section is included in our anthology. The epistle's tripartite division—dealing with *homo animalis, homo rationalis,* and *homo spiritualis*—represents a fundamental structure in William's thought, one which is based scripturally on St. Paul's distinction between body, soul, and spirit at the conclusion of First Thessalonians and patristically on the development of this Pauline theme by Origen and other Fathers. Since William wrote his treatise primarily for the novices of Mont-Dieu, he devotes most of his attention to the state of a beginner—*homo animalis*—showing how through perfect obedience one might reach the point where the habitual exercise of virtue has become a pleasure. His reflections on solitude, spiritual direction, *lectio divina,* the discrete practice of mortification, and other aspects of monastic life in this part of the work have been regarded by generations of monks as a treasury of ascetical wisdom.

William's subsequent treatment of the state of one who is making progress in liv-ing according to the teaching of the faith—*homo rationalis*—and the state of one who is perfect—*homo spiritualis*—is much more condensed and will be read with maximum profit by those who are also familiar with his more extended treatment of these states in his earlier works. In fact, William's prefatory letter, addressed to the prior of Mont-Dieu, explicitly urges that this treatise be read in conjunction with his other works, of which he names twelve(!), including *The Mirror of Faith, The Enigma of Faith,* and the *Exposition on the Song of Songs.* Since a full introduction to his mystical theology is here impossible, we will focus only on themes most directly related to his teaching about *homo spiritualis.*

William's mystical theology is fundamentally what we called in our General Introduction a "mysticism of the image." More precisely, it is based on an understanding that while Christ alone is the full and true image of the Father, we have all been created, in the words of Genesis, *ad imaginem Dei.* For William, this means that we are graced with a radical capacity for participating in God's own life, that we have in the depths of our being a dynamic force impelling us toward such participation. Through sin this capacity or image has been partially lost or tarnished, and its restoration involves the actualization of the "likeness" to which we have also been created: "Faciamus hominem ad imaginem et similitudinem nostram" (Gen 1:26). Attaining the fullness of this likeness could even be called the very heart of the spiritual life according to William, for he writes at the end of *The Golden Epistle* that "resemblance to God is the whole of man's perfection" (n. 259). On one level, this likeness or resemblance is attained through living a virtuous life; as he writes in his commentary on Romans, if we live righteously, "we make progress in our likeness to God and recover his image which, by acting contrarily, we have partially lost" (*Exp. Rom.;* Migne, PL 180, 671A–B). But William writes in *The Golden Epistle* that there is yet another likeness, which "is so close in its resemblance that it is styled not merely a likeness but unity of spirit" (n. 262), a term which implies not simply that the Holy Spirit brings it about but that "it *is* the Holy Spirit himself, the God who is charity" (n. 263). Anyone who is gifted with this unity—and it is always a gift, never something we can acquire by our own efforts—has received the blessed state of not only willing what God wills but of being unable to will anything else.

Now this participation in God's own life and love—the closest possible union in this life, surpassed only by the beatific vision in heaven—is not just a matter of love but also of knowledge. The intimate connection between love and knowledge was, in fact, a constant theme in William's writings from the very beginning, but it was only with the passing years that he expressed himself more and more boldly on this point until he finally arrived at the well-known dictum that love is itself knowledge: *amor ipse intellectus est.*[2] What William means by this phrase (which was certainly influenced by Gregory the Great's similar expression, *amor ipse notitia est*) is not that there is a strict, formal identification between the soul's operations of loving and knowing. His point is rather that by loving God we truly come to know God, not in a rational or conceptual sense but more after the manner of that affective understanding by which we can be said to know a friend or know a work of art. In his own words: "The love of God is itself knowledge of him: unless he is loved, he is not known, and unless he is known, he is not loved" (*Exp. on the Song of Songs,* n. 76). When a person is so centered upon this loving-knowledge that he or she can be said to be one spirit with God, then such a person is "kept at a distance only by the veil of this mortality from the Holy of Holies and from that supreme beatitude of highest heaven" (*Golden Ep.,* n. 275). This, for William of St. Thierry, is the pinnacle of the mystical life.

---

2. This phrase is found literally in the *Exposition on the Song of Songs,* n. 57, but the idea recurs several times in that work, as well as in *The Mirror of Faith,* in *On Contemplating God,* and elsewhere.

Selections

THE GOLDEN EPISTLE*

BOOK TWO: THE SPIRITUAL MAN

The Perfection of Man in This Life

When the object of thought is God and the things which relate to God and the will reaches the stage at which it becomes love, the Holy Spirit, the Spirit of life, at once infuses himself by way of love and gives life to everything, lending his assistance in prayer, in meditation or in study to man's weakness. Immediately the memory becomes wisdom and tastes with relish the good things of the Lord, while the thoughts to which they give rise are brought to the intellect to be formed into affections. The understanding of the one thinking becomes the contemplation of one loving and it shapes it into certain experiences of spiritual or divine sweetness which it brings before the gaze of the spirit so that the spirit rejoices in them.

250. And then, insofar as it is possible for man, worthy thoughts are entertained of God, if indeed the word "thought" *(cogitatio)* is correct where there is no impelling principle *(cogit)* nor anything impelled *(cogitur),* but only awareness of God's abundant sweetness leading to exultation, jubilation and a true experience of the Lord in goodness on the part of the man who has sought him in this simplicity of heart.

251. But this way of thinking about God does not lie at the disposal of the thinker. It is a gift of grace, bestowed by the Holy Spirit who breathes where he chooses, when he chooses, how he chooses and upon whom he chooses. Man's part is continually to prepare his heart by ridding his will of foreign attachments, his reason or intellect of anxieties, his memory of idle or absorbing, sometimes even of necessary business, so that in the Lord's good time and when he sees fit, at the sound of the Holy Spirit's breathing the elements which constitute thought may be free at once to come together and do their work, each contributing its share to the outcome of joy for the soul. The will displays pure affection for the joy which the Lord gives, the memory yields faithful material, the intellect affords the sweetness of experience.

XV. 252. A will that is neglected gives rise to thoughts that are idle and unworthy of God; a will that is corrupted yields thoughts that are perverse and alienated from God; a rightly ordered will leads to thoughts that are necessary for the living of this

*From William of St. Thierry, *The Golden Epistle,* trans. Theodore Berkeley, O.C.S.O., Cistercian Fathers Series, no. 12 (Kalamazoo, Mich.: Cistercian Publications, 1976), 92–105. Reprinted with permission of the publisher. Copyright 1971 by Cistercian Publications, Inc.; W.M.U. Station; Kalamazoo, Michigan 49008.

life; a dutiful will engenders thoughts which are rich in the fruits of the Spirit and bring enjoyment of God. "Now the fruits of the Spirit," the Apostle tells us, "are charity, joy, peace, patience, forbearance, goodness, kindness, meekness, faith, modesty, chastity, continence" (Gal 5:22–23).

253. In every kind of thought all that occurs to the mind conforms to the intention of the will through the intervention of God's mercy and judgment, so that the just man is made still more just and the man who is defiled becomes still more defiled.

254. Therefore the man who desires to love the Lord or already loves him should always question his spirit and examine his conscience as to the object and motive of his basic desire; ask, too, what else the spirit wills or hates and what inordinate desires the flesh entertains in opposition to it.

255. For the desires which make their way in as if from outside and then disappear and those which brush against the soul in passing, so that at one moment it feels desire and at the next moment feels none, are not to be counted among the objects of volition but only among idle thoughts. They may even go as far as to cause the mind some pleasure, but none the less it quickly shakes itself free of them if it is its own master.

256. As to the basic desire, first of all the object of desire should be considered, then the extent to which it is desired and the way in which it is desired. If a man's basic desire is for God he should examine how much and in what way he desires God, whether to the point of despising self and everything which either exists or can exist, and this not only in accordance with the reason's judgment but also following the mind's inclination, so that the will is now something more than will: love, dilection, charity and unity of spirit.

257. For such is the way in which God is to be loved. "Love" is a strong inclination of the will toward God, "dilection" is a clinging to him or a union with him; "charity" is the enjoyment of him. But "unity of spirit" with God for the man who has his heart raised on high is the term of the will's progress toward God. No longer does it merely desire what God desires, not only does it love him, but it is perfect in its love, so that it can will only what God wills.

258. Now to will what God wills is already to be like God, to be able to will only what God wills is already to be what God is; for him, to will and to be are the same thing. Therefore it is well said that we shall see him fully as he is when we are like him, that is when we are what he is. For those who have been enabled to become sons of God have been enabled to become not indeed God, but what God is: holy, and in the future, fully happy as God is. And the source of their present holiness and their future happiness is none other than God himself who is at once their holiness and their happiness.

XVI. 259. Resemblance to God is the whole of man's perfection. To refuse to be perfect is to be at fault. Therefore the will must always be fostered with this perfection in view and love made ready. The will must be prevented from dissipating itself on foreign objects, love preserved from defilement. For to this end alone were we created and do we live, to be like God; for we were created in his image.

260. There is however a likeness to God which is lost only with life itself, left to every man by the Creator of all men as evidence of a better and more sublime likeness that has been lost. It is possessed regardless of acceptance or refusal, alike by the man who is capable of conceiving it and by the man who is so stupid that he cannot conceive it. It consists in the fact that, as God is everywhere, and is present with the whole of his being in his creation, so every living soul is in like manner present in its body. And as God is never unlike himself, and without any unlikeness carries out dissimilar operations in his creation, so, although man's soul vivifies the whole of the body with one and the same life, in the bodily senses and in the thoughts of the heart without any unlikeness it is constantly carrying out dissimilar operations. As far as merit is concerned this likeness to God in man is of no importance with God, since it derives from nature, not from will or effort.

261. But there is another likeness, one closer to God, inasmuch as it is freely willed. It consists in the virtues and inspires the soul as it were to imitate the greatness of Supreme Good by the greatness of its virtue and his unchangeable eternity by its unwearying perseverance in good.

262. In addition to this there is yet another likeness, of which something has been said already. It is so close in its resemblance that it is styled not merely a likeness but unity of spirit. It makes man one with God, one spirit, not only with the unity which comes of willing the same thing but with a greater fullness of virtue, as has been said: the inability to will anything else.

263. It is called unity of spirit not only because the Holy Spirit brings it about or inclines a man's spirit to it, but because it is the Holy Spirit himself, the God who is Charity. He who is the Love of Father and Son, their Unity, Sweetness, Good, Kiss, Embrace and whatever else they can have in common in that supreme unity of truth and truth of unity, becomes for man in regard to God in the manner appropriate to him what he is for the Son in regard to the Father or for the Father in regard to the Son through unity of substance. The soul in its happiness finds itself standing midway in the Embrace and the Kiss of Father and Son. In a manner which exceeds description and thought, the man of God is found worthy to become not God but what God is, that is to say man becomes through grace what God is by nature.

XVII. 264. That is why in his list of spiritual exercises the Apostle prudently inserted the Holy Spirit. He says: "In chastity, in knowledge, in forbearance, in graciousness, in the Holy Spirit, in unfeigned charity, in the word of truth, in the power of God" (2 Cor 6:6–7). See how he put the Holy Spirit in the midst of the good virtues, like the heart in the middle of the body, doing and ordering everything, imparting life to everything.

265. For he is the almighty Artificer who creates man's good will in regard to God, inclines God to be merciful to man, shapes man's desire, gives strength, ensures the prosperity of undertakings, conducts all things powerfully and disposes everything sweetly.

266. He it is who gives life to man's spirit and holds it together, just as it gives life to its body and holds it together. Men may teach how to seek God and angels how to adore him, but he alone teaches how to find him, possess him and enjoy him. He himself is the anxious quest of the man who truly seeks, he is the devotion of the man who adores in spirit and truth, he is the wisdom of the man who finds, the love of him who possesses, the gladness of him who enjoys.

267. Yet whatever he bestows here on his faithful of the vision and the knowledge of God is but as in a mirror and a riddle, as far removed from the vision and the knowledge that is to be in the future as faith is from truth or time from eternity. This is true even when what we read in the book of Job happens: "He hides the light in his hands and commands it to mount on high, then he tells his beloved that it belongs to him and that he can ascend to it" (Job 36:32–33).

XVIII. 268. For the man who is chosen and loved by God is sometimes shown a certain light of God's countenance, just as light that is enclosed in a man's hands appears and is hidden at the will of him who holds it. This is in order that what he is allowed to glimpse for a passing moment may set the soul on fire with longing for full possession of eternal light, the inheritance of full vision of God.

269. To make him realize to some extent what he lacks, grace sometimes as if in passing touches the affections of the lover and takes him out of himself, drawing him into the light of true reality, out of the tumult of affairs into the joys of silence, and to the slight extent of which he is capable, showing him for a moment, for an instant, ultimate reality as it is in itself. Sometimes it even transforms the man into a resemblance of ultimate reality, granting him to be, to the slight extent of which he is capable, such as it is.

270. Then when he has learned the difference between the clean and the unclean he is restored to himself and sent back to cleanse his heart for vision, to fit his spirit for likeness, so that if at some future date he should again be admitted to it he may be the more pure for seeing and able to remain for a longer time in the enjoyment of it.

271. For the limits of human imperfection are never better realized than in the light of God's countenance, in the mirror which is the vision of God. Then in the light of true reality man sees more and more what he lacks and continually corrects

by means of likeness whatever sins he has committed through unlikeness, drawing near by means of likeness to him from whom he has been separated by unlikeness. And so clearer vision is always accompanied by a clearer likeness.

272. It is impossible indeed for the supreme Good to be seen and not loved, or not to be loved to the full extent to which vision of it has been granted. So eventually love arrives at some likeness of that love which made God like to man by accepting the humiliation of our human lot in order that man might be made like to God by receiving the glorification of communion in the divine life. Then indeed it is sweet for man to be abased together with supreme Majesty, to become poor together with the Son of God, to be conformed to divine Wisdom, to make his own the mind which is in Christ Jesus our Lord.

XIX. 273. For here there is wisdom with devotion, love with fear, exultation with trembling, when God is thought of and understood as brought down unto death, the death of the Cross, to the end that man might be exalted to the likeness of the god-head. From here there flows the rushing stream that gladdens God's city, the remembrance of his abounding sweetness in the understanding and consideration of the benefits he has conferred on us.

274. In this regard man is easily led to love God by thinking about or contemplating what is worthy of love in him, which of itself shines upon the affections of the contemplative: his power and strength and glory and majesty and goodness and beatitude. But what especially carries man away in his spiritual love into the object of his love is that God in himself is whatever there is lovable in him; he is in the whole of himself what he is, if one can speak of a whole where there is no part.

275. In his love of this good the devout man who has been so affected centers himself upon it in such a way as not to be distracted from it until he becomes one or one spirit with him. Once arrived at this point he is separated and kept at a distance only by the veil of this mortality from the Holy of Holies and from that supreme beatitude of highest heaven. Yet since he already enjoys it in his soul through his faith and hope in him whom he loves, he is able to bear what is left of this life also with a more ready patience.

XX. 276. This is the goal for which the solitary strives, this is the end he has in view, this is his reward, the rest that comes after his labors, the consolation for his pains; and this is the perfection and the true wisdom of man. It embraces within itself and contains all the virtues, and they are not borrowed from another source but as it were naturally implanted in it, so that it resembles God who is himself whatever he is. Just as God is what he is, so the disposition of the good will in regard to the good of virtue is so firmly established in the good mind and impressed on it that in its ardent clinging to unchangeable Good it seems utterly unable to change from what it is.

277. For when that "taking up by the Lord, the Holy One of Israel, our King" (Ps 88:19), befalls the man of God, the wise and devout soul, with grace to enlighten and assist it, in the contemplation of supreme Good gazes also upon the laws of unchangeable Truth to the extent that it is found worthy to attain to them by means of the understanding that comes of love. From this it forms for itself a way of life which is heavenly and a model of holiness.

For it gazes upon supreme Truth and everything which derives truth from it, upon supreme Good and everything which derives goodness from it, upon supreme Eternity and everything which derives from it. It models itself upon that Truth, that Charity and that Eternity while directing its life here below. It does not fly above those eternal realities in its judgment but gazes up at them in desire or clings to them by love, while it accepts the realities of this created world to adapt and conform itself to them, not without using its judgment to discriminate, its power of reasoning to examine and its mind to appreciate.

278. This process gives rise to holy virtues, the image of God is formed anew in man, and that divine life is set in order from which the Apostle complains that certain men have become estranged. Virtue also takes on its true vigor, those two elements which constitute the perfection of the contemplative and the active life, concerning which, according to the ancient translators, we read in Job: "Behold piety is wisdom, while to abstain from evil is knowledge" (Job 28:28).

279. For wisdom is indeed piety, that is, the worship of God, the love by which we yearn to see him and, seeing him in a mirror obscurely, believe and hope in him and advance even to see him as he reveals himself.

280. But to abstain from evil is the knowledge of temporal matters with which our life here below is concerned. In their regard we abstain from evil to the extent to which we pursue good.

XXI. 281. This knowledge, this abstinence involve in the first place the practice of all the virtues and then the study of all the arts which govern this life which we are living. The former of these, the practice of the virtues, seems to be concerned rather with higher things, as displaying the power of higher wisdom and exhaling its fragrance. The latter, which is concerned with bodily exercises, sinks miserably into the vanity of this world if it is not held back by the bonds of religious faith.

282. In regard to these, since knowledge is something which is grasped either by the reason or by the bodily senses and committed to the memory, upon mature consideration it appears that only what is perceived by the senses can properly

speaking be attributed to knowledge. As for what the reason conceives of itself in such matters, it is already on the borderland between knowledge and wisdom.

283. For whatever is learned from another source, that is, through the bodily senses, is taken into the mind as something foreign, coming from without. But what enters the mind of its own accord, whether through the mere exercise of the reason or by a natural understanding of the unchangeable laws of unchangeable Truth, which sometimes enables the most wicked of men to form a judgment that is wholly right, this is in the reason in such a way as to be identified with the reason. It is not given to it by any process of teaching, so as to be knowledge, but rather is understood to be present naturally either when someone else points this out or when the reason adverts to it itself.

284. The outstanding example of this is when the knowledge of God is revealed to a man, even a godless man, by a natural manifestation on God's part. Then there is the case of a natural inclination to the virtues, of which a pagan poet was able to say that "The good hate sin for love of virtue."[1] Again there are all the distinctions made among the objects of the reason by the processes of investigation and reasoning.

285. The lowest type of knowledge and that which tends downwards is animal experience of sensible objects coming in through the five bodily senses. This is especially so when the lust of the flesh or of the eyes or the pride of this life are involved.

XXII. 286. And so when reason in conformity with wisdom forms a conscience and draws up a rule of life, in the lower kinds of knowledge it avails itself of nature's services and resources, in reasonings and the things of the reason it follows the rule it has laid down, in the acquisition of virtues it obeys its conscience. Thus making progress by means of lower things, finding assistance in higher things, continuing on its way toward what is right it brings into play the judgment of reason, the assent of the will, the inclination of the mind and external activity and so hastens to arrive at liberty and unity of spirit, in order that, as has already been said often, the man of faith may become one spirit with God.

287. Now this is the life of God of which we spoke a little while before, not so much an advance in reason as an attachment of the affections to perfection in wisdom. For the fact that a man relishes these things makes him wise and it is because he has become one spirit with God that he is spiritual. And this is the perfection of man in this life.

---

1. Horace, *Letters* 1.16.

XXIII. 288. Hitherto solitary or alone, now he becomes one and his bodily solitude is changed into unity of spirit. Our Lord's prayer for his disciples, summing up the whole of perfection, is fulfilled in him: "Father, my will is that as I and you are one, so they too may be one in us" (Jn 17:21).

289. For insofar as this unity of man with God or likeness to God draws near to God, it brings into conformity with itself what is inferior to it, and with that what is lower still; so that the spirit, the soul and the body are duly set in order and established in their proper places, rightly appreciated and even thought about in accordance with their several characteristics. So man begins to know himself perfectly, advance through self-knowledge and ascend to the knowledge of God.

290. When the man who is making progress first begins to fix his desire and aspirations on this object he must be on his guard as he ponders on that likeness against the error of unlikeness, that is to say when he compares spiritual things with spiritual and divine things with divine, he must not think of them otherwise than they are in reality.

291. Therefore when the spirit thinks of its likeness to God let it first mold its thought so as wholly to avoid conceiving of itself in terms of a body. Where God is concerned not only must it avoid thinking of him as of a body, as if he were in a place, but also as if he could be represented as a spirit and so changeable. For spiritual things are as different from corporeal things both in quality and in nature as they are remote from all confinement to place. The divine nature, however, transcends both corporeal and spiritual things to the same extent that it is free from all restrictions of time and place and knows nothing of change, remaining changeless and eternal in the beatitude of its own unchangeableness and eternity.

292. Just as the spirit has perception of corporeal things through the bodily senses, so it knows things pertaining to the reason or the spirit only through itself. But the things of God it can seek or expect to understand only by God's gift. Indeed it is lawful and possible for man possessed of reason to think and enquire sometimes of some things which concern God, such as the sweetness of his goodness, the power of his strength and other like matters. But what he is in himself, his essence, can only be grasped by thought at all insofar as the perception of enlightened love reaches out to it.

XXIV. 293. Yet God is to be attained by faith and, to the extent that the Holy Spirit helps our weakness, by thought as Eternal Life living and bestowing life; the Unchangeable and immutably making all changeable things; the Intelligent and creating all understanding and every intellectual being; Wisdom that is the source of all wisdom; fixed Truth that stands fast without any swerving, the Source of all truth and containing from eternity the principles of all things that exist in time.

294. His life itself is his essence, his very nature. He is his own life by which he lives, and it is divinity, eternity, greatness, goodness and strength existing and subsisting in itself, transcending all place in the power of a nature not bounded by place, by its eternity rising above all time that can be conceived by reason or imagination. It exists in a manner that is far more true and excellent than can be grasped by any kind of perception. Yet humble and enlightened love attains to a more certain perception of it than any effort of the reason to grasp it by thought, and it is always better than it is thought to be. Yet it is better thought than spoken of.

295. It is the supreme Essence, from which all being comes forth. It is the supreme Substance, not confined within the predicaments we formulate but the subsistent causal Principle of all things. In it our being does not die, our understanding makes no mistake, our love meets with no offence. It is always sought in order that it may be found with greater pleasure and is found with utmost pleasure in order that it may be sought the more diligently.

XXV. 296. Since this ineffable reality can be seen only in an ineffable way, the man who would see it must cleanse his heart, for it cannot be seen or apprehended by means of any bodily likeness in sleep, any bodily form in waking hours, any investigation of the mind, but only by humble love from a clean heart.

297. For this is the face of God which no one can see and live in the world. This is the Beauty for the contemplation of which everyone sighs who would love the Lord his God with his whole heart and his whole soul and his whole mind and his whole strength. Neither does he cease to arouse his neighbor to the same if he loves him as himself.

298. When eventually he is admitted to this vision he sees without any doubt in the light of truth the grace which forestalls him. When he is thrown back on himself he understands in his blindness that his uncleanness is out of keeping with its purity. And if he loves he takes pleasure in weeping, neither is it without much groaning that he is forced to return to himself.

299. We are wholly unequal to the task of conceiving this reality, but he whom we love forgives us, he of whom we confess we can neither speak nor think worthily. And yet we are stimulated and drawn on by his love or the love of his love to speak and to think of him.

300. It is for one who entertains such thoughts to abase himself in everything and to glorify in himself the Lord his God, to become of no worth in his own eyes as he contemplates God, to subject himself to every human being for the love of his Creator, to offer up his body as a holy victim, living, pleasing to God, the worship due from him as a rational creature. But before everything he should not think highly of

himself, beyond his just estimation but have a sober esteem of himself, according to the measure of faith which God has apportioned to him. He should not entrust his treasures to men's mouths but conceal them in his cell and hide them away in his conscience, so as to have this inscription always in the forefront of his conscience and on the front of his cell: "My secret is my own, my secret is my own" (Is 24:16).

The end of Dom William's epistle to the brethren of Mont Dieu

SELECTED BIBLIOGRAPHY

TEXTS AND TRANSLATIONS

Deux traités sur la foi: La miroir de la foi; L'énigme de la foi. Latin text edited by M. M. Davy. Paris, 1959.

Exposé sur le Cantique des cantiques. Latin text edited by J.-M. Déchanet. Sources chrétiennes, 82. Paris, 1962.

Un traité de la vie solitaire: Epistola ad Fratres de Monte Dei. Edited by M. M. Davy. 2 vols. Paris, 1940.

The Enigma of Faith. Translated by John D. Anderson. Kalamazoo, Mich.: Cistercian Publications, 1974.

Exposition on the Song of Songs. Translated by Mother Columba Hart, O.S.B. Shannon, Ireland: Irish University Press, 1970.

The Golden Epistle: A Letter to the Brethren at Mont Dieu. Translated by Theodore Berkeley, O.C.S.O. Kalamazoo, Mich.: Cistercian Publications, 1976.

The Mirror of Faith. Translated by Thomas X. Davis. Kalamazoo, Mich.: Cistercian Publications, 1979.

STUDIES

Bell, David N. *The Image and Likeness: The Augustinian Spirituality of William of St. Thierry.* Kalamazoo, Mich.: Cistercian Publications, 1984.

Brooke, Odo, O.S.B. "Studies on William of St. Thierry." In his *Studies in Monastic Theology,* 1–216. Kalamazoo, Mich.: Cistercian Publications, 1980. (This section of the book contains articles originally published in various journals.)

Déchanet, J.-M. *Aux sources de la spiritualité de Guillaume de Saint-Thierry. Première série d'études.* Bruges, 1940.

——. *Guillaume de Saint-Thierry: L'homme et son oeuvre.* Bruges, 1942.

Malevez, L. "La doctrine de l'image et de la connaissance mystique chez Guillaume de Saint-Thierry." Parts 1, 2. *Recherches de science religieuse* 22 (1932): 178–205, 257–79.

Bernard of Clairvaux

(1090–1153)

Abbot, ecclesiastical statesman, mediator between warring armies, counselor of popes and kings, champion of orthodoxy, Bernard of Clairvaux was unquestionably the most influential person in Europe in the first half of the twelfth century. But it is perhaps in the stamp he left on Christian spirituality that his most enduring influence is to be found. As already noted in our General Introduction, at one point in the history of Western Christianity love became equated with the very essence of the spiritual life, and if we had to assign the beginning of that movement to one person, that person would have to be Bernard. The passages from his writings included in this anthology are intended above all to illustrate this centrality of love in his mystical theology.

Born the third son of a noble family near Dijon in 1090, Bernard received a broad, humanistic education at Chatillon and then, in the year 1112 and to his parents' dismay, convinced thirty of his relatives and friends to join him in entering the new and struggling reform monastery of Citeaux, a few miles south of his home. This sudden influx breathed new life into a community which had seemed to be on the verge of extinction. A continuing stream of new candidates led to the founding of many daughter houses, including the one at Clairvaux over which Bernard was named abbot after having been a monk for only three years. Gradually Bernard attained a wide reputation for holiness and wisdom and so became more and more involved in the ecclesiastical and political issues of the entire continent. These often drew him away from his monastery for long periods of time and once led him to complain in a letter to his Cistercian confrere Pope Eugene III that "I am a kind of Chimera of my age, living neither as a religious nor as a layman" (*Ep.* 250.4). Toward the end of his life, the failure of the Crusade which he had preached at the request of the same Pope brought much abuse upon him, so that in the eyes of many he died under a cloud of failure. It was, however, only another twenty-one years before he was canonized by Pope Alexander III, and in 1830 he was officially declared a Doctor of the Church.

The close friendship between Bernard and William of St. Thierry was already mentioned in the introduction to our selections from William's writings. In some ways the two men were indeed kindred spirits; they shared the same monastic ideal and communicated or dedicated some of their works to one another. But there were also some important differences, the recognition of which can help us better appreciate Bernard's unique place in the history of Christian spirituality. Perhaps the most significant contrast between the two men was the one summed up in the following words at the congress held at Dijon in 1953 to commemorate the eighth centenary of Bernard's death: "In his work as a whole, St. Bernard was interested less in knowledge than in love, whereas William of St. Thierry was more concerned with joining the one to the other and so arriving at a full knowledge of God."[1] The basic reason for Bernard's proportionately greater emphasis on love was his double conviction that all the disorder and sinfulness of human life is ultimately due to the turning of the will from God to self *(voluntas propria)* and that love alone engages a person at a sufficiently deep level to bring about true conversion to God. As he writes in his treatise *On Loving God:* "It [love] alone can turn the mind from love of itself and the world and direct it to God. Neither fear nor love of self can convert the soul. They change the appearance of one's deeds from time to time, but never one's character. . . . Love truly converts souls because it makes them willing" (*On Loving God,* XII.34; henceforth *Dil.*).

For Bernard, the way to overcome immoderate self-love is not simply to hear and heed the commandment "You shall love your neighbor as yourself." Rather, one must first love God, "so that in him you can love your neighbor too" (*Dil.* VIII.25), and the most effective way to ar-

rive at this love is to reflect not only on God's love for us in general (which even non-Christians can and should do), but on the surpassing love revealed to us in Jesus Christ: "The faithful know how utterly they stand in need of Jesus and him crucified. They wonder at and reach out to that supreme love of his which surpasses all knowledge. . . . The more surely you know yourself loved, the easier you will find it to love in return" (*Dil.* III.7). Knowing himself thus loved, Bernard responded with lyrical expressions of his own love for Christ, as in the following lines from his fifteenth sermon on the Song of Songs: "Write what you will, I shall not relish it unless it tells of Jesus. Talk or argue about what you will, I shall not relish it if you exclude the name of Jesus. Jesus to me is honey in the mouth, music in the ear, a song in the heart" (*Sermons on Song of Songs,* 15.6; henceforth *SC*).

Here is that new note of affectionate love for Jesus which has led so many commentators to speak, with good reason, of Bernard's "affective mysticism." The experiences of the Word's presence which elicited such love from Bernard are movingly described by him in a famous passage from the seventy-fourth sermon on the Song of Songs that we have included in this anthology. At such times, he writes, it is not by any of the five senses but only by the warmth of his heart that he knows the Word is present, and when he afterward suffers the departure of the Word "and all these things become dim and weak and cold," then "I shall not cease to cry, as if after someone who is leaving, begging him with a burning desire to return; I will beseech him to give me the joy of his salvation and return to me" (*SC* 74.7).

1. Jacques Hourlier, O.S.B., "Saint Bernard et Guillaume de Saint Thierry dans le «Liber de amore,»" in *St. Bernard théologien: Actes du Congrès de Dijon,* 2nd ed. (Rome, 1955), 229.

As has been suggested by Professor Andrew Louth, we see in such passages from Bernard a shift in the understanding of the spiritual life.[2] For Augustine (and for Bernard's friend William), the love of God and the knowledge of God go closely together, being united in wisdom *(sapientia),* the contemplation of eternal reality. For Bernard, on the other hand, wisdom is characterized primarily not by the harmonious union of these two components but rather

"by peace of mind and spiritual sweetness"; he even defines wisdom in affective terms as "a taste for goodness" (*SC* 85.7,8). To be sure, neither here nor elsewhere in his writings does Bernard radically disdain knowledge or understanding, but their place in the whole process of turning to and being united with God is nevertheless significantly reduced when compared with their place in Augustine's works. We are still far from the sharp dichotomy between thought and feeling, theology and devotion, which was to become so marked in many writers of the late Middle Ages, but in Bernard's affective mysticism we already sense something of the shape of things to come.

2. Andrew Louth, "Bernard and Affective Mysticism," in *The Influence of St. Bernard: Anglican Essays,* ed. Sister Benedicta Ward (Oxford: SLG Press, 1976), 1–10.

Selections

ON LOVING GOD*

VII.22. I said before that God is the cause of loving God. I spoke the truth, for he is both the efficient and the final cause. He himself provides the occasion. He himself creates the longing. He himself fulfils the desire. He himself causes himself to be (or rather, to be made) such that he should be loved. He hopes to be so happily loved that no one will love him in vain. His love both prepares and rewards ours (cf. 1 Jn 4:19). Kindly, he leads the way. He repays us justly. He is our sweet hope. He is riches to all who call upon him (Rm 10:12). There is nothing better than himself. He gave himself in merit. He keeps himself to be our reward. He gives himself as food for holy souls (Wis 3:13). He sold himself to redeem the captives.

Lord, you are good to the soul which seeks you. What are you then to the soul which finds? But this is the most wonderful thing, that no one can seek you who has not already found you. You therefore seek to be found so that you may be sought for, sought so that you may be found. You can be sought, and found, but not forestalled. For even if we say, "In the morning my prayer will forestall you" (Ps 87:14), it is certain that every prayer which is not inspired is half-hearted. Now let us see where our love begins, for we have seen where it finds its end.

VIII.23. Love is one of the four natural passions. They are well enough known; there is no need to name them. It is clearly right that what is natural should be at the service of the Lord of nature. That is why the first and great commandment is, "You shall love the Lord your God" (Mt 22:37).

THE FIRST DEGREE OF LOVE:
WHEN MAN LOVES HIMSELF FOR HIS OWN SAKE

But because nature has become rather frail and weak, man is driven by necessity to serve nature first. This results in bodily love, by which man loves himself for his own sake. He does not yet know anything but himself, as it is written, "First came what is animal, then what is spiritual" (1 Cor 15:46). This love is not imposed by rule but is innate in nature. For who hates his own flesh? (Eph 5:29). But if that same love begins to get out of proportion and headstrong, as often happens, and it ceases to be satisfied to run in the narrow channel of its needs, but floods out on all sides into the fields of pleasure, then the overflow can be stopped at once by the commandment, "You shall love your neighbor as yourself" (Mt 22:39). . . .

25. But to love one's neighbour with perfect justice it is necessary to be prompted

---

*All selections in this chapter are from *Bernard of Clairvaux: Selected Works,* trans. G. R. Evans, The Classics of Western Spirituality (New York: Paulist, 1987). Reprinted with permission of the publisher.

by God. How can you love your neighbour with purity if you do not love him in God? But he who does not love God cannot love in God. You must first love God, so that in him you can love your neighbour too (Mk 12:30-1).

God therefore brings about your love for him, just as he causes other goods. This is how he does it: He who made nature also protects it. For it was so created that it needs its creator as its protector, so that what could not have come into existence without him cannot continue in existence without him. So that no rational creature might be in ignorance of this fact and (dreadful thought) claim for himself the gifts of the Creator, that same Creator willed by a high and saving counsel that man should endure tribulation; then when man fails and God comes to his aid and sets him free, man will honour God as he deserves. For this is what he says, "Call upon me in the day of tribulation. I will deliver you, and you shall honour me" (Ps 49:15). And so in that way it comes about that man who is a bodily animal (1 Cor 2:14) and does not know how to love anything but himself, begins to love God for his own benefit, because he learns from frequent experience that in God he can do everything which is good for him (Phil 4:13), and that without him he can do nothing (Jn 15:5).

THE SECOND DEGREE OF LOVE:
WHEN MAN LOVES GOD FOR HIS OWN GOOD

IX.26. Man therefore loves God, but as yet he loves him for his own sake, not God's. Nevertheless the wise man ought to know what he can do by himself and what he can do only with God's help; then you will avoid hurting him who keeps you from harm.

If a man has a great many tribulations and as a result he frequently turns to God and frequently experiences God's liberation, surely even if he had a breast of iron or a heart of stone (Ez 11:19; 36:26), must he not soften towards the generosity of the redeemer and love God not only for his own benefit, but for himself?

THE THIRD DEGREE OF LOVE:
WHEN MAN LOVES GOD FOR GOD'S SAKE

Man's frequent needs make it necessary for him to call upon God often, and to taste by frequent contact, and to discover by tasting how sweet the Lord is (Ps 33:9). It is in this way that the taste of his own sweetness leads us to love God in purity more than our need alone would prompt us to do. The Samaritans set us an example when they said to the woman who told them the Lord was there, "Now we believe, not because of your words, but because we have heard him for ourselves and we know that truly he is the Saviour of the world" (Jn 4:42). In the same way, I urge, let us follow their example and rightly say to our flesh, "Now we love God not because he meets your needs; but we have tasted and we know how sweet the Lord is" (Ps 33:9).

There is a need of the flesh which speaks out, and the body tells by its actions of the kindnesses it has experienced. And so it will not be difficult for the man who has had that experience to keep the commandment to love his neighbour (Mk 12:31). He truly loves God, and therefore he loves what is God's. He loves chastely, and to the chaste it is no burden to keep the commandments; the heart grows purer in the obedience of love, as it is written (1 Pet 1:22). Such a man loves justly and willingly keeps the just law.

This love is acceptable because it is given freely. It is chaste because it is not made up of words or talk, but of truth and action (1 Jn 3:18). It is just because it gives back what it has received. For he who loves in this way loves as he is loved. He loves, seeking in return not what is his own (1 Cor 13:5), but what is Jesus Christ's, just as he has sought not his own but our good, or rather, our very selves (2 Cor 12:14). He who says, "We trust in the Lord for he is good" (Ps 117:1) loves in this way. He who trusts in the Lord not because he is good to him but simply because he is good, truly loves God for God's sake and not for his own. He of whom it is said, "He will praise you when you do him favours" (Ps 48:19), does not love him in this way. That is the third degree of love, in which God is already loved for his own sake.

THE FOURTH DEGREE OF LOVE:
WHEN MAN LOVES HIMSELF FOR THE SAKE OF GOD

X.27. Happy is he who has been found worthy to attain to the fourth degree, where man loves himself only for God's sake. "O God, your justice is like the mountains of God" (Ps 35:7). That love is a mountain, and a high mountain of God. Truly, "a rich and fertile mountain" (Ps 67:16). "Who will climb the mountain of the Lord?" (Ps 23:3). "Who will give me wings like a dove, and I shall fly there and rest?" (Ps 54:7). That place was made a place of peace and it has its dwelling-place in Sion (Ps 75:3). "Alas for me, my exile has been prolonged!" (Ps 119:5). When will flesh and blood (Mt 16:17), this vessel of clay (2 Cor 4:7), this earthly dwelling (Wis 9:15) grasp this? When will it experience this kind of love, so that the mind, drunk with divine love and forgetting itself, making itself like a broken vessel (Ps 30:13), may throw itself wholly on God and, clinging to God (1 Cor 6:17), become one with him in spirit and say, "My body and my heart have fainted, O God of my heart; God, my part in eternity" (Ps 72:26)? I should call him blessed and holy to whom it is given to experience even for a single instant something which is rare indeed in this life. To lose yourself as though you did not exist and to have no sense of yourself, to be emptied out of yourself (Phil 2:7) and almost annihilated, belongs to heavenly, not to human love.

And if indeed any mortal is rapt for a moment or is, so to speak, admitted for a moment to this union, at once the world presses itself on him (Gal 1:4), the day's wickedness troubles him, the mortal body weighs him down, bodily needs distract him, he fails because of the weakness of his corruption and—more powerfully than these—brotherly love calls him back. Alas, he is forced to come back to himself, to fall again into his affairs, and to cry out wretchedly, "Lord, I endure violence; fight back for me" (Is 38:14), and, "Unhappy man that I am, who will free me from the body of this death?" (Rom 7:24).

28. But since Scripture says that God made everything for himself (Prov 16:4; Rev 4:11), there will be a time when he will cause everything to conform to its Maker and be in harmony with him. In the meantime, we must make this our desire: that as God himself willed that everything should be for himself, so we, too, will that nothing, not even ourselves, may be or have been except for him, that is according to his will, not ours. The satisfaction of our needs will not bring us happiness, not chance delights, as does the sight of his will being fulfilled in us and in everything which concerns us. This is what we ask every day in prayer when we say, "Your will be done, on earth as it is in heaven" (Mt 6:10). O holy and chaste love! O sweet and tender affection! O pure and sinless intention of the will—the more pure and sinless in that there is no mixture of self-will in it, the more sweet and tender in that everything it feels is divine.

To love in this way is to become like God. As a drop of water seems to disappear completely in a quantity of wine, taking the wine's flavour and colour; as red-hot iron becomes indistinguishable from the glow of fire and its own original form disappears; as air suffused with the light of the sun seems transformed into the brightness of the light, as if it were itself light rather than merely lit up; so, in those who are holy, it is necessary for human affection to dissolve in some ineffable way, and be poured into the will of God. How will God be all in all (1 Cor 15:26), if anything of man remains in man? The substance remains, but in another form, with another glory, another power. When will this be? Who will see this? Who will possess it? "When shall I come and when shall I appear in God's presence?" (Ps 41:3). O Lord my God, "My heart said to you, 'My face has sought you. Lord, I will seek your face'" (Ps 26:8). Shall I see your holy temple? (Ps 26:4).

29. I think that cannot be until I do as I am bid: "Love the Lord your God with all your heart and with all your soul and with all your strength" (Mk 12:30). Then the mind will not have to think of the body. The soul will no longer have to give the body life and feeling, and its power will be set free of these ties and be strength-

ened by the power of God. For it is impossible to draw together all that is in you and turn towards the face of God as long as the care of the weak and miserable body demands one's attention. So it is in a spiritual and immortal body, a perfect body, beautiful and at peace and subject to the spirit in all things, that the soul hopes to attain the fourth degree of love, or rather, to be caught up in it; for it lies in God's power to give it to whom he will. It is not to be obtained by human effort. That, I say, is when a man will easily reach the fourth degree: when no entanglements of the flesh hold him back and no troubles disturb him, as he hurries with great speed and eagerness to the joy of the Lord (Mt 25:21,23).

But do we not think that the holy martyrs received this grace while they were still in their victorious bodies—at least in part? They were so moved within by the great force of their love that they were able to expose their bodies to outward torments and think nothing of them. The sensation of outward pain could do no more than whisper across the surface of their tranquillity; it could not disturb it.

XI.30. But what of those who are already free of the body. We believe that they are wholly immersed in that sea of eternal light and bright eternity.

WHAT IS IMPOSSIBLE FOR SOULS BEFORE THE RESURRECTION

It is not in dispute that they want their bodies back; if they thus desire and hope for them, it is clear that they have not wholly turned from themselves, for it is evident that they are still clinging to something which is their own, even if their desires return to it only a very little. Until death is swallowed up in victory (1 Cor 15:54), and the everlasting light invades the farthest bounds of night and shines everywhere—so that heavenly glory gleams even in bodies—these souls cannot wholly remove themselves and transport themselves to God. They are still too much bound to their bodies, if not in life and feeling, certainly in natural affection. They do not wish to be complete without them, and indeed they cannot be.

And so before the restoration of their bodies souls will not lose themselves, as they will when they are perfect and reach their highest state. If they did so the soul would be complete without its body, and would cease to want it. The body is not laid down nor resumed except for the good of the soul. "Precious in God's sight is the death of his saints" (Ps 115:15). If death is precious, what must life be, and such a life as that? It need not be surprising that the glorified body should seem to confer something on the soul, for it was of use to it when it was weak and mortal. O how truly did he speak who said that all things work together for good to those who love God (Rm 8:28). Its weak body helps the soul to love God; it helps it when it is dead; it helps it when it is resurrected, first in producing fruits of patience, secondly in bringing peace, thirdly in bringing completeness. Truly the soul does not want to be perfected without that which it feels has served it well in every condition.

31. It is clear that the flesh is a good and faithful companion to the good spirit. It helps it if it is burdened, or if it does not help, it relieves it; at any rate, it is an aid and not a burden. The first state is full of labour, but fruitful (Mt 3:8); the second is a time of waiting, but without weariness; the third is glorious. Listen to the Bridegroom in the Song holding out this threefold invitation, "Eat," he says, "and drink, friends; be intoxicated, dearest" (Sg 5:1). He calls those who are labouring in the body to eat. Those who have set aside their bodies he calls to drink. Those who have resumed their bodies, he encourages to drink their fill. These he calls "dearest," for they are filled to overflowing with love. For there is this difference between these and those others he calls "friends," not "dearest," so that those who groan because they are still labouring in the flesh are held dear for the love they have; those who are free from the weight of the flesh are more dear because they are made more ready and quicker to love. More than both are they called "dearest" (and so they are) (1 Jn 3:1) who, having received the second garment, are in their resurrected bodies in glory. They burn the more eagerly and fiercely with love for God because nothing is left to them which can trouble them or hold them back in any way.

SERMON 74 ON THE SONG OF SONGS

1. "Return," she says (Sg 2:17). It is clear that he whom she calls to come back is not present. But he was there, and not long before. Indeed, she seems to be calling him back as he is leaving. She calls him back urgently, and that is a sign of the great love she bears him and of his great loveliness. Who are these who are so wrapped up in love, these unwearying lovers who are driven on by a love which will not let them rest?

It is my task to carry out my promise and to show how these words apply to the Word and the soul. But to do so worthily—or indeed at all—I tell you that I need the help of the Word himself.

That Word ought to be expounded by someone far, far more experienced, who knows more about that holy and mysterious love than I. But I must do my duty—and what you ask. I see the danger, but I ignore it because you force me to (2 Cor 12:11). You oblige me to walk in great things and in wonders which are beyond me (Ps 130:1). O how I fear that I shall suddenly hear, "Why do you speak of my delights and let my secret out in your talk?" (cf Ps 49:16). Hear me, then, as a man who is afraid to speak, but is not able to be silent. That fear of mine may perhaps excuse my boldness; and if you are perhaps edified, that will excuse me further—as perhaps, too, will these tears I shed.

"Return," she says. Good. He was going away; he is called back. Who will explain to me the mystery of this change? Who will give a worthy account of the Word's coming and going? Surely the Bridegroom is not inconstant? Where can he come from or go to, he who fills heaven and earth? (Jer 23:24). How can he who is spirit move from place to place? How can you say that there is any movement of any kind in God? He is unchanging.

2. Let him who is able understand (Mt 19:12). But let us go on carefully (Eph 5:15) and with pure hearts (Prov 11:20) to expound this holy and mysterious utterance (Is 23:3), and do as Scripture does in speaking of the wisdom which is hidden in the mystery (1 Cor 2:7); it speaks of God in images we can understand, in comparisons with things familiar to the senses. By putting what is precious, the unknown and unseen things of God (Rom 1:20) in common vessels (2 Cor 4:7), it brings them within the grasp of human minds.

Let us, then, follow the way of this pure Word (Ps 11:7) and say that the Word of God, God himself, the soul's Bridegroom, comes to the soul as he wishes and leaves it again (1 Cor 12:11). But let us understand that this is only how it feels to the soul; there is no movement of the Word. When the soul is aware of grace, she knows that the Word is with her. When she is not, she seeks him who is absent, and begs him to come to her, saying with the Prophet, "My face has sought you; your face, Lord, will I seek" (Ps 26:8). How could she not? For when so sweet a Bridegroom leaves her, she cannot desire or even think of any other. So she longs for him in his absence, and calls him back as he leaves. So then, the Word is recalled, and by the soul's desire, by that soul which has once tasted his sweetness (Is 26:8). Is longing not a cry? It is a loud one! Then, "the Lord has heard the desire of the poor," says Scripture (Ps 9:38). When the Word goes away, then, the one and continuous cry of the soul, its endless desire, is a repeated "Return," until he comes.

3. And now give me a soul which the Word, the Bridegroom, often visits, to which familiarity has brought courage, which hungers for what it has tasted, and whose contempt for all but him has freed from all other preoccupations. I will unhesitatingly attribute to her the voice and name of Bride, and I shall consider everything this passage says to be applicable to her. For that is how the speaker is portrayed. For she proves that she has deserved the presence of him whom she calls back, even if not his constant presence. Otherwise she would call him, not recall him. For the word "return" is a word of recall.

And perhaps he has withdrawn so that he might the more eagerly be called back and embraced more closely. For once he made as if to go further not because he wished to do so, but because he wanted to hear them say, "Stay with us till morning, for the evening draws on" (Lk 24:28–29). And again, when the Apostles were in a boat and were labouring at the oars, he walked on the water, and seemed to be passing them by; yet he was not going by, but only testing their faith and encouraging their prayers (Mk 6:48). Then, as the Evangelist says, they were troubled and cried out, thinking he was a ghost (Mk 6:49). This holy pretence, this saving contrivance, which the incarnate Word then showed, the same Word still makes as spirit, in his spiritual way, when he wants to stir the soul which loves him. He pretends to pass by, but he goes only to be recalled, for the Word is not irrevocable. He comes and goes as he pleases, as if visiting the soul at dawn (Jb 7:18), and suddenly putting it to the test. His going is part of his purpose; his return is at his will. Both are in perfect wisdom. Only he knows his reasons.

4. Now it is agreed that his comings and goings are the alterations in the soul of which he speaks when he says, "I go away and come to you again" (Jn 14:28), and "A little while and you shall not see me and again a little while and you shall see me" (Jn 16:17). O little and little! Such a long time! Dear Lord, you say it is only for a little while that we do not see you. What you say must be true, yet it is too long, far too long. Both are true: it is a little while in terms of our deserts, and a long time in terms of our desire. You can find both in the prophet: "If he delays, wait for him; for he will come and not delay" (Hab 2:3). How can he not be long, if he delays, unless he comes more quickly than we deserve and yet more slowly than we desire? The loving soul is carried away by longing, swept away by desire; she does not think of what she deserves. She closes her eyes to his majesty and sees only the pleasure he brings; she trusts in his saving grace (Ps 11:6), and puts her faith in him. Boldly and without shame she calls the Word back, and trustingly she asks to have his delights again. She calls him with the freedom we associate not with a Lord but with a lover. "Return, my Beloved." And she adds, "Be like a fawn or a doe on the mountains of Bethel" (Sg 2:17). We shall come back to that later.

5. Now bear with my foolishness for a little while (2 Cor 11:1). I want to tell you, for I promised, about my own experience. It is not important (2 Cor 12:1). But I do so in the hope that it may benefit you, and if it does I shall be content in my foolishness. If not, my foolishness will be plain enough.

I tell you that the Word has come even to me—I speak in my foolishness—and that he has come more than once (2 Cor 11:17). Yet however often he has come, I have never been aware of the moment of his coming. I have known he was there; I have remembered his presence afterwards; sometimes I had an inkling that he was coming. But I never felt it, nor his leaving me (Ps 120:8). And where he comes from when he enters my soul, or where he goes when he leaves it, and how he enters and leaves, I frankly do not know. As it says, "You do not know where he comes from, nor where he goes" (Jn 3:8). That is not surprising, for of him was it said, "Your footsteps will not be known" (Ps 76:20). He did not enter by the eyes, for he has no colour, nor by the ears, for he made no sound; nor by the nostrils, for he is not mingled with the air, but the mind. He did not blend into the air; he created it. His coming was not tasted by the mouth, for he was not eaten or drunk; nor could he be touched, for he is impalpable. So by what route did he enter?

Or perhaps he did not enter at all, because he did not come from outside? For he is not one of those who are without (1 Cor 5:12). Yet he does not come from within me, for he is good (Ps 51:11), and I know that there is no good in me. I have climbed up to the highest that is in me, and see! The Word is far, far above. A curious explorer, I have plumbed my own depths, and he was far deeper than that. If I looked outwards, I saw him far beyond. If I looked inward, he was further in still. And I knew that what I had read was true, that "in him we live and move and have our being" (Acts 17:28). But blessed is he in whom he has his being, who lives for him and is moved by him.

6. You ask me then how I knew he was present, he whose ways cannot be traced (Rm 11:33). He is life and power (Heb 4:12), and as soon as he enters in he stirs my sleeping soul. He moves and soothes and pierces my heart (Sg 4:9), which was as hard as stone and riddled with disease (Si 3:27; Ez 11:19; 36:26). And he begins to root up and destroy, to build and to plant, to water the dry places and light the dark corners (cf. Jer 1:10), to open what was closed, set what was cold on fire, to make the crooked straight and the rough places smooth (Is 40:4), so that my soul may bless the Lord and all that is within me praise his holy name (Ps 102:1).

And so when the Bridegroom, the Word, came to me, he never made any sign that he was coming; there was no sound of his voice, no glimpse of his face, no footfall. There was no movement of his by which I could know his coming; none of my senses showed me that he had flooded the depths of my being. Only by the warmth of my heart, as I said before, did I know that he was there, and I knew the power of his might because my faults were purged and my body's yearnings brought under control. And when my secret faults were revealed (Ps 18:13) and made visible, I have been amazed at the depth of his wisdom. At the slightest sign of amendment of life, I have experienced the goodness of his mercy. In the remaking and renewing of the spirit of my mind (Eph 4:23), that is, the inner man, I perceived the excellence of his glorious beauty (Ps 49:2); and when I contemplate all these things I am filled with awe of his manifold greatness (Ps 150:2).

7. But when the Word has left me, and all these things become dim and weak and cold, as though you had taken the fire from under a boiling pot, I know that he has gone. Then my soul cannot help being sorrowful until he returns, and my heart grows warm within me, and I know he is there.

With such an experience of the Word, is it surprising if I speak the words of the Bride and call him back when he absents himself, when even if I do not burn with an equal desire, I burn with a desire like hers? It will be natural to me as long as I live to speak "Return," the word of recall, to call back the Word.

As often as he slips away from me, so often will I seek him, and I shall not cease to cry, as if after someone who is leaving (Jdg 18:23), begging him, with a burning desire of the heart, to return (Ps 20:3); I will beseech him to give me the joy of his salvation (Ps 50:14) and return to me.

I tell you, children, nothing else gives me joy when he is not with me, who alone is the source of my joy. And I pray that he may not come empty-handed (Is 55:11) but full of grace and truth (Jn 1:14), as is his way, as he did yesterday and the day before (Gen 31:5). In this he is like a roe or a fawn (Sg 2:17), for his truth is like a roe's clear eyes and his grace like the gaiety of a fawn.

8. I need both: truth, so that I cannot hide from him, and grace, so that I do not wish to hide. If either were lacking, his severity might seem heavy without the one and his gaiety frivolous without the other. Truth without grace is bitter; and without the restraint of truth, devotion can be capricious, immoderate and over-confident. How many people have received grace and not benefited, because they did not accept the truth at the same time to temper it? As a result they have been too complacent in their possession of it (Is 42:1), without regard to the truth. They have not imitated the full-grown roe, but behaved like gay and giddy young fawns. So it is that they have lost the grace they wanted to enjoy by itself. It could be said, too late, to them, "Go, then, and learn what it is to serve the Lord in fear, and rejoice in him with awe" (Ps 2:11).

The holy soul once said in her abundance, "I shall never be moved" (Ps 29:7–8), when suddenly she felt the Word turn his face away from her, and she was not only moved but thrown into confusion. And so she sadly learned that she needed not only the gift of devotion but also the gravity of truth. Therefore the fullness of grace lies not in grace alone, nor in truth alone. What profit is it to know what you ought to do if you cannot do it? I have known many who were sadder for knowing the truth, for they did not have the excuse of ignorance when they knew what the Truth wanted them to do and did not do it.

9. So neither is sufficient without the other. I have not put it strongly enough. Neither is of any use without the other. How do we know that? Scripture says, "If anyone knows what is good and does not do it, it counts as sin in him" (Jam 4:17). And again, "A servant who knows his master's will and does not do it as he should, will be soundly beaten (Lk 12:47). That is said of truth. What is said of grace? It is written, "And after the sop Satan entered into him" (Jn 13:27). The reference is to Judas who, having received the gift of grace, did not walk in the truth with the Lord of truth (or rather, with truth as his mistress), but let the devil find a foothold in him (Eph 4:27). . . .

Both grace and truth are found in the Bridegroom. "Grace and truth came by

Jesus Christ" (Jn 1:17), says John the Baptist. If the Lord Jesus knocks at my door with one but not the other—for he is the Word of God, the soul's Bridegroom—he will enter not as a Bridegroom but as a judge. Perish the thought! "Do not enter into judgement with your servant" (Ps 142:2). Let him enter as a bringer of peace, joyous and glad; but may he come grave and adult, too, to purify my joy and restrain my overconfidence with the stern face of truth. Let him enter as a leaping fawn and a sharp-eyed roe, to pass over my blameworthiness at a bound, and look on my faults with pity. Let him enter as one coming down from the mountains of Bethel, full of joy and radiance, descending from the Father (Jn 15:26), sweet and gentle (Ps 85:5), deigning to become the Bridegroom of the soul that seeks him and to be known as such (Lam 3:25), he who is God, blessed above all for ever (Rm 9:5).

SELECTED BIBLIOGRAPHY

TEXTS AND TRANSLATIONS

Opera Omnia. Edited by J. Leclercq, C. H. Talbot, and H. M. Rochais. 8 vols. Rome, 1957–77.

Bernard of Clairvaux: Selected Works. Translated by G. R. Evans. The Classics of Western Spirituality. New York: Paulist; London: SPCK, 1987.

On the Song of Songs. Translated by Kilian Walsh, O.C.S.O., and Irene M. Edmonds. 4 vols. Kalamazoo, Mich.: Cistercian Publications, 1971–80.

STUDIES

Bouton, Jean de la Croix. *Bibliographie bernardine, 1891–1957.* Paris, 1958.

Evans, G. R. *The Mind of St. Bernard of Clairvaux.* Oxford: Clarendon Press, 1983.

Gilson, Etienne. *The Mystical Theology of St. Bernard.* Translated by A. H. C. Downes. London and New York: Sheed and Ward, 1940.

Leclercq, Jean. *Saint Bernard mystique.* Bruges, 1948.

Manning, E. *Bibliographie bernardine, 1957–1970.* Rochefort, 1972.

St. Bernard théologien: Actes du Congrès de Dijon, 15–19 septembre 1953. 2nd ed. Rome, 1955.

Ward, Sister Benedicta, ed. *The Influence of St. Bernard: Anglican Essays.* Oxford: SLG Press, 1976.

Bonaventure

(c.1217–1274)

Offering his readers a rare glimpse into his own past, St. Bonaventure writes in the Prologue to the longer of his two lives of St. Francis: "When I was a boy, as I still vividly remember, I was snatched from the jaws of death by his [Francis'] invocation and merits. . . . I recognize that God saved my life through him, and I realize that I have experienced his power in my very person. This, then, is my principal reason for undertaking this task, that I may gather together the accounts of his virtues . . . so that they may not be lost when those who lived with this servant of God die."[1] Besides praising the power of Francis' intercession, Bonaventure also, and even more insistently, extolled the saint as a living example of how to adhere totally to God through a contemplative way of life. What the Poor Man of Assisi lived, Bonaventure the theologian reflected upon with intellectual acumen and fervent devotion, leaving us a doctrine which, in the opinion of the great medievalist Etienne Gilson, "marks . . . the culminating point of Christian mysticism

and constitutes the completest synthesis it has ever achieved."[2]

Bonaventure was born near Viterbo, probably in 1217. After joining the Roman province of the Franciscans as a young man, he was sent to Paris to complete his education. There he studied under the English Franciscan master Alexander of Hales and began a lifelong friendship with Thomas Aquinas, who joined Bonaventure in helping defend the mendicant ideal of the Franciscans and Dominicans against the attacks of secular masters. Bonaventure himself began teaching in Paris in 1248 and continued doing so until 1257, when he was elected minister general of the entire Franciscan Order, a position he held for the next sixteen years. Much of his work during this period was focused on the delicate task of trying to reconcile sharply divergent factions within the Order, but he also found time to write works of spiritual theology that have become classics, including *The Soul's Journey into God* (whose final two chapters were chosen for this anthology), *The Tree of Life* (meditations on the life of

---

1. Bonaventure, *The Life of St. Francis,* Prol., in *Bonaventure: The Soul's Journey into God; The Tree of Life; The Life of St. Francis,* trans. Ewert Cousins (New York: Paulist; London: SPCK, 1978), 182–83.

2. Etienne Gilson, *The Philosophy of St. Bonaventure,* trans. Dom Illtyd Trethowan and F. J. Sheed (London and New York: Sheed and Ward, 1938), 494.

Christ developed within a theological framework), and *The Triple Way* (a systematic treatment of the stages of the spiritual life). He was made a cardinal in 1273 and died the following year at the Council of Lyons. He was canonized in 1482 and declared a Doctor of the Church in 1588.

We wrote in our General Introduction that the new devotion of twelfth century humanism eventually came to rest in St. Francis and that it was Bonaventure who assigned this new spirituality of creation its place in a traditional mystical theology. One of the best ways to illustrate the extent of this newness is to contrast Bonaventure with the greatest medieval mystical writer before him—Bernard of Clairvaux. For the Cistercian, meditation on the humanity of Christ and on his passion is a profitable but still rather imperfect kind of devotion, belonging to the realm of *amor carnalis* rather than that of *amor rationalis* or *amor spiritualis.* Not surprisingly, meditation on other aspects of the sensible world has even less place in Bernard's mystical theology. His early biographers make much of the fact that Bernard's mental asceticism was such that whatever sensations were produced by exterior stimuli seemed to leave no trace in his memory; it was said that he did not even know the structure of the oratory to which he went every day to pray. In Gilson's striking phrase, "the walls of his mysticism are as bare as the walls of a Cistercian chapel."[3]

Bonaventure's mysticism is of a very different order, in part because of the influence of the mystical treatises of Hugh and Richard of St. Victor, to whom he owed so much, but even more because of the powerful example of his spiritual father, St. Francis. How very unlike Bernard, for example, is Bonaventure in the following passage from *The Life of St. Francis:* "Who can describe the fervent charity which burned within Francis, the friend of the Bridegroom? ... Aroused by all things to the love of God, he rejoiced in all the works of the Lord's hands, and from these joy-producing manifestations he rose to their life-giving principle and cause. In beautiful things he saw Beauty itself, and through his vestiges imprinted on creation he followed his Beloved everywhere, making from all things a ladder by which he could climb up and embrace him who is utterly desirable."[4] Equally great is the contrast with Bernard as regards loving contemplation of the crucifixion of Christ. For Bonaventure, such contemplation is not some beginning step to be later transcended through *amor spiritualis,* but is a distinguishing mark of his entire mystical theology. As he writes in the Prologue to *The Soul's Journey into God* (where he is commenting on the vision Francis saw on the occasion of receiving the stigmata): "The six wings of the seraph can rightly be taken to symbolize the six levels of illumination by which, as if by six steps or stages, the soul can pass over to peace through ecstatic elevations of Christian wisdom. There is no other path but through the burning love of the Crucified."[5] The prevalence of such passages and the prominence they give to Christ Crucified in the description of mystical union distin-

---

3. *Ibid.,* 488.

4. Bonaventure, *The Life of St. Francis,* 9.1, in *Bonaventure,* trans. Cousins, 262–63.

5. Bonaventure, *The Soul's Journey into God,* Prol., in *Bonaventure,* trans. Cousins, 54. Henceforth cited in the text by chapter and section number.

guish the mysticism of St. Bonaventure from that of all his predecessors.[6]

As an aid to understanding the two chapters we have selected from *The Soul's Journey into God* for this anthology, something should be said about the overall structure of the treatise. The first six of its seven chapters deal with six steps or degrees of ascent to mystical union with God: in the first two the mind turns outside itself to find God through his vestiges in the universe (ch. 1) and in the world of the senses (ch. 2); in the next two the mind turns within itself to contemplate God both through his image imprinted on our natural powers of memory, understanding, and will (ch. 3) and in this image reformed and purified by the theological virtues of faith, hope, and charity (ch. 4); and in the last two the mind rises above itself to consider the divine Unity through its primary name, "being" (ch. 5), and also the blessed Trinity through its name, "the good" (ch. 6). Having here reached "the perfection of its illuminations," the mind is drawn on to mystical ecstasy, the subject of chapter seven.

Bonaventure begins his sixth chapter by writing that the good itself is the principal foundation for contemplating the emanations of the Trinity, since (as Dionysius holds) the good is diffusive of itself. As Bonaventure proceeds with his reflections, it might at times seem as though he is claiming to prove the Trinity by natural reason, but in fact he is only offering what might be called proofs of congruency. He next expresses wonder not only at the coincidence of opposites found among the es-

sential attributes and properties of the triune God but also at the union of opposites in the person of Jesus Christ:

The eternal is joined with temporal man,
born of the Virgin in the fulness of time,
the most simple with the most composite,
the most actual with the one who suffered
    supremely and died,
  the most perfect and immense with the
    lowly,
    the supreme and all-inclusive one
with a composite individual distinct from
    others,
    that is, the man Jesus Christ. (6.5)

Here the power of the intellect is at its limit. Just as God rested after the sixth day of creation, so now there is nothing remaining for the mind except "the day of rest on which through mystical ecstasy the mind's discernment comes to rest from all the work which it has done" (6.7). This ecstasy is described in terms borrowed explicitly and at length from *The Mystical Theology* of Pseudo-Dionysius: it occurs in darkness, and consists in the embrace of a Good which transcends thought and would be altogether unattainable were it not for the grace of Christ, who will bestow this gift upon "him who is enflamed in his very marrow by the fire of the Holy Spirit whom Christ sent into the world" (7.4). "This fire," he says some lines later, "is God . . . and Christ enkindles it in the heat of his burning passion. . . . Let us, then, die and enter into the darkness. . . . With Christ crucified, let us pass out of this world to the Father" (7.6).

From even this brief overview of Bonaventure's mysticism, it should be clear that he, perhaps more than any other mys-

---

6. On this point, see Philotheus Boehner, O.F.M., Introduction to *Itinerarium Mentis in Deum*, vol. 2 of *Works of Saint Bonaventure* (St. Bonaventure, N.Y.: Franciscan Institute, 1956), 16.

tic included in our anthology, resists any kind of overly neat categorization. "Image mysticism," "apophatic mysticism," "Trinitarian mysticism," "love mysticism"—all four are *very* prominent in *The Soul's Journey into God*. This, however, is in no sense a problem, but rather a way of corroborating Gilson's claim that Bonaventure provides the most complete synthesis that Christian mysticism has ever achieved.

Selections

THE SOUL'S JOURNEY INTO GOD*

Chapter Six

ON CONTEMPLATING
THE MOST BLESSED TRINITY
IN ITS NAME WHICH IS GOOD

1. After considering the essential attributes of God,
the eye of our intelligence
should be raised to look upon
the most blessed Trinity,
so that the second Cherub
may be placed alongside the first.
Now just as being itself is
the root principle
of viewing the essential attributes,
and the name
through which the others become known,
so the good itself is
the principal foundation
for contemplating the emanations.

2. See, then, and observe
that the highest good is without qualification
that than which no greater can be thought.
And it is such
that it cannot rightly be thought
not to be,
since to be is in all ways better than not to be;[1]
it is such
that it cannot rightly be thought of unless it be thought of
as three and one.
For good is said to be

---

*From *Bonaventure: The Soul's Journey into God; The Tree of Life; The Life of St. Francis,* trans. Ewert Cousins, The Classics of Western Spirituality (New York: Paulist, 1978), 102–16. Reprinted with permission of the publisher.
1. Cf. Anselm, *Proslogion,* c. 2–5, 15.

self-diffusive;[2]
therefore the highest good must be
most self-diffusive.
But the greatest self-diffusion cannot exist unless it is
actual and intrinsic,
substantial and hypostatic,
natural and voluntary,
free and necessary,
lacking nothing and perfect.
Therefore, unless there were eternally in the highest good
a production which is actual and consubstantial,
and a hypostasis as noble as the producer,
as is the case in a producing by way of generation and spiration,
so that it is from an eternal principle eternally coproducing
so that there would be a beloved
and a cobeloved,
the one generated and the other spirated,
and this is
the Father and the Son and the Holy Spirit—
unless these were present,
it would by no means be the highest good
because it would not diffuse itself in the highest degree.
For the diffusion in time in creation
is no more than a center
or point
in relation to the immensity of the divine goodness.
Hence another diffusion can be conceived
greater than this,
namely, one in which
the one diffusing communicates to the other
his entire substance and nature.
Therefore it would not be the highest good
if it could lack this,
either in reality or in thought.
If, therefore, you can behold with your mind's eye
the purity of goodness,
which is the pure act

---

2. Cf. Dionysius, *De caelesti hierarchia,* IV, 1; *De divinis nominibus,* IV, 1, 20.

of a principle loving in charity
with a love
that is both free and due and a mixture of both,
which is the fullest diffusion
by way of nature and will,
which is a diffusion by way of the Word,
in which all things are said,
and by way of the Gift, in which other gifts are given,
then you can see
that through the highest communicability of the good,
there must be
a Trinity of the Father and the Son and the Holy Spirit.
From supreme goodness,
it is necessary that there be in the Persons
supreme communicability;
from supreme communicability, supreme consubstantiality;
from supreme consubstantiality, supreme configurability;
and from these supreme coequality
and hence supreme coeternity;
finally, from all of the above, supreme mutual intimacy,
by which one is necessarily in the other
by supreme interpenetration
and one acts with the other
in absolute lack of division
of the substance, power and operation
of the most blessed Trinity itself.

3. But when you contemplate these things,
do not think
that you comprehend the incomprehensible.
For you still have something else to consider
in these six properties
which strongly leads our mind's eye
to amazement and admiration.
For here is
supreme communicability with individuality of persons,
supreme consubstantiality with plurality of hypostases,
supreme configurability with distinct personality,
supreme coequality with degree,
supreme coeternity with emanation,

supreme mutual intimacy with mission.
Who would not be lifted up in admiration
at the sight of such marvels?
But we understand with complete certitude
that all these things are in the most blessed Trinity
if we lift up our eyes
to the superexcellent goodness.
For if there is here
supreme communication and true diffusion,
there is also here
true origin and true distinction;
and because the whole is communicated and not merely part,
whatever is possessed is given,
and given completely.
Therefore, the one emanating and the one producing
are distinguished by their properties
and are one in essence.
Since, then, they are distinguished by their properties,
they have
personal properties and plurality of hypostases
and emanation of origin
and order, not of posteriority but of origin,
and a sending forth,
not involving a change of place but free inspiration
by reason of the producer's authority
which the sender has in relation to the one sent.
Moreover, because they are one in substance,
there must be unity
in essence, form, dignity, eternity, existence and unlimitedness.
Therefore, when you consider these in themselves one by one,
you have matter for contemplating the truth;
when you compare them with one another,
you have reason to be lifted up to the highest wonder.
Therefore, that your mind may ascend
through wonder to wondering contemplation,
these should be considered together.

4. For the Cherubim who faced each other
also signify this.
The fact that they faced each other,

with their faces turned toward the Mercy Seat,[3]
is not without a mystical meaning,
so that what Our Lord said in John
might be verified:
This is eternal life,
that they may know you, the only true God,
and Jesus Christ, whom you have sent.[4]
For we should wonder
not only at the essential and personal properties of God
in themselves
but also in comparison with
the superwonderful union of God and man
in the unity of the Person of Christ.

5. For if you are the Cherub
contemplating God's essential attributes,
and if you are amazed
because the divine Being is both
first and last,
eternal and most present,
utterly simple and the greatest or boundless,
totally present everywhere and nowhere contained,
most actual and never moved,
most perfect and having nothing superfluous or lacking,
and yet immense and infinite without bounds,
supremely one and yet all-inclusive,
containing all things in himself,
being all power, all truth, all goodness—
if you are this Cherub,
look at the Mercy Seat and wonder
that in him there is joined
the First Principle with the last,
God with man, who was formed on the sixth day;[5]
the eternal is joined with temporal man,
born of the Virgin in the fulness of time,
the most simple with the most composite,

3. Exod 25:20.
4. John 17:3.
5. Cf. Gen 1:26.

the most actual with the one who suffered supremely and died,
the most perfect and immense with the lowly,
the supreme and all-inclusive one
with a composite individual distinct from others,
that is, the man Jesus Christ.

6. But if you are the other Cherub
contemplating the properties of the Persons,
and you are amazed
that communicability exists with individuality,
consubstantiality with plurality,
configurability with personality,
coequality with order,
coeternity with production,
mutual intimacy with sending forth,
because the Son is sent by the Father
and the Holy Spirit by both,
who nevertheless is with them and never departs from them—
if you are this Cherub,
look at the Mercy Seat and wonder
that in Christ
personal union exists
with a trinity of substances and a duality of natures;
that complete agreement exists
with a plurality of wills;
that mutual predication of God and man exists
with a plurality of properties;
that coadoration exists
with a plurality of excellence,
that coexaltation above all things exists
with a plurality of dignity;
that codomination exists
with a plurality of powers.

7. In this consideration is
the perfection of the mind's illumination
when, as if on the sixth day of creation,
it sees man made to the image of God.[6]

---

6. Ibid.

For if an image is an expressed likeness,
when our mind contemplates
in Christ the Son of God,
who is the image of the invisible God by nature,
our humanity
so wonderfully exalted, so ineffably united,
when at the same time it sees united
the first and the last,
the highest and the lowest,
the circumference and the center,
the Alpha and the Omega,[7]
the caused and the cause,
the Creator and the creature,
that is, *the book written within and without,*[8]
it now reaches something perfect.
It reaches the perfection of its illuminations
on the sixth stage,
as if with God on the sixth day of creation;
nor does anything more remain
except the day of rest on which
through mystical ecstasy
the mind's discernment comes to rest
from all the work which it *has done.*[9]

*   *   *

Chapter Seven

ON SPIRITUAL AND MYSTICAL ECSTASY
IN WHICH REST IS GIVEN TO OUR INTELLECT
WHEN THROUGH ECSTASY OUR AFFECTION
PASSES OVER ENTIRELY INTO GOD

1. We have, therefore, passed through
these six considerations.
They are like

---

7. Apoc 1:8, 21:6, 22:13.
8. Apoc 5:1; Ezech 2:9.
9. Gen 2:2.

the six steps of the true Solomon's throne,
by which we arrive
at peace,
where the true man of peace
rests in a peaceful mind
as in the interior Jerusalem.

They are also like
the six wings of the Seraph[1]
by which the mind of the true contemplative
can be borne aloft,
filled with the illumination of heavenly wisdom.

They are also like the first six days,
in which the mind has been trained so that it may reach
the sabbath of rest.

After our mind has beheld God
outside itself
through his vestiges and in his vestiges,
within itself
through his image and in his image,
and above itself
through the similitude of the divine Light shining above us
and in the Light itself,
insofar as this is possible in our state as wayfarers
and through the exercise of our mind,
when finally in the sixth stage
our mind reaches that point
where it contemplates
in the First and Supreme Principle
and in the *mediator of God and men,*[2]
Jesus Christ,
those things whose likenesses can in no way be found
in creatures
and which surpass all penetration
by the human intellect,

---

1. Although the critical text has "Cherub," we have read "Seraph," since Bonaventure is clearly referring to the six-winged Seraph of Francis's vision (cf. prologue, 2–3), which serves as the symbolic matrix of the entire treatise.
   2. 1 Tim 2:5.

it now remains for our mind,
by contemplating these things,
to transcend and pass over not only this sense world
but even itself.
In this passing over,
Christ is the *way and the door;*[3]
Christ is the ladder and the vehicle,
like the Mercy Seat placed above the ark of God[4]
and the *mystery hidden from eternity.*[5]

2. Whoever turns his face fully to the Mercy Seat
and with faith, hope and love,
devotion, admiration, exultation,
appreciation, praise and joy
beholds him hanging upon the cross,
such a one makes the Pasch, that is, the passover,
with Christ.
By the staff of the cross
he passes over the Red Sea,[6]
going from Egypt into the desert,
where he will taste the *hidden manna;*[7]
and with Christ
he rests in the tomb,
as if dead to the outer world,
but experiencing,
as far as is possible in this wayfarer's state,
what was said on the cross
to the thief who adhered to Christ:
Today you shall be with me in paradise.[8]

3. This was shown also
to blessed Francis,
when in ecstatic contemplation

---

3. Cf. John 14:6, 10:7.
4. Cf. Exod 25:21.
5. Eph 3:9.
6. Cf. Exod 12:11.
7. Apoc 2:17.
8. Luke 23:43.

on the height of the mountain—
where I thought out these things I have written—
there appeared to him
a six-winged Seraph fastened to a cross,
as I and several others heard
in that very place
from his companion who was with him then.[9]
There he passed over into God in ecstatic contemplation
and became an example of perfect contemplation
as he had previously been of action,
like another Jacob and Israel,[10]
so that through him,
more by example than by word,
God might invite all truly spiritual men
to this kind of passing over
and spiritual ecstasy.

4. In this passing over,
if it is to be perfect,
all intellectual activities must be left behind
and the height of our affection
must be totally transferred and transformed
into God.
This, however, is mystical and most secret,
which *no one knows
except him who receives it,*[11]
no one receives
except him who desires it,
and no one desires except him
who is inflamed in his very marrow by the fire of the Holy Spirit
whom Christ sent into the world.[12]
And therefore the Apostle says that
this mystical wisdom is revealed
by the Holy Spirit.[13]

---

9. Cf. Bonaventure's *Life of St. Francis,* XIII, 3.
10. Cf. Gen 35:10.
11. Apoc 2:17.
12. Cf. Luke 12:49.
13. Cf. 1 Cor 2:10ff.

5. Since, therefore, in this regard
nature can do nothing
and effort can do but little,
little importance should be given to inquiry,
but much to unction;
little importance should be given to the tongue,
but much to inner joy;
little importance should be given to words and to writing,
but all to the gift of God,
that is, the Holy Spirit;
little or no importance should be given to creation,
but all to the creative essence,
the Father, Son and Holy Spirit,
saying with Dionysius
to God the Trinity:
"Trinity,
superessential, superdivine and supereminent
overseer of the divine wisdom of Christians,
direct us into
the super-unknown, superluminous and most sublime
summit
of mystical communication.
There
new, absolute and unchangeable mysteries of theology
are hidden
in the superluminous darkness
of a silence
teaching secretly in the utmost obscurity
which is supermanifest—
a darkness which is super-resplendent
and in which everything shines forth
and which fills to overflowing
invisible intellects
with the splendors of invisible goods
that surpass all good."[14]
This is said to God.
But to the friend to whom these words were written,
let us say with Dionysius:

---

14. Dionysius, *De mystica theologia*, I, 1.

"But you, my friend,
concerning mystical visions,
with your journey more firmly determined,
leave behind
your senses and intellectual activities,
sensible and invisible things,
all nonbeing and being;
and in this state of unknowing
be restored,
insofar as is possible,
to unity with him
who is above all essence and knowledge.
For transcending yourself and all things,
by the immeasurable and absolute ecstasy of a pure mind,
leaving behind all things
and freed from all things,
you will ascend
to the superessential ray
of the divine darkness."[15]

6. But if you wish to know how these things come about,
ask grace not instruction,
desire not understanding,
the groaning of prayer not diligent reading,
the Spouse not the teacher,
God not man,
darkness not clarity,
not light but the fire
that totally inflames and carries us into God
by ecstatic unctions and burning affections.
This fire is God,
and *his furnace is in Jerusalem;*[16]
and Christ enkindles it
in the heat of his burning passion,
which only he truly perceives who says:
My soul chooses hanging and my bones death.[17]
Whoever loves this death

15. *Ibid.*
16. Isa 31:9.
17. Job 7:15.

can see God
because it is true beyond doubt that
man will not see me and live.[18]
Let us, then, die
and enter into the darkness;
let us impose silence
upon our cares, our desires and our imaginings.
With Christ crucified
let us pass *out of this world to the Father*[19]
so that when the Father is shown to us,
we may say with Philip:
It is enough for us.[20]
Let us hear with Paul:
My grace is sufficient for you.[21]
Let us rejoice with David saying:
My flesh and my heart have grown faint;
You are the God of my heart,
and the God that is my portion forever.
Blessed be the Lord forever
and all the people will say:
Let it be; let it be.
Amen.[22]

HERE ENDS THE SOUL'S JOURNEY INTO GOD.

---

18. Exod 33:20.
19. John 13:1.
20. John 14:8.
21. 2 Cor 12:9.
22. Ps 72:26, 105:48.

SELECTED BIBLIOGRAPHY

TEXTS AND TRANSLATIONS

Opera Omnia. 10 vols. Quaracchi, 1882–1902.

Itinerarium Mentis in Deum. Edited and translated by Philotheus Boehner, O.F.M. Vol. 2 of *Works of Saint Bonaventure.* St. Bonaventure, N.Y.: Franciscan Institute, 1956.

Bonaventure: The Soul's Journey into God; The Tree of Life; The Life of St. Francis. Translated by Ewert Cousins. The Classics of Western Spirituality. New York: Paulist; London: SPCK, 1978.

The Works of Bonaventure. Translated by José de Vinck. 5 vols. Paterson, N.J.: St. Anthony Guild Press, 1960–70.

STUDIES

Bougerol, Jacques Guy, O.F.M. *Introduction to the Works of Bonaventure.* Translated by José de Vinck. Paterson, N.J.: St. Anthony Guild Press, 1964.

————, ed. *S. Bonaventura, 1274–1974.* 5 vols. Grottaferrata, 1972–74.

Gilson, Etienne. *The Philosophy of St. Bonaventure.* Translated by Dom Illtyd Trethowan and F. J. Sheed. London and New York: Sheed and Ward, 1938; Paterson, N.J.: St. Anthony Guild Press, 1965.

Landsberg, P.-L. "La philosophie d'une expérience mystique: L'itinerarium." *La vie spirituelle, Suppl.* 51 (1937): [71]–[85].

Tavard, George, A.A. "St. Bonaventure as Mystic and Theologian." In *The Heritage of the Early Church,* edited by David Neiman and Margaret Schatkin, 289–306. Orientalia Christiana Analecta, 195. Rome, 1973.

Meister Eckhart

(c.1260–c.1329)

Today Eckhart may well be the most-quoted Christian mystic. His name appears not only in theological studies but, perhaps even more, in philosophical, literary, and historical ones. We may doubt, however, whether his popularity is matched by a correct understanding of his thought. Symptomatic for what is at least a one-sided presentation of it is that, until recent years, the bold German sermons received all the attention while the Latin works remained unread. Two volumes of The Classics of Western Spirituality, as well as a few monographs, have begun to remedy the lack of balance. A more thorough acquaintance with his work reveals next to the obvious influence of Neoplatonic (Christian) sources that of Aristotelian–Thomist ones as well. Their simultaneous presence gives Eckhart's thought a complexity unparalleled in the ecstatic tradition. On the one hand, the Meister places God beyond Being (in Neoplatonic fashion), while, on the other, he defines God as *esse simpliciter*—Being-as-such (a Thomist position). Clearly, Being for Eckhart means not the supreme intelligible, or the act of existing, but that ultimately real which lies beyond all names. Indeed, with the concept of Being Eckhart attempts to surpass even Dionysius' One (which he regards as still a category of cognition) and to overcome the very opposition between transcendence and immanence, for it is the point in which God and the ground of the soul coincide.

Nor should we be surprised by this prevalence of Thomist terminology in the writings of a Dominican friar who lived only a few decades after Saint Thomas and consistently claimed to be a disciple of the Angelic Doctor. Far from being an outsider, Eckhart enjoyed a high, lifelong esteem in his order. Born near Erfurt in Thuringia he joined the Dominicans at an early age, studied in Cologne and Paris, and lectured in the theology faculties at Paris, Strasbourg, and Cologne. Eckhart enjoyed a great success as a preacher—especially in Cologne. He was appointed to several positions of authority, including that of general vicar of the Dominican provinces of Saxony and Bohemia. Though given to the highest theological speculation, he nevertheless seems to have been a quite practical person gifted with a great deal of common sense. Moreover, honoring the Dominican ideal of *contemplata tradere,* he literally "preached" mysticism in sermons that, however sublime and often abstruse, were nevertheless directed to all devout believers, not to a few privileged souls. Though his spirituality decidedly belongs to the intellectual type introduced by Dionysius, many of his most spiritual sermons deal with moral virtues—poverty, humility, resignation—preparing the soul to pass beyond all cognitive endeavor.

His efforts to stress the total transcendence of God as well as His total immanence resulted more in a dynamic tension than in a balanced synthesis. Toward the end of his life his doctrine came under severe attack by the archbishop of Cologne, whose assembled theologians condemned a number of theses attributed to Eckhart. His defense combines denials of ever having held some of the theses with somewhat disingenuously innocuous interpretations of others. Pope John XXII, in his Bull *In agro dominico,* ratified the Cologne condemnations. But some of the members of the papal commission (possibly John XXII's own successor, Benedict XII) appeared to have felt serious misgivings about the juridical procedure. Awaiting the verdict at the papal court in Avignon, Eckhart died having professed his loyalty to the Church and, according to the Bull, "revoked and deplored the twenty-six articles which he admitted that he had preached." At the time of this writing Rome appears to consider lifting the condemnations (which contain some clear misreadings of his work) and restoring him to full ecclesiastical honor.

Eckhart took apophatic theology to an unprecedented extreme where it surpassed even the Persons in the Trinity. The mystical journey leads "into the simple ground, into the quiet desert, into which distinction never gazed, not the Father, nor the Son, nor the Holy Spirit."[1] The innermost ground of the Godhead leaves no room for distinctions. At the same time, Eckhart's theology of the Image may well count as one of the first important trinitarian spiritual theologies in Latin Christianity and was to give the main impulse to trinitarian mysticism in the Rhineland and Flanders. Indeed, more than his negation, his doctrine of the birth of the Son in the soul was singled out for doctrinal criticism by both the Cologne and the Avignon commissions. In his *Commentary on Genesis* Eckhart had written: "In one and the same time in which He was God and in which He begat His coeternal Son as God equal to Himself in all things, He also created the world."[2] Eckhart defended himself against charges of having held the eternity of creation by distinguishing the eternal *now* of God's creative activity and the temporal result of that creative act. Whether his reply adequately settles the matter or not, his intention to present the creature as in some manner eternally present in the divine *Image* of the Son is clear enough. His sixth sermon, one daring speculation on the birth of the Son in the soul, fully highlights the central importance of the Image theology in Eckhart's mysticism. But most of the texts here reproduced reflect that theology. Especially the famous sermon 52 on spiritual poverty points the way toward a decreation which would allow the divine Image to occupy the empty space.

---

1. Sermon 48, in *Meister Eckhart: The Essential Sermons, Commentaries, Treatises, and Defense,* trans. Edmund Colledge and Bernard McGinn, The Classics of Western Spirituality (New York: Paulist, 1981), 198.

2. *Commentary on Genesis,* ibid., 85.

Eckhart never fully integrated the two aspects of God's essence and His manifestation with one another. This failure may well be responsible for some of the doctrinal difficulties he brought upon himself. His theology moves, often abruptly, between the extremes of religious atheism and pantheism without lapsing into either one, but also without ever achieving an harmonious synthesis. This unsurmounted dualism renders his doctrine as controversial today as in his own time, but its dynamic opposition of the two major tendencies of Western mysticism also conveys to that doctrine its striking power.

Selections

SERMON SIX*

Justi vivent in aeternum (Wis 5:16)

"The just will live forever, and their reward is with God." See exactly what this means; though it may sound simple and commonplace, it is really noteworthy and excellent.

"The just will live." Which are the just? Somewhere it is written: "That man is just who gives everyone what belongs to him";[1] those who give God what is his, and the saints and the angels what is theirs, and their fellow man what is his.

Honor belongs to God. Who are those who honor God? Those who have wholly gone out of themselves, and who do not seek for what is theirs in anything, whatever it may be, great or little, who are not looking beneath themselves or above themselves or beside themselves or at themselves, who are not desiring possessions or honors or ease or pleasure or profit or inwardness or holiness or reward or the kingdom of heaven, and who have gone out from all this, from everything that is theirs, these people pay honor to God, and they honor God properly, and they give him what is his.

People ought to give joy to the angels and the saints. What, does this amaze you? Can a man in this life give joy to those who are in everlasting life? Yes, indeed, he can! Every saint has such great delight and such unspeakable joy from every good work; from a good will or an aspiration they have such great joy that no tongue can tell, no heart can think how great is the joy they have from this. Why is that? Because their love for God is so immeasurably great, and they have so true a love for him, that his honor is dearer to them than their blessedness. And not only the saints or the angels, for God himself takes such delight in this, just as if it were his blessedness; and his being depends upon it, and his contentment and his well-being. Yes, mark this well: If we do not want to serve God for any other reason than the great joy they have in this who are in everlasting life, and that God himself has, we could do it gladly and with all our might.

And one ought also to give help and support to those who are in purgatory, and improvement and edification to those who are still living.

Such a man is just in one way, and so in another sense are all those who accept all things alike from God, whatever it may be, great or small, joy or sorrow, all of it

---

*The three sermons in this chapter are from *Meister Eckhart: The Essential Sermons, Commentaries, Treatises, and Defense,* trans. Edmund Colledge, O.S.A., and Bernard McGinn, The Classics of Western Spirituality (New York: Paulist, 1981), 185–89, 197–203. Reprinted with permission of the publisher.

1. Justinian, *Institutes* I, 1.

alike, less or more, one like the other. If you account anything more than something else, you do wrong. You ought to go wholly out from your own will.

Recently I had this thought: If God did not wish as I do, then I would still wish as he does. There are some people who want to have their own will in everything; that is bad, and there is much harm in it. Those are a little better who do want what God wants, and want nothing contrary to his will; if they were sick, what they would wish would be for God's will to be for them to be well. So these people want God to want according to their will, not for themselves to want according to his will. One has to endure this, but still it is wrong. The just have no will at all; what God wills is all the same to them, however great distress that may be.

For just men, the pursuit of justice is so imperative that if God were not just, they would not give a fig for God; and they stand fast by justice, and they have gone out of themselves so completely that they have no regard for the pains of hell or the joys of heaven or for any other thing. Yes, if all the pains that those have who are in hell, men or devils, or all the pains that have ever been or ever will be suffered on earth were to be joined on to justice, they would not give a straw for that, so fast do they stand by God and by justice. Nothing is more painful or hard for a just man than what is contrary to justice. In what way? If one thing gives them joy and another sorrow, they are not just; but if on one occasion they are joyful, then they are always joyful; and if on one occasion they are more joyful and on others less, then they are wrong. Whoever loves justice stands so fast by it that whatever he loves, that is his being; nothing can deflect him from this, nor does he esteem anything differently. Saint Augustine says: "When the soul loves, it is more properly itself than when it gives life."[2] This sounds simple and commonplace, and yet few understand what it means, and still it is true. Anyone who has discernment in justice and in just men, he understands everything I am saying.

"The just will live." Among all things there is nothing so dear or so desirable as life. However wretched or hard his life may be, a man still wants to live. It is written somewhere that the closer anything is to death, the more it suffers. Yet however wretched life may be, still it wants to live. Why do you eat? Why do you sleep? So that you live. Why do you want riches or honors? That you know very well; but— why do you live? So as to live; and still you do not know why you live. Life is in itself so desirable that we desire it for its own sake. Those in hell are in everlasting torment, but they would not want to lose their lives, not the devils or the souls of men, for their life is so precious that it flows without any medium from God into the soul. And because it flows from God without medium they want to live. What

---

2. This is actually from Bernard of Clairvaux, *Of Precept and Dispensation* 20.60.

is life? God's being is my life. If my life is God's being, then God's existence must be my existence and God's is-ness is my is-ness, neither less nor more.

They live eternally "with God," directly close to God, not beneath or above. They perform all their works with God, and God with them. Saint John says: "The Word was with God" (Jn. 1:1). It was wholly equal, and it was close beside, not beneath there or above there, but just equal. When God made man, he made woman from man's side, so that she might be equal to him. He did not make her out of man's head or his feet, so that she would be neither woman nor man for him, but so that she might be equal. So should the just soul be equal with God and close beside God, equal beside him, not beneath or above.

Who are they who are thus equal? Those who are equal to nothing, they alone are equal to God. The divine being is equal to nothing, and in it there is neither image nor form. To the souls who are equal, the Father gives equally, and he withholds nothing at all from them. Whatever the Father can achieve, that he gives equally to this soul, yes, if it no longer equals itself more than anything else, and it should not be closer to itself than to anything else. It should desire or heed its own honor, its profit and whatever may be its own, no more than what is a stranger's. Whatever belongs to anyone should not be distant or strange to the soul, whether this be evil or good. All the love of this world is founded on self-love. If you had forsaken that, you would have forsaken the whole world.

The Father gives birth to his Son in eternity, equal to himself. "The Word was with God, and God was the Word" (Jn. 1:1); it was the same in the same nature. Yet I say more: He has given birth to him in my soul. Not only is the soul with him, and he equal with it, but he is in it, and the Father gives his Son birth in the soul in the same way as he gives him birth in eternity, and not otherwise. He must do it whether he likes it or not. The Father gives birth to his Son without ceasing; and I say more: He gives me birth, me, his Son and the same Son. I say more: He gives birth not only to me, his Son, but he gives birth to me as himself and himself as me and to me as his being and nature. In the innermost source, there I spring out in the Holy Spirit, where there is one life and one being and one work. Everything God performs is one; therefore he gives me, his Son, birth without any distinction. My fleshly father is not actually my father except in one little portion of his nature, and I am separated from him; he may be dead and I alive. Therefore the heavenly Father is truly my Father, for I am his Son and have everything that I have from him, and I am the same Son and not a different one. Because the Father performs one work, therefore his work is me, his Only-Begotten Son without any difference.

"We shall be completely transformed and changed into God" (2 Co. 3:18). See a comparison. In the same way, when in the sacrament bread is changed into the Body of our Lord, however many pieces of bread there were, they still become one Body. Just so, if all the pieces of bread were changed into my finger, there would still not be more than one finger. But if my finger were changed into the bread, there would be as many of one as of the other. What is changed into something else becomes one with it. I am so changed into him that he produces his being in me as one, not just similar. By the living God, this is true! There is no distinction.

The Father gives his Son birth without ceasing. Once the Son has been born he receives nothing from the Father because he has it all, but what he receives from the Father is his being born. In this we ought not to ask for something from God as if he were a stranger. Our Lord said to his disciples: "I have not called you servants, but friends" (Jn. 15:14). Whoever asks for something from someone else is a servant, and he who grants it is a master. Recently I considered whether there was anything I would take or ask from God. I shall take careful thought about this, because if I were accepting anything from God, I should be subject to him as a servant, and he in giving would be as a master. We shall not be so in life everlasting.

Once I said here, and what I said is true: If a man obtains or accepts something from outside himself, he is in this wrong. One should not accept or esteem God as being outside oneself, but as one's own and as what is within one; nor should one serve or labor for any recompense, not for God or for his honor or for anything that is outside oneself, but only for that which one's own being and one's own life is within one. Some simple people think that they will see God as if he were standing there and they here. It is not so. God and I, we are one. I accept God into me in knowing; I go into God in loving. There are some who say that blessedness consists not in knowing but in willing. They are wrong; for if it consisted only in the will, it would not be one. Working and becoming are one. If a carpenter does not work, nothing becomes of the house. If the axe is not doing anything, nothing is becoming anything. In this working God and I are one; he is working and I am becoming. The fire changes anything into itself that is put into it and this takes on fire's own nature. The wood does not change the fire into itself, but the fire changes the wood into itself. So are we changed into God, that we shall know him as he is (1 Jn. 3:2). Saint Paul says: "So shall we come to know him, I knowing him just as he knows me" (1 Co. 13:12), neither less nor more, perfectly equal. "The just will live forever, and their reward is with God," perfectly equal.

That we may love justice, for its own sake and for God, without asking return, may God help us to this. Amen.

SERMON FORTY-EIGHT

Ein meister sprichet: alliu glichiu dinc minnent sich under einander.

An authority says: "All things that are alike love one another and unite with one another, and all things that are unlike flee from one another and hate one another."[1] And one authority says that nothing is so unlike as are heaven and earth.[2] The kingdom of earth was endowed by nature with being far off from heaven and unlike it. This is why earth fled to the lowest place and is immovable so that it may not approach heaven. Heaven by nature apprehended that the earth fled from it and occupied the lowest place. Therefore heaven always pours itself out fruitfully upon the kingdom of earth; and the authorities maintain that the broad and wide heaven does not retain for itself so much as the width of a needle's point, but rather bestows it upon the earth. That is why earth is called the most fruitful of all created things that exist in time.

I say the same about the man who has annihilated himself in himself and in God and in all created things; this man has taken possession of the lowest place, and God must pour the whole of himself into this man, or else he is not God. I say in the truth, which is good and eternal and enduring, that God must pour out the whole of himself with all his might so totally into every man who has utterly abandoned himself that God withholds nothing of his being or his nature or his entire divinity, but he must pour all of it fruitfully into the man who has abandoned himself for God and has occupied the lowest place.

As I was coming here today I was wondering how I should preach to you so that it would make sense and you would understand it. Then I thought of a comparison: If you could understand that, you would understand my meaning and the basis of all my thinking in everything I have ever preached. The comparison concerns my eyes and a piece of wood. If my eye is open, it is an eye; if it is closed, it is the same eye. It is not the wood that comes and goes, but it is my vision of it. Now pay good heed to me! If it happens that my eye is in itself one and simple (Mt. 6:22), and it is opened and casts its glance upon the piece of wood, the eye and the wood remain what they are, and yet in the act of vision they become as one, so that we can truly say that my eye is the wood and the wood is my eye. But if the wood were immaterial, purely spiritual as is the sight of my eye, then one could truly say that in the act of vision the wood and my eye subsisted in one being. If this is true of physical objects, it is far truer of spiritual objects. You should know that my eye has far more in common with the eye of a sheep which is on the other side of the sea and which I never saw, than it has in common with my ears, with which, however, it shares its

---

1. Of the possible sources indicated by Quint in his critical edition, the closest is Thomas Aquinas, *STh* IaIIae.29.1.
2. The "authority" seems to be Aristotle, *On Heaven and Earth,* passim.

being; and that is because the action of the sheep's eye is also that of my eye. And so I attribute to both more in common in their action than I do to my eyes and my ears, because their actions are different.

Sometimes I have spoken of a light that is uncreated and not capable of creation and that is in the soul. I always mention this light in my sermons; and this same light comprehends God without a medium, uncovered, naked, as he is in himself; and this comprehension is to be understood as happening when the birth takes place. Here I may truly say that this light may have more unity with God than it has with any power of the soul, with which, however, it is one in being. For you should know that this light is not nobler in my soul's being than is the feeblest or crudest power, such as hearing or sight or anything else which can be affected by hunger or thirst, frost or heat; and the simplicity of my being is the cause of that. Because of this, if we take the powers as they are in our being, they are all equally noble; but if we take them as they work, one is much nobler and higher than another.

That is why I say that if a man will turn away from himself and from all created things, by so much will you be made one and blessed in the spark in the soul, which has never touched either time or place. This spark rejects all created things, and wants nothing but its naked God, as he is in himself. It is not content with the Father or the Son or the Holy Spirit, or with the three Persons so far as each of them persists in his properties. I say truly that this light is not content with the divine nature's generative or fruitful qualities. I will say more, surprising though this is. I speak in all truth, truth that is eternal and enduring, that this same light is not content with the simple divine essence in its repose, as it neither gives nor receives; but it wants to know the source of this essence, it wants to go into the simple ground, into the quiet desert, into which distinction never gazed, not the Father, nor the Son, nor the Holy Spirit. In the innermost part, where no one dwells, there is contentment for that light, and there it is more inward than it can be to itself, for this ground is a simple silence, in itself immovable, and by this immovability all things are moved, all life is received by those who in themselves have rational being.

May that enduring truth of which I have spoken help us that we may so have rational life. Amen.

SERMON FIFTY-TWO

Beati pauperes spiritu, quoniam ipsorum est regnum caelorum (Mt 5:3)

Blessedness opened its mouth to wisdom and said: "Blessed are the poor in spirit, for the kingom of heaven is theirs" (Mt. 5:3).

All angels and all saints and all who were ever born must keep silent when the

Wisdom of the Father speaks, for all the Wisdom of the angels and of all created beings is mere folly before the unfathomable Wisdom of God. It has said that the poor are blessed.

Now there are two kinds of poverty. There is an external poverty, which is good and is greatly to be esteemed in a man who voluntarily practices it for the love of our Lord Jesus Christ, for he himself used it when he was on earth. I do not now want to say anything more about this poverty. But there is a different poverty, an inward poverty, and it is of this that we must understand that our Lord is speaking: "Blessed are the poor in spirit."

Now I beg you to be disposed to what I say; for I say to you in everlasting truth that if you are unlike this truth of which we want to speak, you cannot understand me. Various people have asked me what poverty may be in itself and what a poor man may be. Let us try to answer this.

Bishop Albert says that a poor man is one who does not find satisfaction in all the things God created;[1] and this is well said. But we can put it even better, and take poverty in a higher sense. A poor man wants nothing, and knows nothing, and has nothing. Let us now talk about these three points; and I beg you for the sake of God's love that you understand this truth, if you can, and if you do not understand it, do not burden yourself with it, for the truth I want to expound is such that there will be few good people to understand it.

First let us discuss a poor man as one who wants nothing. There are some people who do not understand this well. They are those who are attached to their own penances and external exercises, which seem important to people. God help those who hold divine truth in such low esteem! Such people present an outward picture that gives them the name of saints; but inside they are donkeys, for they cannot distinguish divine truth. These people say that a man is poor who wants nothing; but they interpret it in this way, that a man ought to live so that he never fulfills his own will in anything, but that he ought to comport himself so that he may fulfill God's dearest will. Such people are in the right, for their intention is good. For this let us commend them. May God in his mercy grant them the kingdom of heaven. But I speak in the divine truth when I say that they are not poor men, nor do they resemble poor men. They have great esteem in the sight of men who know no better, but I say that they are donkeys who have no understanding of divine truth. They deserve the kingdom of heaven for their good intention, but of the poverty of which we want to talk they know nothing.

If someone asks me now what kind of poor man he is who wants nothing, I reply in this way. So long as a man has this as his will, that he wants to fulfill God's dearest

---

1. Albert the Great, *Commentary on Matthew* 5.3.

will, he has not the poverty about which we want to talk. Such a person has a will with which he wants to fulfill God's will, and that is not true poverty. For if a person wants really to have poverty, he ought to be as free of his own created will as he was when he did not exist. For I tell you by the truth that is eternal, so long as you have a will to fulfill God's will, and a longing for God and for eternity, then you are not poor; for a poor man is one who has a will and longing for nothing.

When I stood in my first cause, I then had no "God," and then I was my own cause. I wanted nothing, I longed for nothing, for I was an empty being, and the only truth in which I rejoiced was in the knowledge of myself. Then it was myself I wanted and nothing else. What I wanted I was, and what I was I wanted; and so I stood, empty of God and of everything. But when I went out from my own free will and received my created being, then I had a "God," for before there were any creatures, God was not "God," but he was what he was. But when creatures came to be and received their created being, then God was not "God" in himself, but he was "God" in the creatures.

Now I say that God, so far as he is "God," is not the perfect end of created beings. The least of these beings possesses in God as much as he possesses. If it could be that a fly had reason and could with its reason seek out the eternal depths of the divine being from which it issued, I say that God, with all that he has as he is "God," could not fulfill or satisfy the fly. So therefore let us pray to God that we may be free of "God," and that we may apprehend and rejoice in that everlasting truth in which the highest angel and the fly and the soul are equal—there where I was established, where I wanted what I was and was what I wanted. So I say: If a man is to become poor in his will, he must want and desire as little as he wanted and desired when he did not exist. And in this way a man is poor who wants nothing.

Next, a man is poor who knows nothing. Sometimes I have said that a man ought to live so that he did not live for himself or for the truth or for God. But now I say something different and something more, that a man who would possess this poverty ought to live as if he does not even know that he is not in any way living for himself or for the truth or for God. Rather, he should be so free of all knowing that he does not know or experience or grasp that God lives in him. For when man was established in God's everlasting being, there was no different life in him. What was living there was himself. So I say that a man should be set as free of his own knowing as he was when he was not. Let God perform what he will, and let man be free.

Everything that ever came from God is directed into pure activity. Now the actions proper to a man are loving and knowing. The question is: In which of these does blessedness most consist? Some authorities have said that it consists in knowing, others say that it consists in loving; others that it consists in knowing and loving, and what they say is better. But I say that it does not consist in either knowing or loving, but that there is that in the soul from which knowing and loving flow; that something does not know or love as do the powers of the soul. Whoever knows this knows in what blessedness consists. That something has neither before nor after, and it is not waiting for anything that is to come, for it can neither gain nor lose. So it is deprived of the knowledge that God is acting in it; but it is itself the very thing that rejoices in itself as God does in himself. So I say that a man ought to be established, free and empty, not knowing or perceiving that God is acting in him; and so a man may possess poverty. The authorities say that God is a being, and a rational one, and that he knows all things. I say that God is neither being nor rational, and that he does not know this or that.[2] Therefore God is free of all things, and therefore he is all things. Whoever will be poor in spirit, he must be poor of all his own knowledge, so that he knows nothing, not God or created things or himself. Therefore it is necessary for a man to long not to be able to know or perceive God's works. In this way a man can be poor of his own knowledge.

Third, a man is poor who has nothing. Many people have said that it is perfection when one possesses no material, earthly things, and in one sense this is indeed true, if a man does this voluntarily. But this is not the sense in which I mean it.

I have said just now that a man is poor who does not want to fulfill God's will, but who lives so that he may be free both of his own will and of God's will, as he was when he was not. About this poverty I say that it is the highest poverty. Second, I say that a man is poor who knows nothing of God's works in him. A man who is so established is as free of knowing and perceiving as God is free of all things, and this is the purest poverty. But a third form is the most intimate poverty, on which I now want to speak; and this is when a man has nothing.

Now pay great attention and give heed! I have often said, and great authorities say, that a man should be so free of all things and of all works, both interior and exterior, that he might become a place only for God, in which God could work. Now I say otherwise. If it be the case that man is free of all created things and of God and of himself, and if it also be that God may find place in him in which to work, then I say that so long as that is in man, he is not poor with the most intimate poverty. For it is not God's intention in his works that man should have in himself a place for God to work in. Poverty of spirit is for a man to keep so free of God and of all his works that if God wishes to work in the soul, he himself is the place in which he wants to work; and that he will gladly do. For if he finds a man so poor as this, then God performs his own work, and the man is in this way suffering God to work, and God is his own place to work in, and so God is his own worker in himself. Thus in

---

2. "This or that," that is, particular things.

this poverty man pursues that everlasting being which he was and which he is now and which he will evermore remain.

It is Saint Paul who says: "All that I am, I am by God's grace" (1 Co. 15:10). But if what I say transcends grace and being and understanding and will and longing, how then can Paul's words be true? People show that what Paul said is true in this way. That the grace of God was in him was necessarily so, for it was God's grace working in him that brought what was accidental to the perfection of the essential. When grace had finished and had perfected its work, then Paul remained what he was.

So I say that man should be so poor that he should not be or have any place in which God could work. When man clings to place, he clings to distinction. Therefore I pray to God that he may make me free of "God," for my real being is above God if we take "God" to be the beginning of created things. For in the same being of God where God is above being and above distinction, there I myself was, there I willed myself and committed myself to create this man. Therefore I am the cause of myself in the order of my being, which is eternal, and not in the order of my becoming, which is temporal. And therefore I am unborn, and in the manner in which I am unborn I can never die. In my unborn manner I have been eternally, and am now, and shall eternally remain. What I am in the order of having been born, that will die and perish, for it is mortal, and so it must in time suffer corruption. In my birth all things were born and I was the cause of myself and of all things; and if I would have wished it, I would not be nor would all other things be. And if I did not exist, "God" would also not exist. That God is "God," of that I am a cause; if I did not exist, God too would not be "God." There is no need to understand this.

A great authority says that his breaking through is nobler than his flowing out;[3] and that is true. When I flowed out from God, all things said: "God is." And this cannot make me blessed, for with this I acknowledge that I am a creature. But in the breaking-through, when I come to be free of will of myself and of God's will and of all his works and of God himself, then I am above all created things, and I am neither God nor creature, but I am what I was and what I shall remain, now and eternally. Then I received an impulse that will bring me up above all the angels. Together with this impulse, I receive such riches that God, as he is "God," and as he performs all his divine works, cannot suffice me; for in this breaking-through I receive that God and I are one. Then I am what I was, and then I neither diminish nor increase, for I am then an immovable cause that moves all things. Here God finds no place in man, for with this poverty man achieves what he has been eternally

---

3. The "great authority" may be Eckhart himself.

and will evermore remain. Here God is one with the spirit, and that is the most intimate poverty one can find.

Whoever does not understand what I have said, let him not burden his heart with it; for as long as a man is not equal to this truth, he will not understand these words, for this is a truth beyond speculation that has come immediately from the heart of God. May God help us so to live that we may find it eternally. Amen.

COMMENTARY ON THE BOOK OF WISDOM*

"And since it is one, it can do all things" (Wis 7:27a)

144. The wise man makes two statements about Wisdom: first, that it is one; second, a hint that because it is one it can do all things. As far as Wisdom being one is concerned, I have amply treated the matter [in commenting on] Deuteronomy 6 and Galatians 3, "God is one." It should be noted in the case of this text that when God is said to be one by Moses speaking in God's name, this is not the only thing that God intended to teach Israel (that is, those who see God). He intimated something deeper to us, beyond the fact that God is one and not many as the sun is one and not many, though this is also true.

We must understand that the term "one" is the same as indistinct,[1] for all distinct things are two or more, but all indistinct things are one. Furthermore, there is an indistinction that concerns God's nature, both because he is infinite, and also because he is not determined by the confines or limits of any genera or beings. But it is the nature of any created being to be determined and limited by the fact that it is created, as we read in Chapter 11, "You have ordered all things in measure, and number and weight" (Ws. 11:21). Therefore, saying that God is one is to say that God is indistinct from all things, which is the property of the highest and first existence and its overflowing goodness. For this reason later in the same eleventh chapter there follows, "You love all things which are" (Ws. 11:25).

145. A further, third argument. God is one which is indistinct. This signifies the highest divine perfection by which nothing exists or is able to exist without him or distinct from him. This is most clear if in place of the word "God" we use the word "existence." God is existence. It is clear that existence is indistinct from everything

---

*From *Meister Eckhart: Teacher and Preacher,* ed. and trans. Bernard McGinn with the collaboration of Frank Tobin and Elvira Borgstädt, The Classics of Western Spirituality (New York: Paulist, 1986), 166–71. Reprinted with permission of the publisher.
1. "Indistinct," that is, "not-to-be-distinguished."

which exists and that nothing exists or can exist that is distinct and separated from existence. John 1 says, "All things were made through him and without him nothing was made" (Jn. 1:3); and Augustine speaking to God says, "You were with me and I was not with you."[2] "You were with me," because indistinct from all things; "I was not with you," because I am distinct as something created. Therefore, here where the discussion concerns Wisdom which is "one," the fullness and purity of its own existence is shown, and also the goodness by which it loves all things, and thirdly its highest and primal perfection, as well as the imperfection of every created thing in that they are made from it and without it are nothing in themselves.

146. From these observations the common understanding according to the literal sense of the text "God is one" (Ga. 3:20) is well proven. This is the first way. It is impossible for there to be two infinite things. This is immediately evident to anyone who understands the terms, because the infinite is that outside of which there is nothing. But God, as contained and limited by no genus or comprehended by no limits, is infinite, as said above. Therefore, he is one and unique. The second argument runs thus. It is impossible for there to be two or more indistinct things, for the indistinct and the One are the same, as was also said above. But God is indistinct and the Indistinct Itself. Therefore, it is impossible for there to be many gods.

Yet a third argument comes from the fact that God is Existence Itself (Ex. 3:14). Granted this, it follows that it is impossible for there to be two or more gods. Rather, if two gods are admitted, there will not be two gods: Either none or one of them will be God. Again, it would follow that there will be two acts of existence in any creature, and consequently any being will [actually] be two beings. The conclusion of all these premises will be clear enough to one who understands the terms. Nevertheless, the consequence has been demonstrated [in the explanation] of Galatians 3, "God is one" (Ga. 3:20).

147. Again, the statement that Wisdom is one is proven from the nature of this term, that is, "one." Indeed, the first three proofs are derived from the nature of the term Wisdom or God. Therefore, it should be recognized now that the term "one" is a negative word but is in reality affirmative. Moreover, it is the negation of negation which is the purest form of affirmation and the fullness of the term affirmed. Fullness, superabundance, and "what is said by way of superabundance belong to the One alone," as the Philosopher says.[3]

148. Still, the One descends totally into all things which are beneath it, which are many and which are enumerated. In these individual things the One is not divided, but remaining the incorrupt One, it flows forth into every number and informs it

---

2. Augustine, *Conf.* 10.27.
3. Aristotle, *Top.* 5.5.

with its own unity. So, the One is necessarily found prior to any duality or plurality both in reality and understanding. Thus the term "one" adds nothing beyond existence, not even conceptually, but only according to negation. This is not so in the case of "true" and "good." For this reason it is most immediately related to existence in that it signifies the purity and core and height of existence itself, something which even the term "existence" does not do. The term "one" signifies Existence Itself in itself along with the negation and exclusion of all nonbeing, which [nonbeing], I say, every negation entails. Every negation denies the existence of a thing whose very existence bespeaks privation. The negation of negation (which the term "one" signifies) denotes that everything which belongs to the term is present in the signified and everything which is opposed to it is absent. This is necessarily the One. It is impossible for any being or nature to be multiplied unless something of its nature is either lacking to a second being or there is something added to the second being from another source, or both together, that is, there is both lack and addition.[4]

149. It is therefore evident from all the premises that unity or the One most properly belongs to God, even more than the terms "the True" and "the Good," and this is what is said here of Wisdom ("since it is one"), and in Galatians 3, "God is one" (Ga. 3:20). The sense is not only that God is one, but also that he is the only one or that he is alone. "God," he says, "is one," that is, he is the one God. Macrobius says this plainly in the first book of his *Commentary on the Dream of Scipio,* a good bit before the middle, in these words: "The One which is called the Monad, that is, unity, is not a number, but the source and origin of all number. The beginning and the end of all things, itself not knowing beginning nor end, it refers to the supreme God. You would seek it in vain in an inferior stage below God. Since it is one, it cannot be numbered itself; nevertheless, it creates innumerable kinds of genera from itself and contains them within itself."[5] Thus far the words of Macrobius, from which it is clear that God is one and is one Wisdom, as it says here, "since it is one, it can do all things."

150. From Macrobius's words, especially the last sentence, it is seen that the One, in that it is one, is formally distinguished from number as an opposed principle. This is the greatest distinction. Therefore Boethius in his *Trinity* says, "That is truly one in which there is no number,"[6] as if we were to say, "That is truly gold in which there is nothing foreign or opposed to gold."

151. The One itself also gives number existence, for number is a multitude com-

---

4. The meaning of this convoluted sentence is that there can be only one "One."
5. Macrobius, *Comm. on the Dream of Scipio* 1.6.7.
6. Boethius, *Trinity* 2.

posed of unities. The One even conserves number and multitude in existence; "Every multitude participates in the One," as Proclus says.[7] And this is what Macrobius states: "Unity cannot be numbered itself." Observe the opposition and distinction. There follows: "It creates innumerable kinds from itself and contains them within itself." Observe the indistinction.

152. From these two points I form two new arguments to prove from the nature of the One that God, Wisdom, is one. The first is this: "The One is that in which there is no number." But in God there is no number, as Macrobius says here. The reason is that number is a falling away, and falling away does not pertain to God, since he is the First and also since he is existence. Therefore, God is one. This second [argument] is this. The One and the Many are opposed. But in God there is no number (as was said and proved above), because there is no falling away in him and because he is the First and is existence. Therefore, God is one.

153. What Augustine says in *True Religion,* Chapter 11, speaks to this: "All agree that what is preferred to everything else is God." Immediately prior to this he says, "All created things eagerly compete [in describing] the excellence of God."[8] From this it is evident that there is no falling away or retreat in him; consequently, there is neither number nor multitude. Therefore, God is one, for that is one in which there is no number. Again, [the same follows] because the One and the Many are opposed.

154. Accordingly, it should be noted that nothing is so distinct from number and the thing numbered or what is numerable (the created thing, that is) as God is. And yet nothing is so indistinct.

The first proof is because the indistinct is more distinguished from the distinct than any two distinct things are from each other. For example, something not colored is further from a colored thing than two colored things are from each other. But indistinction belongs to God's nature; distinction to the created thing's nature and idea, as was said above. Therefore, God is most distinct from each and every created thing.

Further, the second argument goes this way. Nothing is further from something than its opposite. But God and the creature are opposed as the One and Unnumbered is opposed to number, the numerated, and the numerable. Therefore, nothing is as distinct from any created being.

The third argument goes thus. Everything which is distinguished by indistinction is the more distinct the more indistinct it is, because it is distinguished by its own indistinction. Conversely, it is the more indistinct the more distinct it is, because it

---

7. Proclus, *Elements of Theology,* prop. 1.
8. The text is actually from Augustine, *Christ. Doct.* 1.7.7.

is distinguished by its own distinction from what is indistinct. Therefore, it will be the more indistinct insofar as it is distinct and vice versa, as was said.[9] But God is something indistinct which is distinguished by his indistinction, as Thomas says in Ia, q. 7, a. 1, at the end. For God is a sea of infinite substance, and consequently indistinct, as Damascene says.[10]

155. On the other hand, it must be noted that nothing is so one and indistinct as God and every created being. There is a threefold reason for this, as proven before in the opposite sense.

First, because nothing is as indistinct as being and existence, potency and its act, form and matter. This is how God and every creature are related. Second, nothing is so much one and indistinct as a thing that is composed and that from which, through which, and in which it is composed and subsists. But, as said above, number or multitude, the numbered or the numerable as such, is composed and subsists from unities. Therefore, nothing is as indistinct as the one God or Unity and the numbered created thing. The third argument is this. Nothing is as indistinct from anything as from that from which it is indistinguished by its own distinction. But everything that is numbered or created is indistinguished from God by its own distinction, as said above. Therefore, nothing is so indistinct and consequently one, for the indistinct and the One are the same. Wherefore, God and any creature whatever are indistinct. The text of Romans 11 speaks to this: "From him, through him and in him are all things" (Rm. 11:36). Therefore, the first principal point is evident, namely that Wisdom is one, as it says here, "since it is one."

156. The second principal point follows, namely that because it is one "it can do all things." For it would not be able to do anything were it not one, much less do all things. It should be recognized that insofar as a thing is more simple and more unified, it is more powerful and more strong, able to do more things. The reason is that every composite thing draws its power and strength from the other things composing it. Clearly, therefore, power and strength in a composite being are alien to it insofar as it is composite, but are proper to simple beings. This is what we want, because the simpler a thing is, the more powerful and strong it is, able to work in more things and upon more things. That with us the more composite beings are more perfect is not against our position, but in its favor. This happens not because they are more composite (for as such they are later and dependent), but because there are more simple things that compose them. A thing is more powerful, able to work more things, insofar as power descends upon it from many [simple] sources.

---

9. To facilitate understanding of this difficult dialectical text, one can substitute "transcendent" for "distinct" and "immanent" for "indistinct."

10. John Damascene, *Orthodox Faith* 1.9.

157. In summary, the argument may be briefly put in this way. The more a thing is one, the more powerful it is, as said. Therefore, what is simply one, and it alone, can do all things. The *Topics* say: "When more results in more, then what is simple results in simplicity."[11] But Wisdom is simply one, as it says here. Therefore, it can do all things. This is the meaning of "Since it is one, it can do all things."

Furthermore, the second argument—from the *Book of Causes*— runs thus, "Every unified power is more infinite,"[12] able to work more things and in more things. But the Wisdom which is God is especially one in that it is the First. Therefore, it is simply infinite and is able to do all things.

Further, the third argument runs this way. Form and act are always directed to one thing and exist in one thing. What is potential and material is in potency to many things, but in a passive and negative way. Each thing acts insofar as it is in act and is one. Therefore, the more anything is one, the more it will be in act, as was said. Then the conclusion is as before. Divine Wisdom, "since it is one," has power and ability to act in that it is one and through the fact that it is one. Because it is simply and especially one, as being the First, it has the power to do all things. "It has the power," because it is one; "it has the power to do all things," because it is the First One. It also follows that nothing else can do all things.

---

11. Aristotle, *Top.* 2.11 and 5.8.
12. *Book of Causes,* prop. 17(16).

SELECTED BIBLIOGRAPHY

TEXTS AND TRANSLATIONS

Meister Eckhart: Die deutschen und lateinischen Werke. Edited by Josef Quint, Josef Koch, *et al.* Stuttgart and Berlin: W. Kohlhammer, 1936–.

Meister Eckhart: The Essential Sermons, Commentaries, Treatises, and Defense. Translated by Edmund Colledge, O.S.A., and Bernard McGinn. The Classics of Western Spirituality. New York: Paulist; London: SPCK, 1981.

Meister Eckhart: German Sermons and Treatises. Translated by M. O'C. Walshe. 2 vols. London and Dulverton: Watkins, 1979 and 1981.

Meister Eckhart: Teacher and Preacher. Translated by Bernard McGinn, Frank Tobin, and Elvira Borgstädt. The Classics of Western Spirituality. New York: Paulist; London: SPCK, 1986.

STUDIES

Caputo, John. "Fundamental Themes in Meister Eckhart's Mysticism." *The Thomist* 42 (1978): 197–225.

Gandillac, Maurice de. "La 'dialectique' de Maître Eckhart." In *La mystique rhénane: Colloque de Strasbourg, 1961,* 59–94. Paris, 1963.

Kelley, C. F. *Meister Eckhart on Divine Knowledge.* New Haven: Yale University Press, 1977.

Kertz, Karl G. "Meister Eckhart's Teaching on the Birth of the Divine Word in the Soul." *Traditio* 15 (1959): 327–63.

Libera, Alain de. *Introduction à la mystique rhénane d'Albert le Grand à Maître Eckhart.* Paris, 1984.

Lossky, Vladimir. *Théologie négative et connaissance de Dieu chez Maître Eckhart.* Paris, 1960.

Schürmann, Reiner. *Meister Eckhart: Mystic and Philosopher.* Bloomington and London: Indiana University Press, 1978.

Woods, Richard, O. P. *Eckhart's Way.* The Way of the Christian Mystics, vol. 2. Wilmington, Del.: Michael Glazier, 1986.

Jan van Ruusbroec

(1293–1381)

The greatest of the Flemish mystics, Jan van Ruusbroec was conversant not only with the main currents of mystical theology in the medieval Low Countries and Rhineland but also with the patristic heritage of both the East and the West. His personal appropriation of this legacy, together with a keen sensitivity to the needs of all the members of the Church of his day and a rare gift for describing the highest levels of mystical experience, enabled Ruusbroec to produce treatises of unsurpassed beauty, perspicuity, and synthetic power.

Ordained a priest in Brussels at the age of twenty-four, Ruusbroec spent the next twenty-six years of his life there, serving as a chaplain at the large collegiate church of St. Gudula (which has since become a cathedral church under the new title of St. Michael). Although his early biographers are silent about most details of his life during this period, we do know that he began writing his first treatises out of a conscious desire to combat an unorthodox movement of quietistic and sometimes pantheistic tendencies which is generally known as the movement of the Free Spirit. These early works, however, are by no means written in a primarily polemical style. On the contrary, they are marked above all by a pro-

foundly positive presentation of all that was best in the Christian spiritual tradition, from the humblest ascetic strivings in what he called "the active life," through those diverse stages of fervent longing for God that he termed collectively "the interior life," up to that rare state of the most intimate union with God that he named the contemplative or "God-seeing life."

Altogether Ruusbroec completed five treatises during his years in Brussels (including his masterpiece, *The Spiritual Espousals*) and had begun a sixth when, with two like-minded priests, he retired in 1343 to a more solitary, forested setting at Groenendaal, about ten kilometers southeast of the city. Others were soon attracted to join the original group of three, and on March 10, 1349, they were clothed in the habit of the canons regular of St. Augustine, with Ruusbroec being named prior of the community under the man whom the bishop of Cambrai appointed provost. It was in this setting that he spent the final thirty-two years of his life. When not engaged in community duties he would regularly go out alone into the forest and there compose further mystical treatises on wax tablets, which he would then bring back to the monastery to be copied by others. Some of

these later treatises were written in the first
instance for a Poor Clare nun in Brussels,
another was an attempt to clarify some passages from an earlier work which had puz-
zled and even disturbed some of his Carthusian friends at a nearby charterhouse,
and a final treatise seems to be a posthu-
mous collection of writings that Ruusbroec
had left unfinished at the time of his death
in 1381. He was buried in the monastery
chapel, but his remains were later removed
to the church in Brussels where he had long
served as a chaplain. He was beatified in
1909 and his feastday is observed in the diocese of Mechelen-Brussels on the anniversary of his death, December 2.

As is the case with all the introductions
to the mystics in this anthology, we can
here discuss only some of the most fundamental points which might help bring the
reader to a fuller understanding of the texts
themselves. In the General Introduction to
this volume we have already noted that for
Ruusbroec the Trinity is the very essence of
the spiritual life. What cannot be emphasized too strongly is that for him, as for the
Flemish mystics in general, the inner life of
the Trinity is marked by a twofold movement: at one pole there is a movement toward "the dark silence" and toward rest in
the "superessential Unity" (terminology
reminiscent of Pseudo-Dionysius, Eckhart,
and other followers of the *via negativa*),
while at the other pole there is, simultaneously, a movement outward in the generation of the Son by the Father and the
breathing forth of the Holy Spirit as the
bond of love between them both. Of equal
importance is Ruusbroec's claim that our
being created in the divine image means
precisely that we partake of this same si-

multaneous interplay between repose and
activity, rest and work. In other words, the
soul's relation to God partakes in the very
movements that are within the triune God.

Only if this is clearly understood will the
reader be able to attain a firm grasp of our
first two selections from Ruusbroec and of
their interrelationship. In the first selection
(drawn, like the second, from the final part
of book two of *The Spiritual Espousals*),
Ruusbroec writes of various ways of meeting God: "with intermediary" (referring
above all to the gifts of God and our response to them through virtuous activity)
and "without intermediary" (referring to a
"blissful unity [where] we will constantly
rest in a state transcending ourselves and
all things"). Since the second selection
deals with three manners or modes of
meeting God "without intermediary," one
might assume that it will be concerned only
with various forms of that blissful rest already referred to. But of the three modes
that Ruusbroec ascribes to this union without intermediary, the second is explicitly
said to be "*with* intermediary," while the
third is in large measure based on the intermediary of virtuous activity. This is not,
however, in any way a sign of inconsistency
on Ruusbroec's part, but is rather one more
manifestation of his basic principle that
such realities are complementary and concomitant rather than separated from one
another by temporal succession. As Paul
Henry observes in a long and carefully rea-
soned essay on Ruusbroec's Trinitarian
mysticism:

The reader familiar with other mystics,
such as St. Teresa of Avila, for whom
the spiritual "marriage" comes after

the "full union" and the latter comes after the state of "quiet," will derive [from Ruusbroec] an impression of confusion and of disorder. But in fact *the concomitance of "intermediary" mystical states* at even the highest level is only a consistent corollary of his doctrine of the complementarity of divine moments [in the Trinity].[1]

Ruusbroec himself makes the same point with all possible clarity at the end of our second selection when he writes that "anyone who does not possess both rest and activity in one and the same exercise has not attained this righteousness."

Our final selection from Ruusbroec reproduces in its entirety the third and last book of *The Spiritual Espousals,* the most important of his many descriptions of the contemplative life. He himself was well aware that his attempt to articulate the nature of the deepest possible experience of union with God would appear overly bold and even unorthodox to persons who had not themselves experienced such union. He was in fact posthumously attacked by Jean Gerson, the late fourteenth century chancellor of the University of Paris, for such statements as that the contemplative life means "to be God with God, without intermediary or any element of otherness which could constitute an obstacle or impediment." A careful reading of such statements in their full context, however, shows clearly enough that Ruusbroec is writing of mystical *consciousness,* of how a true contemplative may no longer "feel" or "perceive" any distinction from God. He is, in other words, writing as a phenomenologist of mystical experience and is not making claims of ontological identity with God.

A final point to be made concerning Ruusbroec's description of the contemplative life is that here, too, is to be found that same dialectical relationship between rest and activity which we noted earlier. He speaks of a state of darkness that, in itself, sounds as utterly formless and ineffable as anything ever written by the most rigorous advocate of the *via negativa,* but for Ruusbroec this state of darkness is in no sense absolute. Rather, "in this darkness an incomprehensible light is born and shines forth; this is the Son of God, in whom a person becomes able to see and to contemplate eternal life." So, too, "the eternal state of rest" in which even the divine Persons give way before the essential Unity is not utterly divorced from all activity, for it is at all times the very ground of what the mystic calls "the active meeting of the Father and the Son, in which we are lovingly embraced by means of the Holy Spirit in eternal love." In sum, even if the notes of ineffability, modelessness, rest, and Unity predominate in the final paragraphs of the *Espousals,* they always remain in dialectical relationship with the notes of effability, distinctness, activity, and Trinity. This could hardly be more beautifully expressed than by the words with which Ruusbroec concludes his entire treatise: "That we might blissfully possess the essential Unity and clearly contemplate the Unity in the Trinity—may the divine love grant us this, for it turns no beggar away. Amen. Amen."

From this, it should be clear why Louis

---

1. Paul Henry, "La mystique trinitaire du bienheureux Jean Ruusbroec: II," *Recherches de science religieuse* 41 (1953): 62.

Cognet, the highly respected twentieth century historian of spirituality, spoke of Ruusbroec's work as "one of the most exceptional achievements that Western mysticism has produced,"[2] and why Evelyn Underhill regarded him as "one of the greatest—perhaps the very greatest—of the mystics of the Church."[3]

2. Louis Cognet, *Introduction aux mystiques rhéno-flamands* (Paris: Desclée, 1968), 281.

3. Evelyn Underhill, *The Mystics of the Church* (Cambridge, England, 1925; Greenwood, S.C.: Attic Press, 1975), 148.

Selections

THE SPIRITUAL ESPOUSALS*

BOOK TWO: THE INTERIOR LIFE

Part Four: "To Meet Him."

I have now shown you how a free and uplifted person becomes able to see by the help of God's grace in interior exercises. This is the first thing that Christ requires and desires of us when he says, "See." As regards the second and third points (when he says, "The Bridegroom is coming. Go out."), I have described three manners in which Christ comes interiorly, of which the first manner has four different modes; I have also shown how we are to go out through exercises that are in accordance with all the ways in which God interiorly enkindles, teaches, and moves us by his coming. It remains for us to consider the fourth and last point, which is a meeting with Christ our Bridegroom. All of our interior, spiritual seeing, whether in grace or in glory, and all of our going out through the practice of virtue in various exercises are all for the purpose of meeting and being united with Christ our Bridegroom, for he is our eternal rest and the goal and reward of all our activity.

A. INTRODUCTORY REMARKS ON THE VARIOUS WAYS OF MEETING GOD

As you know, every meeting is an encounter between two persons coming from different places which are separate from and set over against one another. Now Christ comes from above as an almighty Lord and generous Benefactor, while we come from below as poor servants who can do nothing of ourselves but have need of everything. Christ comes to us from within outward, while we come to him from without inward. It is this which gives rise to a spiritual meeting. This coming, this meeting between ourselves and Christ, occurs in two ways, namely, with intermediary and without intermediary.

Natural union with God, without intermediary

Now understand and note carefully that the unity of our spirit exists in two ways, namely, as it is in its essential being and as it is in its activity. According to its essential being, you should know that the spirit receives Christ's coming in its bare nature without intermediary and without interruption, for the being and life that we

*From *John Ruusbroec: The Spiritual Espousals and Other Works,* trans. James A. Wiseman, O.S.B., The Classics of Western Spirituality (New York: Paulist, 1985), 116–21, 132–36, 145–52. Reprinted with permission of the publisher.

are in God, in our eternal image, is immediately and indivisibly united with the being and life that we possess in ourselves and that we are according to our essential being. For this reason the spirit, in the most intimate and highest part of its being, in its bare nature, ceaselessly receives the imprint of its eternal image and of the divine resplendence and becomes an eternal dwelling place of God. God possesses this dwelling place with his eternal presence and constantly comes to it afresh with new resplendence radiating anew from his eternal birth.[1] Where he comes, there he is present, and where he is present, there he comes. But he will never come where he has never been, for in him there is nothing fortuitous or changeable. Everything in which he is present is also present in him, for he never goes outside himself.

For this reason the spirit possesses God essentially in its bare nature, and God possesses the spirit, for it lives in God and God in it. In the highest part of its being it is also capable of receiving God's resplendence without intermediary, together with all that God can accomplish. By means of the resplendence of its eternal image, which shines within it both essentially and personally, the spirit immerses itself in the divine being as regards the highest part of its own vital being and there possesses in an enduring way its eternal blessedness. It then flows out again with all other creatures through the eternal birth of the Son and is established in its created being by the free will of the Holy Trinity. It here bears a likeness to the image of the sublime Trinity and Unity, according to which it was made. In its creatureliness it ceaselessly receives the imprint of its eternal image, just like a spotless mirror in which the image always remains and in which knowledge of it is ceaselessly renewed with fresh clarity each time you look at it. This essential unity of our spirit with God does not subsist in itself but remains in God, flows forth from God, depends upon God, and turns back to God as to its eternal cause. Accordingly it has never been separated from God and never will be, for this unity exists within us in our bare nature, and if a creature were to be separated from God in this respect it would fall into pure nothingness. This unity transcends time and place and is ceaselessly active according to God's own manner of acting, but it passively receives the imprint of its eternal image inasmuch as it is like God but is in itself a creature.

This is the nobility which we naturally possess in the essential unity of our spirit, which is at this level naturally united with God. This renders us neither holy nor blessed, for all persons, both good and bad, possess this unity within themselves; it is, however, the first principle of all holiness and blessedness. This, then, is the meeting and union between God and our spirit in our bare nature.

---

1. This teaching about the birth of Christ in the soul, even more prominent in the writings of Eckhart, has its roots in the earliest Christian theology and is found in many of the Greek Fathers. The best modern study of the doctrine, from its beginnings up to Eckhart, is Hugo Rahner, "Die Gottesgeburt," in *Symbole der Kirche* (Salzburg: Otto Múller, 1964), pp. 13–87.

Meeting God with intermediary

Now pay careful attention to the meaning of my words, for if you understand well what I now wish to say as well as what I have already said, then you will have understood all the divine truth which any creature could teach you—and much more besides. In this same unity our spirit also exists in a second way, namely, as it is in its activity. In this respect it subsists in itself as in its created, personal mode of being. This is the originating source of the higher powers and the beginning and end of all creaturely activity which is performed in a creaturely manner, whether in the natural or the supernatural order. Nevertheless the unity is not active insofar as it is unity; it is the powers of the soul which act, but in whatever way they act they derive their power and potency from their originating source, that is, from the unity of the spirit, where the spirit subsists in its personal mode of being.

In this unity the spirit must always be either like God by means of grace and virtue or else unlike God because of mortal sin. This is because human beings have been created to the likeness of God, that is, in the grace of God, for grace is a deiform light which shines through us and makes us like God, so that without this light which makes us like God we cannot attain supernatural union with him. Even though we cannot lose God's image or our natural unity with God, if we lose our likeness to him, which is his grace, then we will suffer damnation.

For this reason, whenever God finds in us some capacity for receiving his grace, he wishes out of gratuitous goodness to give us life and make us like himself by means of his gifts. This happens whenever we turn to him with all our will, for in one and the same moment Christ comes to us and enters within us with intermediary and without intermediary (that is, with his gifts and above all gifts), and we come to him and enter within him with intermediary and without intermediary (that is, with our virtues and above all virtues). He imprints his image and likeness upon us, namely, himself and his gifts, delivers us from our sins, sets us free, and makes us like himself.

Meeting God without intermediary

In this same activity whereby God delivers us from sin, sets us free, and makes us like himself in charity, the spirit immerses itself in blissful love. Here there occurs a meeting and a union which are without intermediary and supernatural, and in this is found our highest blessedness. Although from God's side it is natural that he bestows gifts out of love and gratuitous goodness, from our side this is something accidental and supernatural, for previously we were strangers and unlike him, while afterward we attained a likeness to God and unity with him. This meeting and unity which the loving spirit attains in God and possesses without intermediary must take place in the essential ground of our being; it therefore remains a deep mystery to our understanding, unless the understanding apprehends it essentially in an utterly simple way.

In this blissful unity we will constantly rest in a state transcending ourselves and all things. All natural and supernatural gifts flow forth from this unity, and yet the loving spirit rests in this unity above all gifts. Here there is nothing but God and the spirit united with God without intermediary. In this unity we are received by the Holy Spirit, and we ourselves receive the Holy Spirit, the Father, the Son, and the divine nature in its entirety, for God cannot be divided. The spirit's inclination to blissful enjoyment seeks rest in God above all likeness. In the spirit's essential being, this inclination obtains and possesses in a supernatural way all that the spirit ever received there in a natural way.

All good persons possess this, but its nature remains hidden to them all their lives if they are not interiorly fervent and empty of all creatures. In the very moment in which a person turns from sin, he is received by God in the essential unity of his being, the topmost part of his spirit, so that he might rest in God now and forevermore. He also receives grace and a likeness to God in the ground of his powers, so that he might constantly grow and increase in new virtues. As long as this likeness exists through charity and the practice of virtue, just so long does this unity in rest perdure, for it cannot be lost except through mortal sin.

The absolute necessity of God's grace and our response to it

Now all holiness and blessedness lie in the spirit's being led, by means of likeness and the mediation of grace or glory, to a state of rest in the essential unity. The grace of God is the path we must always follow if we are to arrive at that bare being in which God gives himself to us without intermediary in all his richness. Sinners and the damned spirits are in darkness precisely because they lack God's grace, which would have enlightened them, instructed them, and led them to this blissful unity. Nevertheless the essential being of the spirit is so noble that the damned cannot will their own annihilation, but sin causes such a state of darkness and unlikeness and raises so great a barrier between the spirit's powers and the essential being where God dwells that the spirit cannot attain union in its own being, which would be the spirit's proper place of eternal rest if it were not for sin. Whoever lives apart from sin lives in the likeness and grace of God and has God as his own possession. Grace is therefore necessary, for it drives away sin, prepares the way for us, and makes our entire life fruitful.

For this reason Christ is constantly coming to us through the mediation of grace and manifold gifts, while we in turn go to him through the mediation of our virtues and various exercises. The more interior the gifts he bestows and the more finely wrought his movements within us, the more interior and delightful will be the exercises of our spirit, as you have already heard concerning all the ways which have previously been described. There is in all this a constant renewal, for God is always giving new gifts and our spirit is always turning back to God in accordance with the ways in which it has been called and gifted by God, and in this encounter it constantly receives new and higher gifts. In this way a person is constantly advancing to a higher form of life.

This active meeting is always with intermediary, since God's gifts, together with our virtues and the activity of our spirit, constitute this intermediary. Such mediation is necessary for all persons and all spirits, for without the mediation of God's grace and of our freely willed and loving conversion no one can be saved. . . .

C. MEETING GOD WITHOUT INTERMEDIARY, IN THREE DIFFERENT MODES

Now understand well what follows: The measureless illumination of God which, together with his incomprehensible resplendence, is a cause of all gifts and virtues is the same incomprehensible light which transforms and pervades our spirit's inclination toward blissful enjoyment. It does this in a way which is devoid of all particular form, since it occurs in incomprehensible light. In this light the spirit immerses itself in a rest of pure bliss, for this rest is modeless and fathomless. It cannot be known except through itself, for if we could know and comprehend it by ourselves it would lapse into some particular form or measure and would then not be able to satisfy us; instead, this rest would become an eternal state of restlessness. For this reason the simple, loving inclination of our spirit, immersed in rest, produces in us a blissful love, and such love is fathomless. Here, God's deep calls to deep (cf. Ps 42:8), that is, calls to all who are united with the Spirit of God in blissful love. This call is an overflow of essential resplendence, and this essential resplendence, enveloping us in fathomless love, makes us lose ourselves and flow forth into the wild darkness of the Godhead. Thus united—one with the Spirit of God, without intermediary—we are able to meet God with God and endlessly possess our eternal blessedness with him and in him. This most interior way of life is practiced in three manners or modes.

The first mode: emptiness

Sometimes a person living the interior life turns within himself in a simple way in accordance with his inclination toward blissful enjoyment. This occurs above and beyond all activity and all virtue, by means of a simple, inward act of gazing in blissful love. Here such a person meets God without intermediary, and an ample light, shining from out of God's Unity, reveals to him darkness, bareness, and nothingness. He is enveloped by the darkness and falls into a modeless state, as though he were completely lost; through the bareness he loses the power of observing all things in their distinctness and becomes transformed and pervaded by a simple resplendence; in the nothingness all his activity fails him, for he is overcome by the activity of God's fathomless love, while in the inclination of his spirit toward blissful enjoyment he overcomes God and becomes one spirit with him (cf. 1 Cor 6:17).

Through this unity in the Spirit of God such a person enters a state of blissful savor and there possesses God's essential being. Being immersed in his own essential being, this person becomes filled with the fathomless delights and riches of God. From out of these riches there flow into the unity of the higher powers an embrace and a fullness of felt love, and from this fullness of felt love there flows into the heart and into the corporeal powers a felt and deeply penetrating savor. By means of this influx such a person becomes interiorly unable to move and powerless over himself and all his activity. In the inmost part of his being, in both soul and body, he neither knows nor feels anything except a unique resplendence accompanied by a felt sense of well-being and a penetrating savor.

This is the first mode, which is characterized by emptiness, for it empties a person of all things, lifts him up above all virtues and activities, unites him with God, and provides a firm and stable basis for the most fervent interior exercises which a person can practice. When, therefore, any restlessness or any virtuous practice sets up an obstacle or interposes images between a good person and the bare introversion which he desires, then he will be hindered in this mode, since it consists in transcending all things to enter a state of emptiness. This is the first mode in the practice of the most interior exercises.

The second mode: active desire

At times this interiorly fervent person turns to God in a way characterized by desire and activity, so that he might give God glory and honor and might offer him both himself and all his works, letting them be consumed in the love of God. At such times he meets God with intermediary, namely, the intermediary of the gift of savorous wisdom. This gift is the ground and source of all virtue, for it urges and moves every good person toward virtue in accordance with the degree of his love. It sometimes touches an interior person so deeply and enkindles his love so intensely that all God's gifts and all that God can bestow apart from himself are too small and unsatisfying and serve only to increase his restlessness. Such a person has an interior perception or feeling in the ground of his being, where all virtues have their beginning and end, where with ardent desire he offers God all these virtues, and where love has its abode. Here the hunger and thirst of love are so great that he surrenders himself at every moment and is unable to work any further, but rather transcends his activity and comes to nought in love. He hungers and thirsts for the taste of God and at each sudden illumination of God is seized by him and touched by him anew in love. Though living he dies; though dying he comes back to life. In this way the yearning hunger and thirst of love are constantly renewed within him.

This is the second mode, one which is characterized by desire. In it, love stands in a state of likeness and yearningly desires to be united with God. This mode is more honorable and more beneficial to us than the first since it is the cause of the first, for no one can enter a state of rest transcending activity unless he has previously loved in a way characterized by desire and activity. For this reason God's grace and our active love must both precede and follow, that is, must be practiced both before and after, for without works of love we cannot merit or attain God nor can we retain what we have gained by means of the works of love. Therefore no one should be empty of activity if he is master of himself and can give himself to the works of love. But whenever a good person lingers somewhat over any of God's gifts or over any creature, he will be hindered in this most interior exercise, for it is a hunger which cannot be satisfied by anything or anyone except God alone.

The third mode: both resting and working in accordance with righteousness

From these first two modes there arises the third, which is an interior life in accordance with righteousness. You should understand that God comes ceaselessly to us both with intermediary and without intermediary and calls us both to blissful enjoyment and to activity in such a way that the one will not be hindered by the other but rather constantly strengthened by it. An interior person therefore possesses his life in these two ways, that is, in rest and in activity, and in each he is whole and undivided, for he is completely in God when he blissfully rests and is completely in himself when he actively loves. He is exhorted and called by God at all times to renew both his rest and his activity, and his spirit's righteousness wishes to pay at each instant whatever God asks of it. For this reason the spirit turns inward both actively and with blissful enjoyment each time it experiences God's sudden illumination. In this way it is constantly renewed in all the virtues and becomes more deeply immersed in blissful rest, for each time God bestows something on us he gives himself as well as his gifts, while in each of its inward movements the spirit gives itself as well as all its works. By means of God's simple illumination and the spirit's inclination to be blissfully immersed in love, the spirit is united with God and is ceaselessly transported into a state of rest. In addition, by means of the gifts of understanding and of savorous wisdom, it is actively touched and at all times enlightened and enkindled in love.

To a person in this state there is spiritually revealed and held out before him all that one could desire. He is hungry and thirsty, for he sees angelic food and heavenly drink; he works intensely in love, for he sees his rest; he is a pilgrim and sees his fatherland; he strives for victory in love, for he sees his crown. Consolation, peace, joy, beauty, riches, and everything else that brings delight is revealed in God to the enlightened reason without measure in spiritual likenesses. Through this revelation and God's touch love remains active, for this righteous person has established for himself a truly spiritual life in both rest and activity; such a life will continue forever, though after this present life it will be transformed into a higher state.

It is in all this that a person's righteousness consists. He goes toward God with fervent interior love through his eternal activity, enters into God with his blissful inclination toward eternal rest, remains in God, and nevertheless goes out to creatures in virtue and righteousness through a love which is common to all. This is the highest point of the interior life. Anyone who does not possess both rest and activity in one and the same exercise has not attained this righteousness, while a person who has attained it cannot be hindered when he turns inward, for he does so both actively and in blissful enjoyment.

A person is, however, like a double mirror, receiving images on both sides, for in the higher part of his being he receives God with all his gifts and in the lower part he receives corporeal images through the senses. Now he can turn inward whenever he wishes and so practice righteousness without hindrance. But in this life a person is inconstant and accordingly often turns outward; without necessity or the direction of his enlightened reason he gets caught up in the activities of the senses and so falls into daily faults. Still, in the loving inward movement of a righteous person these daily faults are just like a drop of water in a red-hot furnace. With this I conclude the description of the interior life. . . .

BOOK THREE: THE CONTEMPLATIVE LIFE

A fervent lover of God who possesses God in blissful rest, who possesses himself in dedicated and active love, and who possesses his entire life in virtues and righteousness will—by means of these three points and the hidden revelation of God— enter the contemplative life. Indeed, God freely desires to choose this fervent and righteous lover and raise him to a state of superessential contemplation in the divine light in accordance with the divine mode of being. This contemplation establishes us in a state of purity which transcends all our understanding, for it is a special adornment and heavenly crown and is, in addition, an eternal reward for all our virtues and for our entire life. No one can attain this through knowledge or subtle reasoning or through any exercises; the only persons who can attain divine contemplation are those whom God wishes to unite with himself in his Spirit and to enlighten through himself—no one else can attain this.

The hidden divine nature is eternally active in contemplation and love as regards the Persons and is constantly in a state of blissful enjoyment insofar as the Persons are embraced in the Unity of the divine being.[2] All interior spirits are one with God through their loving immersion in this embrace, which takes place within God's essential Unity; they are that same oneness which the divine being is in itself according to the mode of blessedness. In this sublime Unity of the divine nature, the heavenly Father is the origin and beginning of every work which is wrought in heaven and on earth. In the hidden depths in which our spirit is immersed, he speaks the words: "See, the bridegroom is coming. Go out to meet him." We wish to explain and clarify these words as they relate to the state of superessential contemplation, which is the ground of all holiness and of all the life which can ever be lived.

Few persons can attain this divine contemplation because of their own incapacity and because of the hidden, mysterious nature of the light in which one contemplates. For this reason no one can properly or thoroughly understand its meaning through any learning or subtle reflections of his own, for all words and all that can be learned or understood in a creaturely manner are alien to and far beneath the truth which I mean. However, a person who is united with God and enlightened in this truth can understand the truth through itself. To comprehend and understand God as he is in himself, above and beyond all likenesses, is to be God with God, without intermediary or any element of otherness which could constitute an obstacle or impediment. I therefore beseech everyone who does not understand this or feel it in the blissful unity of his spirit not to take offense at it but simply to let it be as it is. What I want to say is true; Christ, the eternal truth, said it himself at many places in his teaching, if only we are able to manifest and express it well. Whoever, then, wishes to under-

---

2. For a proper understanding of book three of the *Espousals,* it is important to note the constant allusions to the dialectical relationship between work and rest, a relationship so very evident in the two clauses of this particular sentence of Ruusbroec. As regards God's own life, the active pole of the dialectic is characterized by such notes as the distinctions among the three Persons, the begetting of the Son, the creation of all things in the Son, the breathing forth of the Holy Spirit, and the Father and the Son's love of all things in the Spirit. On the other hand, the pole of blissful rest is characterized by the Persons' being embraced in the divine Unity, "beyond the distinction of Persons," in a state of "essential bareness" where all names and distinctions "pass away into simple ineffability, without mode and without reason." As noted in the Introduction to this chapter, much of the strength of Ruusbroec's mystical theology lies in his insistence that both poles are always present, both in God's life and in the life of contemplatives.

stand it must have died to himself and be living in God and must turn his gaze to that eternal light which is shining in the ground of his spirit, where the hidden truth is revealing itself without intermediary.

Part One: "See."

Our heavenly Father wishes us to see, for he is the Father of light (cf. Jas 1:17). Accordingly, in the hidden depths of our spirit he eternally, ceaselessly, and without intermediary utters a single, fathomless word, and only that word. In this word he gives utterance to himself and all things. This word, which is none other than "See," is the generation and birth of the Son, the eternal light, in whom all blessedness is seen and known.

If our spirit is to contemplate God with God without intermediary in this divine light, three things are necessary. The first is that a person must be exteriorly well ordered, interiorly unhindered, and as empty of all his exterior works as if he were not even performing them, for if he is interiorly disturbed through any virtuous work he will be troubled by images, and as long as this lasts he will not be able to contemplate. Secondly, he must interiorly cleave to God with devoted intention and love, just as if he were a burning, glowing fire which can never be extinguished. As long as he feels himself to be in this state, he will be able to contemplate. Thirdly, he must lose himself in a state devoid of particular form or measure, a state of darkness in which all contemplatives blissfully lose their way and are never again able to find themselves in a creaturely way.

In the abyss of this darkness in which the loving spirit has died to itself, God's revelation and eternal life have their origin, for in this darkness an incomprehensible light is born and shines forth; this is the Son of God, in whom a person becomes able to see and to contemplate eternal life. This divine light is shed upon a person in the simple being of his spirit, where the spirit receives the resplendence which is God himself above and beyond all gifts and creaturely activity in the empty idleness of the spirit, where the spirit has lost itself in blissful love and receives God's resplendence without intermediary. The spirit ceaselessly becomes the very resplendence which it receives. See, this hidden resplendence, in which a person contemplates all that he desires in accordance with his spirit's mode of emptiness, is so great a resplendence that the loving contemplative neither sees nor feels in the ground of his being, in which he is at rest, anything other than an incomprehensible light. In the simple bareness which envelops all things, he feels and finds himself to be nothing other than the same light with which he sees.

This is the first point, describing how a person is made capable of seeing in the divine light. Blessed are the eyes that see in this way, for they possess eternal life.

Part Two: "The Bridegroom Is Coming."

When we have thus become able to see, we can joyfully contemplate the eternal coming of our Bridegroom, which is the second point of which we wish to speak. What is this eternal coming of our Bridegroom? It is a new birth and a new illumination which knows no interruption, for the ground out of which the resplendence shines forth and which is the resplendence itself is both living and fruitful. The revelation of the eternal light is therefore ceaselessly renewed in the hidden depths of the spirit. See, all creaturely activity and all exercises of virtue must here cease, for here God works himself alone in the most sublime nobility of the spirit, where there is only an eternal contemplating of and gazing at the light with the light and in the light. The coming of the Bridegroom is so fast that he has always come and is always abiding with fathomless richness and yet is personally and ceaselessly coming anew with such new resplendence that it seems as if he had never previously come. This is because his coming occurs beyond time in an eternal now, which is ever received with new pleasure and new joy.

See, the delight and joy which the Bridegroom brings at his coming is fathomless and without measure, for it is his very self. For this reason the spirit's eyes, with which it contemplates and gazes at its Bridegroom, are opened so wide that they will never again be closed, for the spirit's gaze and contemplation remain eternally caught up in God's hidden revelation, and the spirit's capacity for comprehending is opened so wide for the coming of the Bridegroom that the spirit itself becomes the very breadth which it comprehends. In this way God is comprehended and seen with God; in this lies all our blessedness.

This is the second point, describing how we ceaselessly receive the eternal coming of our Bridegroom into our spirit.

Part Three: "Go Out."

A. OUR ETERNAL BEING IN GOD
BEFORE OUR CREATION IN TIME

The Spirit of God now speaks within our own spirit in its hidden immersion: "Go out, into a state of eternal contemplation and blissful enjoyment after God's own manner." All the richness which is in God by nature is something which we lovingly possess in God—and God in us—through the infinite love which is the Holy Spirit. In this love a person savors all that he can desire. By means of this love we have died to ourselves and through a loving immersion of ourselves have gone out into a state of darkness devoid of particular form. There the spirit is caught up in the embrace of the Holy Trinity and eternally abides within the superessential Unity in a state of rest and blissful enjoyment. In this same Unity, considered now as regards its fruitfulness, the Father is in the Son and the Son in the Father, while all creatures are in them both. This is beyond the distinction of Persons, for here we can only make distinctions of reason between fatherhood and sonship in the living fecundity of the divine nature.

This is the origin and beginning of an eternal going forth and an eternal activity which is without beginning, for it is a beginning without beginning. Since the almighty Father has perfectly comprehended himself in the ground of his fruitfulness, the Son, who is the Father's eternal Word, goes forth as another Person within the Godhead. Through this eternal birth all creatures have gone forth eternally before their creation in time. God has thus seen and known them in himself—as distinct in his living ideas and as different from himself, though not different in every respect, for all that is in God is God.

This eternal going forth and this eternal life which we eternally have and are in God apart from ourselves is a cause of our created being in time. Our created being depends upon this eternal being and is one with it in its essential subsistence. This eternal being and life which we have and are in God's eternal wisdom is like God, for it both abides eternally and without distinction in the divine essence and, through the birth of the Son, flows forth eternally as a distinct entity, its distinctness being in accordance with God's eternal idea of it. In these two ways it is so like God that he ceaselessly knows and expresses himself in this likeness as regards both the divine essence and the Persons. Although there are here distinctions and differences of a rational kind, this likeness is nevertheless one with the very image of the Holy Trinity which is the wisdom of God, in which God contemplates himself and all things in an eternal now that has no before or after. He sees himself and all things in a single act of seeing; this is God's image and likeness as well as our image and likeness, for in this act God expresses both himself and all things. In this divine image all creatures have an eternal life apart from themselves, as in their eternal Exemplar.

B. ATTAINING OUR ETERNAL IMAGE
IN THE CONTEMPLATIVE LIFE

It is to this eternal image and likeness that the Holy Trinity has created us. God therefore wills that we go out from ourselves into this divine light, supernaturally pursuing this image which is our own life and possessing it with him both actively and blissfully in a state of eternal blessedness. We will find that the bosom of the

Father is our own ground and origin, in which our life and being have their beginning. From out of this ground, that is, from out of the Father and all that lives in him, there shines an eternal resplendence, which is the birth of the Son. In this resplendence, that is, in the Son, the Father is himself revealed together with all that lives in him, for he gives to the Son all that he is and all that he has, with the single exception of the property of fatherhood, which he retains himself. For this reason all that in the Father lives still concealed in unity lives also in the Son as having flowed forth in open manifestation; so too, the simple ground of our eternal image constantly abides in a state of darkness devoid of particular form, while the infinite resplendence which shines forth from there reveals and manifests the hidden mystery of God in particular forms.

All persons who have been raised above their creaturely state into the contemplative life are one with this divine resplendence and are this resplendence itself. Through this divine light—and as regards their uncreated being—they see, feel, and find themselves to be the same simple ground from out of which the resplendence shines without measure in a divine way and in which it eternally abides devoid of particular form according to the simplicity of the divine essence. For this reason interior, contemplative persons will go out in accordance with the mode of their contemplation, above and beyond reason and distinction and their own created being. Through an eternal act of gazing accomplished by means of the inborn light, they are transformed and become one with that same light with which they see and which they see. It is in this way that contemplatives pursue the eternal image to which they have been created; they contemplate God and all things without distinction in a simple act of seeing in the divine resplendence.

This is the noblest and most beneficial contemplation which a person can attain in this life, for in such contemplation a person remains free and master of himself in the best possible way. With each loving movement within, he is able to grow in nobility of life beyond anything that is humanly understandable: He remains free and master of himself in the practice of the interior life and of virtue; in addition, his gazing into the divine light raises him above all interiority, all virtue, and all acquisition of merit, for it is the crown and reward to which we aspire and which we now have and possess in a certain way, for the contemplative life is a heavenly life. If, however, we were set free from this present exile, we would have a still greater capacity in our creatureliness to receive this resplendence, and then God's glory would in every respect shine through us in a better and nobler way.

All this is the way above all ways in which a person goes out into a state of divine contemplation and an eternal act of gazing and in which he is transformed and formed over in the divine resplendence.

Part Four: "To Meet Him."

This going forth of a contemplative also takes place in love, for by means of blissful love he transcends his creaturely state and finds and savors the riches and delight which God is himself and which he causes ceaselessly to flow forth into the hidden depths of the spirit, where the spirit bears a likeness to God's own nobility.[3]

When an interior, contemplative person has thus attained his eternal image and, in this purity and by means of the Son, has possessed the Father's bosom, then he is enlightened with divine truth. He continually receives the eternal birth and goes out into a state of divine contemplation in accordance with the mode of the light. Here arises the fourth and last point, which is a meeting in love; it is in this more than anything else that our highest blessedness resides.

You should know that the heavenly Father, as a living ground and with all that lives in him, has turned actively toward his Son as toward his own eternal wisdom, and that this same wisdom, together with all that lives in it, has actively turned back toward the Father, that is, toward that same ground from which it comes forth. In this meeting between the Father and the Son there arises the third Person, the Holy Spirit, who is the love of them both and who is one with them in the same nature. In a way characterized by both activity and blissful enjoyment, the Spirit embraces and penetrates the Father and Son and all that lives in both of them with such great riches and joy that all creatures must remain silent before this, for the incomprehensible wonder which resides in this love eternally transcends the understanding of all creatures. But when a person understands this wonder and savors it without amazement, then has his spirit been raised above itself and been made one with the Spirit of God; it savors and sees—without measure, like God himself—the riches which it has itself become in the Unity of the living ground where it possesses itself in accordance with the mode of its uncreated being.

Now this blessed meeting is actively renewed in us without ceasing in accordance with God's own mode of being, for the Father gives himself to the Son and the Son to the Father in an eternal sense of well-being and a loving embrace. This is con-

---

3. The close parallelism between this fourth part of book three and the preceding third part should be noted. In part three, Ruusbroec writes that contemplatives "are transformed and become one with that same light with which they see and which they see," that light being the Son of God. In part four, there is a similar transformation—only this time through the Holy Spirit—whereby a person's spirit is "raised above itself and . . . made one with the Spirit of God," who is the love of the Father and Son. These two transformations are clearly on the level of what the mystic calls an "active meeting," characterized by distinction of Persons. In the same two parts of the book there is also a meeting or union that is not active, but "blissful," occurring "beyond distinction." In part three, contemplatives are said to feel themselves to be the same simple ground from out of which the divine resplendence shines forth but which itself is in a state of darkness, devoid of particular form, while in part four contemplatives are described as encompassed in "that dark stillness in which all lovers lose their way."

stantly renewed in the bond of love, for just as the Father ceaselessly sees all things anew in the birth of the Son, so too are all things loved anew by the Father and the Son in the flowing forth of the Holy Spirit. This is the active meeting of the Father and the Son, in which we are lovingly embraced by means of the Holy Spirit in eternal love.

Now this active meeting and this loving embrace are in their ground blissful and devoid of particular form, for the fathomless, modeless being of God is so dark and so devoid of particular form that it encompasses within itself all the divine modes and the activity and properties of the Persons in the rich embrace of the essential Unity; it thereby produces a divine state of blissful enjoyment in this abyss of the ineffable. Here there is a blissful crossing over and a self-transcending immersion into a state of essential bareness, where all the divine names and modes and all the living ideas which are reflected in the mirror of divine truth all pass away into simple ineffability, without mode and without reason. In this fathomless abyss of simplicity all things are encompassed in a state of blissful blessedness, while the ground itself remains completely uncomprehended, unless it be through the essential Unity. Before this the Persons must give way, together with all that lives in God, for here there is nothing other than an eternal state of rest in a blissful embrace of loving immersion.

This is that modeless being which all fervent interior spirits have chosen above all things, that dark stillness in which all lovers lose their way. But if we could prepare ourselves through virtue in the ways I have shown, we would at once strip ourselves of our bodies and flow into the wild waves of the Sea, from which no creature could ever draw us back.

That we might blissfully possess the essential Unity and clearly contemplate the Unity in the Trinity—may the divine love grant us this, for it turns no beggar away. Amen. Amen.

SELECTED BIBLIOGRAPHY

TEXTS AND TRANSLATIONS

Opera Omnia. Edited by the Ruusbroecgenootschap. 3 vols. to date. Tielt and Leiden, 1981; Turnhout, 1988–.

John Ruusbroec: The Spiritual Espousals and Other Works. Translated by James A.

Wiseman, O.S.B. The Classics of Western Spirituality. New York: Paulist; London: SPCK, 1985.

Ruysbroeck: Oeuvres choisies. Translated by J.-A. Bizet. Paris, 1946.

STUDIES

Ampe, Albert. "La théologie mystique de l'ascension de l'âme selon le bienheureux Jean de Ruusbroec." Parts 1, 2. *Revue d'ascétique et de mystique* 36 (1960): 188–201, 303–22.

Bonny, Johan. "Jan van Ruusbroec." *La vie spirituelle,* no. 136 (Nov.–Dec. 1982): 666–94.

Dupré, Louis. *The Common Life: The Origins of Trinitarian Mysticism and Its Development by Jan Ruusbroec.* New York: Crossroad, 1984.

Henry, Paul. "La mystique trinitaire du bienheureux Jean Ruusbroec." Parts 1, 2. *Recherches de science religieuse* 39–40 (1951–52): 335–68; 41 (1953): 51–75.

Mommaers, Paul, and Norbert De Paepe, eds. *Jan van Ruusbroec: The Sources, Content, and Sequels of His Mysticism.* Mediaevalia Lovaniensia, ser. 1, stud. 12. Louvain, 1984.

Teasdale, Wayne. "Ruysbroeck's Mystical Theology." Parts 1, 2. *American Benedictine Review* 35 (1984): 82–96, 176–93.

Underhill, Evelyn. *Ruysbroeck.* London, 1915.

Gregory Palamas

(1296–1359)

Gregory Palamas is a controversial figure. Proclaimed a saint by the Synod of Constantinople in 1368, he became for many in the Latin Church the paragon of what separated them from the East. Even within the Orthodox Church resistance to his theology remained fierce during his lifetime and never entirely subsided. Yet whatever interpretation theologians may give to his distinction between God's essence and God's energies, the mystical insight behind it should be a source of inspiration to the West as well as to the East. Palamas' main contribution lies in his attempt to provide a theological justification for the direct *experience* of God which some of his contemporaries claimed to enjoy and which all mystics in one form or another aspire to.

Unfortunately, his theology as articulated in the *Triads* (three essays written at different stages of the same controversy) is highly polemical and often tediously repetitive. The Calabrian monk Barlaam (who resided in Constantinople), in defending the Orthodox interpretation of the Creed, had concluded that theology could reach only "dialectical," that is, probable rather than absolutely certain conclusions, since the divine mystery remains inaccessible to the human mind. His main antagonists were the hesychast monks who claimed that, in the practice of the "Jesus Prayer" (a constant repetition of the word "Jesus" or of a one-phrase invocation of Jesus' name), both body and mind were transformed by the divine light and the direct presence of God. Palamas himself, though born of a noble family close to the Byzantine Court, had joined the monastic community of the "Great Lavra" on Mount Athos where he assiduously practiced the hesychastic prayer. When Barlaam attacked the hesychasts' claim of a "spiritual knowledge" of God, Palamas rose to their defense. To him the issue concerned the very essence of faith. His defense became heatedly polemical after Barlaam branded the hesychasts with the name of the condemned sect of the "Messalians" (who had held that we may "see" God with our eyes). At this point Palamas felt it necessary to distinguish God's *essence* (which is and remains unknown, as Greek theologians had persistently maintained) from God's *energies*. These energies, which transform the praying person, are themselves *uncreated*. Not only Barlaam but also some Greek theologians objected that no such distinction could be made between God's essence and energies. Whatever did not belong to the essence *had* to be created.

To most Latin theologians that principle settled the case, until recently the question of "uncreated grace" emerged in occidental theology. Is grace merely a creation, an "accident," as Scholastics would claim, or is it a form of "theosis," a transformation of my entire being, as the Greek Fathers and a number of Western mystics since Eckhart and Ruusbroec had implied? Palamas' expression may not be theologically the most felicitous, for it is hard to see how God's "energy" can be distinguished from his nature. Yet the mystical vision upon which it is based remains profound and convincing. John Meyendorff perceptively describes it: "The darkness of the cloud surrounding God is not an empty darkness. While eliminating all perceptions of the senses, or of the mind, it nevertheless places man before a Presence, revealed to a transfigured mind and purified body. . . . The theological principle presupposed by Palamas is that God, even when He communicates Himself to the purified body and mind, *remains transcendent* in His essence. In this, Palamas follows St. Gregory of Nyssa, who spoke of mystical experience in terms of an experience of divine inexhaustability, and used the term 'tension' *(epektasis)* to describe it."[1] The image of light, symbol of God's glory, illuminating both the mind and the body, originated in a spiritual reading of the Gospel pericope of Jesus' transfiguration on Mount Thabor.

The contrast between light and darkness, introduced in the Fourth Gospel, pervades the entire Eastern spirituality. Yet for Greek theologians darkness itself assumes a positive, spiritual meaning: it is the cloud which surrounds God's nature and subtracts it from our understanding. Even as the divine light transformed the body of Jesus, so it transforms those who become united with Him. Yet that light itself was nothing less than the divine glory itself shining through His human appearance. Palamas insists throughout the *Triads* that this divine light does not originate in the mind's natural aptitude. The mind is not capable of *understanding* God in any way; only uncreated grace can enable it to *experience* God's glory. Even as the apostles' eyes and minds were transformed by grace, so our bodies and minds may be transformed beyond their natural capacities to receive the divine light. Only in this light can we see the Light (Ps. 36). "For it is in light that light is seen, and that which sees operates in a similar light, since this faculty has no other way in which to work. . . . If it sees itself, it sees light; if it beholds the object of its vision, that too is light; and if it looks at the means by which it sees, again it is light" (*Triads* 2.3.36). The Thaboric light is not "knowledge," in the ordinary sense, though it is refracted into cognition both in the mind and the senses.

The tension in Palamas' mystical theology arises from the fact that it supports a direct experience of God, translatable into language, while remaining within the confines of a strictly negative theology. This paradox has inhered in Neoplatonic mysticism since the beginning. For Plotinus the One stands beyond all knowledge, yet remains immediately present to the lower hypostases and may even be directly experi-

1. *Gregory of Palamas: The Triads,* ed. with an introduction by John Meyendorff, The Classics of Western Spirituality (New York: Paulist, 1983), 14.

enced by the soul. What distinguishes Palamas' theology is that its basis lies in experience, rather than in speculation. As such, it remains a rich, yet in the West inadequately explored source of inspiration.

Selections

THE TRIADS*

A. TEXTS ON APOPHATIC THEOLOGY AS POSITIVE EXPERIENCE

I. iii. 4.

The human mind also, and not only the angelic, transcends itself, and by victory over the passions acquires an angelic form. It, too, will attain to that light[1] and will become worthy of a supernatural vision of God, not seeing the divine essence, but seeing God by a revelation appropriate and analogous to Him. One sees, not in a negative way—for one does see something—but in a manner superior to negation. For God is not only beyond knowledge, but also beyond unknowing;[2] His revelation itself is also truly a mystery of a most divine and an extraordinary kind, since the divine manifestations, even if symbolic, remain unknowable by reason of their transcendence. They appear, in fact, according to a law which is not appropriate to either human or divine nature—being, as it were, for us yet beyond us—so that no name can properly describe them. And this God indicated when, in reply to Manoe's question, "What is your name?", He replied, "It is marvellous" (Jdg 13:17–18); for that vision, being not only incomprehensible but also unnameable, is no less wonderful. However, although vision be beyond negation, yet the words used to explain it are inferior to the negative way. Such explanations proceed by use of examples or analogies, and this is why the word "like", pointing to a simile, appears so often in theological discourse; for the vision itself is ineffable, and surpasses all expression.

5

So, when the saints contemplate this divine light within themselves, seeing it by the divinising communion of the Spirit, through the mysterious visitation of perfecting illuminations—then they behold the garment of their deification, their mind being glorified and filled by the grace of the Word, beautiful beyond measure in His splendour;[3] just as the divinity of the Word on the mountain glorified with divine

---

*From *Gregory Palamas: The Triads,* ed. John Meyendorff, trans. Nicholas Gendle, The Classics of Western Spirituality (New York: Paulist, 1983), 32–40, 57–63. Reprinted with permission of the publisher.

1. That is, the divine uncreated light of Thabor, God Himself in His outward manifestation (or "energies").

2. A key idea in Palamas, deriving ultimately from Pseudo-Dionysius. The Divine Reality transcends not only the positive concepts we may hold of God (cataphatic theology), but also the negations of the apophatic way. The "knowledge" of the utterly unknowable God is a supremely positive experience, not a cognitive void, for it is the superabundance of light and being in God that dazzles the created mind. God, as Dionysius says, is beyond unknowability, beyond the human antithesis of affirmation and negation. Similarly the vision of such a God must be ineffable, yet it is less misleading to say what it is not than what it is.

3. The vision of God for Palamas is not an intellectual grasp of an external object, but an interior participation in the life of the Holy Spirit: to see God is to share in this life, i.e., to become divinized. This involves a complete transfiguration of the whole person, body and soul together.

light the body conjoined to it. For "the glory which the Father gave Him", He Himself has given to those obedient to Him, as the Gospel says, and "He willed that they should be with Him and contemplate His glory" (Jn 17:22, 24).

How can this be accomplished corporeally, now that He Himself is no longer corporeally present after His ascension to the heavens? It is necessarily carried out in a spiritual fashion, for the mind becomes supercelestial, and as it were the companion of Him who passed beyond the heavens for our sake, since it is manifestly yet mysteriously united to God, and contemplates supernatural and ineffable visions, being filled with all the immaterial knowledge of a higher light. Then it is no longer the sacred symbols accessible to the senses that it contemplates, nor yet the variety of Sacred Scripture that it knows; it is made beautiful by the creative and primordial Beauty, and illumined by the radiance of God.[4]

In the same way, according to the revealer and interpreter of their hierarchy,[5] the ranks of supracosmic spirits above are hierarchically filled, in a way analogous to themselves, not only with the first-given knowledge and understanding, but with the first light in respect of the sublimest triadic initiation. Not only do they [the angels] participate in, and contemplate, the glory of the Trinity, but they likewise behold the manifestation of the light of Jesus, revealed to His disciples on Thabor. Judged worthy of this vision, they are initiated into Him, for He is Himself deifying light: They truly draw near to Him, and enjoy direct participation in His divinising rays. This is why the blessed Macarius calls this light "the food of the supracelestial beings".[6] And here is what another theologian says: "All the intelligible array of supracosmic beings, immaterially celebrating this light, give us a perfect proof of the love which the Word bears towards us."[7] And the great Paul, at the moment of encountering the invisible and supracelestial visions that are in Christ, was "ravished"[8] and became himself supracelestial, without his mind needing to pass beyond the heavens by actually changing place. This "ravishment" denotes a mystery of an entirely different order, known only to those who have experienced it. But it is not necessary to mention that we ourselves have heard the testimony of Fathers who have had this experience, so as not to expose these things to calumny. But what has already been said should suffice to demonstrate easily to the unconvinced that there is indeed an intellectual illumination, visible to those whose hearts have been purified, and utterly different from knowledge, though productive of it. . . .

---

4. That is, the transfigured spiritual intellect is able to apprehend directly the transcendent realities figured forth symbolically in Scripture and the liturgy.

5. That is, Pseudo-Dionysius, the author of *The Celestial Hierarchy*.

6. Macarius, Hom. 12.14.

7. St. Andrew of Crete, Hom. 7 on the transfiguration.

8. 2 Cor 12:2. Paul's ecstasy is frequently cited by the Greek Fathers as a paradigm of mystical experience.

18

Do you now understand that in place of the intellect, the eyes and ears, they acquire the incomprehensible Spirit and by Him hear, see and comprehend? For if all their intellectual activity has stopped, how could the angels and angelic men see God except by the power of the Spirit? This is why their vision is not a sensation, since they do not receive it through the senses; nor is it intellection, since they do not find it through thought or the knowledge that comes thereby, but after the cessation of all mental activity. It is not, therefore, the product of either imagination or reason; it is neither an opinion nor a conclusion reached by syllogistic argument.

On the other hand, the mind does not acquire it simply by elevating itself through negation. For, according to the teaching of the Fathers, every divine command and every sacred law has as its final limit purity of heart; every mode and aspect of prayer reaches its term in pure prayer;[9] and every concept which strives from below towards the One Who transcends all and is separated from all comes to a halt once detached from all created beings. However, it is erroneous to say that over and above the accomplishment of the divine commands, there is nothing but purity of heart. There *are* other things, and many of them: There is the pledge of things promised in this life, and also the blessings of the life to come, which are rendered visible and accessible by this purity of heart. Thus, beyond prayer, there is the ineffable vision, and ecstasy in the vision, and the hidden mysteries. Similarly, beyond the stripping away of beings, or rather after the cessation [of our perceiving or thinking of them] accomplished not only in words, but in reality, there remains an unknowing which is beyond knowledge; though indeed a darkness, it is yet beyond radiance, and, as the great Denys says, it is in this dazzling darkness that the divine things are given to the saints.

Thus the perfect contemplation of God and divine things is not simply an abstraction; but beyond this abstraction, there is a participation in divine things, a gift and a possession rather than just a process of negation. But these possessions and gifts are ineffable: If one speaks of them, one must have recourse to images and analogies—not because that is the way in which these things are seen, but because one cannot adumbrate what one has seen in any other way. Those, therefore, who do not listen in a reverent spirit to what is said about these ineffable things, which are necessarily expressed through images, regard the knowledge that is beyond wisdom as foolishness; trampling under foot the intelligible pearls, they strive also to destroy as far as possible by their disputations those who have shown them to them.

---

9. A technical phrase deriving from Evagrius, "pure prayer" means the state of undifferentiated consciousness when the mind is "naked" of all images and earthly notions. But, Palamas insists, it is not enough to abstract oneself from creation; the mind must be emptied of contingent things so as to be filled with divine ones.

19

As I have said, it is because of their love of men that the saints speak, so far as this is possible, about things ineffable, rejecting the error of those who in their ignorance imagine that, after the abstraction from beings, there remains only an absolute inaction, not an inaction surpassing all action. But, I repeat, these things remain ineffable by their very nature. This is why the great Denys says that after the abstraction from beings, there is no word but "an absence of words"; he also says, "After every elevation, we will be united with the Inexpressible."[10] But, despite this inexpressible character, negation alone does not suffice to enable the intellect to attain to superintelligible things. The ascent by negation is in fact only an apprehension of how all things are distinct from God; it conveys only an image of the formless contemplation and of the fulfillment of the mind in contemplation, not being itself that fulfillment.[11]

But those who, in the manner of angels, have been united to that light celebrate it by using the image of this total abstraction. The mystical union with the light teaches them that this light is superessentially transcendent to all things. Moreover, those judged worthy to receive the mystery with a faithful and prudent ear can also celebrate the divine and inconceivable light by means of an abstraction from all things. But they can only unite themselves to it and see if they have purified themselves by fulfillment of the commandments and by consecrating their mind to pure and immaterial prayer, so as to receive the supernatural power of contemplation.

20

What then shall we call this power which is an activity neither of the senses nor of the intellect? How else except by using the expression of Solomon, who was wiser than all who preceded him: "a sensation intellectual and divine".[12] By adding those two adjectives, he urges his hearer to consider it neither as a sensation nor as an intellection, for neither is the activity of the intelligence a sensation, nor that of the senses an intellection. The "intellectual sensation" is thus different from both. Following the great Denys, one should perhaps call it union, and not knowledge. "One should realise," he says, "that our mind possesses both an intellectual power which permits it to see intelligible things, and also a capacity for that union which surpasses the nature of the intellect and allies it to that which transcends it."[13] And

---

10. Both quotations are from *The Mystical Theology,* ch. 3.

11. The cardinal point about the *via negativa* is that it is neither a species of agnosticism nor itself the vision of God, but rather a necessary preliminary process of mental detachment from created things which provides an image of the otherness of divine ones.

12. In fact, the phrase "divine sense" *(aisthēsis theia)* is an Origenist version of Prov 2:5 (LXX: *epignōsis theou*).

13. *The Divine Names* 7.1.

again: "The intellectual faculties become superfluous, like the senses, when the soul becomes deiform, abandoning itself to the rays of the inaccessible light in an unknown union by blind advances."[14] In this union, as St. Maximus puts it, "the saints by beholding the light of the hidden and more than ineffable glory themselves become capable of receiving blessed purity, together with the celestial powers".[15]

Let no one think that these great men are referring here to the ascent through the negative way. For the latter lies within the powers of whoever desires it; and it does not transform the soul so as to bestow on it the angelic dignity. While it liberates the understanding from other beings, it cannot by itself effect union with transcendent things. But purity of the passionate part of the soul effectively liberates the mind from all things through impassibility, and unites it through prayer to the grace of the Spirit; and through this grace the mind comes to enjoy the divine effulgence, and acquires an angelic and godlike form.

21

This is why the Fathers, following the great Denys, have called this state "spiritual sensation", a phrase appropriate to, and somehow more expressive of, that mystical and ineffable contemplation. For at such a time man truly sees neither by the intellect nor by the body, but by the Spirit, and he knows that he sees supernaturally a light which surpasses light. But at that moment he does not know by what organ he sees this light, nor can he search out its nature, for the Spirit through whom he sees is untraceable. This was what Paul said when he heard ineffable words and saw invisible things: "I know not whether I saw out of the body or in the body" (2 Cor 12:2). In other words, he did not know whether it was his intellect or his body which saw.

Such a one does not see by sense perception, but his vision is as clear as or clearer than that by which the sight clearly perceives sensibilia. He sees by going out of himself, for through the mysterious sweetness of his vision he is ravished beyond all objects and all objective thought, and even beyond himself.[16]

Under the effect of the ecstasy, he forgets even prayer to God. It is this of which St. Isaac speaks, confirming the great and divine Gregory: "Prayer is the purity of the intellect which is produced with dread only from the light of the Holy Trinity."[17] And again, "Purity of spiritual mind is what allows the light of the Holy Trinity to

---

14. *Ibid.* 4.11.
15. Cf. *Chapters on Knowledge* 2.70, 76.
16. *Ecstasis* in the Greek Fathers need not imply any kind of paranormal psychological state or loss of consciousness. It is (literally) a "going-out" from oneself, a self-transcendence under the influence of love and divine grace. It enables a supernatural mode of cognition of divine things, which is mystical knowledge, after one has ceased to know and see through the functions of the discursive intellect and the senses.
17. Isaac of Nineveh, Hom. 32.

shine forth at the time of prayer. . . . The mind then transcends prayer, and this state should not properly be called prayer, but a fruit of the pure prayer sent by the Holy Spirit. The mind does not pray a definite prayer, but finds itself in ecstasy in the midst of incomprehensible realities. It is indeed an ignorance superior to knowledge."[18]

This most joyful reality, which ravished Paul, and made his mind go out from every creature but yet return entirely to himself—this he beheld as a light of revelation, though not of sensible bodies; a light without limit, depth, height or lateral extension. He saw absolutely no limit to his vision and to the light which shone round about him; but rather it was as it were a sun infinitely brighter and greater than the universe, with himself standing in the midst of it, having become all eye.[19] Such, more or less, was his vision.

22

This is why the great Macarius says that this light is infinite and supercelestial.[20] Another saint, one of the most perfect, saw the whole universe contained in a single ray of this intelligible sun—even though he himself did not see this light as it is in itself, in its full extent, but only to that extent that he was capable of receiving it.[21] By this contemplation and by his supra-intelligible union with this light, he did not learn what it is by nature, but he learnt that it really exists, is supernatural and superessential, different from all things; that its being is absolute and unique, and that it mysteriously comprehends all in itself. This vision of the Infinite cannot permanently belong to any individual or to all men.

He who does not see understands that he is himself incapable of vision because not perfectly conformed to the Spirit by a total purification, and not because of any limitation in the Object of vision. But when the vision comes to him, the recipient knows well that it *is* that light, even though he sees but dimly; he knows this from the impassible joy akin to the vision which he experiences, from the peace which fills his mind, and the fire of love for God which burns in him. The vision is granted him in proportion to his practice of what is pleasing to God, his avoidance of all that is not, his assiduity in prayer, and the longing of his entire soul for God; always he is being borne on to further progress and experiencing even more resplendent contemplation. He understands then that his vision is infinite because it *is* a vision

---

18. *Ibid.*

19. The image of becoming "all eye," entirely subsumed in the vision that consumes and unites, goes back to Plotinus.

20. Cf. Macarius-Symeon, *De libert. mentis* 21.

21. An episode in Gregory the Great's *Life* of St. Benedict, whose biography was popular among Byzantine monks. At a time of theological tension between Latins and Greeks, it is pleasing to find Palamas describing a Western saint as "one of the most perfect."

of the Infinite, and because he does not see the limit of that brilliance; but, all the more, he sees how feeble is his capacity to receive the light.

23

But he does not consider that the vision of which he has been deemed worthy *is* simply the Divine Nature. Just as the soul communicates life to the animated body—and we call this life "soul", while realising that the soul which is in us and which communicates life to the body is distinct from that life—so God, Who dwells in the God-bearing soul, communicates the light to it. However, the union of God the Cause of all with those worthy transcends that light. God, while remaining entirely in Himself, dwells entirely in us by His superessential power; and communicates to us not His nature, but His proper glory and splendour.[22]

The light is thus divine, and the saints rightly call it "divinity", because it is the source of deification. It is not only "divinity", but "deification-in-itself",[23] and thearchy. While it appears to produce a distinction and multiplication within the one God, yet it is nonetheless the Divine Principle, more-than-God, and more-than-Principle. The light is one in the one divinity, and therefore is itself the Divine Principle, more-than-God and more-than-Principle, since God is the ground of subsistence of divinity. Thus the doctors of the Church, following the great Areopagite Denys, call "divinity" the deifying gift that proceeds from God. So when Gaius asked Denys how God could be beyond the thearchy, he replied in his letter: "If you consider as 'divinity' the reality of the deifying gift which divinises us, and if this Gift is the principle of divinisation, then He Who is above all principle is also above what you thus call 'divinity'."[24] So the Fathers tell us that the divine grace of the suprasensible light is God. But God in his nature does not simply identify Himself with this grace, because He is able not only to illumine and deify the mind, but also to bring forth from nonbeing every intellectual essence.

B. TEXTS ON DEIFICATION IN CHRIST

II. iii: 8

... The monks know that the essence of God transcends the fact of being inaccessible to the senses, since God is not only above all created things, but is even

---

22. This touches on the cardinal doctrine of Palamas, that God, utterly and permanently unknowable and inaccessible in His essence, yet comes to us and shares His life with us in His energies. Palamas insists that the energies *are* God, personally present, not just a created grace in us, yet he also affirms that the energies are distinct from the essence, without implying division in God.

23. The language in this paragraph is Dionysian. The light, energy, or grace is indeed "divinity," a communication of the life of God, yet God as the source of that life may be termed "beyond being," or even "beyond divinity."

24. Epistle 2.

beyond Godhead. The excellence of Him Who surpasses all things is not only beyond all affirmation, but also beyond all negation; it exceeds all excellence that is attainable by the mind. This hypostatic light, seen spiritually by the saints, they know by experience to exist, as they tell us, and to exist not symbolically only, as do manifestations produced by fortuitous events; but it is an illumination immaterial and divine, a grace invisibly seen and ignorantly known.[25] *What* it is, they do not pretend to know.[26]

9

. . . This light is not the essence of God, for that is inaccessible and incommunicable; it is not an angel, for it bears the marks of the Master. Sometimes it makes a man go out from the body or else, without separating him from the body, it elevates him to an ineffable height. At other times, it transforms the body, and communicates its own splendour to it when, miraculously, the light which deifies the body becomes accessible to the bodily eyes. Thus indeed did the great Arsenius appear when engaged in hesychastic combat; similarly Stephen, whilst being stoned, and Moses, when he descended from the mountain. Sometimes the light "speaks" clearly, as it were with ineffable words, to him who contemplates it. Such was the case with Paul. According to Gregory the Theologian, "It descends from the elevated places where it dwells, so that He who in His own nature from eternity is neither visible to nor containable by any being may in a certain measure be contained by a created nature."[27] He who has received this light, by concentrating upon himself, constantly perceives in his mind that same reality which the children of the Jews called *manna,* the bread that came down from on high. . . .

10

. . . The hesychasts in fact never claim that this light is an angel. Having been initiated by the teaching of the Fathers, they know that the vision of angels takes place in various ways, according to the capacities of those who behold it: sometimes in the form of a concrete essence, accessible to the senses, and visible even to creatures full of passions and totally foreign to all initiation; sometimes under the form of an ethereal essence which the soul itself can only see in part; sometimes as a true vision, which only those who are purified and who see spiritually are worthy to be-

---

25. A classic example of deliberately paradoxical language, of the kind common in Gregory of Nyssa and Pseudo-Dionysius (cf. "learned ignorance" and "sober drunkenness") when referring to mystical knowledge or experience.

26. The divine subject of such illumination constitutes an overwhelming experiential impact, yet permanently defies intellectual analysis. True mystical cognition is darkness to the discursive mind, since it is by definition ineffable and incomprehensible.

27. Gregory Nazianzen, Hom. 45.11.

hold. But you,[28] who have not been initiated into these different modes of seeing angels, think to show that the angels are invisible to one another not because they are incorporeal, but in their essence; and implicitly you class the contemplators of God with Balaam's ass, which also is said to have seen an angel (Num 22:25, 27)!

11

Elsewhere you claim that the mind contemplates God "not in some other hypostasis; but when purified at once of passions and ignorance, in beholding itself, it sees God in itself, since it is made in His image."[29] You also believe that those who claim to see in this way the very essence of the mind under the form of light are in accord with the most mystical Christian tradition. But hesychasts know that the purified and illuminated mind, when clearly participating in the grace of God, also beholds other mystical and supernatural visions—for in seeing itself, it sees more than itself: It does not simply contemplate some other object, or simply its own image, but rather the glory impressed on its own image by the grace of God. This radiance reinforces the mind's power to transcend itself, and accomplish that union with those better things which is beyond understanding. By this union, the mind sees God in the Spirit in a manner transcending human powers. . . .

15

It is our purpose to communicate the teaching on the light of grace of those long-revered saints whose wisdom comes from experience, proclaiming that "such is the teaching of Scripture". Thus we set forth as a summary the words of Isaac, the faithful interpreter of these things: "Our soul", he affirms, "possesses two eyes, as all the Fathers tell us. . . . Yet the sight which is proper to each 'eye' is not for the same use: with one eye, we behold the secrets of nature, that is to say, the power of God, His wisdom and providence towards us, things comprehensible by virtue of the greatness of His governance. With the other eye, we contemplate the glory of His holy nature, since it pleases God to introduce us to the spiritual mysteries."[30]

Since then these are eyes, what they see is a light; but since each possesses a power of vision designed for a particular use, a certain duality appears in the contemplation

---

28. Addressing Barlaam directly, who was prepared to accept the hesychasts' claim to have seen the divine light if this were admitted to be an angel.

29. The vision of God in the mirror of the purified soul is a commonplace of patristic spiritual teaching. The doctrine stems from the biblical view of man as created in the divine image and therefore originally capable of reflecting the splendor of God Himself. But, as a result of the Fall, the image has become tarnished and corroded, and must undergo restoration and cleaning in order once again to mediate the vision of God.

30. Isaac of Nineveh, Hom. 72. He contrasts two kinds of religious knowledge: "natural contemplation" (physike theōria), knowledge of God in creation; and direct vision of God's uncreated energies or glory (theologia in the strict sense).

of this light, since each eye sees a different light, invisible to the other eye. As the divine Isaac has explained, the one is the apprehension of the power, wisdom and providence of God, and in general, knowledge of the Creator through the creatures; the other is contemplation, not of the divine nature ... but of the *glory* of His nature, which the Saviour has bestowed on His disciples, and through them, on all who believe in Him and have manifested their faith through their works. This glory He clearly desired them to see, for He says to the Father, "I will that they contemplate the glory You have given Me, for You have loved Me since the foundation of the world" (Jn 17:24). And again, "Glorify Me, Father, with that glory I have had from You since before the world began" (Jn 17:5).

Thus to our human nature He has given the glory of the Godhead, but not the divine nature; for the nature of God is one thing, His glory another, even though they be inseparable one from another. However, even though this glory is different from the divine nature, it cannot be classified amongst the things subject to time, for in its transcendence "it is not", because it belongs to the divine nature in an ineffable manner.

Yet it is not only to that human composite which is united to His hypostasis[31] that He has given this glory which transcends all things, but also to His disciples. "Father," He says, "I have given them the glory which You gave Me, so that they may be perfectly one" (Jn 17:22–23). But He wishes also that they should see this glory, which we possess in our inmost selves and through which properly speaking we see God.

16

How then do we possess and see this glory of the divine nature? Is it in examining the causes of things and seeking through them the knowledge of the power, wisdom and providence of God? But, as we have said, it is another eye of the soul which sees all this, which does not see the divine light, "the glory of his nature" (in St. Isaac's words). This light is thus different from the light synonymous with knowledge.

Therefore, not every man who possesses the knowledge of created things, or who sees through the mediation of such knowledge has God dwelling in him; but he merely possesses knowledge of creatures, and from this by means of analogy he infers the existence of God. As to him who mysteriously possesses and sees this light, he knows and possesses God in himself, no longer by analogy, but by a true contem-

---

31. That is, the created (and therefore composite) human nature united to Christ as Second Person *(hypostasis)* of the Trinity. Participation in Christ's divine glory is not limited to His own individual humanity, but is shared by those incorporated into His Body by grace.

plation, transcendent to all creatures, for he is never separated from the eternal glory.

Let us not, then, turn aside incredulous before the superabundance of these blessings; but let us have faith in Him who has participated in our nature and granted it in return the glory of His own nature, and let us seek how to acquire this glory and see it. How? By keeping the divine commandments. For the Lord has promised to manifest Himself to the man who keeps them, a manifestation He calls His own indwelling and that of the Father, saying, "If anyone loves Me, he will keep My word, and My Father will love him, and We will come to him and will make our abode with him" (Jn 14:23) and "I will manifest Myself to him" (Jn 14:21). And it is clear that in mentioning His "word", He means His commandments, since earlier He speaks of "commandments" in place of "word": "He who possesses and keeps My commandments, that is the man who loves Me" (Jn 14:21).

17

We have here a proof . . . that this contemplation of God is not a form of knowledge,[32] even though Barlaam's greatest desire is that the opposite should be true. For our own part, if we refuse to call this contemplation "knowledge", it is by reason of its transcendence—just as we also say that God is not being, for we believe Him to be above being. . . .

18

. . . But let us also hear what certain saints . . . have to say of the glory of God, mysteriously and secretly visible to the initiated alone. Let us look first at the eyewitnesses and apostles of our one God and Father Jesus Christ, from Whom all paternity in the fulness of Holy Church is derived. And, first among them, let us listen to their leader Peter, who says, "It is not by following improbable fables that we have come to know the power and presence of Our Lord Jesus Christ, but because we have ourselves become witnesses of His greatness" (2 Pet 1:16). And here is another apostolic eyewitness of this glory: "Keeping themselves awake, Peter and his companions beheld the glory of Christ" (Lk 9:32). What glory? Another evangelist testifies: "His face shone like the sun, and His garments became white like the light" (Mt 17:2), showing them that He was Himself the God Who, in the Psalmist's words, "wraps himself in light as in a mantle" (Ps 104:2).

But, after having testified to his vision of Christ's glory on the holy mountain—

---

32. In the sense of a field of human knowledge naturally accessible to the reason. Infused illumination is different in kind from that sort of knowledge, and as such is "not-knowledge" or "learned ignorance." It is in this respect that Palamas affirms that "contemplation is not knowledge."

of a light which illumines, strange though it may be, the ears themselves (for they contemplated also a luminous cloud from which words reverberated)—Peter goes on to say, "This confirms the prophetic word" (2 Pet 1:19). What is this prophetic word which the vision of light confirms for you, O contemplators of God? What if not that verse that God "wraps Himself in light as in a mantle"? He continues, "You would do well to pay attention to that prophetic word, as to a lamp which shines in a dark place till the day dawns." What day, if not that which dawned in Thabor? "Let the morning star arise!" What star, if not that which illuminated Peter there, and also James and John? And where will that star rise, but "in your hearts"?

Do you not see how this light shines even now in the hearts of the faithful and perfect? Do you not see how it is superior to the light of knowledge? It has nothing to do with that which comes from Hellenic studies, which is not worthy to be called light, being but deception or confounded with deception, and nearer to darkness than light. Indeed, this light of contemplation even differs from the light that comes from the holy Scriptures, whose light may be compared to "a lamp that shines in an obscure place", whereas the light of mystical contemplation is compared to the star of the morning which shines in full daylight, that is to say, to the sun.[33]

---

33. That is, the truth of Scripture is not self-explanatory, but remains an "obscure light" until the Holy Spirit illuminates our hearts to perceive its inner meaning. By contemplation, the inner eye is purified and we are assimilated to Christ, who is all truth. Thus the hesychast is able to see the divine light directly ("in full daylight"), not only as mediated through the veils of Scripture.

SELECTED BIBLIOGRAPHY

TEXTS AND TRANSLATIONS

Gregoriou tou Palama Syngrammata. Edited by P. K. Chrestou. 3 vols. to date. Thessalonica, 1962–. Projected to be a six-volume, complete edition of Palamas' theological writings.

Défense des saints hésychastes: Introduction, texte critique, traduction et notes. Edited by J. Meyendorff. Spicilegium Sacrum Lovaniense, fasc. 30–31. 2nd ed. Louvain, 1973.

Gregory Palamas: The Triads. Edited by John Meyendorff. Translated by Nicholas Gendle. The Classics of Western Spirituality. New York: Paulist; London: SPCK, 1983.

STUDIES

Kern, Cyprien. "Les éléments de la théologie de Grégoire Palamas." Parts 1, 2. *Irenikon* 20 (1947): 6–33, 164–93.

Krivochéine, Basile. "The Ascetic and Theological Teaching of Gregory Palamas." Parts 1–4. *Eastern Churches Quarterly* 3 (1938–39): 26–33, 71–84, 138–56, 193–214.

Mantzarides, G. I. *The Deification of Man: St. Gregory Palamas and the Orthodox Tradition.* Crestwood, N.Y.: St. Vladimir's Seminary Press, 1984.

Meyendorff, John. *St. Gregory Palamas and Orthodox Spirituality.* Translated by Adele Fiske. Crestwood, N.Y.: St. Vladimir's Seminary Press, 1974.

————. *A Study of Gregory Palamas.* Translated by G. Lawrence. 2nd ed. Crestwood, N.Y.: St. Vladimir's Seminary Press; London: Faith Press, 1974.

Ware, Kallistos. "The Debate about Palamism." *Eastern Churches Review* 9 (1977): 45–63.

Julian of Norwich

(c.1342–c.1416)

The suspicion with which the writings of women mystics have often been viewed surely discouraged some women from writing at all, while those who did publish their reflections regularly did so only with diffidence and self-depreciation. Such disparagement appears at times in the writings of Julian of Norwich, who protests that she has no pretensions of being a teacher, "for I am a woman, ignorant, weak and frail."[1] Fortunately for us, she did not allow such diffidence to keep her from writing down her revelations or "showings," for she was convinced that she had received them "by the revelation of him who is the sovereign teacher" (135) and that they would lead her fellow Christians to a deeper knowledge and love of God.

Of Julian's life we know little more than may be gleaned from her *Showings.* Born toward the end of 1342 or the beginning of 1343, she writes that as a young woman she had desired three graces: recollection of Christ's passion, a bodily sickness, and the three "wounds" of contrition, compassion for the sufferings of Christ, and longing for God. She had forgotten all about the first two of these desires when, toward the middle of May 1373, she suddenly fell so ill that after three days she received the last rites of the Church and prepared herself for imminent death. After two more days, however, she suddenly recovered and thereupon thought to wish for the second of the three wounds, "for I wished that his [Christ's] pains might be my pains, with compassion which would lead to longing for God" (180). With this, she suddenly began having (in the course of a single day) a series of sixteen revelations which, after some initial hesitation, she concluded had truly been given her by God. Some time later—we do not know just when—she began living as an anchoress in a cell attached to the church of St. Julian in Norwich, apparently taking for herself the name of that saint in accordance with anchoritic custom.[2] During her many years of living in this anchor-

---

1. *Julian of Norwich: Showings,* trans. Edmund Colledge, O.S.A., and James Walsh, S.J., The Classics of Western Spirituality (New York: Paulist, 1978), 135. All subsequent citations of this work will be given in the text, the numbers being page references.

2. For a helpful description of the way of life of a medieval anchoress, see Margaret Wade Labarge, "Women Who Prayed: Recluses and Mystics," chap. 6 in *A Small Sound of the Trumpet: Women in Medieval Life* (Boston: Beacon Press, 1986).

hold, she wrote two versions of her showings: the first a relatively short text in which
she primarily limits herself to the description of what she had experienced, and
twenty years later a much longer text containing extended reflections on its meaning.
It is above all in virtue of this longer text
that she has come to be regarded not simply
as a visionary possessed of rare literary gifts
for describing her experiences but as a mystical theologian of the highest order, able to
correlate her experiences with the teaching
of Scripture and the Christian mystical tradition in a way that is comprehensive, sane,
and in some respects strikingly original.

Before we consider her teaching itself,
something should be said about the nature
of her revelations. Anyone reading her description of the first showing, in which she
"saw the red blood running down from
under the crown, hot and flowing freely and
copiously, a living stream, just as it was at
the time when the crown of thorns was
pressed on his blessed head" (181), might
be led to expect that the remaining fifteen
were also of this sort, which in traditional
theological language would be called an
"imaginative vision." In fact, only five others are of this type, while a second category
is made up of what Julian calls "words
formed in my understanding" (tradition-
ally called "locutions") and a third is com-
prised of those intellectual visions (her
term is "spiritual vision") of which Augustine had written centuries before in *The
Literal Meaning of Genesis* and which Teresa of Avila and John of the Cross would
discuss with such acumen two centuries
after Julian. Our first selection from the
Showings is Julian's account of just such a
vision of the glorified Christ, one which she

herself recalls a number of times in her
work as she tries to fathom all that was intended there in the constantly repeated
words of Christ: "I am he, I am he, I am he
who is highest" (223).

Since only the briefest of summaries of
Julian's mystical theology is possible here,
it may be best to focus first on a pair of con-
trasted terms which keep recurring in the
other chapters from the long text included
in this anthology—the terms "substance"
and "sensuality." Although she under-
standably does not attempt to give a pre-
cise, scholastic definition of these terms, by
"substance" she seems to mean what other
mystical writers have called the "ground"
of the soul, that aspect of our being which
is in immediate contact with God and
which, even though "a creature in God"
(285), is so like its Creator that Julian "saw
no difference between God and our substance, but, as it were, all God" (285). The
other element of the human person according to her theological anthropology is what
she calls "sensuality" or the "sensual soul"
(sensualyte), designating by this term all
that depends on the body; she speaks, for
example, of that moment "when our soul is
breathed into our body, at which time we
are made sensual" (286). Certainly there is
nothing negative or pejorative about sensuality for Julian, for she writes: "I saw
very surely that our substance is in God,
and I also saw that God is in our sensuality,
for in the same instant and place in which
our soul is made sensual, in that same instant and place exists the city of God, ordained for him from without beginning"
(287). It is sin alone which has disrupted
the original harmony between our substance and our sensuality, but if from one

point of view sin is "incomparably worse, more vile and painful than Hell," since it is so unnatural, so much "in opposition to our fair nature" (304), from another point of view it is a *felix culpa,* since "the goodness of [God's] mercy and grace opposed that wickedness and turned everything to goodness and honor for all who will be saved" (295).

This mercy and grace were, of course, manifested above all in the incarnation and redemption, but it is precisely in her magnificent treatment of these themes that Julian shows herself to be not simply a Christocentric mystic but one of the most profound trinitarian mystics in the history of the Church. Already in commenting on her first vision of the thorn-crowned head of Christ, Julian had said that "where Jesus appears, the blessed Trinity is understood" (181). Later in the work, as part of her lengthy reflections on the meaning of the fourteenth showing, she declares that the words of the glorified Christ in the twelfth revelation ("I am he, I am he . . .") are in fact to be understood not simply of the second Person of the Trinity but of the triune God *in toto:*

As truly as God is our Father, so truly is God our Mother, and he revealed that in everything, and especially in these sweet words where he says: I am he; that is to say: I am he, the power and goodness of fatherhood; I am he, the wisdom and lovingness of motherhood; I am he, the light and grace which is all blessed love; I am he, the Trinity; I am he, the unity; I am he, the supreme goodness of every kind of thing; I am he who makes you to love;

I am he who makes you to long; I am he, the endless fulfillment of all true desires. (296)

Our final point by way of introduction to Julian concerns her declaration at the beginning of the passage just quoted that God is "truly . . . our Mother." This theme, and particularly her attribution of motherhood to Jesus, is very prominent in the chapters here presented. Recent scholarship has shown that the allusions to God's motherhood in Scripture had already been elaborated by some of the Fathers of the Church and that the motherhood of Jesus was a favorite subject of many Cistercian writers of the twelfth century.[3] Seldom, however, had this theme received the extended treatment that it has in Julian's *Showings,* nor had the obviously maternal aspects of Christ as the one who feeds us in the Eucharist and saves us from perishing through his own suffering and death been complemented in the writings of Julian's predecessors by a parallel emphasis on the maternal aspects of Christ's role (as eternal Wisdom) in our *creation.* In Julian, the creative and redemptive works of "Jesus our Mother" are regularly brought together, as when she writes that "Jesus is our true Mother in nature by our first creation, and he is our true Mother in grace by his taking our created nature. All the lovely works and all the sweet loving offices of beloved motherhood

---

3. See Ritamary Bradley, "Patristic Background of the Motherhood Similitude in Julian of Norwich," *Christian Scholar's Review* 8 (1978): 101–13, and Caroline Walker Bynum, "Jesus as Mother and Abbot as Mother: Some Themes in Twelfth-Century Cistercian Writing," chap. 4 in *Jesus as Mother: Studies in the Spirituality of the High Middle Ages* (Berkeley and Los Angeles: University of California Press, 1983).

are appropriated to the second person . . ." (296).[4]

Even with the good, modern English translations now available, reading Julian is not particularly easy, which is perhaps one reason why, at least up to the present time, her *Showings* have not been as widely read as the works of other major fourteenth century mystics. But those who take the time to read her carefully and reflectively will understand why Thomas Merton once wrote that she "is without doubt one of the most wonderful of all Christian voices. She gets greater and greater in my eyes as I grow older. . . . I think that Julian of Norwich is, with Newman, the greatest English theologian."[5]

4. On this point, see J. P. H. Clark, "Nature, Grace and the Trinity in Julian of Norwich," *Downside Review* 100 (1982): 211.

5. From a letter of Merton's quoted in Robert Llewelyn, *All Shall Be Well: The Spirituality of Julian of Norwich for Today* (New York: Paulist, 1982), 137.

Selections

SHOWINGS (LONG TEXT)*

The Twenty-Sixth Chapter

And after this our Lord showed himself to me, and he appeared to me more glorified than I had seen him before, in which I was taught that our soul will never have rest till it comes into him, acknowledging that he is full of joy, familiar and courteous and blissful and true life. Again and again our Lord said: I am he, I am he, I am he who is highest. I am he whom you love. I am he in whom you delight. I am he whom you serve. I am he for whom you long. I am he whom you desire. I am he whom you intend. I am he who is all. I am he whom Holy Church preaches and teaches to you. I am he who showed himself before to you. The number of the words surpasses my intelligence and my understanding and all my powers, for they were the most exalted, as I see it, for in them is comprehended I cannot tell what; but the joy which I saw when they were revealed surpasses all that the heart can think or the soul may desire. And therefore these words are not explained here, but let every man accept them as our Lord intended them, according to the grace God gives him in understanding and love. . . .

The Fifty-Eighth Chapter

God the blessed Trinity, who is everlasting being, just as he is eternal from without beginning, just so was it in his eternal purpose to create human nature, which fair nature was first prepared for his own Son, the second person; and when he wished, by full agreement of the whole Trinity he created us all once. And in our creating he joined and united us to himself, and through this union we are kept as pure and as noble as we were created. By the power of that same precious union we love our Creator and delight in him, praise him and thank him and endlessly rejoice in him. And this is the work which is constantly performed in every soul which will be saved, and this is the godly will mentioned before.

And so in our making, God almighty is our loving Father, and God all wisdom is our loving Mother, with the love and the goodness of the Holy Spirit, which is all one God, one Lord. And in the joining and the union he is our very true spouse and we his beloved wife and his fair maiden, with which wife he was never displeased; for he says: I love you and you love me, and our love will never divide in two.

---

*From *Julian of Norwich: Showings,* trans. Edmund Colledge, O.S.A., and James Walsh, S.J., The Classics of Western Spirituality (New York: Paulist, 1978), 223–24, 293–305. Reprinted with permission of the publisher.

I contemplated the work of all the blessed Trinity, in which contemplation I saw and understood these three properties: the property of the fatherhood, and the property of the motherhood, and the property of the lordship in one God. In our almighty Father we have our protection and our bliss, as regards our natural substance, which is ours by our creation from without beginning; and in the second person, in knowledge and wisdom we have our perfection, as regards our sensuality, our restoration and our salvation, for he is our Mother, brother and saviour; and in our good Lord the Holy Spirit we have our reward and our gift for our living and our labour, endlessly surpassing all that we desire in his marvellous courtesy, out of his great plentiful grace. For all our life consists of three: In the first we have our being, and in the second we have our increasing, and in the third we have our fulfillment. The first is nature, the second is mercy, and the third is grace.

As to the first, I saw and understood that the high might of the Trinity is our Father, and the deep wisdom of the Trinity is our Mother, and the great love of the Trinity is our Lord; and all these we have in nature and in our substantial creation. And furthermore I saw that the second person, who is our Mother, substantially the same beloved person, has now become our mother sensually, because we are double by God's creating, that is to say substantial and sensual. Our substance is the higher part, which we have in our Father, God almighty; and the second person of the Trinity is our Mother in nature in our substantial creation, in whom we are founded and rooted, and he is our Mother of mercy in taking our sensuality. And so our Mother is working on us in various ways, in whom our parts are kept undivided; for in our Mother Christ we profit and increase, and in mercy he reforms and restores us, and by the power of his Passion, his death and his Resurrection he unites us to our substance. So our Mother works in mercy on all his beloved children who are docile and obedient to him, and grace works with mercy, and especially in two properties, as it was shown, which working belongs to the third person, the Holy Spirit. He works, rewarding and giving. Rewarding is a gift for our confidence which the Lord makes to those who have laboured; and giving is a courteous act which he does freely, by grace, fulfilling and surpassing all that creatures deserve.

Thus in our Father, God almighty, we have our being, and in our Mother of mercy we have our reforming and our restoring, in whom our parts are united and all made perfect man, and through the rewards and the gifts of grace of the Holy Spirit we are fulfilled. And our substance is in our Father, God almighty, and our substance is in our Mother, God all wisdom, and our substance is in our Lord God, the Holy Spirit, all goodness, for our substance is whole in each person of the Trinity, who is one God. And our sensuality is only in the second person, Christ Jesus, in whom is the Father and the Holy Spirit; and in him and by him we are powerfully taken out of hell and out of the wretchedness on earth, and gloriously brought up into heaven, and blessedly united to our substance, increased in riches and nobility by all the power of Christ and by the grace and operation of the Holy Spirit.

The Fifty-Ninth Chapter

And we have all this bliss by mercy and grace, and this kind of bliss we never could have had and known, unless that property of goodness which is in God had been opposed, through which we have this bliss. For wickedness has been suffered to rise in opposition to that goodness; and the goodness of mercy and grace opposed that wickedness, and turned everything to goodness and honour for all who will be saved. For this is that property in God which opposes good to evil. So Jesus Christ, who opposes good to evil, is our true Mother. We have our being from him, where the foundation of motherhood begins, with all the sweet protection of love which endlessly follows.

As truly as God is our Father, so truly is God our Mother, and he revealed that in everything, and especially in these sweet words where he says: I am he; that is to say: I am he, the power and goodness of fatherhood; I am he, the wisdom and the lovingness of motherhood; I am he, the light and the grace which is all blessed love; I am he, the Trinity; I am he, the unity; I am he, the great supreme goodness of every kind of thing; I am he who makes you to love; I am he who makes you to long; I am he, the endless fulfilling of all true desires. For where the soul is highest, noblest, most honourable, still it is lowest, meekest and mildest.

And from this foundation in substance we have all the powers of our sensuality by the gift of nature, and by the help and the furthering of mercy and grace, without which we cannot profit. Our great Father, almighty God, who is being, knows us and loved us before time began. Out of this knowledge, in his most wonderful deep love, by the prescient eternal counsel of all the blessed Trinity, he wanted the second person to become our Mother, our brother and our saviour. From this it follows that as truly as God is our Father, so truly is God our Mother. Our Father wills, our Mother works, our good Lord the Holy Spirit confirms. And therefore it is our part to love our God in whom we have our being, reverently thanking and praising him for our creation, mightily praying to our Mother for mercy and pity, and to our Lord the Holy Spirit for help and grace. For in these three is all our life: nature, mercy and grace, of which we have mildness, patience and pity, and hatred of sin and wickedness; for the virtues must of themselves hate sin and wickedness.

And so Jesus is our true Mother in nature by our first creation, and he is our true Mother in grace by his taking our created nature. All the lovely works and all the sweet loving offices of beloved motherhood are appropriated to the second person, for in him we have this godly will, whole and safe forever, both in nature and in grace, from his own goodness proper to him.

I understand three ways of contemplating motherhood in God. The first is the foundation of our nature's creation; the second is his taking of our nature, where the motherhood of grace begins; the third is the motherhood at work. And in that, by the same grace, everything is penetrated, in length and in breadth, in height and in depth without end; and it is all one love.

The Sixtieth Chapter

But now I should say a little more about this penetration, as I understood our Lord to mean: How we are brought back by the motherhood of mercy and grace into our natural place, in which we were created by the motherhood of love, a mother's love which never leaves us.

Our Mother in nature, our Mother in grace, because he wanted altogether to become our Mother in all things, made the foundation of his work most humbly and most mildly in the maiden's womb. And he revealed that in the first revelation, when he brought that meek maiden before the eye of my understanding in the simple stature which she had when she conceived; that is to say that our great God, the supreme wisdom of all things, arrayed and prepared himself in this humble place, all ready in our poor flesh, himself to do the service and the office of motherhood in everything. The mother's service is nearest, readiest and surest: nearest because it is most natural, readiest because it is most loving, and surest because it is truest. No one ever might or could perform this office fully, except only him. We know that all our mothers bear us for pain and for death. O, what is that? But our true Mother Jesus, he alone bears us for joy and for endless life, blessed may he be. So he carries us within him in love and travail, until the full time when he wanted to suffer the sharpest thorns and cruel pains that ever were or will be, and at the last he died. And when he had finished, and had borne us so for bliss, still all this could not satisfy his wonderful love. And he revealed this in these great surpassing words of love: If I could suffer more, I would suffer more. He could not die any more, but he did not want to cease working; therefore he must needs nourish us, for the precious love of motherhood has made him our debtor.

The mother can give her child to suck of her milk, but our precious Mother Jesus can feed us with himself, and does, most courteously and most tenderly, with the blessed sacrament, which is the precious food of true life; and with all the sweet sacraments he sustains us most mercifully and graciously, and so he meant in these blessed words, where he said: I am he whom Holy Church preaches and teaches to you. That is to say: All the health and the life of the sacraments, all the power and the grace of my word, all the goodness which is ordained in Holy Church for you, I am he.

The mother can lay her child tenderly to her breast, but our tender Mother Jesus can lead us easily into his blessed breast through his sweet open side, and show us there a part of the godhead and of the joys of heaven, with inner certainty of endless bliss. And that he revealed in the tenth revelation, giving us the same understanding in these sweet words which he says: See how I love you, looking into his blessed side, rejoicing.

This fair lovely word 'mother' is so sweet and so kind in itself that it cannot truly be said of anyone or to anyone except of him and to him who is the true Mother of life and of all things. To the property of motherhood belong nature, love, wisdom and knowledge, and this is God. For though it may be so that our bodily bringing to birth is only little, humble and simple in comparison with our spiritual bringing to birth, still it is he who does it in the creatures by whom it is done. The kind, loving mother who knows and sees the need of her child guards it very tenderly, as the nature and condition of motherhood will have. And always as the child grows in age and in stature, she acts differently, but she does not change her love. And when it is even older, she allows it to be chastised to destroy its faults, so as to make the child receive virtues and grace. This work, with everything which is lovely and good, our Lord performs in those by whom it is done. So he is our Mother in nature by the operation of grace in the lower part, for love of the higher part. And he wants us to know it, for he wants to have all our love attached to him; and in this I saw that every debt which we owe by God's command to fatherhood and motherhood is fulfilled in truly loving God, which blessed love Christ works in us. And this was revealed in everything, and especially in the great bounteous words when he says: I am he whom you love.

The Sixty-First Chapter

And in our spiritual bringing to birth he uses more tenderness, without any comparison, in protecting us. By so much as our soul is more precious in his sight, he kindles our understanding, he prepares our ways, he eases our conscience, he comforts our soul, he illumines our heart and gives us partial knowledge and love of his blessed divinity, with gracious memory of his sweet humanity and his blessed Passion, with courteous wonder over his great surpassing goodness, and makes us to love everything which he loves for love of him, and to be well satisfied with him and with all his works. And when we fall, quickly he raises us up with his loving embrace and his gracious touch. And when we are strengthened by his sweet working, then we willingly choose him by his grace, that we shall be his servants and his lovers, constantly and forever.

And yet after this he allows some of us to fall more heavily and more grievously than ever we did before, as it seems to us. And then we who are not all wise think that everything which we have undertaken was all nothing. But it is not so, for we need to fall, and we need to see it; for if we did not fall, we should not know how feeble and how wretched we are in ourselves, nor, too, should we know so completely the wonderful love of our Creator.

For we shall truly see in heaven without end that we have sinned grievously in this life; and notwithstanding this, we shall truly see that we were never hurt in his love, nor were we ever of less value in his sight. And by the experience of this falling we shall have a great and marvellous knowledge of love in God without end; for enduring and marvellous is that love which cannot and will not be broken because of offences.

And this was one profitable understanding; another is the humility and meekness which we shall obtain by the sight of our fall, for by that we shall be raised high in heaven, to which raising we might never have come without that meekness. And therefore we need to see it; and if we do not see it, though we fell, that would not profit us. And commonly we first fall and then see it; and both are from the mercy of God.

The mother may sometimes suffer the child to fall and to be distressed in various ways, for its own benefit, but she can never suffer any kind of peril to come to her child, because of her love. And though our earthly mother may suffer her child to perish, our heavenly Mother Jesus may never suffer us who are his children to perish, for he is almighty, all wisdom and all love, and so is none but he, blessed may he be.

But often when our falling and our wretchedness are shown to us, we are so much afraid and so greatly ashamed of ourselves that we scarcely know where we can put ourselves. But then our courteous Mother does not wish us to flee away, for nothing would be less pleasing to him; but he then wants us to behave like a child. For when it is distressed and frightened, it runs quickly to its mother; and if it can do no more, it calls to the mother for help with all its might. So he wants us to act as a meek child, saying: My kind Mother, my gracious Mother, my beloved Mother, have mercy on me. I have made myself filthy and unlike you, and I may not and cannot make it right except with your help and grace.

And if we do not then feel ourselves eased, let us at once be sure that he is behaving as a wise Mother. For if he sees that it is profitable to us to mourn and to weep, with compassion and pity he suffers that until the right time has come, out of his love. And then he wants us to show a child's characteristics, which always naturally trusts in its mother's love in well-being and in woe. And he wants us to commit ourselves fervently to the faith of Holy Church, and find there our beloved Mother in consolation and true understanding, with all the company of the blessed. For one single person may often be broken, as it seems to him, but the entire body of Holy

Church was never broken, nor ever will be without end. And therefore it is a certain thing, and good and gracious to will, meekly and fervently, to be fastened and united to our mother Holy Church, who is Christ Jesus. For the flood of mercy which is his dear blood and precious water is plentiful to make us fair and clean. The blessed wounds of our saviour are open and rejoice to heal us. The sweet gracious hands of our Mother are ready and diligent about us; for he in all this work exercises the true office of a kind nurse, who has nothing else to do but attend to the safety of her child.

It is his office to save us, it is his glory to do it, and it is his will that we know it; for he wants us to love him sweetly and trust in him meekly and greatly. And he revealed this in these gracious words: I protect you very safely.

The Sixty-Second Chapter

For at that time he revealed our frailty and our falling, our trespasses and our humiliations, our chagrins and our burdens and all our woe, as much as it seemed to me could happen in this life. And with that he revealed his blessed power, his blessed wisdom, his blessed love, and that he protects us at such times, as tenderly and as sweetly, to his glory, and as surely to our salvation as he does when we are in the greatest consolation and comfort, and raises us to this in spirit, on high in heaven, and turns everything to his glory and to our joy without end. For his precious love, he never allows us to lose time; and all this is of the natural goodness of God by the operation of grace.

God is essence in his very nature; that is to say, that goodness which is natural is God. He is the ground, he is the substance, he is very essence or nature, and he is the true Father and the true Mother of natures. And all natures which he has made to flow out of him to work his will, they will be restored and brought back into him by the salvation of man through the operation of grace. For all natures which he has put separately in different creatures are all in man, wholly, in fulness and power, in beauty and in goodness, in kingliness and in nobility, in every manner of stateliness, preciousness and honour.

Here we can see that we are all bound to God by nature, and we are bound to God by grace. Here we can see that we do not need to seek far afield so as to know various natures, but to go to Holy Church, into our Mother's breast, that is to say into our own soul, where our Lord dwells. And there we should find everything, now in faith and understanding, and afterwards truly, in himself, clearly, in bliss.

But let no man or woman apply this particularly to himself, because it is not so. It is general, because it is our precious Mother Christ, and for him was this fair nature prepared for the honour and the nobility of man's creation, and for the joy and the bliss of man's salvation, just as he saw, knew and recognized from without beginning.

The Sixty-Third Chapter

Here we may see that truly it belongs to our nature to hate sin, and truly it belongs to us by grace to hate sin, for nature is all good and fair in itself, and grace was sent out to save nature and destroy sin, and bring fair nature back again to the blessed place from which it came, which is God, with more nobility and honour by the powerful operation of grace. For it will be seen before God by all his saints in joy without end that nature has been tried in the fire of tribulation, and that no lack or defect is found in it.

So are nature and grace of one accord; for grace is God, as uncreated nature is God. He is two in his manner of operation, and one in love, and neither of these works without the other, and they are not separated. And when we by the mercy of God and with his help reconcile ourselves to nature and to grace, we shall see truly that sin is incomparably worse, more vile and painful than hell. For it is in opposition to our fair nature; for as truly as sin is unclean, so truly is sin unnatural. All this is a horrible thing to see for the loving soul which would wish to be all fair and shining in the sight of God, as nature and grace teach. But do not let us be afraid of this, except insofar as fear may be profitable; but let us meekly lament to our beloved Mother, and he will sprinkle us all with his precious blood, and make our soul most pliable and most mild, and heal us most gently in the course of time, just as it is most glory to him and joy to us without end. And from this sweet and gentle operation he will never cease or desist, until all his beloved children are born and brought to birth; and he revealed that when he gave understanding of the spiritual thirst which is the longing in love which will last till the day of judgment.

So in our true Mother Jesus our life is founded in his own prescient wisdom from without beginning, with the great power of the Father and the supreme goodness of the Holy Spirit. And in accepting our nature he gave us life, and in his blessed dying on the Cross he bore us to endless life. And since that time, now and ever until the day of judgment, he feeds us and fosters us, just as the great supreme lovingness of motherhood wishes, and as the natural need of childhood asks. Fair and sweet is our heavenly Mother in the sight of our soul, precious and lovely are the children of grace in the sight of our heavenly Mother, with gentleness and meekness and all the lovely virtues which belong to children by nature. For the child does not naturally despair of the mother's love, the child does not naturally rely upon itself, naturally the child loves the mother and either of them the other.

These, and all others that resemble them, are such fair virtues, with which our heavenly Mother is served and pleased. And I understood no greater stature in this life than childhood, with its feebleness and lack of power and intelligence, until the time that our gracious Mother has brought us up into our Father's bliss. And there it will truly be made known to us what he means in the sweet words when he says: All will be well, and you will see it yourself; that every kind of thing will be well. And then will the bliss of our motherhood in Christ be to begin anew in the joys of our Father, God, which new beginning will last, newly beginning without end.

SELECTED BIBLIOGRAPHY

TEXTS AND TRANSLATIONS

A Book of Showings to the Anchoress Julian of Norwich. Edited by Edmund Colledge, O.S.A., and James Walsh, S.J. 2 vols. Toronto: Pontifical Institute of Medieval Studies, 1978. A critical edition of the Middle English text.

Julian of Norwich: Showings. Translated by Edmund Colledge, O.S.A., and James Walsh, S.J. The Classics of Western Spirituality. New York: Paulist; London: SPCK, 1978.

Revelations of Divine Love. Translated by Clifton Wolters. Harmondsworth and New York: Penguin, 1966.

STUDIES

Allchin, A.M., and the Sisters of the Love of God. *Julian of Norwich: Four Studies to Commemorate the Sixth Centenary of the Revelations of Divine Love.* Oxford: Fairacres, 1975.

Llewelyn, Robert. *All Shall Be Well: The Spirituality of Julian of Norwich for Today.* New York: Paulist, 1985. Originally published as *With Pity Not Blame* (London: Darton, Longman and Todd, 1982).

Molinari, Paul. *Julian of Norwich: The Teaching of a Fourteenth-Century English Mystic.* London: Longmans, 1958; Darby, Pa.: Arden Library, 1978.

Pelphrey, Brant. *Julian of Norwich.* The Way of the Christian Mystics. Wilmington, Del.: Michael Glazier, 1988.

————. *Love Was His Meaning: The Theology and Mysticism of Julian of Norwich.* Salzburg Studies in English Literature, 92:4. Salzburg, 1982.

The Cloud of Unknowing

(14th Century)

We may distinguish three kinds of mystical writings: theological (the earliest), existential (the latest), and practical (how to become a spiritual person). The *Cloud* belongs entirely to the latter category. Yet its rather down-to-earth pedagogy has not rendered the reading of it tedious. Nor can one classify its content as "common," for its attempt to give the ecstatic ideal of negative theology an earthly concreteness makes it unique in our spiritual literature. The anonymous, fourteenth century Englishman who wrote it—most likely a priest in a religious order, possibly a Carthusian—must have been a wise director as well as a true visionary.

How thoroughly he had assimilated the spiritual currents of his day appears in the remarkable synthesis he accomplished between Dionysius' negative theology and medieval love mysticism. The work's main authority is unquestionably Dionysius' *Mystical Theology,* which the author paraphrased[1] under the title *Deonise Hid Divin-*ite. He refers exclusively to Dionysius and defines the mystical life in his terms. Having asserted that by the knowledge of created things man can never reach the uncreated, he adds: "But by the failing of it [knowledge], he can. For where his understanding fails is in nothing except God alone; and it was for this reason that Saint Denis said, 'The truly divine knowledge of God is that which is known by unknowing'" (Ch. 71). As William Johnston writes, "the very heart of this work is love."[2] Indeed, unknowing itself here appears as a means to purify the soul and thus to prepare it for the union of love. The author adds to the "cloud of ignorance" what he quaintly terms the "cloud of forgetting," the ascetic move whereby the soul abandons interest—both theoretical and practical—in creatures for their own sake.

Love, then, transforms this *apophatic* mysticism into a *kataphatic* (one that does speak about God). The author thereby escapes a number of nettlesome problems inherent in strictly Dionysian theology. In fact, he never ceases to caution his readers against premature ambitions toward ecstatic prayer. Whoever presumes to aban-

1. He introduces his work as "the English translation of a book written by Saint Denis to Timothy, the title of which in the Latin is *Mistica Theologia.*" But apart from the fact that he used the existing Latin translation by Sarracenus (he may never have seen the Greek text), he amply borrows from Thomas Gallus' extensive commentary. On the historical sources the reader may consult the excellent introduction by James Walsh, S.J., to The Classics of Western Spirituality edition.

2. *The Cloud of Unknowing and The Book of Privy Counseling,* newly edited, with an introduction by William Johnston (New York: Doubleday, Image Books, 1973), 21.

don humble prayer and spiritual discipline
will experience nothing but "nervous exaltation," the quickest way to death both of
body and of soul, "for it is madness and not
wisdom, and leads a man to madness" (Ch.
51). Prayer begins with meditation, that is,
according to our author, with discursive
"reading" and "thinking." Despite his dis-
claimer that God can in any way be
"heard" or "seen," the author also grants a
real significance to visions. Above all, he
places Christ's humanity in a central position, as no negative theologian would ever
have done.[3]

Still, the emphasis remains on passivity,
on the soul's impotence to conquer what
lies entirely beyond its powers. The *Cloud*
succeeds in expressing accurately and simply the concepts of moral passivity and
"pure love" around which the Quietist
movement would arouse such strident controversies. Thus the author recommends
not to resist distractions in contemplative
prayer, but "to say to oneself: It is futile to
contend with them any longer," and then
fall down before them like a captive or a
coward. "For in doing this you commend
yourself to God in the midst of your enemies and admit the radical impotence of
your nature" (Ch. 32).

The doctrine of love is equally far re-

moved from exaltation or sentimentality,
and solidly rooted in orthodoxy and common sense. Basically love means "a radical
commitment to God" (Ch. 49), and it matters little whether a person thereby experiences the consolations of feeling or not.
The union of the spirit remains anchored
exclusively in the commitment of the will.

In later years the author composed yet
another short essay on contemplation, *The
Book of Privy Counseling*. This treatise is
not directed to a general, spiritual reader-
ship, but to one person ready for contemplative prayer: "You have reached a point
where your further growth in perfection demands that you do not feed your mind with
meditations on the multiple aspects of your
being. In the past these meditations helped
you to understand something of God. . . .
But now it is important that you seriously
concentrate on the effort to abide continually in the deep center of your spirit, offering to God that naked blind awareness of
your being which I call your first fruit" (Ch.
5). The entire letter, an argument for re-
placing discursive meditation through "the
faculties" by a state of inner quiet, comes
as close as any spiritual work in our past to
Buddhist and Yoga methods. Yet the author constantly attaches it to established
Christian doctrine. As such, it remains a
tour de force and somewhat of an oddity in
our tradition, but one that strongly appeals
to Christians of our time.

---

3. Harvey Egan, S.J., "Christian Apophatic and Kataphatic Mysticisms," *Theological Studies* 39 (1978):
409–13.

Selections

THE CLOUD OF UNKNOWING*

CHAPTER III
How this exercise is to be made; how it is worth more than all other exercises.

Lift up your heart to God with a humble impulse of love; and have himself as your aim, not any of his goods. Take care that you avoid thinking of anything but himself, so that there is nothing for your reason or your will to work on, except himself. Do all that in you lies to forget all the creatures that God ever made, and their works, so that neither your thought nor your desire be directed or extended to any of them, neither in general nor in particular. Let them alone and pay no attention to them. This is the work of the soul that pleases God most. All saints and angels take joy in this exercise, and are anxious to help it on with all their might. All the devils are furious when you undertake it, and make it their business, insofar as they can, to destroy it. We cannot know how wonderfully all people dwelling on earth are helped by this exercise. Yes, and the souls in purgatory are eased of their pain, and you yourself are purified and made virtuous, much more by this work than by any other. Yet it is the easiest exercise of all and most readily accomplished when a soul is helped by grace in this felt desire; otherwise, it would be extraordinarily difficult for you to make this exercise. Do not hang back then, but labour in it until you experience the desire. For when you first begin to undertake it, all that you find is a darkness, a sort of cloud of unknowing; you cannot tell what it is, except that you experience in your will a simple reaching out to God. This darkness and cloud is always between you and your God, no matter what you do, and it prevents you from seeing him clearly by the light of understanding in your reason, and from experiencing him in sweetness of love in your affection. So set yourself to rest in this darkness as long as you can, always crying out after him whom you love. For if you are to experience him or to see him at all, insofar as it is possible here, it must always be in this cloud and in this darkness. So if you labour at it with all your attention as I bid you, I trust, in his mercy, that you will reach this point.

CHAPTER IV
The brief nature of this exercise; it cannot be attained by intellectual study or through the imaginative faculty.

To prevent you from making mistakes in this exercise, and from thinking that it is other than it actually is, I am going to tell you a little more about it, as I believe

---

*From *The Cloud of Unknowing,* ed. James Walsh, S.J., The Classics of Western Spirituality (New York: Paulist, 1981), 119–23, 127–41. Reprinted with permission of the publisher.

it to be. It is an exercise that does not need a long time before it can be truly done, as some men seem to think; for it is the shortest possible of all exercises that men can imagine. It is neither longer nor shorter than an atom. The atom, if we follow the definition of good philosophers in the science of astronomy, is the smallest particle of time. It is so little that, because of its littleness, it is indivisible and almost unperceivable. It is the time of which it is written: "All time is given to you, it shall be asked of you how you have spent it." And it is right that you should give account of it, for it is neither longer nor shorter but exactly equal to each single stirring that is in the chief working power of your soul, that is, your will. For as many choices and desires, no more and no less, as there can be and are in your will in one hour, so are there atoms in an hour. If you were reformed by grace according to the primal state of man's soul as it was before sin, you would always, by the help of that grace, be in control of that impulse or of those impulses. None of them would go unheeded, but all would reach out to the preeminent and supreme object of your will and your desire, which is God himself.

He fits himself exactly to our souls by adapting his Godhead to them; and our souls are fitted exactly to him by the worthiness of our creation after his image and his likeness. He, by himself alone, and no one but he, is fully sufficient, and much more so, to fulfil the will and the desire of our souls. And our soul, because of his reforming grace, is wholly enabled to comprehend by love the whole of him who is incomprehensible to every created knowing power: that is, to the souls of angels and of men. I speak of their knowing and not of their loving; that is why I call their souls in this case knowing powers.

Now all rational creatures, angels and men alike, have in them, each one individually, one chief working power, which is called a knowing power, and another chief working power called a loving power; and of these two powers, God, who is the maker of them, is always incomprehensible to the first, the knowing power. But to the second, which is the loving power, he is entirely comprehensible in each one individually; in so much that one loving soul of itself, because of love, would be able to comprehend him who is entirely sufficient, and much more so, without limit, to fill all the souls of men and angels that could ever exist. This is the everlastingly wonderful miracle of love, which shall never have an end. For he shall ever work it and shall never cease to do so. Let him understand it who can do so by grace; for the experience of this is endless happiness, and its contrary is endless suffering. . . .

Whoever hears this exercise read or spoken of may think that he can or ought to achieve it by intellectual labour; and so he sits and racks his brains how it can be achieved, and with such ingenious reasonings he does violence to his imagination, perhaps beyond its natural ability, so as to fashion a false way of working which fits neither body nor soul. Truly such a man, whoever he be, is perilously deluded; and so much so that unless God in his great goodness show him his wondrous mercy, and quickly lead him away from his imaginings, to put himself meekly under direction of those experienced in the exercise, he shall be overcome by frenzies or else fall into other great mischief, spiritual sins and the devil's deceits; and through these he may easily be robbed of body and soul for all eternity. So for the love of God, take care in this exercise and do not labour with your senses or with your imagination in any way at all. For I tell you truly, this exercise cannot be achieved by their labour; so leave them and do not work with them.

Now when I call this exercise a darkness or a cloud, do not think that it is a cloud formed out of the vapours which float in the air, or a darkness such as you have in your house at night, when your candle is out. For such a darkness or such a cloud you can certainly imagine by subtle fancies, as though it were before your eyes, even on the clearest day of summer; and likewise, on the darkest night of winter, you can imagine a clear shining light. But leave such falsehood alone. I mean nothing of that sort. When I say "darkness," I mean a privation of knowing, just as whatever you do not know or have forgotten is dark to you, because you do not see it with your spiritual eyes. For this reason, that which is between you and your God is termed, not a cloud of the air, but a cloud of unknowing.

CHAPTER V
During this exercise, all creatures and all the works of creatures, past, present or future, must be hidden in the cloud of forgetting.

If ever you come to this cloud, and live and work in it as I bid you, just as this cloud of unknowing is above you, between you and your God, in the same way you must put beneath you a cloud of forgetting, between you and all the creatures that have ever been made. It seems to you, perhaps, that you are very far from him, because this cloud of unknowing is between you and your God. However, if you give it proper thought, you are certainly much further away from him when you do not have the cloud of forgetting between you and all the creatures that have ever been made. Whenever I say "all the creatures that have ever been made," I mean not only the creatures themselves, but also all their works and circumstances. I make no exceptions, whether they are bodily creatures or spiritual, nor for the state or activity of any creature, whether these be good or evil. In short, I say that all should be hid under the cloud of forgetting.

For though it is very profitable on some occasions to think of the state and activities of certain creatures in particular, nevertheless in this exercise it profits little or nothing. Being mindful or thinking of any creature that God ever made, or of any of their works either, is a sort of spiritual light. The eye of your soul is opened on it and fixed upon it, like the eye of the bowman upon the eye of the target that he is shooting at. I have one thing to say to you: Everything that you think of is above you during this time, and between you and your God. Insofar as there is anything in your mind except God alone, in that far you are further from God.

Yes, and if one may say it courteously and fittingly, in this exercise it is of little or no profit to think of the kindness or the worthiness of God, or of our Lady or the saints or angels in heaven, or even of the joys of heaven; that is to say, with a special concentration upon them, as though you wished by that concentration to feed and increase your purpose. I believe that it would in no wise be so in this case and in this exercise, for though it is good to think of the kindness of God and to love him and to praise him for that, yet it is far better to think upon his simple being and to love him and praise him for himself.

CHAPTER VI
A short appreciation of this exercise by means of question and answer.

But now you put me a question and say: "How might I think of him in himself, and what is he?" And to this I can only answer thus: "I have no idea." For with your question you have brought me into that same darkness, into that same cloud of unknowing where I would you were yourself. For a man may, by grace, have the fulness of knowledge of all other creatures and their works, yes, and of the works of God's own self, and he is well able to reflect on them. But no man can think of God himself. Therefore, it is my wish to leave everything that I can think of and choose for my love the thing that I cannot think. Because he can certainly be loved, but not thought. He can be taken and held by love but not by thought. Therefore, though it is good at times to think of the kindness and worthiness of God in particular, and though this is a light and a part of contemplation, nevertheless, in this exercise, it must be cast down and covered over with a cloud of forgetting. You are to step above it stalwartly but lovingly, and with a devout, pleasing, impulsive love strive to pierce that darkness above you. You are to smite upon that thick cloud of unknowing with a sharp dart of longing love. Do not leave that work for anything that may happen.

CHAPTER VII
How to deal with all thoughts during this exercise, particularly those which result from one's own investigation, knowledge and natural acumen.

If any thought should rise and continue to press in, above you and between you and that darkness, and should ask you and say: "What do you seek and what would you have?" you must say that it is God whom you would have. "Him I covet, him I seek, and nothing but him." And if the thought should ask you who that God is, you must answer that it is the God who made you and ransomed you, and with his grace has called you to his love. And say: "You have no part to play." So say to the thought: "Go down again." Tread it down quickly with an impulse of love, even though it seems to you to be very holy; even though it seems that it could help you to seek him. Perhaps the thought will bring to your mind a variety of excellent and wonderful instances of his kindness; it will say that he is most sweet and most loving, gracious and merciful. The thought will want nothing better than that you should listen to it; for in the end it will increase its chattering more and more until it brings you lower down to the recollection of his passion. There it will let you see the wonderful kindness of God; it looks for nothing better than that you should listen to it. For soon after that he will let you see your former wretched state of life; and perhaps as you see and think upon it, the thought will bring to your mind some place in which you used to live. And so at the end, before you are even aware of it, your concentration is gone, scattered about you know not where. The cause of this dissipation is that in the beginning you deliberately listened to the thought, answered it, took it to yourself and let it continue unheeded.

Yet what it said was nonetheless both good and holy. Yes indeed, so holy that if any man or woman should think to come to contemplation without many sweet meditations of this sort, on their own wretched state, on the passion, the kindness and the great goodness and the worthiness of God, they will certainly be deceived and fail in their purpose. At the same time, those men and women who are long practised in these meditations must leave them aside, put them down and hold them far under the cloud of forgetting, if they are ever to pierce the cloud of unknowing between them and their God.

Therefore, when you set yourself to this exercise, and experience by grace that you are called by God to it, then lift up your heart to God by a humble impulse of love, and mean the God who made you and ransomed you, and has in his grace called you to this exercise. Have no other thought of God; and not even any of these thoughts unless it should please you. For a simple reaching out directly towards God is sufficient, without any other cause except himself. If you like, you can have this reaching out, wrapped up and enfolded in a single word. So as to have a better grasp of it, take just a little word, of one syllable rather than of two; for the shorter it is the better it is in agreement with this exercise of the spirit. Such a one is the word "God" or the word "love." Choose which one you prefer, or any other according to your liking—the word of one syllable that you like best. Fasten this word to your heart, so that whatever happens it will never go away. This word is to be your shield and your spear, whether you are riding in peace or in war. With this word you are to beat upon this cloud and this darkness above you. With this word you are to strike down every kind of thought under the cloud of forgetting; so that if any thought should press upon you and ask you what you would have, answer it with no other word but with this one. If the thought should offer you, out of its great learning, to analyse that word for you and to tell you its meanings, say to the thought that you want to keep it whole, and not taken apart or unfastened. If you will hold fast to this purpose, you may be sure that the thought will not stay for very long. And why? Because you will not allow it to feed itself on the sort of sweet meditations that we mentioned before.

CHAPTER VIII
An accurate treatment, by question and answer, of certain doubts that may arise during this exercise; the suppression of rational investigation, knowledge and intellectual acumen; distinguishing the various levels and divisions of the active and contemplative lives.

But now you will ask, "What is this thought that presses upon me in this work, and is it a good or an evil thing?" "If it is an evil thing," you say, "then I am very much surprised, because it serves so well to increase a man's devotion; and at times I believe that it is a great comfort to listen to what it has to say. For I believe that sometimes it can make me weep very bitterly out of compassion for Christ in his passion, and sometimes for my own wretched state, and for many other reasons. All these, it seems to me, are very holy and do me much good. And therefore I believe that these thoughts can in no way be evil; and if it is good, and their sweet tales do me so much good, then I am very surprised why you bid me put them deep down under the cloud of forgetting!"

This strikes me as being a very good question. And so I must reflect in order to answer it as well as my feebleness permits. First, when you ask me what this thought is that presses so hard upon you in this exercise, offering to help you in this work, I answer that it is a well-defined and clear sight of your natural intelligence imprinted upon your reason within your soul. And when you ask me whether it is good or evil, I say that it must of necessity be always good in its nature, because it is a ray of God's likeness. But the use of it can be both good and evil. It is good when it is illuminated by grace, so that you may see your wretched state, the passion, the kindness and the wonderful works of God in his creatures, bodily and spiritual. And so it is no wonder that it increases your devotion as much as you say. But the use of it is evil when it is swollen with pride, and with the curiosity which comes from the subtle speculation and learning, such as theologians have, which makes them want to be known not as humble clerics and masters of divinity or of devotion, but proud scholars of the devil and masters of vanity and falsehood. And in other men and women, whether they be religious or seculars, the use and exercise of this natural understanding is evil when it is swollen with proud and clever learning of worldly things and earthly ideas, for the coveting of worldly honours and rich possessions, and the pleasure and vainglory which comes from men's flatterings.

Next, you ask me why you should put down such thoughts under the cloud of forgetting, since it is true that they are good of their kind, and when well used they do you so much good and greatly increase your devotion. My answer is that you must clearly understand that there are two kinds of lives in holy Church. One is the active life, and the other is the contemplative life. The active life is the lower and the contemplative life is the higher. Active life has two degrees, a higher and a lower; and the contemplative life also has two degrees, a lower and a higher. Further, these two lives are so joined together that though in part they are different, neither of them can be lived fully without having some part in the other. For the higher part of the active life is the same as the lower part of the contemplative life. Hence, a man cannot be fully active unless he is partly a contemplative, nor can he be fully contemplative here below unless he is in some way active. It is the nature of the active life both to be begun and ended in this life. Not so, however, of the contemplative life, which is begun in this life and shall last without end. That is why the part that Mary chose shall never be taken away. The active life is troubled and anxious about many things; but the contemplative sits in peace, intent only on one thing.

The lower part of the active life consists in good and honest corporal works of mercy and of charity. The higher part of the active life, and the lower part of the contemplative, consists in good spiritual meditations and earnest consideration of a man's own wretched state with sorrow and contrition, of the passion of Christ and of his servants with pity and compassion, and of the wonderful gifts, kindness, and works of God in all his creatures, corporeal and spiritual, with thanksgiving and praise. But the higher part of contemplation, insofar as it is possible to possess it here below, consists entirely in this darkness and in this cloud of unknowing, with a loving impulse and a dark gazing into the simple being of God himself alone.

In the lower part of the active life, a man is outside himself and beneath himself. In the higher part of the active life, and the lower part of the contemplative life, a man is within himself and on a par with himself. But in the higher part of the contemplative life, a man is above himself and under his God. He is above himself, because he makes it his purpose to arrive by grace whither he cannot come by nature: that is to say, to be knit to God in spirit, in oneness of love and union of wills.

One can understand that it is impossible for a man to come to the higher part of the active life unless he leaves, for a time, the lower part. In the same way, a man cannot come to the higher part of the contemplative life unless he leaves for a time the lower part. It would be a wrong thing for a man engaged on meditation, and a hindrance to him, to turn his mind to the outward corporal works which he had done or should do, even though in themselves they are very holy works. In the same way, it would be very inappropriate and a great hindrance to a man who ought to be working in this darkness and in this cloud of unknowing, with an affective impulse of love to God for himself alone, to permit any thought or any meditation on God's wonderful gifts, kindness or his work in any of his creatures, bodily or spiritual, to rise up in his mind so as to press between him and his God, even if they should be very holy thoughts, and give him great happiness and consolation.

This is the reason why I bid you put down any such clear and insinuating thought, and cover it up with a thick cloud of forgetting, no matter how holy it might be, and no matter how well it might promise to help you in your endeavour. Because it is love alone that can reach God in this life, and not knowing. For as long as the soul dwells in this mortal body, the clarity of our understanding in the contemplation of all spiritual things, and especially of God, is always mixed up with some sort of imagination; and because of it this exercise of ours would be tainted, and it would be very surprising if it did not lead us into great error.

CHAPTER IX
During this exercise, the calling to mind of the holiest creature God ever made is a hindrance rather than a help.

The intense activity, therefore, of your understanding, which will always press upon you when you set yourself to this dark contemplation, must always be put down. For if you do not put it down it will put you down; so much so that when you imagine that you can best abide in this darkness, and that nothing is in your mind except God alone, if you take a close look, you will find that your mind is occupied, not with this darkness, but with a clear picture of something beneath God. If this is in fact so, then indeed that thing is above you for the moment, and between you and your God. So set yourself to put down such clear pictures, no matter how holy or how pleasant they may be.

One thing I must tell you. This blind impulse of love towards God for himself alone, this secret love beating on this cloud of unknowing, is more profitable for the salvation of your soul, more worthy in itself, and more pleasing to God, and to all the saints and angels in heaven; yes and of more use to all your friends both bodily and spiritually, whether they are alive or dead. And it is better for you to experience this spiritually in your affection than it is to have the eye of your soul opened in contemplation either in seeing all the angels and the saints in heaven, or in hearing all the mirth or the melody that is amongst those who are in bliss.

Nor need you be surprised at what I say; for if you could once see it as clearly as you can come by grace to touch it and to experience it in this life, you would think as I do. But take it for granted that no man shall ever have such clear sight here in this life; but the feeling—that a man can have through grace, when God deigns to grant it. So lift up your love to that cloud; or rather, if I am to speak more truthfully, let God draw your love up to that cloud; and try, through the help of his grace, to forget every other thing.

A simple awareness of anything under God, which forces itself upon your will and consciousness, puts you further away from God than you would be if it did not exist; it hinders you and makes you less able to feel, by experience, the fruit of his love. How much more, then, do you think that an awareness which is drawn to yourself knowingly and deliberately, will hinder you in your purpose? And if the consciousness of any particular saint or pure spiritual thing hinders you so much, how do you think that the consciousness of any living person in this wretched life or any corporal or worldly thing will hinder you and be an obstacle to you in this exercise?

I am not saying that any such simple, sudden thought of any good and pure spiritual thing under God which presses against your will or your understanding, or is wilfully drawn into your mind deliberately in order to increase your devotion, is therefore evil, even though it is a hindrance to this sort of exercise; and God forbid that you should understand it so! But I do say that in spite of its goodness and holiness, in this exercise it is more of a hindrance than a help—I mean during the time of the exercise. For certainly, he who seeks to have God perfectly will not take his rest in the consciousness of any angel or any saint that is in heaven.

SELECTED BIBLIOGRAPHY

TEXTS AND TRANSLATIONS

The Cloud of Unknowing. Edited by Phyllis Hodgson. London and New York: Early English Text Society, 1944. Rev. ed. Oxford: Oxford University Press, 1958. A critical edition, containing also *The Epistle of Privy Counsel.*

The Cloud of Unknowing and Related Treatises. Edited by Phyllis Hodgson. Analecta Cartusiana, 3. Salzburg, 1982.

The Cloud of Unknowing. Translated by James Walsh, S.J. The Classics of Western Spirituality. New York: Paulist; London: SPCK, 1981.

The Cloud of Unknowing and Other Works. Translated by Clifton Wolters. Harmondsworth and New York: Penguin, 1978.

STUDIES

Egan, Harvey, S.J. "Mystical Crosscurrents." *Communio* 7 (1980): 4–20.

Johnston, William, S.J. *The Mysticism of the Cloud of Unknowing.* New York: Harper and Row, 1967.

Knowles, David, O.S.B. "The Excellence of the *Cloud.*" *Downside Review* 52 (1934): 71–92.

Nieva, Constantino S. *This Transcending God: The Teaching of the Author of the Cloud of Unknowing.* London: Mitre, 1970.

Strolle, Charles P. "The Primacy of Love in *The Cloud of Unknowing.*" *Review for Religious* 40 (1981): 736–58.

Catherine of Siena

(1347–1380)

St. Catherine (Caterina di Giacomo di Benincasa) was born in Siena in 1347. When seven she vowed herself to virginity and when sixteen joined an Order of Penance (the *Mantellate*) affiliated to the Order of Preachers founded by St. Dominic. She lived in seclusion for a while, but soon became active in society and politics. She worked among the sick and the poor of Siena, acted as ambassador between the papacy and the city-state of Florence, and encouraged a Crusade to the Holy Land. She was also an influence on the move of the papacy from Avignon to Rome.[1]

Catherine died in 1380, so her life was a short, though remarkable one, much noticed by contemporaries.[2] On subsequent generations, however, her impact has been chiefly literary. Today she is best known for her *Dialogue,* probably begun in 1377.[3] Extracts from this appear below, together with characteristic material derived from the letters of St. Catherine, which are, in their way, as famous as the *Dialogue,* for Catherine was one of the great letter-writers of her century. Some four hundred remain, and they provide a splendid glimpse both of her character and her theology. The same can be said of her prayers, not reproduced here but in which readers will find much that is already familiar from Catherine's more systematic writings.[4]

Certain schools of thought sharply distinguish between mysticism and theology, and by their canons the description of Catherine as chiefly a mystic is not without foun-

---

1. For a general, though antique, account of Catherine's life, see A. T. Drane, *The History of St. Catherine of Siena and Her Companions* (London, 1880). Other biographical sources are cited in Noffke (see note 3 below).

2. She attracted a large following which included Raymond of Capua (c.1330–1399), who became Master General of the Dominican Order and whose program of reform for the Order was influenced by her. His *Legenda* is the earliest biography of Catherine. See *The Life of Catherine of Siena by Raymond of Capua,* trans. Conleth Kearns, O.P. (Wilmington, Del., and Dublin, 1980).

3. *Catherine of Siena: The Dialogue,* trans. Suzanne Noffke, O.P. (New York, 1980). References to the *Dialogue* are to this edition, abbreviated "D," and are page references.

4. For some of Catherine's letters see *I, Catherine: Selected Writings of St. Catherine of Siena,* ed. and trans. Kenelm Foster, O.P., and Mary John Ronayne, O.P. (London, 1980), which also contains a summary of Catherine's life and spiritual teaching. For her prayers see *The Prayers of Catherine of Siena,* ed. Suzanne Noffke, O.P. (New York, 1983). References to the letters and prayers here are to these editions, abbreviated "L" and "P," and are page references.

dation. She was severely ascetic throughout a life marked by a series of dramatic religious experiences, including a "mystical espousal" to Christ in 1368, a "mystical death" in 1370, and the reception of the stigmata in 1380. But in 1970 she was proclaimed a Doctor of the Roman Catholic Church, for she was a great teacher, offering a consistent Christian vision. In this sense, she is very much a theologian, arguably a very good one.

As with her fellow Dominican St. Thomas Aquinas (1224/5–1273), behind everything Catherine writes is an insistence on creation. For both writers, everything totally depends on God for its being as long as it lasts (D, 56–57, 95, 114; P, 18, 122–23, 186; cf. *Summa Theologiae,* Ia.44–45), which in Catherine's judgment has implications: it throws light on sin and suffering. Sin, she concludes, is a kind of non-being, and the sinner is somehow unreal (D, 73, 76, 95; P, 18). In the end, she argues, suffering must be a means to something good, something which falls within the providence of God (D, 142, 187, 226; L, 147–49). This, in turn, leads her to a note of optimism. With no doctrine of universal salvation, she sometimes dwells on hell in a way which might make one uncomfortable (D, 78–82). But, like her contemporary Julian of Norwich, from the concept of God's providence, and of God as Creator, Catherine concludes that creation tends to what is good (D, 226; in Julian cf. *Showings* [Long Text], ch. 11). So she maintains that it would be wrong to be utterly dismayed even by the awfulness of sin. Marks of discernment for her include patience and resistance to scandal (D, 282–93). Like Jean-Pierre de Caussade (1675–1751), she emphasizes that everything should be held in

reverence (D, 142, 187, 194, 283). God's nature and providence imply that we may simply not be the best judges concerning what we find around us. Our business is trustingly to leave things to God. He knows what he is doing, and he is to be trusted because he loves us.

On the theme of God's love, Catherine waxes long and eloquently, taking the familiar biblical teaching that God is Love (1 Jn 4:16) and presenting it in a way both theologically reflective and practically applicable. God as the unchangeable source of everything has nothing to gain from his creatures and everything is as nothing by comparison with him. But this does not mean that he is distant, remote. He is, on the contrary, the "mad lover" (D, 325). He has no need of us, but the moral to draw is that his love is therefore total since nothing wrings it from him and he has nothing to gain from it. Given this conclusion she can develop two main points. First, we have a reason for loving which is grounded in the nature of God himself; we can be what God is (D, 58; P, 90–91, 101–2). Second, from eternity God has found us in himself, which for Catherine implies that we are, in a sense, by nature divine, loved by God as he loves himself and made in his image as Trinity, an image progressively restored in us as we come to know Christ (D, 46, 49–50, 58, 63, 117, 205, 297). In this scheme, creation and redemption form a unity where redemption restores that for which creation was intended (D, 71, 273). Here there are two senses in which we can speak of God's image, for if it is something given *to* humanity by God, in the person of Christ it is also something taken by God *from* humanity (D, 46 and 205).

"Christian mystics" vary in approaching

the incarnation. We should therefore stress that Catherine (unlike, say, the author of *The Cloud of Unknowing*) is "manifestly 'christocentric,' in that the Incarnate God is right in the centre of her vision; . . . reflections on the soul's way to God are very largely a minute and extraordinarily physical, incarnational study of Christ himself, especially of Christ bleeding on the cross."[5] We cannot know God in his essence, Catherine concedes, but in Christ we have a clue to what God is: Christ is God and God in Christ reveals himself to be Love. "The fiery chariot of my only begotten Son came to bring the fire of my charity," says the Father in the *Dialogue* (D, 112), a teaching to which Catherine constantly returns. Christ is the Bridge between God and humanity (D, 64–160), the embodiment of God's love for people, while those who love him are "one thing" with God (D, 116–17; cf. 26).

Not surprisingly, Catherine's criterion of Christian perfection is charity. She emphasizes the value of faith, hope, and prayer (L, 65–66; D, 122–27), but finds the life of God in the practice of charity, which serves as a means of defining "sin." Anyone with charity is "another" Christ (D, 26); "all virtues are built on charity"; and "every sin committed against me is done by means of your neighbors" (D, 35–36; cf. 33–34, 45–46, 218).[6] And for Catherine it is important that this is something we should *know.* Wickedness is essentially a form of *stupidity,* or *ignorance,* and a dominant theme in her teaching is the need to know ourselves, which means recognizing the nature of God and how we are united with him. In Catherine's judgment, knowing the significance of charity is essentially to know everything, to know God, whom Catherine frequently refers to simply as "Truth."[7] We are reasoning creatures made for Truth (D, 26, 131–32, 173–74; L, 104, 136, 143; P, 35, 193–94). Or, as she also puts it, we are made for Love, and insofar as we know that, we also have knowledge of God (L, 207–8, 89–91, 111–13).

The *Dialogue* begins by stressing the need for self-knowledge and it ends by saying that this is achieved only by finding oneself in the context of the God revealed in Christ. And that, in a nutshell, is the teaching of St. Catherine. She spices it with a good deal of practical counsel and admonition. But it is the nerve of her doctrine. For it we are indebted to her.

5. Kenelm Foster, O.P., "St. Catherine's Teaching on Christ," *Life of the Spirit* 16 (1962): 313.

6. The concept of charity has an effect on Catherine's teaching on prayer, which she identifies with charity (D, 122–27). Her views on charity also lead her sometimes to favor apostolic activity over devout seclusion (L, 226–27).

7. *Prima Verità* and *prima dolce Verità* are among Catherine's favorite names for God and Christ (D, 27, 48, 160, 163, 187).

Selections

THE DIALOGUE*

73

Up to now I have shown you in many ways how the soul rises up from imperfection and comes to perfect love, and what she does after she has attained the love of friendship and filial love.

I told you that she came this far by dint of perseverance and shutting herself up in the house of self-knowledge. (But this self-knowledge must be seasoned with knowledge of me, or it would end in confusion.) For through self-knowledge the soul learns contempt for her selfish sensual passion and for pleasure in her own consolation. And from contempt grounded in humility she draws patience, which will make her strong in the face of the devil's attacks and other people's persecutions, and strong in my presence when for her own good I take away her spiritual pleasure. With this power she will endure it all.

And if difficulties make her selfish sensuality want to rise up against reason, her conscience must use [holy] hatred to pronounce judgment and not let any impulse pass uncorrected. Indeed the soul who lives in [holy] hatred finds self-correction and self-reproach in everything—not only in those [movements] which are against reason but often even in those which come from me. This is what my gentle servant Gregory meant when he said that a holy and pure conscience makes sin where there is no sin. In other words, the soul in the purity of her conscience sees guilt even where there was no guilt.

Now the soul who would rise up from imperfection by awaiting my providence in the house of self-knowledge with the lamp of faith ought to do and does just as the disciples did. They waited in the house and did not move from there, but persevered in watching and in constant humble prayer until the coming of the Holy Spirit.

This, as I have told you, is what the soul does when she has risen from imperfection and shuts herself up at home to attain perfection. She remains watching, gazing with her mind's eye into the teaching of my Truth. She is humbled, for in constant prayer (that is, in holy and true desire) she has come to know herself, and in herself she has come to know my affectionate charity.

74

Now it remains to say how one can tell that a soul has attained perfect love. The sign is the same as that given to the holy disciples after they had received the Holy

---

*From *Catherine of Siena: The Dialogue,* trans. Suzanne Noffke, O.P., The Classics of Western Spirituality (New York: Paulist, 1980), 135–37, 144–47, 363–66. Reprinted with permission of the publisher.

Spirit. They left the house and fearlessly preached my message by proclaiming the teaching of the Word, my only-begotten Son. They had no fear of suffering. No, they even gloried in suffering. It did not worry them to go before the tyrants of the world to proclaim the truth to them for the glory and praise of my name.

So it is with the soul who has waited for me in self-knowledge: I come back to her with the fire of my charity. In that charity she conceived the virtues through perseverance when she stayed at home, sharing in my power. And in that power and virtue she mastered and conquered her selfish sensual passion.

In that same charity I shared with her the wisdom of my Son, and in that wisdom she saw and came to know, with her mind's eye, my truth and the delusions of spiritual sensuality, that is, the imperfect love of one's own consolation. And she came to know the malice and deceit the devil works on the soul who is bound up in that imperfect love. So she rose up in contempt of that imperfection and in love for perfection.

I gave her a share in this love, which is the Holy Spirit, within her will by making her will strong to endure suffering and to leave her house in my name to give birth to the virtues for her neighbors. Not that she abandons the house of self-knowledge, but the virtues conceived by the impulse of love come forth from that house. She gives birth to them as her neighbors need them, in many different ways. For the fear she had of not showing herself lest she lose her own consolations is gone. After she has come to perfect, free love, she lets go of herself and comes out, as I have described.

And this brings her to the fourth stage. That is, after the third stage, the stage of perfection in which she both tastes and gives birth to charity in the person of her neighbor, she is graced with a final stage of perfect union with me. These two stages are linked together, for the one is never found without the other any more than charity for me can exist without charity for one's neighbors or the latter without charity for me. The one cannot be separated from the other. Even so, neither of these two stages can exist without the other. . . .

78

Now I would not refrain from telling you with what delight these souls enjoy me while still in their mortal bodies. For having arrived at the third stage, as I have told you, they now reach the fourth. Not that they leave the third. The two are joined together, nor can the one exist without the other any more than charity for me without charity for your neighbor. But there is a fruit that comes from this third stage, from the soul's perfect union with me. She receives strength upon strength until she no longer merely suffers with patience, but eagerly longs to suffer for the glory and praise of my name.

Such souls glory in the shame of my only-begotten Son, as my trumpeter the glorious Paul said: "I glory in the hardships and shame of Christ crucified." And in another place he says, "I bear in my body the marks of Christ crucified." So these also run to the table of the most holy cross, in love with my love and hungry for the food of souls. They want to be of service to their neighbors in pain and suffering, and to learn and preserve the virtues while bearing the marks of Christ in their bodies. In other words, their anguished love shines forth in their bodies, evidenced in their contempt for themselves and in their delight in shame as they endure difficulties and suffering however and from whatever source I grant them.

To such very dear children as these, suffering is a delight and pleasure is wearisome, as is every consolation or delight the world may offer them. And not only what the world gives them through my dispensation (for my kindness sometimes constrains the world's servants to hold them in reverence and help them in their physical needs) but even the spiritual consolation they receive from me, the eternal Father—even this they scorn because of their humility and contempt for themselves. It is not, however, the consolation, my gift and grace, that they scorn, but the pleasure their soul's desire finds in that consolation. This is because of the true humility they have learned from holy hatred, which humility is charity's governess and wet nurse, and is learned in truly knowing themselves and me. So you see how virtue and the wounds of Christ crucified shine forth in their bodies and spirits.

To such as these it is granted never to feel my absence. I told you how I go away from others (in feeling only, not in grace) and then return. I do not act thus with these most perfect ones who have attained great perfection and are completely dead to every selfish impulse. No, I am always at rest in their souls both by grace and by feeling. In other words, they can join their spirits with me in loving affection whenever they will. For through loving affection their desire has reached such union that nothing can separate it [from me]. Every time and place is for them a time and place of prayer. For their conversation has been lifted up from the earth and has climbed up to heaven. In other words, they have shed every earthly affection and sensual selfishness and have risen above themselves to the height of heaven by the stairway of virtue, having climbed the three stairs that I symbolized for you in the body of my only-begotten Son.

At the first step they put off love of vice from the feet of their affection. At the second they taste the secret and the love of his heart and there conceive love in virtue. At the third step of spiritual peace and calm they prove their virtue, and rising up from imperfect love they come to great perfection. Thus have these found rest in the teaching of my Truth. They have found table and food and waiter, and they taste this food through the teaching of Christ crucified, my only-begotten Son.

I am their bed and table. This gentle loving Word is their food, because they taste the food of souls in this glorious Word and because he himself is the food I have given you: his flesh and blood, wholly God and wholly human, which you receive in the sacrament of the altar, established and given to you by my kindness while you are pilgrims and travelers, so that you may not slacken your pace because of weakness, nor forget the blessing of the blood poured forth for you with such burning love, but may be constantly strengthened and filled with pleasure as you walk. The Holy Spirit, my loving charity, is the waiter who serves them my gifts and graces.

This gentle waiter carries to me their tender loving desires, and carries back to them the reward for their labors, the sweetness of my charity for their enjoyment and nourishment. So you see, I am their table, my Son is their food, and the Holy Spirit, who proceeds from me the Father and from the Son, waits on them.

You see, then, how they feel me constantly present to their spirits. And the more they have scorned pleasure and been willing to suffer, the more they have lost suffering and gained pleasure. Why? Because they are enflamed and on fire in my charity,where their own will is consumed. So the devil is afraid of the club of their charity, and that is why he shoots his arrows from far off and does not dare come near. The world strikes at the husk of their bodies, but though it thinks it is hurting, it is itself hurt, for the arrow that finds nowhere to enter returns to the one who shot it. So it is with the world and its arrows of insult and persecution and grumbling: When it shoots them at my most perfect servants, they find no place at all where they can enter because the soul's orchard is closed to them. So the arrow poisoned with the venom of sin returns to the one who shot it.

You see, they cannot be struck from any side, because what may strike the body cannot strike the soul, which remains at once happy and sad: sad because of her neighbor's sin, happy because of the union [with me] and the loving charity she has received for herself.

These souls follow the spotless Lamb, my only-begotten Son, who was both happy and sad on the cross. He was sad as he carried the cross of his suffering body and the cross of his longing to make satisfaction for the sin of humankind. And he was happy because his divine nature joined with his human nature could not suffer and made his soul always happy by showing itself to him unveiled. This is why he was at once happy and sad, because his flesh bore the pain the Godhead could not suffer—nor even his soul, so far as the superior part of his intellect was concerned.

So it is with these very dear children. When they have attained the third and fourth stage they are sad as they carry their actual and spiritual cross by actually enduring physical pain as I permit it, and the cross of desire, their crucifying sorrow at the offense done to me and the harm done to their neighbors. They are happy, I say, because the delight of charity that makes them happy can never be taken away from them, and in this they receive gladness and blessedness. Therefore their sadness is called not "distressing sadness" that dries up the soul, but "fattening sadness" that fattens the soul in loving charity, because sufferings increase and strengthen virtue, make it grow and prove it.

So their suffering is fattening, not distressing, because no sadness or pain can drag them out of the fire. They are like the burning coal that no one can put out once it is completely consumed in the furnace, because it has itself been turned into fire. So it is with these souls cast into the furnace of my charity, who keep nothing at all, not a bit of their own will, outside of me, but are completely set afire in me. There is no one who can seize them or drag them out of my grace. They have been made one with me and I with them. I will never withdraw from their feelings. No, their spirits always feel my presence within them, whereas of the others I told you that I come and go, leaving in terms of feeling, not in terms of grace, and I do this to bring them to perfection. When they reach perfection I relieve them of this lover's game of going and coming back. I call it a "lover's game" because I go away for love and I come back for love—no, not really I, for I am your unchanging and unchangeable God; what goes and comes back is the feeling my charity creates in the soul. . . .

167

Now that soul had seen the truth and the excellence of obedience with the eye of her understanding, and had known it by the light of most holy faith; she had heard it with feeling and tasted it with anguished longing in her will as she gazed into the divine majesty. So she gave him thanks, saying:

Thanks, thanks be to you, eternal Father, that you have not despised me, your handiwork, nor turned your face from me, nor made light of these desires of mine. You, Light, have disregarded my darksomeness; you, Life, have not considered that I am death; nor you, Doctor, considered these grave weaknesses of mine. You, eternal Purity, have disregarded my wretched filthiness; you who are infinite have overlooked the fact that I am finite, and you, Wisdom, the fact that I am foolishness.

For all these and so many other endless evils and sins of mine, your wisdom, your kindness, your mercy, your infinite goodness have not despised me. No, in your light you have given me light. In your wisdom I have come to know the truth; in your mercy I have found your charity and affection for my neighbors. What has compelled you? Not my virtues, but only your charity.

Let this same love compel you to enlighten the eye of my understanding with the light of faith, so that I may know your truth, which you have revealed to me. Let my memory be great enough to hold your favors, and set my will ablaze in your charity's fire. Let that fire burst the seed of my body and bring forth blood; then with that blood, given for love of your blood, and with the key of obedience, let me unlock heaven's gate.

I heartily ask the same of you for every reasoning creature, all and each of them, and for the mystic body of holy Church. I acknowledge and do not deny that you loved me before I existed, and that you love me unspeakably much, as one gone mad over your creature.

O eternal Trinity! O Godhead! That Godhead, your divine nature, gave the price of your Son's blood its value. You, eternal Trinity, are a deep sea: The more I enter you, the more I discover, and the more I discover, the more I seek you. You are insatiable, you in whose depth the soul is sated yet remains always hungry for you, thirsty for you, eternal Trinity, longing to see you with the light in your light. Just as the deer longs for the fountain of living water, so does my soul long to escape from the prison of my darksome body and see you in truth. O how long will you hide your face from my eyes?

O eternal Trinity, fire and abyss of charity, dissolve this very day the cloud of my body! I am driven to desire, in the knowledge of yourself that you have given me in your truth, to leave behind the weight of this body of mine and give my life for the glory and praise of your name. For by the light of understanding within your light I have tasted and seen your depth, eternal Trinity, and the beauty of your creation. Then, when I considered myself in you, I saw that I am your image. You have gifted me with power from yourself, eternal Father, and my understanding with your wisdom—such wisdom as is proper to your only-begotten Son; and the Holy Spirit, who proceeds from you and from your Son, has given me a will, and so I am able to love.

You, eternal Trinity, are the craftsman; and I your handiwork have come to know that you are in love with the beauty of what you have made, since you made of me a new creation in the blood of your Son.

O abyss! O eternal Godhead! O deep sea! What more could you have given me than the gift of your very self?

You are a fire always burning but never consuming; you are a fire consuming in your heat all the soul's selfish love; you are a fire lifting all chill and giving light. In your light you have made me know your truth: You are that light beyond all light who gives the mind's eye supernatural light in such fullness and perfection that you bring clarity even to the light of faith. In that faith I see that my soul has life, and in that light receives you who are Light.

In the light of faith I gain wisdom in the wisdom of the Word your Son; in the light of faith I am strong, constant, persevering; in the light of faith I have hope: It does not let me faint along the way. This light teaches me the way, and without this light I would be walking in the dark. This is why I asked you, eternal Father, to enlighten me with the light of most holy faith.

Truly this light is a sea, for it nourishes the soul in you, peaceful sea, eternal Trinity. Its water is not sluggish; so the soul is not afraid because she knows the truth. It distills, revealing hidden things, so that here, where the most abundant light of your faith abounds, the soul has, as it were, a guarantee of what she believes. This water is a mirror in which you, eternal Trinity, grant me knowledge; for when I look into this mirror, holding it in the hand of love, it shows me myself, as your creation, in you, and you in me through the union you have brought about of the Godhead with our humanity.

This light shows you to me, and in this light I know you, highest and infinite Good: Good above every good, joyous Good, Good beyond measure and understanding! Beauty above all beauty; Wisdom above all wisdom—indeed you are wisdom itself! You who are the angels' food are given to humans with burning love. You, garment who cover all nakedness, pasture the starving within your sweetness, for you are sweet without trace of bitterness.

O eternal Trinity, when I received with the light of most holy faith your light that you gave me, I came to know therein the way of great perfection, made smooth for me by so many wonderful explanations. Thus I may serve you in the light, not in the dark; and I may be a mirror of a good and holy life; and I may rouse myself from my wretched life in which, always through my own fault, I have served you in darkness. I did not know your truth, and so I did not love it. Why did I not know you? Because I did not see you with the glorious light of most holy faith, since the cloud of selfish love darkened the eye of my understanding. Then with your light, eternal Trinity, you dispelled the darkness.

But who could reach to your height to thank you for so immeasurable a gift, for such generous favors, for the teaching of truth that you have given me? A special grace, this, beyond the common grace you give to other creatures. You willed to bend down to my need and that of others who might see themselves mirrored here.

You responded, Lord; you yourself have given and you yourself answered and satisfied me by flooding me with a gracious light, so that with that light I may return thanks to you. Clothe, clothe me with yourself, eternal Truth, so that I may run the course of this mortal life in true obedience and in the light of most holy faith. With that light I sense my soul once again becoming drunk! Thanks be to God! Amen.

LETTER 55*

To: *Monna Catella, Monna Cecia Planula and Monna Caterina Dentice, of Naples.*[1]

Date: May/June 1379.

---

*From I, Catherine: Selected Writings of St. Catherine of Siena, ed. and trans. Kenelm Foster, O.P., and Mary John Ronayne, O.P. (London: Collins, 1980), 239–41. Reprinted with permission of the publisher.

1. Little is known about these three women except that they were devoted to Catherine. She acquired a number of disciples in Naples, mainly perhaps through her contacts in Rome, with emissaries from Queen Joanna and her Court.

I say then that when a soul has tasted this angelic food it sees by the light [of holy faith] that to love and associate with creatures apart from the Creator is to put an obstacle between itself and this food. So it makes every effort to avoid them, and also to love and pursue anything that will make it grow and abide in virtue. Realizing, too, that this food is best savoured through prayer based on self-knowledge, it practises this continually, as it practises all other ways of drawing closer to God.

There are three ways of praying. The first is that abiding holy desire which prays to God in everything we creatures do, for it directs all our spiritual and bodily actions in his honour, and so is called continuous. The glorious Saint Paul seems to have meant this kind of prayer when he said: "Pray without ceasing." Then there is vocal prayer, as when the tongue is used in reciting the Office or other vocal prayers. This is a preparation for the third kind of prayer, namely mental, which the soul comes to when it practises vocal prayer prudently and humbly; that is when, as the tongue prays, the heart is not far from God.

But one must endeavour to establish the heart firmly in a love for divine Charity. And whenever one feels God visiting one's mind, drawing it in some way to think of the Creator, one should stop praying vocally and rest lovingly in whatever one feels this visitation to be. If there is still time when this has passed, the soul should resume its vocal prayer so that the mind will always be full and not empty. And even if the prayer abounds in battles of all kinds, in darkness and great confusion of mind, with the devil suggesting that our prayer is not pleasing to God, we must not give up prayer on this account, but persist with fortitude and unfailing perseverance, realizing that this is the devil's way of enticing us away from our mother, prayer; and that God permits this to test in us our fortitude and constancy and also so that, in the struggles and darkness, we may know our own nothingness, while in the good will [that we perceive in ourselves] we know the goodness of God, who gives and upholds our good and holy desires, and will not refuse this gift to those who ask him.

The soul thus comes to the third and last kind of [fully] mental prayer, in which it receives the fruit of the efforts it has put into the less perfect vocal prayer, for it now savours the milk of fidelity to prayer. It lifts itself above the crude level of feeling and with the mind as of an angel is made one with God by love; by the light of its understanding it sees, knows and is clothed with the Truth. Made now sister to the angels, seated with the Bridegroom at the table of crucified desire, it delights in seeking God's honour and the salvation of souls for which, it now sees clearly, the eternal Bridegroom ran to meet the shameful death of the cross and, in so doing, obeyed his Father's will and achieved our salvation. Such prayer is indeed a mother, conceiving her children, the virtues, in God's love, and giving birth to them in love for others. Where do you find the light that guides you in the way of truth? In prayer. And where do you display love, faith, hope and humility? Again, in prayer. You would not be doing these things unless you loved them, and it is because a creature loves that it seeks to be one with the thing it loves, [that is, with God]. By prayer you ask him for what you need. Knowing yourself—and true prayer is founded on this knowledge—you see you are in great need and feel surrounded by your enemies: the world, with its hurts; the devil, with all his temptations; and the flesh, ever warring against the spirit by rebelling against reason. You see, too, that of yourself you are not; and since you are not, you cannot help yourself; so you turn, with faith, to him who IS; who knows your needs and can and will help you in them. You ask with hope, then wait for his help. This is how we must pray if we are to get what we desire. No right thing will ever be denied us if we ask the divine Goodness for it in this way, but we would get very little benefit from praying in any other.

Where shall we sense the fragrance of obedience, if not in prayer? Where strip ourselves of the self-love that makes us impatient when insulted or made to suffer? Or put on a divine love that will make us patient, and ready to glory in the cross of Christ crucified? In prayer. And where shall we sense the sweet perfume of virginity and purity, and a hunger for martyrdom that will make us ready to give our lives for the honour of God and the salvation of souls? In this sweet mother, prayer. She will make us obey God's holy commandments, and seal her counsels into our hearts and minds by imprinting on us the desire to keep them until death. She withdraws us from the company of creatures and gives us the Creator as companion. She fills the vessel of our heart with the blood of the humble spotless Lamb and clothes it in Fire, for by the fire of Love was it shed.

A soul will of course receive and savour this mother, prayer, more or less perfectly according as it feeds on the angelic food of true and holy desire for God, raising itself up, as I said, to take it from the table of the most sweet cross. And that is why I said I wanted to see each of you partaking of this angelic food, for you could not have the life of grace or be true servants of Christ crucified in any other way. I will say no more. Abide in the sweet and holy love of God. . . .

SELECTED BIBLIOGRAPHY

TEXTS AND TRANSLATIONS

Il Dialogo della Divina Provvidenza. Edited by Giuliana Cavallini. Rome, 1968.
Epistolario di santa Caterina. Edited by D. U. Meattini. Rome, 1966.
Le Orazioni. Edited by Giuliana Cavallini. Rome, 1978.

Catherine of Siena: The Dialogue. Translated by Suzanne Noffke, O.P. The Classics of Western Spirituality. New York: Paulist; London: SPCK, 1980.

I, Catherine: Selected Writings of St Catherine of Siena. Translated by Kenelm Foster, O.P., and Mary John Ronayne, O.P. London: Collins, 1980.

The Prayers of Catherine of Siena. Translated by Suzanne Noffke, O.P. New York: Paulist, 1983.

STUDIES

Fatula, Mary Ann, O.P. *Catherine of Siena's Way.* The Way of the Christian Mystics. Wilmington, Del.: Michael Glazier, 1987.

Fawtier, Robert. *Sainte Catherine de Sienne: Essaie de critique des sources.* 2 vols. Paris, 1921 and 1930.

Foster, Kenelm, O.P. "St. Catherine's Teaching on Christ." *Life of the Spirit* 16 (1962): 310–23.

Gardner, Edmund G. *Saint Catherine of Siena: A Study in the Religion, Literature and History of the Fourteenth Century in Italy.* London: E. P. Dent, 1907.

Perrin, Joseph Marie. *Catherine of Siena.* Translated by Paul Barrett. Westminster, Md.: Newman, 1965.

Raymond of Capua. *The Life of Catherine of Siena by Raymond of Capua.* Translated by Conleth Kearns. Wilmington, Del.: Michael Glazier; Dublin: Dominican Publications, 1980.

Ignatius of Loyola

(1491–1556)

Only in recent years have we witnessed serious efforts to restore St. Ignatius to the place of honor he deserves in the development of Western mysticism. Formerly the man tended to disappear behind his formidable accomplishment: the inspiration and organization of that most versatile of all religious orders, the Society of Jesus, with its legions of saints, scholars, spiritual directors, teachers, and missionaries. Often the spiritual writings of this poor stylist were eclipsed by those of his more eloquent followers. Ignatius wrote little and, we must confess, badly. Moreover, he succeeded in destroying all but one small part of his diaries. Still we may justifiably claim that his own mystical vision stands at the origin of one of the greatest outbursts of spiritual energy in the history of the Catholic Church.

His early years as a Basque soldier serving in the Emperor's army held little promise of any spiritual future, active or contemplative. Only after having been wounded in the defense of the Pamplona fortress and finding nothing better to read than Ludolph the Saxon's *Life of Christ* and Jacobus de Voragine's *Golden Legend* (the lives of the saints) did the prospect of any but a military career first appear worth considering.

A little more than a year later he received his first great mystical revelation in Manresa on the bank of the River Cardoner:

> As he sat there, the eyes of his understanding began to open. It was not that he beheld any vision, but rather, he comprehended, understood many things about the spiritual life as well as about faith and learning. This took place with an illumination so great that all these things appeared to be something new.[1]

It was what the schools have come to call an intellectual "vision," that is, a sudden insight without sense impression or dominating image. In Elmer O'Brien's well-chosen words, "It was not knowledge delimited and defined and accorded in concepts: his inability then or later to express it in so many words is sufficient indication that it was a question of a direct *experience* in the order of knowing quite as that of other mystics is a direct experience in the order

---

1. Ignacio de Loyola, *Obras Completas* (Madrid: Biblioteca de autores Christianos, 1952), 50. *Saint Ignatius' Own Story as Told to Luis González de Cámara,* trans. William J. Young, S.J. (Chicago: Henry Regnery, 1956).

of loving."[2] Thus began a mystical life that would become ever more continuous until in the final years of Ignatius' life it was virtually uninterrupted. The constant presence of God, far from distracting him from what he understood to be his task, inspired him even in the details of its organization. But not until he had articulated the various aspects of his "vision" in the *Spiritual Exercises* could it effectively coordinate his apostolic activity. This mighty spiritual synthesis he wrought in the solitude of Manresa (1522–23).

For a long time the *Spiritual Exercises* enjoyed a rather dubious reputation among writers on contemplative prayer. As late as the beginning of this century some dismissed it as a mere technique, perhaps useful for bringing the recently converted to an elementary form of prayer but clearly not conducive to higher contemplation. Fortunately, such evaluations no longer appear in print today. Yet some of the difficulties that gave rise to them remain. The *Spiritual Exercises,* for all their simplicity, are an exceedingly difficult book to read. Indeed, they are not a book to read at all, but a manual of instructions about how to behave while entering into, and progressing in, the spiritual life. What Ignatius provides in the dry form of "annotations" and "points" for meditation constitutes in fact an effective method for opening the aspirant to receive the contemplative grace he is capable of receiving and not to prevent its effect in any way. It holds a delicate balance between eliciting the kind of active endeavor ("exercise") without which no spiritual life is possible, and cautioning the exercitant to become utterly passive when

2. *Varieties of Mystic Experience* (New York: Holt, Rinehart & Winston, 1964), 249.

divine grace invites him or her. Throughout, the work bears the mark of Ignatius' own mystical progress.

Since the *Exercises* are essentially a process, its individual parts taken separately will not convey their full meaning, nor will they attain their intended effect. The three outlines of meditations, then, which we reproduce in the following selection must be interpreted as way-stations or cardinal moments of that process. In the "Foundation" the "facts" of human life are reduced to their stark simplicity in order to awaken the exercitant from his distracted existence. The meditation on the divine King, the centerpiece of the *Exercises,* already conceived in Manresa, must turn his entire life to one, spiritual purpose. The "contemplation to attain divine love" allows the exercitant to return to the world he has abandoned without being distracted from his adopted spiritual goal. The terms of the *Exercises* are carefully chosen and serve a purpose in the overall attempt to lead the retreatant into less discursive prayer. "Contemplation" differs from "meditation." Frequently, in the course of either, Ignatius suggests an "application of the senses," as when he invites the exercitant in the meditation on hell "to see in imagination the great fires," "to hear the wailing, the screaming, cries and blasphemies," "to smell the smoke, the brimstone, the corruption, rottenness," "to taste bitter things, as tears, sadness, and remorse of conscience," "with the sense of touch to feel how the flames surround and burn souls." Concrete presentations such as these may not be to the modern taste, but the idea behind them remains an essential part of contemplative life. They play a particularly significant role in the meditations on the life of Christ.

IGNATIUS OF LOYOLA

Commentators have rightly pointed out the similarity that links them to the Christocentric tradition initiated by St. Francis, which via the *Meditations on the Life of Christ* (formerly attributed to St. Bonaventure) found their way into Ludolph the Saxon's *Life of Christ.* Yet in the context of the *Exercises* the applications of the senses fulfill a different, more self-conscious function. They appear in places where a direct exposure to the human Christ is expected to have a maximum impact upon the retreatant's "election" of an appropriate state of perfection. At the same time, they are intended to introduce him or her to a more contemplative mode of praying.

The meditation on the divine King, placed at a strategic position after the Foundation and the purgation of the "first week," when the candidate is ready for a positive illumination, also betrays the impact of an earlier work of piety. On the title page of the Spanish translation of *The Golden Legend* which Ignatius read during his convalescence, Christ appears as the King of Kings. His cross is described as a "royal standard" and He Himself invites Christians to follow Him in the "conquest of the world."[3] Yet again, Ignatius transforms the metaphor in a sense at once more practical and more contemplative. Its practical aim consists in leading the candidate, now in a state of holy "indifference," to follow Christ alone. Beyond that immediate goal, however, the meditation aims at establishing a bond of prayerful and affective intimacy with the Christ whose life, death,

and resurrection the retreatant is about to contemplate.

Finally, the "contemplation to attain divine love" fully reveals Ignatius' intentions. That a "contemplation," unrelated to any direct plan of action, should conclude the *Exercises* shows their ultimate purpose to consist in bringing generous Christians to a point where they may live in the constant presence of God and work under the exclusive guidance of His Spirit, whatever the circumstances of their task may be. In a few dry sentences Ignatius here sketches what John of the Cross was to announce and develop poetically in the *Spiritual Canticle:* "The soul is able to see in that tranquil wisdom how all the creatures . . . raise their voice in testimony to that which God is. She sees that each one after its manner exalts God, since it has God in itself according to its capacity" (*Sp. Cant.,* st. 14/15). Even while stating this contemplative ideal Ignatius keeps it united with the world of action. This mysticism of creation may well, and, in the case of the Society (which he had foremost in his mind), *must* allow the retreatant to become a "contemplative *in action.*" Precisely this unique combination of contemplation with an apostolic orientation made great men of action out of great contemplatives—missionaries like Francis Xavier or Peter Canisius; philosophers and scientists like Francisco Suárez, Joseph Maréchal, Karl Rahner, Petavius, Pierre Teilhard de Chardin; spiritual directors like Louis Lallemant, Balthasar Alvarez, Jean de Caussade.

Our final selection consists of a passage taken from Ignatius' *Spiritual Diary.* The entries in this journal (of which only seventy pages have been preserved) are extremely short, written in telegram style, and

---

3. Robert W. Gleason, S.J., Introduction to *The Spiritual Exercises of Saint Ignatius,* trans. Anthony Mottola (New York: Doubleday, Image Books, 1964), 19.

clearly not destined to be read by others. Only the entries here reproduced, between February 19 and 29, describe at any length the nature of the experience. Together with the few visions Ignatius reported to Gon-zález de Cámara in his narrated autobiography, they permit us to conclude that this reticent man of action was one of the giants of contemplation in the Western Church.

Selections

AUTOBIOGRAPHY*

Chapter Three

27   ... At this time God treated him just as a schoolmaster treats a little boy when he teaches him.[1] This perhaps was because of his rough and uncultivated understanding, or because he had no one to teach him, or because of the firm will God Himself had given him in His service. But he clearly saw, and always had seen that God dealt with him like this. Rather, he thought that any doubt about it would be an offense against His Divine Majesty. Something of this can be gathered from the five following points.

28   *First.* He had a great devotion to the Most Holy Trinity, and thus daily prayed to the Three Persons distinctly. While he was also praying to the Most Holy Trinity, the objection occurred to him as to how he could say four prayers to the Trinity.[2] But this thought gave him little or no trouble, as being something of only slight importance. One day while he was reciting the Hours of our Lady on the steps of the same monastery, his understanding began to be elevated as though he saw the Holy Trinity under the figure of three keys. This was accompanied with so many tears and so much sobbing that he could not control himself. That morning he accompanied a procession which left the monastery and was not able to restrain his tears until dinner time. Nor afterwards could he stop talking about the Most Holy Trinity. He made use of many different comparisons and experienced great joy and consolation. The result was that all through his life this great impression has remained with him, to feel great devotion when he prays to the Most Holy Trinity.

29   *Second.* Another time there was represented to his understanding with great spiritual delight the manner in which God had created the world. It had the appearance of something white out of which rays were coming, and it was out of this that God made light. But he did not know how to explain these things, nor did he remember well the spiritual illumination which at that time God impressed upon his soul.

Third. At Manresa also, where he remained almost a year, after he began to feel God's consolations and saw the fruit produced in the souls with whom he dealt, he gave up those outward extremes he formerly adopted, and trimmed his nails and hair. One day, in this town, when he was hearing Mass in the church of the mon-

---

*From *St. Ignatius' Own Story as Told to Luis González de Cámara,* trans. William J. Young, S.J. (Chicago: Loyola University Press, 1980), nos. 27–30. Reprinted with permission of the publisher.

1. Ignatius is referring to the time he spent at Manresa, in the year 1522.

2. In Books of Hours, three prayers were frequently given, one to each of the divine Persons, and then a fourth to the Most Holy Trinity.

astery already mentioned, during the elevation he saw with the inner eyes of the soul something like white rays that came from above. Although he cannot explain this after so long a time, yet what he clearly saw with his understanding was how Jesus Christ our Lord is present in that most holy sacrament.

Fourth. When he was at prayer, he often and for a long time saw with the inner eyes the humanity of Christ. The shape which appeared to him was like a white body, not very large or very small, but he saw no distinction of members. He often saw this in Manresa. If he were to say twenty, or even forty times, he would not venture to say that it was an untruth. He saw it another time when he was in Jerusalem, and still another when he was on the road near Padua. He has also seen our Lady in like form, without distinction of parts. These things which he saw gave him at the time great strength, and were always a striking confirmation of his faith, so much so that he has often thought to himself that if there were no Scriptures to teach us these matters of faith, he was determined to die for them, merely because of what he had seen.

30 *Fifth.* Once out of devotion he was going to a church which was about a mile distant from Manresa, and which I think was called St. Paul. The road ran along close to the river. Moving along intent on his devotion, he sat down for a moment with his face towards the river which there ran deep. As he sat, the eyes of his understanding began to open. He beheld no vision, but he saw and understood many things, spiritual as well as those concerning faith and learning. This took place with so great an illumination that these things appeared to be something altogether new. He cannot point out the particulars of what he then understood, although they were many, except that he received a great illumination in his understanding. This was so great that in the whole course of his past life right up to his sixty-second year, if he were to gather all the helps he had received from God, and everything he knew, and add them together, he does not think that they would equal all that he received at that one time.

THE SPIRITUAL EXERCISES*

23. FIRST PRINCIPLE AND FOUNDATION
Man is created to praise, reverence, and serve God our Lord, and by this means to save his soul.

*From *The Spiritual Exercises of St. Ignatius,* trans. Louis J. Puhl, S.J. (Chicago: Loyola University Press, 1968), nos. 23, 91–100, 230–37. Reprinted with permission of the publisher.

The other things on the face of the earth are created for man to help him in attaining the end for which he is created.

Hence, man is to make use of them in as far as they help him in the attainment of his end, and he must rid himself of them in as far as they prove a hindrance to him.

Therefore, we must make ourselves indifferent to all created things, as far as we are allowed free choice and are not under any prohibition. Consequently, as far as we are concerned, we should not prefer health to sickness, riches to poverty, honor to dishonor, a long life to a short life. The same holds for all other things.

Our one desire and choice should be what is more conducive to the end for which we are created. . . .

THE KINGDOM OF CHRIST

91. THE CALL OF AN EARTHLY KING
This will help us to contemplate the life of the eternal king

PRAYER.   The preparatory prayer will be as usual.

FIRST PRELUDE.   This is a mental representation of the place. Here it will be to see in imagination the synagogues, villages, and towns where Jesus preached.

SECOND PRELUDE.   I will ask for the grace I desire. Here it will be to ask of our Lord the grace not to be deaf to His call, but prompt and diligent to accomplish His holy will.

FIRST PART

92. FIRST POINT.   This will be to place before my mind a human king, chosen by God our Lord Himself, to whom all Christian princes and people pay homage and obedience.

93. SECOND POINT.   This will be to consider the address this king makes to all his subjects, with the words: "It is my will to conquer all infidel lands. Therefore, whoever wishes to join with me in this enterprise must be content with the same food, drink, clothing, etc. as mine. So, too, he must work with me by day, and watch with me by night, etc., that as he has had a share in the toil with me, afterwards, he may share in the victory with me."

94. THIRD POINT.   Consider what the answer of good subjects ought to be to a king so generous and noble-minded, and consequently, if anyone would refuse the invi-

tation of such a king, how justly he would deserve to be condemned by the whole world, and looked upon as an ignoble knight.

95. SECOND PART

The second part of this exercise will consist in applying the example of the earthly king mentioned above to Christ our Lord according to the following points:

FIRST POINT.   If such a summons of an earthly king to his subjects deserves our attention, how much more worthy of consideration is Christ our Lord, the Eternal King, before whom is assembled the whole world. To all His summons goes forth, and to each one in particular He addresses the words: "It is my will to conquer the whole world and all my enemies, and thus to enter into the glory of my Father. Therefore, whoever wishes to join me in this enterprise must be willing to labor with me, that by following me in suffering, he may follow me in glory."

96. SECOND POINT.   Consider that all persons who have judgment and reason will offer themselves entirely for this work.

97. THIRD POINT.   Those who wish to give greater proof of their love, and to distinguish themselves in the service of the eternal King and the Lord of all, will not only offer themselves entirely for the work, but will act against their sensuality and carnal and worldly love, and make offerings of greater value and of more importance in words such as these:

98. ETERNAL LORD OF ALL THINGS

Eternal Lord of all things, in the presence of Thy infinite goodness, and of Thy glorious mother, and of all the saints of Thy heavenly court, this is the offering of myself which I make with Thy favor and help. I protest that it is my earnest desire and my deliberate choice, provided only it is for Thy greater service and praise, to imitate Thee in bearing all wrongs and all abuse and all poverty, both actual and spiritual, should Thy most holy majesty deign to choose and admit me to such a state and way of life

NOTES

99. NOTE I.   This exercise should be gone through twice during the day, that is, in the morning on rising, and an hour before dinner, or before supper.

100. NOTE II.   During the Second Week and thereafter, it will be very profitable to read some passages from the *Following of Christ,* or from the Gospels, and from the *Lives of the Saints. . . .*

230. CONTEMPLATION TO ATTAIN THE LOVE OF GOD

NOTE.   Before presenting this exercise it will be good to call attention to two points:

1. The first is that love ought to manifest itself in deeds rather than in words.

231. 2. The second is that love consists in a mutual sharing of goods, for example, the lover gives and shares with the beloved what he possesses, or something of that which he has or is able to give; and vice versa, the beloved shares with the lover. Hence, if one has knowledge, he shares it with the one who does not possess it; and so also if one has honors, or riches. Thus, one always gives to the other.

PRAYER.   The usual prayer.

232. FIRST PRELUDE.   This is the representation of the place, which here is to behold myself standing in the presence of God our Lord and of His angels and saints, who intercede for me.

233. SECOND PRELUDE.   This is to ask for what I desire. Here it will be to ask for an intimate knowledge of the many blessings received, that filled with gratitude for all, I may in all things love and serve the Divine Majesty.

234. FIRST POINT.   This is to recall to mind the blessings of creation and redemption, and the special favors I have received.

I will ponder with great affection how much God our Lord has done for me, and how much He has given me of what He possesses, and finally, how much, as far as He can, the same Lord desires to give Himself to me according to His divine decrees.

Then I will reflect upon myself, and consider, according to all reason and justice, what I ought to offer the Divine Majesty, that is, all I possess and myself with it. Thus, as one would do who is moved by great feeling, I will make this offering of myself:

TAKE, LORD, AND RECEIVE
Take, Lord, and receive all my liberty, my memory, my understanding, and my entire will, all that I have and possess. Thou hast given all to me. To Thee, O Lord, I return it. Dispose of it wholly according to Thy will. Give me Thy love and Thy grace, for this is sufficient for me.

235. SECOND POINT.   This is to reflect how God dwells in creatures: in the elements giving them existence, in the plants giving them life, in the animals conferring upon them sensation, in man bestowing understanding. So He dwells in me and gives me being, life, sensation, intelligence, and makes a temple of me, besides having created me in the likeness and image of the Divine Majesty.

Then I will reflect upon myself again in the manner stated in the first point, or in some other way that may seem better.

The same should be observed with regard to each of the points given below.

236. THIRD POINT.   This is to consider how God works and labors for me in all creatures upon the face of the earth, that is, He conducts Himself as one who labors. Thus, in the elements, the plants, the fruits, the cattle, etc., He gives being, conserves them, confers life and sensation, etc.

Then I will reflect on myself.

237. FOURTH POINT.   This is to consider all blessings and gifts as descending from above. Thus, my limited power comes from the supreme and infinite power above, and so, too, my justice, goodness, mercy, etc., descend from above as the rays of light descend from the sun, and as the waters flow from their fountains, etc.

Then I will reflect on myself, as has been said.

Conclude with a colloquy and the *Our Father.*

THE SPIRITUAL JOURNAL*

The Trinity, 1st.[1]

18. Tuesday [February 19th].—Last night I went to bed with the thought of examining what I would do in celebrating Mass or how. On awaking in the morning and beginning my examination of conscience and prayer, with a great and abundant flood of tears, I felt much devotion with many intellectual lights and spiritual remembrances of the Most Holy Trinity, which quieted me and delighted me immensely, even to producing a pressure in my chest, because of the intense love I felt for the Most Holy Trinity. This gave me confidence, and I determined to say the Mass of the Most Holy Trinity, to see what I should do later. I had the same feelings while vesting, with lights from the Trinity. I got up and made a short meditation not without tears, and later much devotion and spiritual confidence to say successively six or more Masses of the Most Holy Trinity.

On the way to Mass and just before it, I was not without tears; an abundance of them during it, but very peacefully, with very many lights and spiritual memories concerning the Most Holy Trinity which served as a great illumination to my mind, so much so that I thought I could never learn so much by hard study, and later, as

*From *The Spiritual Journal of St. Ignatius Loyola, February 1544-45,* trans. William J. Young, S.J. (Rome: Centrum Ignatianum Spiritualitatis, 1974), nos. 18–28. Reprinted with permission of the publisher.
1. The reference is to the first of a series of Masses in honor of the Holy Trinity.

I examined the matter more closely, I felt and understood, I thought, more than if I had studied all my life.

I finished the Mass and spent a short time in vocal prayer: "Eternal Father, confirm me; Son, confirm me"; with a flood of tears spreading over my face and a growing determination to go on with their Masses (thinking of putting some limit to their number), with much heavy sobbing, I drew very near, and became assured in an increased love of His Divine Majesty.

In general, the intellectual lights of the Mass, and those preceding it, were with regard to choosing the proper orations of the Mass, when one speaks with God, with the Father or the Son, etc., or deals with the operations ad extra of the Divine Persons, or their processions more by feeling and seeing than by understanding. All these experiences corroborated what I had done and encouraged me to continue. Today, even as I walked through the city, with much joy of soul, I represented the Most Holy Trinity to myself, now when I met with three rational creatures, or three animals, or again, three other things, and so on.

The Trinity, 2nd.

19. Wednesday [February 20th].—Before beginning my meditation, I felt a devout eagerness to do so, and, after having begun it, a great devotion that was warm, or light and sweet, but without any intellectual lights, tending rather to a feeling of security without terminating in any Divine Person.

Later, I felt confirmed about the past, in recognizing the evil spirit of the past, namely, the spirit who wished to make me doubt and caused me to be impatient with the Blessed Trinity, as I have said in paragraph 17. With this recognition, I felt a fresh interior movement to tears, and so later, before Mass, and during it with an increased quiet and tranquil devotion together with tears, and some lights, feeling and thinking both before and after, when the desire of going on left me, particularly later, with that great quiet or satisfaction of soul, as I thought that I should not go on with the Masses of the Most Holy Trinity, unless it were in thanksgiving, and for the completion of the matter but not out of any need of confirming what had passed.

The Most Holy Trinity, 3rd.

20. Thursday [February 21st].—In the meditation, I had on the whole very great and continuous devotion, a warm brightness and spiritual relish, drawing partly to a certain elevation. Later, while getting ready in my room, at the altar and while vesting, I felt a few interior movements and inclination to tears. In this state I finished Mass and remained in great spiritual repose. In the Mass there were tears in greater abundance than the day before, and for the most part with a loss of speech. Once or twice I also felt spiritual lights, to such an extent that I seemed thus to

understand that there was nothing more to learn from the Most Holy Trinity in this matter. This took place because, as formerly I sought to find devotion in the Trinity in the prayers to the Father, I did not want, nor did I prepare myself, either to search for it or to find it, as it did not seem to me that consolation or illumination was to come from the Most Holy Trinity. But in this Mass I recognized, felt or saw, the Lord knows, that in speaking to the Father, in seeing that He was a Person of the Most Holy Trinity, I was moved to love the Trinity all the more that the other Persons were present in It essentially. I felt the same in the prayer to the Son, and the same in the prayer to the Holy Spirit, rejoicing in any One of Them and feeling consolations, attributing it to and rejoicing in the Being of all Three. In untying this knot, or something similar, the fact seemed so great to me that I never got through saying to myself: "Who are you? Where do you come from? etc. How did you deserve this? or whence did it come?" and so on.

The Trinity, 4th.

21. Friday [February 22nd].—In the customary prayer I had much assistance on the whole from the warming grace, partly brilliant, and with much devotion, although for my part I found it easy a few times to lose the thread of my thought, in spite of the continual assistance of grace.

Later, while preparing the altar, there were certain movements to tears with a tendency to repeat over and over again to myself: "I am not worthy of invoking the Name of the Most Holy Trinity," which thought and multiplication moved me to greater interior devotion. On vesting, with this and other considerations, my soul opened wider to tears and sobbing. Beginning Mass and going on to the Gospel, I said it with deep devotion and a great assistance from a warming grace, which later seemed to struggle with some thoughts, as fire with water.

The Trinity, 5th.

22. Saturday [February 23rd].—In the customary prayer, at the beginning, nothing, but from midway to the end, I found much satisfaction of soul, with some indication of brilliant clearness.

While preparing the altar, the thought of Jesus occurring to me, I felt a movement to follow Him, it seemed to me interiorly, since He was the head of the Society, a greater argument to proceed in complete poverty than all the other human reasons, although I thought that all the reasons of the past elections tended towards the same decision. This thought moved me to devotion and to tears, and to a firmness which, although I had no tears in the Mass, or Masses, etc., I thought that this feeling was enough to keep me firm in time of temptation or trial.

I went along with these thoughts and vested while they increased, and took them as a confirmation, although I received no consolations on this point, and thinking that the appearance of Jesus was in some way from the Most Holy Trinity, I recalled the day when the Father placed me with the Son. As I finished vesting with this intention of impressing on my mind the name of Jesus, and trying to think that a confirmation for the future, a fresh attack of tears and sobbing came upon me, as I began Mass helped with much grace and devotion, and with quiet tears for the most part, and even when I had finished, the great devotion and movement to tears lasted until I had unvested.

Throughout the Mass, I had various feelings in confirmation of what I had said, and, as I held the Blessed Sacrament in my hands, the word came to me with an intense interior movement never to leave Him for all heaven and earth, etc., while I felt fresh movements of devotion and spiritual joy. For my part, I added, doing as much as I could, and this last step was directed to the companions who had given their signatures.[2] Later in the day, as often as I thought of Jesus, or remembered Him, I had a certain feeling, or saw with my understanding, with a continuous and confirming devotion.

Of the day.

23. Sunday [February 24th].—In the usual prayer, from beginning to end, I had the help of a very interior and gentle grace, full of warm devotion and very sweet. While preparing the altar and vesting, I saw a representation of the name of Jesus with much love, confirmation and increased desire to follow Him, accompanied by tears and sobs.

All through the Mass very great devotion, on the whole, with many tears, and several times loss of speech, all devotion and feeling being directed to Jesus. I could not apply myself to the other Persons, except to the First Person as Father of such a Son, with spiritual answers, How He is Father, How He is Son!

Having finished Mass, I had during the prayer that same feeling towards the Son, and how I would have desired the confirmation of the Most Holy Trinity, and felt that it was given to me through Jesus, when He showed Himself to me and gave me such interior strength and certainty of the confirmation, without any fear of the future. The thought suggested itself to me to beg Jesus to obtain pardon for me from the Most Holy Trinity. I felt an increased devotion, tears and sobs, and the hope of obtaining the grace, when I found myself so vigorous and strengthened concerning the future.

---

2. Ignatius is speaking of his determination against having any revenues, as far as it depended on him. But he would have to submit the election to the judgment of his companions who, in the first draft of the *Constitutions*, had decided that the sacristies of Jesuit churches, as distinct from the Society itself, might have a revenue.

Later, at the fire,[3] there was a fresh representation of Jesus with great devotion and movement to tears. Later, as I walked through the street, I had a vivid representation of Jesus with interior movements and tears. After I had spoken with [Cardinal] Carpi, and was on the way home, I felt great devotion. After dinner, especially when I passed through the door of the Vicar, in the house of the Cardinal of Trani, I felt or saw Jesus, had many interior movements and many tears, begging and praying Jesus to obtain pardon for me from the Most Holy Trinity, while I felt remaining in me a great confidence of being heard.

At these times, when I sensed or saw Jesus, I felt so great a love within me that I thought that nothing could happen in the future that would separate me from Him, or cause me to doubt about the graces or confirmation I had received.

St. Matthias.

24. Monday [February 25th].—The first part of the prayer was with much devotion, and thereafter a warmth and an assisting grace, although on my part, and because of some obstacles I felt on the part of others to hold me back, I neither asked nor sought confirmation, but desired to be reconciled with the Three Divine Persons. Later on, vesting for Mass, not knowing to whom to commend myself, or where to begin, the thought came to me while Jesus was communicating Himself: "I want to go on," and with that I began the *Confiteor* "Confiteor Deo," as Jesus said in the Gospel for the day, "Confiteor tibi," etc.[4]

However, I began the confession with fresh devotion, and not without movements to tears, entering on the Mass with much devotion, warmth and tears, and occasional loss of speech. I thought that Jesus presented the orations that were addressed to the Father, or that He was accompanying those which I was saying to the Father. I felt and saw this in a way that I cannot explain.

When the Mass was finished I wanted to be reconciled with the Most Holy Trinity, and I begged this of Jesus, not without tears and sobbing, assuring myself and not asking or feeling the need of any confirmation, or of saying Masses for this purpose, but only to be reconciled.

Of the Trinity, 6th.

25. Tuesday [February 26th].—The first prayer was without disturbance, nor did I withdraw from it. There was much devotion and from the middle on, devotion was much increased, although I felt in it, especially in the first part, some physical weakness or indisposition.

---

3. This expression occurs a number of times between the 24th and 27th of February. Ignatius appears to have had a brazier in his room at the time because of the extraordinary cold.

4. This passage is read at the Mass of St. Matthias (Mt 11:25).

After dressing and while still in my room preparing with fresh and interior movements to tears, when I recalled Jesus, I felt much confidence in Him, and I thought
He was ready to intercede for me; yet I did not seek or ask further confirmation
concerning the past, remaining quiet and restful in this regard. But the thought came
to ask and beg Jesus to make me conformable with the will of the Most Holy Trinity,
in the way He thought best.

Later, while vesting, as this representation of the love and help of Jesus grew, I
began Mass, not without much quiet and restful devotion and with a slight inclination to tears, thinking that with even less I would be more satisfied and contented
in allowing myself to be governed by the Divine Majesty, Who bestows and withdraws His graces as He thinks best. After this I went to the fire, the contentment
growing, with a fresh interior movement and love for Jesus. I noticed the absence
of that former opposition regarding the Most Holy Trinity, and thus during the Mass
I continued with great devotion towards It.

The beginning of Lent.
26. Wednesday [February 27th].—In the customary prayer I felt quite well, as I
usually do, but towards the middle and then on to the end great devotion, spiritual
quiet and sweetness, followed by a continuous devotion which remained. As I got
ready in my room, asking Jesus, not in any way for a confirmation, but that He do
me His best service in the presence of the Most Holy Trinity, etc., and by the most
suitable manner, provided I find myself in His grace.

In this I received some light and strength, and going into the chapel and praying,
I felt or rather saw beyond my natural strength the Most Holy Trinity and Jesus,
presenting me, or placing me, or simply being the means of union in the midst of
the Most Holy Trinity in order that this intellectual vision be communicated to me.
With this knowledge and sight, I was deluged with tears and love, directing to Jesus
and to the Most Holy Trinity a respectful worship which was more on the side of a
reverential love than anything else.

Later, I thought of Jesus doing the same duty in thinking of praying to the Father,
thinking and feeling interiorly that He was doing everything with the Father and the
Most Holy Trinity. I began Mass with many tears, great devotion and tears continuing all through it. Likewise all of a sudden, I clearly saw the same vision of the
Most Holy Trinity as before, with an ever increasing love for His Divine Majesty,
and several times losing the power of speech.

The Mass finished, in my prayer and later at the fire, several times I felt great and
intense devotion, terminating in Jesus, and not without special movements to tears
later. Even while writing this, I feel a drawing of my understanding to behold the
Most Holy Trinity, and beholding, although not as distinctly as formerly, Three Per-

sons; and at the time of Mass, at the prayer, *"Domine Jesu Christe, Fili Dei vivi,"* etc., I thought in spirit that I saw just Jesus, that is, the humanity, and at this other time I felt it in my soul in another way, namely, not the humanity alone, but the whole Being of my God, etc., with a fresh flood of tears and great devotion, etc.

Of the Trinity, 7th.

27. Thursday [February 28th].—Through the whole of the customary prayer, much devotion and grace, warm and helpful, bright and loving. Entering the chapel, fresh devotion, and as I knelt a revelation or a vision of Jesus at the feet of the Most Holy Trinity, and with this, movements and tears. This vision did not last so long, nor was it so clear as that of Wednesday, although it seems to have taken place in the same way. Later, at Mass, tears with deep devotion and profitable thoughts, and some also after Mass.[5]

Of the Wounds.[6]

28. Friday [February 29th].—In the customary prayer, from beginning to end very great devotion, which was very bright, covered my sins and did not allow me to think of them. Outside the house, in the church, before Mass, a sight of the heavenly fatherland, or of its Lord, after the manner of an intellectual vision of the Three Persons, and in the Father the Second and the Third.

At times during the Mass great devotion, but without any lights or movements to tears. After it was over, a vision likewise of the fatherland, or of its Lord, indistinctly but clearly, as frequently happens at other times, sometimes more, sometimes less, and the whole day with special devotion.

---

5. This exceptional representation of the one Mediator between God and man "at the foot of the Most Holy Trinity" was a source of scandal to some of the early opponents of the *Spiritual Exercises,* who looked with suspicion on the role there given to the Son in the Triple Colloquy. But see 1 Timothy 2:5–6.

6. The reference is to the Mass of the Five Wounds, which at that time was celebrated on the first Friday after Ash Wednesday.

SELECTED BIBLIOGRAPHY

TEXTS AND TRANSLATIONS

Obras completas de San Ignacio de Loyola. Edited by I. Iparraguirre, S.I., and C. de Dalmases, S.I. Rev. ed. Madrid, 1963.

Letters of St. Ignatius of Loyola. Translated by William J. Young, S.J. Chicago: Loyola University Press, 1959.

A Pilgrim's Journey: The Autobiography of Ignatius of Loyola. Translated by Joseph N. Tylenda, S.J. Wilmington, Del.: Michael Glazier, 1985.

St. Ignatius' Own Story as Told to Luis González de Cámara. Chicago: Regnery, 1956. Reprint. Chicago: Loyola University Press, 1980.

The Spiritual Exercises of St. Ignatius. Translated by Louis Puhl, S.J. Westminster, Md.: Newman, 1951. Reprint. Chicago: Loyola University Press, 1968.

The Spiritual Journal of St. Ignatius of Loyola: February, 1544–45. Translated by William J. Young, S.J. Woodstock, Md.: Woodstock College Press, 1958. Reprint. Rome: Centrum Ignatianum Spiritualitatis, 1974.

STUDIES

Egan, Harvey, S.J. *The Spiritual Exercises and the Ignatian Mystical Horizon.* St. Louis: Institute of Jesuit Sources, 1976.

————. "The *Spiritual Exercises* of Saint Ignatius of Loyola." In Egan's *Christian Mysticism,* 30–79. New York: Pueblo, 1984.

Guibert, Joseph de, S.J. *The Jesuits: Their Spiritual Doctrine and Practice.* Translated by William J. Young, S.J. St. Louis: Institute of Jesuit Sources, 1972.

Rahner, Hugo, S.J. *Ignatius the Theologian.* Translated by Michael Barry. New York: Herder and Herder, 1968.

————. *The Spirituality of St. Ignatius Loyola: An Account of Its Historical Development.* Translated by Francis J. Smith, S.J. Westminster, Md.: Newman, 1953.

Rahner, Karl, S.J. *Spiritual Exercises.* Translated by Kenneth Baker, S.J. New York: Herder and Herder, 1965.

Wulf, Friedrich, S.J., ed. *Ignatius of Loyola: His Personality and Spiritual Heritage, 1556–1956.* St. Louis: Institute of Jesuit Sources, 1977.

Teresa of Avila

(1515–1582)

Entering the town of Avila on the Castilian plateau of central Spain where Teresa was born and lived most of her life, one cannot but be struck by its similarity with the birthplace of the other female "Doctor of the Church"—Siena. Safely snuggled within elegantly fortified walls, both compact cities appear to have endowed their native saints with a sense of security and a clearly defined identity. Their physical dwelling, quite naturally, came to symbolize God's presence in the soul. There the similarity between Teresa's and Catherine's living conditions ends. Teresa's family, well-to-do, belonged to the lower nobility. Her father's father had converted from Judaism, as many Jews had done after the laws of Ferdinand and Isabella. But in his case, more than moral pressure appears to have been involved, for both his sons became unusually devout Christians. Teresa's paternal uncle played a significant role both in her decision to enter a convent and, later, in her conversion to a life of genuine piety. The *Reconquista* was still in the air, even though the Catholic kings had recently (1492) and forcefully united the peninsula in the Christian faith. The seven year old Teresa, apparently not fully acquainted with the latest political developments, once left home with her brother to go "to the land of the Moors" in order "to be decapitated" and thus find the shortest path to heaven. This early drive to heroic sanctity soon gave way to an interest in the more profane heroism of chevaleresque novels. The young teenager started work on such a novel herself, but this premature expression of her literary inclinations never reached completion. All such mundane activities came abruptly to a halt when her father brought her, much against her will, at age seventeen, to a convent of Augustinian nuns. After less than two years Teresa became sick and left the convent school for a prolonged stay with her uncle. While reading to him St. Jerome's *Letters* she, surprisingly enough, decided to enter a convent. Her father, though deeply pious, drew the line at that point. Teresa, in her characteristically dramatic, somewhat Quixotic style, eloped to the Carmelite convent of the Incarnation in Avila. In retrospect we may find it difficult to appreciate this grand gesture made in order to join a community as open to the world as a dovecote: the nuns spent much of their time in the parlor gossiping with city acquaintances and frequently returned to their families for special care or even for a good meal.

To one such excursion from the convent Teresa owed what could be called her second conversion—not yet the definitive one! Shortly after her profession she fell seriously ill. Was her sickness psychosomatic? Possibly, but the forceful treatment of her "wonder doctor" would have sufficed to kill a healthy patient. Once more she ended in her uncle's home, and again a book from his well-stocked spiritual library deeply touched her. Francisco de Osuna's *Third Spiritual Alphabet* initiated her into the method of "recollection." Franciscans had devised a mode of interior prayer which would enable lay men and women to practice in the world the kind of mental discipline which professed religious were expected to practice in their monasteries. Concentrating on the imitation of Christ as a means to total union with God, "recollection" was intended to bring the soul from discursive meditation to passive contemplation. In Spain Francisco de Osuna had been one of its most effective expositors. The reform movement inspired by the new piety had affected religious orders as well. Occasionally it had shown some affinity with the so-called *Alumbrados* who, favoring interior abandonment to God's will over any traditional form of piety, tended to discredit discursive or liturgical prayer altogether. Ecclesiastical authorities, suspecting some link with the emerging Reformation in northern Europe, became increasingly suspicious. After the Council of Trent, fear led to repressive action. The Spanish Inquisitor General placed a number of devotional works on the Index of Forbidden Books—among them Francisco de Osuna's *Third Alphabet*. Teresa, distressed about seeing some of her favorite authors thus being taken out of circulation,

felt comforted only when the Lord promised her a living book instead.

But much had occurred between her recovery and this event of her forty-fourth year. The facts, as filtered through her own penitent autobiography, may have been somewhat distorted but appear essentially trustworthy. Having passed through a prolonged period of desolation she seems to have become discouraged in pursuing internal prayer and, in her outward conduct, to have followed the rather relaxed standards of discipline that prevailed at the Incarnation, including the frequent visits to the parlor for hours of idle conversation. In 1554, when thirty-nine years old, she experienced her definitive conversion. There appear to have been two stages: the first one occurred when she was suddenly struck by the sight of a statue of Christ after his flagellation, tied to a pole and mocked by soldiers; the second was occasioned by the reading of Augustine's conversion. An interior life that had lain dormant during the preceding years instantly blossomed into a flowering spring. The subterranean development of her spiritual life during the "infertile" period allowed her to enter immediately into the passive state of prayer.

With these events, as narrated in her *Life,* begins an episode often distressing, but occasionally comical—troubles with spiritual directors. The first to whom she confided her particular experiences promptly informed her that they all came from the devil. The next one, relenting somewhat on the source, nevertheless advised her to resist passive recollection. Fortunately, all such interpretations and counsels turned out to be marvelously ineffective while Teresa kept waiting for God's Providence to send her the right confessor. Eventually she did indeed encounter confessors, mostly Jesuits, who fully realized the extraordinary nature of the person they were called to direct. One of them, Balthasar Alvarez, a very articulate mystic himself, left a remarkable diary of his own spiritual experience. Teresa respected him well enough, but by that time she had become highly critical of these men appointed by authority to "guide" her along a path totally unfamiliar to them. She sums up her twenty years of travails with incapable confessors: "Through them I suffered so much that I now wonder how I could endure it." Nor were there many books on prayer left to assist her after most of the good ones had been removed from the library. Thus Teresa found herself compelled to seek her own way. In the process of doing so she took others along, because she wrote—easily and well.

But before introducing Teresa's writings, we must say something about her activities. Despairing of her ability to lead a genuinely contemplative life in the company of so many women hostile to any tightening of convent discipline, Teresa conceived the plan of founding another, unsubsidized, house where cloister, poverty, and prayer would be enforced according to the original rule of the Carmel. Despite almost universal resistance in the beginning, she obtained permission in 1562 to move with four postulants to a small house in Avila. There matters rested several years, for Teresa had no intention of founding another "branch" of Carmelites. But during a visit to her new foundation of Saint Joseph, the Superior General in 1567 granted Teresa authority to start "as many houses as she had hairs on her head." That decision transformed the life of the woman who had pursued a strictly cloistered life into one of traveling thousands of miles, by two-wheel cart and by mule, of sleeping in dubious, mostly untidy inns, bothered by "fleas, poltergeists, and all the inconveniences of travel," of suffering from extreme heat and cold, from fever and angina. By one of those ironical twists of fortune to which saints appear to be particularly prone, the authorities anxious to halt, at least temporarily, her controversial foundations, appointed her prioress of her former "Incarnation" convent. The unreformed nuns received their unelected prioress with howls of indignation. Defusing the explosive situation, Teresa placed a statue of the Virgin on the prioress' seat and exclaimed, "Mary will be our prioress; I shall be a sister among sisters." Not only did she survive the opposition of her former fellow sisters, she "converted" the entire convent! The confessor who assisted her in this turmoil was John of the Cross, a man who was to suffer as much as Teresa in the course of reforming the male Carmel.

Under such uncontemplative circumstances Teresa wrote her books on contemplation. They reveal a person of extraordinary religious sensitivity, endowed with an earthly realism and a refreshing ability to see the comical side of her own and other people's struggle through life. Having always been an avid reader and being capable of expressing even the subtlest experiences in words, she would have seemed predestined to become a writer. That she actually became one, however, we owe in the first place to some of her more "enlightened" directors who ordered her to write. Once she started, there was no way of stopping her. Among her works: a spiritual autobiography, reports on her foundations, and, while her *Life* was "at the Inquisition" for examination, a treatise on prayer that was to formulate her experience in an impersonal, objective mode. About this final project she felt plenty of misgivings, which she unambiguously expressed to Father Jeronimo Gracian, who had suggested the writing:

> There are more than enough books written on prayer already. For the love of God, let me get on with my spinning and go to the choir and do my religious duties like the other sisters. I am not meant for writing. I have neither the health nor the wits for it.

The overcoming of her resistance resulted in that accomplished spiritual masterpiece, *The Interior Castle.* In it Teresa attempted to be systematic and impersonal. She did not altogether succeed in the former and, fortunately for us, completely failed in the latter.

In judging her work we should remain aware of the circumstances of its composition: surrounded by all the cares and confusion accompanying what amounted to the erection of a new religious order, ceaselessly traveling under conditions hard to imagine today, constantly plagued by ill health. She herself occasionally reminds the reader of the fragmented, improvised composition of her work:

> God help me in this task which I have embarked upon. I had quite forgotten what I was writing about, for business matters and ill health forced me to postpone continuing it until a more suitable time, and, as I have a poor

memory, it will all be very confused for I cannot read it through again (*The Interior Castle,* 4.2.1).

Yet, precisely this marvelous directness of her writing has defined her unique, inimitable style.

No writings in this collection have proven more resistant to being anthologized than Teresa's. One should read them from one end to the other—repetitions, excursions, inconsistencies, and all. We would render a disservice if the reader were to consider the following excerpts to be more than an invitation to read the whole work from which they were taken—and some others as well.

The image of an interior castle came to Teresa in a vision of "a most beautiful crystal globe, made in the shape of a castle, and containing seven mansions, in the seventh and innermost of which was the King of Glory, in the greatest splendor, illuming and beautifying them all." Teresa herself in her description of the first mansion alludes to the word of John 14:2: "In my Father's house are many mansions...." The first three prepare the higher spiritual life by means of prayer, pious readings, and the practice of love. In the fourth mansion the prayer of quiet introduces the mystical grace. That grace proper consists of a state of infused contemplation, described in mansions five and six. Initially the soul's faculties are asleep, as the silkworm lies dormant in the cocoon before turning into a butterfly. In the sixth mansion Teresa describes the development of the mystical life up to the permanent union—the mystical betrothal. Here also occurs that very painful purgation of the soul to which Saint

John of the Cross refers as the dark night. The work concludes with the short seventh mansion wherein the soul is permanently transformed into God—the spiritual marriage.

THE INTERIOR CASTLE*

The Fifth Dwelling Places

CHAPTER ONE

Begins to deal with how the soul is united to God in prayer. Tells how one discerns whether there is any illusion.

1. O Sisters, how can I explain the riches and treasures and delights found in the fifth dwelling places? I believe it would be better not to say anything about these remaining rooms, for there is no way of learning how to speak of them; neither is the intellect capable of understanding them nor can comparisons help in explaining them; earthly things are too coarse for such a purpose.

Send light from heaven, my Lord, that I might be able to enlighten these Your servants—for You have been pleased that some of them ordinarily enjoy these delights—so that they may not be deceived by the devil transforming himself into an angel of light. For all their desires are directed toward pleasing You.

2. And although I have said "some," there are indeed only a few who fail to enter this dwelling place of which I shall now speak. There are various degrees, and for that reason I say that most enter these places. But I believe that only a few will experience some of the things that I will say are in this room. Yet even if souls do no more than reach the door, God is being very merciful to them; although many are called few are chosen. So I say now that all of us who wear this holy habit of Carmel are called to prayer and contemplation. This call explains our origin; we are the descendants of men who felt this call, of those holy fathers on Mount Carmel who in such great solitude and contempt for the world sought this treasure, this precious pearl of contemplation that we are speaking about. Yet few of us dispose ourselves that the Lord may communicate it to us. In exterior matters we are proceeding well so that we will reach what is necessary; but in the practice of the virtues that are necessary for arriving at this point we need very, very much and cannot be careless in either small things or great. So, my Sisters, since in some way we can enjoy heaven on earth, be brave in begging the Lord to give us His grace in such a way that nothing will be lacking through our own fault; that He show us the way and strengthen the soul that it may dig until it finds this hidden treasure. The truth

*From *The Collected Works of St. Teresa of Avila,* vol. 2, trans. Kieran Kavanaugh, O.C.D., and Otilio Rodriguez, O.C.D. (Washington, D.C.: Institute of Carmelite Studies, 1980), 335–40, 366–69, 405–8, 432–38. Reprinted with permission of the publisher. Copyright © 1980 by Washington Province of Discalced Carmelites, ICS Publications, 2131 Lincoln Rd., N.E., Washington, D.C. 20002.

is that the treasure lies within our very selves. This is what I would like to know how to explain, if the Lord would enable me to do so.

3. I said "strengthen the soul" so that you will understand that bodily strength is not necessary for those to whom God does not give it. He doesn't make it impossible for anyone to buy His riches. He is content if each one gives what he has. Blessed be so great a God. But reflect, daughters, that He doesn't want you to hold on to anything, for if you avoid doing so you will be able to enjoy the favors we are speaking of. Whether you have little or much, He wants everything for Himself; and in conformity with what you know you have given you will receive greater or lesser favors. There is no better proof for recognizing whether our prayer has reached union or not. Don't think this union is some kind of dreamy state like the one I mentioned before.[1] I say "dreamy state" because it seems that the soul is as though asleep; yet neither does it really think it is asleep nor does it feel awake. There is no need here to use any technique to suspend the mind since all the faculties are asleep in this state—and truly asleep—to the things of the world and to ourselves. As a matter of fact, during the time that the union lasts the soul is left as though without its senses, for it has no power to think even if it wants to. In loving, if it does love, it doesn't understand how or what it is it loves or what it would want. In sum, it is like one who in every respect has died to the world so as to live more completely in God. Thus the death is a delightful one, an uprooting from the soul of all the operations the latter can have while being in the body. The death is a delightful one because in truth it seems that in order to dwell more perfectly in God the soul is so separated from the body that I don't even know if it has life enough to breathe. (I was just now thinking about this, and it seems to me that it doesn't—at least if it does breathe, it is unaware that it is doing so.) Nonetheless, its whole intellect would want to be occupied in understanding something of what is felt. And since the soul does not have the energy to attain to this, it is so stunned that, even if it is not completely lost, neither a hand nor a foot stirs, as we say here below when a person is in such a swoon that we think he is dead. . . .

5. . . . This union is above all earthly joys, above all delights, above all consolations, and still more than that. It doesn't matter where those spiritual or earthly joys come from, for the feeling is very different, as you will have experienced. I once said that the difference is like that between feeling something on the rough outer covering of the body or in the marrow of the bones. And that was right on the mark, for I don't know how to say it better.

6. It seems to me that you're still not satisfied, for you will think you can be mistaken and that these interior things are something difficult to examine. What was

---

1. She is referring to the "prayer of recollection" as discussed in IV, ch. 3, no. 11.

said will be sufficient for anyone who has experienced union. Yet, because the difference between union and the previous experience is great, I want to mention a clear sign by which you will be sure against error or doubts about whether the union is from God. His Majesty has brought it to my memory today, and in my opinion it is the sure sign. In difficult matters, even though it seems to me that I understand and that I speak the truth, I always use this expression "it seems to me." For if I am mistaken, I'm very much prepared to believe what those who have a great deal of learning say. . . .

7. I have had a great deal of experience with learned men, and have also had experience with half-learned, fearful ones; these latter cost me dearly. At least I think that anyone who refuses to believe that God can do much more or that He has considered and continues to consider it good sometimes to communicate favors to His creatures has indeed closed the door to receiving them. Therefore, Sisters, let this never happen to you, but believe that God can do far more and don't turn your attention to whether the ones to whom He grants His favors are good or bad; for His Majesty knows this, as I have told you. There is no reason for us to meddle in the matter, but with humility and simplicity of heart we should serve and praise Him for His works and marvels.

8. Now then, to return to the sign that I say is the true one: you now see that God has made this soul a fool with regard to all so as better to impress upon it true wisdom. For during the time of this union it neither sees, nor hears, nor understands, because the union is always short and seems to the soul even much shorter than it probably is. God so places Himself in the interior of that soul that when it returns to itself it can in no way doubt that it was in God and God was in it. This truth remains with it so firmly that even though years go by without God's granting that favor again, the soul can neither forget nor doubt that it was in God and God was in it. This is what matters now, for I shall speak of the effects of this prayer afterward. . . .

10. Don't be mistaken by thinking that this certitude has to do with a corporal form, as in the case of the bodily presence of our Lord Jesus Christ in the Most Blessed Sacrament even though we do not see Him. Here the matter isn't like that; it concerns only the divinity. How, then, is it that what we do not see leaves this certitude? I don't know; these are His works. But I do know I speak the truth. And I would say that whoever does not receive this certitude does not experience union of the whole soul with God, but union of some faculty, or that he experiences one of the many other kinds of favors God grants souls. In regard to all these favors we have to give up looking for reasons to see how they've come about. Since our intellect cannot understand this union, why do we have to make this effort? It's enough for us to see that He who is the cause of it is almighty. Since we have no part at all

to play in bringing it about no matter how much effort we put forth, but it is God who does so, let us not desire the capacity to understand this union. . . .

The Sixth Dwelling Places

CHAPTER TWO

Deals with some of the ways in which our Lord awakens the soul. It seems that there is nothing in these awakenings to fear even though the experience is sublime and the favors are great.

1. . . . Let us begin, then, to discuss the manner in which the Spouse deals with it [the soul] and how before He belongs to it completely He makes it desire Him vehemently by certain delicate means the soul itself does not understand. (Nor do I believe I'll be successful in explaining them save to those who have experienced them.) These are impulses so delicate and refined, for they proceed from very deep within the interior part of the soul, that I don't know any comparison that will fit.

2. They are far different from all that we can acquire of ourselves here below and even from the spiritual delights that were mentioned. For often when a person is distracted and forgetful of God, His Majesty will awaken it. His action is as quick as a falling comet. And as with a thunderclap, even though no sound is heard, the soul understands very clearly that it was called by God. So well does it understand that sometimes, especially in the beginning, it is made to tremble and even complain without there being anything that causes it pain. It feels that it is wounded in the most delightful way, but it doesn't learn how or by whom it was wounded. It knows clearly that the wound is something precious, and it would never want to be cured. It complains to its Spouse with words of love, even outwardly, without being able to do otherwise. It knows that He is present, but He doesn't want to reveal the manner in which He allows Himself to be enjoyed. And the pain is great, although delightful and sweet. And even if the soul does not want this wound, the wound cannot be avoided. But the soul, in fact, would never want to be deprived of this pain. The wound satisfies it much more than the delightful and painless absorption of the prayer of quiet.

3. I am struggling, Sisters, to explain for you this action of love, and I don't know how. For it seems a contradiction that the Beloved would give the soul clear understanding that He is with it and yet make it think that He is calling it by a sign so certain that no room is left for doubt and a whisper so penetrating that the soul cannot help but hear it. For it seems that when the Spouse, who is in the seventh dwelling place, communicates in this manner (for the words are not spoken), all the people in the other dwelling places keep still; neither the senses, nor the imagination, nor the faculties stir.

O my powerful God, how sublime are your secrets, and how different spiritual things are from all that is visible and understandable here below. There is nothing that serves to explain this favor, even though the favor is a very small one when compared with the very great ones You work in souls.

4. This action of love is so powerful that the soul dissolves with desire, and yet it doesn't know what to ask for since clearly it thinks that its God is with it.

You will ask me: Well, if it knows this, what does it desire or what pains it? What greater good does it want? I don't know. I do know that it seems this pain reaches to the soul's very depths and that when He who wounds it draws out the arrow, it indeed seems in accord with the deep love the soul feels that God is drawing these very depths after Him. I was thinking now that it's as though from this fire enkindled in the brazier that is my God a spark leapt forth and so struck the soul that the flaming fire was felt by it. And since the spark was not enough to set the soul on fire, and the fire is so delightful, the soul is left with that pain; but the spark merely by touching the soul produces that effect. It seems to me this is the best comparison I have come up with. This delightful pain—and it is not pain—is not continuous, although sometimes it lasts a long while; at other times it goes away quickly. This depends on the way the Lord wishes to communicate it, for it is not something that can be procured in any human way. But even though it sometimes lasts for a long while, it comes and goes. To sum up, it is never permanent. For this reason it doesn't set the soul on fire; but just as the fire is about to start, the spark goes out and the soul is left with the desire to suffer again that loving pain the spark causes.

5. Here there is no reason to wonder whether the experience is brought on naturally or caused by melancholy, or whether it is some trick of the devil or some illusion. It is something that leaves clear understanding of how this activity comes from the place where the Lord, who is unchanging, dwells. The activity is not like that found in other feelings of devotion, where the great absorption in delight can make us doubtful. Here all the senses and faculties remain free of any absorption, wondering what this could be, without hindering anything or being able, in my opinion, to increase or take away that delightful pain.

Anyone to whom our Lord may have granted this favor—for if He has, that fact will be recognized on reading this—should thank Him very much. Such a person doesn't have to fear deception. Let his great fear be that he might prove ungrateful for so generous a favor, and let him strive to better his entire life, and to serve, and he will see the results and how he receives more and more. In fact, I know a person[2] who received this favor for some years and was so pleased with it that had she served the Lord through severe trials for a great number of years she would have felt well repaid by it. May He be blessed forever, amen.

---

2. She is alluding to herself. See her *Spir. Test.,* 59, no. 13.

6. You may wonder why greater security is present in this favor than in other things. In my opinion, these are the reasons: First, the devil never gives delightful pain like this. He can give the savor and delight that seem to be spiritual, but he doesn't have the power to join pain—and so much of it—to the spiritual quiet and delight of the soul. For all of his powers are on the outside, and the pains he causes are never, in my opinion, delightful or peaceful, but disturbing and contentious. Second, this delightful tempest comes from a region other than those regions of which he can be lord. Third, the favor brings wonderful benefits to the soul, the more customary of which are the determination to suffer for God, the desire to have many trials, and the determination to withdraw from earthly satisfactions and conversations and other similar things. . . .

CHAPTER EIGHT

Discusses how God communicates Himself to the soul through an intellectual vision; gives some counsels. Tells about the effects such a vision causes if it is genuine. Recommends secrecy concerning these favors.

1. For you to see, Sisters, that what I have told you is true and that the further a soul advances the more it is accompanied by the good Jesus, we will do well to discuss how, when His Majesty desires, we cannot do otherwise than walk always with Him. This is evident in the ways and modes by which His Majesty communicates Himself to us and shows us the love He bears us. He does this through some very wonderful apparitions and visions. That you might not be frightened if He grants you some of these, I want briefly to mention something about these visions— if the Lord be pleased that I succeed—so that we might praise Him very much even though He may not grant them to us. We would praise Him because being so filled with majesty and power He nonetheless desires to communicate thus with a creature.

2. It will happen while the soul is heedless of any thought about such a favor being granted to it, and though it never had a thought that it deserved this vision, that it will feel Jesus Christ, our Lord, beside it. Yet, it doesn't see Him, neither with the eyes of the body nor with those of the soul. This is called an intellectual vision; I don't know why. I saw the person[3] to whom God granted this favor, along with other favors I shall mention further on, quite worried in the beginning because, since she didn't see anything, she couldn't understand the nature of this vision. However, she knew so certainly that it was Jesus Christ, our Lord, who showed Himself to her in that way that she couldn't doubt; I mean she couldn't doubt the vision was there. As to whether it was from God or not, even though she carried with her great effects

---

3. This person is Teresa herself. See *Life,* ch. 27, nos. 2–5.

to show that it was, she nonetheless was afraid. She had never heard of an intellectual vision, nor had she thought there was such a kind. But she understood very clearly that it was this same Lord who often spoke to her in the way mentioned. For until He granted her this favor I am referring to, she never knew who was speaking to her, although she understood the words.

3. I know that since she was afraid about this vision (for it isn't like the imaginative one that passes quickly, but lasts many days and sometimes even more than a year), she went very worried to her confessor. He asked her how, since she didn't see anything, she knew that it was our Lord—what kind of face He had. She told him she didn't know, that she didn't see any face, and that she couldn't say any more than what she had said, that what she did know was that He was the one who spoke to her and that the vision had not been fancied. And although some persons put many fears in her, she was still frequently unable to doubt, especially when the Lord said to her: "Do not be afraid, it is I."[4] These words had so much power that from then on she could not doubt the vision, and she was left very much strengthened and happy over such good company. She saw clearly that the vision was a great help toward walking with a habitual remembrance of God and a deep concern about avoiding anything displeasing to Him, for it seemed to her that He was always looking at her. And each time she wanted to speak with His Majesty in prayer, and even outside of it, she felt He was so near that He couldn't fail to hear her. But she didn't hear words spoken whenever she wanted; only unexpectedly when they were necessary. She felt He was walking at her right side, but she didn't experience this with those senses by which we can know that a person is beside us. This vision comes in another unexplainable, more delicate way. But it is so certain and leaves much certitude; even much more than the other visions do because in the visions that come through the senses one can be deceived, but not in the intellectual vision. For this latter brings great interior benefits and effects that couldn't be present if the experience were caused by melancholy; nor would the devil produce so much good; nor would the soul go about with such peace and continual desires to please God, and with so much contempt for everything that does not bring it to Him. Afterward she understood clearly that the vision was not caused by the devil, which became more and more clear as time went on.

4. Nonetheless, I know that at times she went about very much frightened; other times, with the most intense confusion, for she didn't know why so much good had come to her. We were so united, she and I, that nothing took place in her soul of which I was ignorant; so I can be a good witness, and believe me all I have said of this matter is the truth.

---

4. See *Life,* ch. 25, no. 18.

It is a favor from the Lord that she bears in herself the most intense confusion and humility. If the vision were from the devil, the effects would be contrary. And since the vision is something definitely understood to be a gift from God and human effort would not be sufficient to produce this experience, the one who receives it can in no way think it is his own good but a good given through the hand of God. And even though, in my opinion, some of those favors that were mentioned are greater, this favor bears with it a particular knowledge of God. This continual companionship gives rise to a most tender love for His Majesty, to some desires even greater than those mentioned to surrender oneself totally to His service, and to a great purity of conscience because the presence at its side makes the soul pay attention to everything. For even though we already know that God is present in all we do, our nature is such that we neglect to think of this. Here the truth cannot be forgotten, for the Lord awakens the soul to His presence beside it. And even the favors that were mentioned became much more common since the soul goes about almost continually with actual love for the One who it sees and understands is at its side.

5. In sum, with respect to the soul's gain, the vision is seen to be a most wonderful and highly valuable favor. The soul thanks the Lord that He gives the vision without any merits on its part and would not exchange that blessing for any earthly treasure or delight. Thus, when the Lord is pleased to take the vision away, the soul feels very much alone. But all the efforts it could possibly make are of little avail in bringing back that companionship. The Lord gives it when He desires, and it cannot be acquired. Sometimes also the vision is of some saint, and this too is most beneficial.

6. You will ask how if nothing is seen one knows that it is Christ, or a saint, or His most glorious Mother. This, the soul will not know how to explain, nor can it understand how it knows, but it does know with the greatest certitude. It seems easier for the soul to know when the Lord speaks; but what is more amazing is that it knows the saint, who doesn't speak but seemingly is placed there by the Lord as a help to it and as its companion. Thus there are other spiritual things that one doesn't know how to explain, but through them one knows how lowly our nature is when there is question of understanding the sublime grandeurs of God, for we are incapable even of understanding these spiritual things. But let the one to whom His Majesty gives these favors receive them with admiration and praise for Him. Thus He grants the soul particular graces through these favors. For since the favors are not granted to all, they should be highly esteemed; and one should strive to perform greater services since God in so many ways helps the soul to perform these services. Hence the soul doesn't consider itself to be any greater because of this, and it thinks that it is the one who serves God the least among all who are in the world. This soul thinks that it is more obligated to Him than anyone, and any fault it commits pierces to the core of its being, and very rightly so.

The Seventh Dwelling Places

CHAPTER TWO

Explains the difference between spiritual union and spiritual marriage. Describes this difference through some delicate comparisons.

1. Now then let us deal with the divine and spiritual marriage, although this great favor does not come to its perfect fullness as long as we live; for if we were to withdraw from God, this remarkable blessing would be lost.

The first time the favor is granted, His Majesty desires to show Himself to the soul through an imaginative vision of His most sacred humanity so that the soul will understand and not be ignorant of receiving this sovereign gift; with other persons the favor will be received in another form. With regard to the one of whom we are speaking, the Lord represented Himself to her, just after she had received Communion, in the form of shining splendor, beauty, and majesty, as He was after His resurrection, and told her that now it was time that she consider as her own what belonged to Him and that He would take care of what was hers, and He spoke other words destined more to be heard than to be mentioned.

2. It may seem that this experience was nothing new since at other times the Lord had represented Himself to the soul in such a way. The experience was so different that it left her indeed stupefied and frightened: first, because this vision came with great force; second, because of the words the Lord spoke to her and also because in the interior of her soul, where He represented Himself to her, she had not seen other visions except the former one. You must understand that there is the greatest difference between all the previous visions and those of this dwelling place. Between the spiritual betrothal and the spiritual marriage the difference is as great as that which exists between two who are betrothed and between two who can no longer be separated.

3. I have already said that even though these comparisons are used, because there are no others better suited to our purpose, it should be understood that in this state there is no more thought of the body than if the soul were not in it, but one's thought is only of the spirit. In the spiritual marriage, there is still much less remembrance of the body because this secret union takes place in the very interior center of the soul, which must be where God Himself is, and in my opinion there is no need of any door for Him to enter. I say there is no need of any door because everything that has been said up until now seems to take place by means of the senses and faculties, and this appearance of the humanity of the Lord must also. But that which comes to pass in the union of the spiritual marriage is very different. The Lord appears in this center of the soul, not in an imaginative vision but in an intellectual

one, although more delicate than those mentioned, as He appeared to the apostles without entering through the door when He said to them *pax vobis*.[5] What God communicates here to the soul in an instant is a secret so great and a favor so sublime—and the delight the soul experiences so extreme—that I don't know what to compare it to. I can say only that the Lord wishes to reveal for that moment, in a more sublime manner than through any spiritual vision or taste, the glory of heaven. One can say no more—insofar as can be understood—than that the soul, I mean the spirit, is made one with God. For since His Majesty is also spirit, He has wished to show His love for us by giving some persons understanding of the point to which this love reaches so that we might praise His grandeur. For He has desired to be so joined with the creature that, just as those who are married cannot be separated, He doesn't want to be separated from the soul.

4. The spiritual betrothal is different, for the two often separate. And the union is also different because, even though it is the joining of two things into one, in the end the two can be separated and each remains by itself.[6] We observe this ordinarily, for the favor of union with the Lord passes quickly, and afterward the soul remains without that company; I mean, without awareness of it. In this other favor from the Lord, no. The soul always remains with its God in that center. Let us say that the union is like the joining of two wax candles to such an extent that the flame coming from them is but one, or that the wick, the flame, and the wax are all one. But afterward one candle can be easily separated from the other and there are two candles; the same holds for the wick. In the spiritual marriage the union is like what we have when rain falls from the sky into a river or fount; all is water, for the rain that fell from heaven cannot be divided or separated from the water of the river. Or it is like what we have when a little stream enters the sea, there is no means of separating the two. Or, like the bright light entering a room through two different windows; although the streams of light are separate when entering the room, they become one.

5. Perhaps this is what Saint Paul means in saying *He that is joined or united to the Lord becomes one spirit with him* (1 Cor 6:17), and is referring to this sovereign marriage, presupposing that His Majesty has brought the soul to it through union. And he also says: *For me to live is Christ, and to die is gain* (Phil 1:21). The soul as well, I think, can say these words now because . . . its life is now Christ.

---

5. Jn 20:19–21. The earlier-mentioned intellectual visions are those in VI, ch. 8.

6. For the proper understanding of this paragraph, it should be noted that the word "union" is here used in two different senses. In the first three uses of the word, Teresa is referring to the "prayer of union" treated in the Fifth Dwelling Places—a form of contemplative prayer in which the faculties of memory, understanding, and will become completely silent for a time. Teresa then contrasts this temporary experience with what she calls the "union" that occurs "in the spiritual marriage," where there is no longer any division or separation.

6. And that its life is Christ is understood better, with the passing of time, by the effects this life has. Through some secret aspirations the soul understands clearly that it is God who gives life to our soul. These aspirations come very, very often in such a living way that they can in no way be doubted. The soul feels them very clearly even though they are indescribable. But the feeling is so powerful that sometimes the soul cannot avoid the loving expressions they cause, such as: O Life of my life! Sustenance that sustains me! and things of this sort. For from those divine breasts where it seems God is always sustaining the soul there flow streams of milk bringing comfort to all the people of the castle. It seems the Lord desires that in some manner these others in the castle may enjoy the great deal the soul is enjoying and that from that full-flowing river, where this tiny fount is swallowed up, a spurt of that water will sometimes be directed toward the sustenance of those who in corporeal things must serve these two who are wed. Just as a distracted person would feel this water if he were suddenly bathed in it, and would be unable to avoid feeling it, so are these operations recognized, and even with greater certitude. For just as a great gush of water could not reach us if it didn't have a source, as I have said, so it is understood clearly that there is Someone in the interior depths who shoots these arrows and gives life to this life, and that there is a Sun in the interior of the soul from which a brilliant light proceeds and is sent to the faculties. The soul, as I have said, does not move from that center nor is its peace lost; for the very One who gave peace to the apostles when they were together can give it to the soul. . . .

10. . . . This center of our soul, or this spirit, is something so difficult to explain, and even believe in, that I think, Sisters, I'll not give you the temptation to disbelieve what I say, for I do not know how to explain this center. That there are trials and sufferings and that at the same time the soul is in peace is a difficult thing to explain. I want to make one or more comparisons for you. Please God, I may be saying something through them; but if not, I know that I'm speaking the truth in what I say.

11. The King is in His palace and there are many wars in his kingdom and many painful things going on, but not on that account does he fail to be at his post. So here, even though in those other dwelling places there is much tumult and there are many poisonous creatures and the noise is heard, no one enters that center dwelling place and makes the soul leave. Nor do the things the soul hears make it leave; even though they cause it some pain, the suffering is not such as to disturb it and take away its peace. The passions are now conquered and have a fear of entering the center because they would go away from there more subdued.

Our entire body may ache; but if the head is sound, the head will not ache just because the body aches.

I am laughing to myself over these comparisons for they do not satisfy me, but I don't know any others. You may think what you want; what I have said is true.

SELECTED BIBLIOGRAPHY

TEXTS AND TRANSLATIONS

Obras Completas de Santa Teresa de Jesús. Edited by Efrén de la Madre de Dios, Otilio del Niño Jesús, and Otger Stegginck. 3 vols. Madrid, 1951–59.

The Collected Works of St. Teresa of Avila. Translated by Kieran Kavanaugh and Otilio Rodriguez. 3 vols. Washington, D.C.: Institute of Carmelite Studies, 1976–85.

The Complete Works of St. Teresa of Jesus. Translated by E. Allison Peers. 3 vols. London and New York: Sheed and Ward, 1946.

STUDIES

Dicken, E. W. Trueman. *The Crucible of Love.* New York: Sheed and Ward; London: Darton, Longman and Todd, 1963.

Marie-Eugène de l'Enfant Jesus. *I Want to See God.* Translated by Sister M. Verda Clare. Chicago: Fides, 1953.

————. *I Am a Daughter of the Church.* Translated by Sister M. Verda Clare. Chicago: Fides, 1955.

Peers, E. Allison. *Handbook to the Life and Times of St. Teresa and St. John of the Cross.* London: Burns and Oates, 1954.

Ramge, Sebastian. *An Introduction to the Writings of St. Teresa.* Chicago: Regnery, 1963.

Renault, Emmanuel. *Ste Thérèse d'Avila et l'expérience mystique.* Paris, 1970.

John of the Cross

(1542–1591)

No one reading John of the Cross is likely to attribute the text to another author. Not only does he write in a distinctly personal style (as most great writers do), but his entire approach to the mystical life differs from that of others. Bossuet's saying that St. John's works enjoy the same authority in mystical theology as Thomas Aquinas' writings do in the dogmatic branch both reveals and conceals his literary identity. Certainly, no mystic wrote about spiritual life in a more scholastic way, doggedly pursuing the last Aristotelian distinction in a matter so reluctant to submit to such distinctions. Yet the reader never feels left with the dry bones of conceptualization long deserted by contemplative life. The poet's passion constantly reanimates the language of the School, allowing the living experience to radiate through the cold concepts. Nor does John ever sacrifice personal experience to theological *apriori*. He has been called the greatest psychologist in the history of mysticism.[1] Indeed, we may regard him as one of the first theologians to follow the modern "turn to the subject." Yet, he belongs to the small company of modern writers who succeeded in conveying a genuine content to that subject, rather than restricting it to its objective functions. The life of this withdrawn contemplative was as filled with controversy and sensational developments as that of any statesman of his age.

Born as Juan de Ypes at Fontiveros near Avila in 1542, he moved with his mother to Medina del Campo after the death of his father. A clerical benefactor took him in at the local hospital and allowed him to study at the town's Jesuit College. In 1562 he entered the Carmel in Medina. After his profession he studied three years in the "Arts" faculty at the University of Salamanca. At the end of this period he was ordained a priest, apparently with little formal training in theology. Desirous to devote himself to a life of total silence and solitude, he decided to join the Carthusian Order. When he revealed this plan to Saint Teresa, who had founded a reformed convent in Medina, she replied that he could do exactly what he wanted to do within the reformed branch of the Carmel. The problem was that no reformed houses for men existed. So, with her characteristic mixture of cunning and boldness, Teresa suggested

---

1. E. Allison Peers, General Introduction to John of the Cross, *Ascent of Mount Carmel* (New York: Doubleday, Image Books, 1958), 42.

that Juan reform the male Carmel as she had done for the female branch. One may doubt whether the shy, unworldly Carmelite would have accepted this substitute to the peace of a Carthusian monastery if he had foreseen even part of the troubles that were awaiting him. Yet Juan proved as persistent as he was innocent. After one year of theology at Salamanca—the total extent of the formal education in theology of this *Doctor Ecclesiae*—he accompanied Teresa. In 1568 he started with two other priests the first "discalced" house in Duruelo. Soon Mother Teresa came to visit them. No stranger to evangelical poverty herself, she was nevertheless aghast when she saw the place—"a true stable of Bethlehem."

These were the happy years of the reformed Carmel's honeymoon. Teresa, perceiving the spiritual potential of the man she had so expeditiously hitched to her cause, was determined to use him for all he was worth. She succeeded in having him as confessor of the convent of the Incarnation in Avila where she had been appointed prioress by the General of the Order. From that period on he would become her theological and mystical guide, while she would provide him with practical counsel in the reform project. The "calced" Carmelites, perceiving enough trouble in the Order with Teresa alone, decided to stop Juan in his attempts to extend the reform to the male branch. They abducted him from his Avila house and kept him imprisoned in Medina del Campo until the papal nuncio ordered his release. Two years later they repeated their assault and took him to a dark room in the Toledo convent. When Teresa heard about it, she wrote that she would have preferred him to have fallen "into the hands of the Moors." Juan spent over eigh-

teen months in captivity and might have ended his days there had he not in an ingenious plot (of which few would have thought him capable) planned his escape. He waited for the full moon, then carefully unscrewed the lock of the door with previously assembled and hidden tools, lowered himself from the city wall by means of his bed sheets, took one bold leap for the remaining distance, and ran to a nearby reformed convent. For posterity the Toledo captivity turned out to be an unmixed blessing. In his cell he started writing and—what he might never have done without the imposed leisure and scarcity of writing material—composing poetry. There he created the first part of his magnificent *Spiritual Canticle* as well as several other poems— among them, "One Dark Night." During the following period of relative quiet when he served as vicar at the reformed convent of El Calvario, as rector of the college he founded in nearby Baeza, and as prior of Los Mártires convent in Granada, he wrote his two long mystical commentaries in prose on the Toledo poem: *Ascent of Mount Carmel* and *The Dark Night of the Soul*.

His trials might have seemed to be ending when the Pope officially divided the Order into the autonomous branches. Such was far from being the case. John never gained the authority over the discalced friars to which his early initiative, numerous foundations, and constant inspiration would appear to have entitled him. Instead the General Chapter of 1591 deprived him of all offices and intended to send him to Mexico. John, fallen ill, spent his final months at the reformed convent of Ubeda, where his hostile brothers refused him proper care. Covered with sores, he died a lonely death—as he had wished to do.

It would be impossible to summarize his theology—for a veritable theology it is—in two pages. Some of its spirit, however, may be captured in a letter he wrote to a Carmelite nun: "Our most important task consists in remaining silent before this great God, silent with our desires as well as with our tongue. He understands only one language, that of silent love." Spiritual life for John of the Cross aims at an ever deeper negation—not only the negation of knowing, as for Dionysius, but also the abnegation of willing and feeling: "The road to Mount Carmel: the spirit of perfection, nothing, nothing, nothing, and even on the mountain nothing." Yet the ultimate motive in all of these negative endeavors is an eminently positive one: to attain the unconditioned, unqualified love that refuses to be distracted from its object, even for a moment.

Neither the absoluteness of that love ideal nor the negation of all relative values prevented John from being extremely methodic and meticulously concrete in his instructions for the spiritual life. *Ascent of Mount Carmel* and *The Dark Night of the Soul* together constitute the most systematic account of the mystical ascent in the spiritual literature of the modern age. To call it systematic, however, is not to say that the division between the various stages or even the coherence between the two works may be readily perceived. The poem "One Dark Night," featured at the beginning of each book, describes the mystical journey according to the traditional succession of purgation, illumination, and union. In *Ascent* John expresses his intention to follow the entire journey suggested in the stanzas "to the summit of the Mount, which is the high state of perfection which

we here call union of the soul with God." Yet the following commentary discusses only the first two stanzas which deal with purgation: illumination and union appear as modes of purifying the soul. The Prologue to *The Dark Night* states even more explicitly that all the stanzas of the poem will be expounded, not only the first two but also the six which treat "the wondrous effects of the spiritual illumination and union of love with God." Have those works remained incomplete or, as a few commentators have suggested, was part of them lost?

The relation between *Ascent* and *The Dark Night* appears even more complex. At first reading *Ascent* seems to treat the active purgation of the senses (Bk. I) and of the mind (Bks. II–III), while *The Night* deals with the passive one. *The Night* could then be considered the fourth part of *Ascent* to which John alludes in *Ascent* I, 1, 2. But the first seven chapters of *The Night* do not fit this scheme. Were they meant to recapitulate very briefly the subject matter of *Ascent* once the promised fourth part was made into an independent work? Possibly. But the later part of Bk. II of *Ascent* (especially Ch. 24–26) presents new problems, since it deals with what in John's scheme would have to be called *passive illumination*. Also, how do "the touches engendering sweetness and intimate delight" (II, 26) differ from what occurs in the *unitive* way? John himself informs us that "these lofty manifestations of knowledge can come only to the soul that attains to union with God, for they are themselves that union" (II, 26, 5). We may further wonder whether the term *purgation* still adequately defines the unitive love described in *The Night* II, 11, 2: "Inasmuch as this love is informed, it is passive rather than active, and thus it begets in the soul a strong passion of love. This love has in it something of union with God. . . ." All this should caution us that for St. John "systematic" does not necessarily mean "consistent." Yet, more importantly, it shows how in the highest mystical stages the traditional division between cognitive and appetitive states of mind collapses altogether.

The excerpts taken from Book I of *Ascent* compactly describe the general attitude John considers indispensable to a contemplative life. Of Book II, chapter 23 introduces the so-called "intellectual visions," modes of passive illumination in which the senses and the imagination play no role or a purely subordinate one. To these total apprehensions none of the terms derived from the language of ordinary experience properly applies—not even that of "vision." Nevertheless, St. John uses visionary terminology because, as he explains in the following chapter, they show a certain analogy with bodily visions: "Just as the eyes see bodily visions by means of natural light, so does the soul, by means of supernaturally derived light, see those same things inwardly" (ch. 24). The difference between the two lies in the mode of percep-

tion. John cautions against *all* visions of the created world—even the spiritual ones. To stay with them is to encumber one's spiritual progress and to expose oneself to delusions. Still, among intellectual visions he excepts one kind from these reservations—the so-called "knowledge of naked truths" described in chapter 26. Among them we also find insights concerning the created world—not, however, of creatures as they exist in themselves, but as they derive from their divine source. Only the latter "visions" of creation are safe from illusions. (Similar distinctions appear in Ignatius of Loyola and Teresa of Avila, though both seem more readily inclined to ascribe the former directly to the devil.) Infused awareness of naked truths about God John equates with "touches" of substantial union. In that supreme state the distinction between illumination and union breaks down and this highest contemplation coincides with total darkness. The second Book of *The Dark Night of the Soul* deals with this "dark contemplation" of the mind. Yet gradually John extends the subject beyond singular "visions" and "touches" to the entire mental state of the mystic who has attained that level of illumination.

Selections

THE ASCENT OF MOUNT CARMEL*

BOOK ONE

Chapter One

Some remarks about the two different nights through which spiritual persons pass in both the lower and higher parts of their nature. A commentary on the first stanza.

First Stanza

One dark night,
Fired with love's urgent longings
—Ah, the sheer grace!—
I went out unseen,
My house being now all stilled;

1. The soul sings in this first stanza of its good luck and the grace it had in departing from its inordinate sensory appetites and imperfections. To understand this departure one should know that a soul must ordinarily pass through two principal kinds of night—which spiritual persons call purgations or purifications of the soul—in order to reach the state of perfection. Here we will term these purgations "nights" because in both of them the soul journeys in darkness as though by night.

2. The first night or purgation, to which this stanza refers and which will be under discussion in the first section of this book, concerns the sensory part of the soul. The second night, to which the second stanza refers, concerns the spiritual part. We will deal with this second night, insofar as it is active, in the second and third sections of the book. In the fourth section we will discuss the night insofar as it is passive.

3. This first night is the lot of beginners, at the time God commences to introduce them into the state of contemplation. It is a night in which their spirit also participates, as we will explain in due time. The second night or purification takes place in those who are already proficients, at the time God desires to lead them into the state of divine union. This purgation, of course, is more obscure, dark, and dreadful, as we will subsequently point out. . . .

---

*All selections in this chapter are from *John of the Cross: Selected Writings,* ed. and trans. Kieran Kavanaugh, O.C.D., The Classics of Western Spirituality (New York: Paulist, 1987), 61–62, 76–79, 81–82, 137–40, 178–80, 200–03, 208–09. Reprinted with permission of the publisher.

Chapter Thirteen

The manner and method of entering this night of sense.

1. Some counsels are in order now that the individual may both know the way of entering this night and be able to do so. It should be understood, consequently, that a person ordinarily enters this night of sense in two ways: active and passive.

The active way, which will be the subject of the following counsels, comprises what one can do and does by oneself to enter this night. The passive way is that in which one does nothing, but God accomplishes the work in the soul, while the soul acts as the recipient. This will be the subject of the fourth book where we will discuss beginners.[1] Since, with God's help, I will there give counsels pertinent to the numerous imperfections beginners ordinarily possess on this road, I will not take the time to offer many here. Nor is this the proper place to give them, since presently we are dealing only with the reasons for calling this journey a night, and with the nature and divisions of this night.

Nevertheless, if we do not offer some immediate remedy or counsel, this part would seem very short and less helpful. Therefore I want to set down the following abridged method. And I will do the same at the end of my discussion of each of the next two parts (or reasons for the use of the term "night") which, with God's help, will follow.

2. Though these counsels for the conquering of the appetites are brief and few in number, I believe they are as profitable and efficacious as they are concise. A person who sincerely wants to practice them will need no others since all the others are included in these.

3. First, have a habitual desire to imitate Christ in all your deeds by bringing your life into conformity with His. You must then study His life in order to know how to imitate Him and behave in all events as He would.

4. Second, in order to be successful in this imitation, renounce and remain empty of any sensory satisfaction that is not purely for the honor and glory of God. Do this out of love for Jesus Christ. In His life He had no other gratification, nor desired any other, than the fulfillment of His Father's will, which He called His meat and food [Jn 4:34]. . . .

5. Many blessings flow from the harmony and tranquillity of the four natural passions: joy, hope, fear, and sorrow. The following maxims contain a complete remedy for mortifying and pacifying the passions. If put into practice these maxims will give rise to abundant merit and great virtues.

---

1. John never got to this fourth book as promised; however he did deal in *The Dark Night* with what he mentions here.

6. Endeavor to be inclined always:

> not to the easiest, but to the most difficult;
> not to the most delightful, but to the harshest;
> not to the most gratifying, but to the less pleasant;
> not to what means rest for you, but to hard work;
> not to the consoling, but to the unconsoling;
> not to the most, but to the least;
> not to the highest and most precious, but to the lowest and most
>   despised;
> not to wanting something, but to wanting nothing;
> do not go about looking for the best of temporal things, but for
>   the worst, and desire to enter for Christ into complete nudity,
>   emptiness, and poverty in everything in the world.

7. You should embrace these practices earnestly and try to overcome the repugnance of your will toward them. If you sincerely put them into practice with order and discretion, you will discover in them great delight and consolation. . . .

10. As a conclusion to these counsels and rules it would be appropriate to repeat the verses in "The Ascent of Mount Carmel" (the drawing at the beginning of the book), which are instructions for climbing to the summit, the high state of union. Although in the drawing we admittedly refer to the spiritual and interior aspect, we also deal with the spirit of imperfection existent in the sensory and exterior part of the soul, as is evident by the two roads, one on each side of that path that leads to perfection. Consequently, these verses will here bear reference to the sensory part. Afterward, in the second division of this night, they may be interpreted in relationship to the spiritual part.

11. The verses are as follows:

> To reach satisfaction in all
>   desire its possession in nothing.
> To come to possess all
>   desire the possession of nothing.
> To arrive at being all
>   desire to be nothing.
> To come to the knowledge of all
>   desire the knowledge of nothing.
> To come to the pleasure you have not
>   you must go by a way in which you enjoy not.

To come to the knowledge you have not
  you must go by a way in which you know not.
To come to the possession you have not
  you must go by a way in which you possess not.
To come to be what you are not
  you must go by a way in which you are not.
When you turn toward something
  you cease to cast yourself upon the all.
For to go from all to the all
  you must deny yourself of all in all.
And when you come to the possession of the all
  you must possess it without wanting anything.
Because if you desire to have something in all
  your treasure in God is not purely your all.

12. In this nakedness the spirit finds its quietude and rest. For in coveting nothing, nothing raises it up and nothing weighs it down, because it is in the center of its humility. When it covets something, in this very desire it is wearied.

BOOK TWO

This book is a treatise on faith, the proximate means of ascent to union with God. It consequently considers the second part of this night, the night of spirit to which the following stanza refers.[2]

Chapter One

The Second Stanza

In darkness and secure,
By the secret ladder, disguised,
—Ah, the sheer grace!—
In darkness and concealment,
My house being now all stilled;

1. This second stanza tells in song of the sheer grace that was the soul's in divesting the spirit of all its imperfections and appetites for spiritual possessions. This

---

2. John gives an explanation of the second stanza in this chapter, but then never returns to it until his work *The Dark Night*. There he interprets it from a different perspective and also explains the stanza verse by verse.

grace is far greater here because of the greater hardship involved in quieting the house of one's spiritual nature and entering this interior darkness (the spiritual nudity of all sensory and immaterial things), leaning on pure faith alone, in an ascent by it to God.

The secret ladder represents faith, because all the rungs or articles of faith are secret to and hidden from both the senses and the intellect. Accordingly the soul lived in darkness, without the light of the senses and intellect, and went out beyond every natural and rational boundary to climb the divine ladder of faith that leads up to and penetrates the deep things of God [1 Cor 2:10].

The soul declares that it was disguised because in the ascent through faith its garments, apparel, and capacities were changed from natural to divine. On account of this disguise, neither the devil, nor temporal, nor rational things recognized or detained it. None of these can do harm to the one who walks in faith. . . .

Chapter Twenty-Six

The two kinds of knowledge of naked truths. The proper conduct of the soul in their regard.

1. For an adequate exposition of this subject (the knowledge of naked truths), God would have to move my hand and pen. For you should know, beloved reader, that what they in themselves are for the soul is beyond words. Since, however, I intentionally speak of these only so as to impart instruction and guide the soul through them to the divine union, let me discuss them in a brief and restricted way, which will be sufficient for our purpose.

2. . . . This intellectual vision is not like the vision of corporal objects, but rather consists in an intellectual understanding or vision of truths about God, or to a vision of present, past, or future events, which bears great resemblance to the spirit of prophecy, as we shall perhaps explain later.

3. This type of knowledge is divided into two kinds: The object of the one kind is the Creator; and that of the other is the creature, as we said. Both kinds bring intense delight to the soul. Yet those of God produce an incomparable delight; there are no words or terms to describe them, for they are the knowledge and delight of God Himself. And as David says: *There is nothing like unto Him* [Ps 40:6]. God is the direct object of this knowledge in that one of His attributes (His omnipotence, fortitude, goodness, sweetness, and so on) is sublimely experienced. And as often as this experience occurs, it remains fixed in the soul. Since this communication is pure contemplation, the soul clearly understands that it is ineffable. People are capable of describing it only through general expressions—expressions caused by the abun-

dance of the delight and good of these experiences. But they realize the impossibility of explaining with these expressions what they tasted and felt in this communication.

4. David, after having received a similar experience, spoke in these unprecise terms: *Judicia Domini vera, justificata in semetipsa. Desiderabilia super aurum et lapidem pretiosum multum, et dulciora super mel et favum* (God's judgments—the virtues and attributes we experience in God—are true, in themselves justified, more desirable than gold and extremely precious stone, and sweeter than the honey and the honeycomb) [Ps 19:11].

We read that Moses spoke only in general terms of the lofty knowledge that God, while passing by, gave him. And it happened that when the Lord passed before him in that knowledge, Moses quickly prostrated himself, crying: *Dominator Domine Deus, misericors et clemens, patiens, et multae miserationis, ac verax. Qui custodis misericordiam in millia,* and so on (Sovereign Lord God, merciful and clement, patient, and of great compassion, and true. You guard the mercy that you promise to thousands) [Ex 34:6–7]. Evidently, since Moses could not express with one concept what he knew in God, he did so through an overflow of words.

Although at times individuals use words in reference to this knowledge, they clearly realize that they have said nothing of what they experienced, for no term can give adequate expression to it. And thus when St. Paul experienced that lofty knowledge of God, he did not care to say anything else than that it was not licit for humans to speak of it [2 Cor 12:4].

5. This divine knowledge of God never deals with particular things, since its object is the Supreme Principle. Consequently one cannot express it in particular terms, unless a truth about something less than God is seen together with this knowledge of Him. But in no way can anything be said of that divine knowledge.

This sublime knowledge can be received only by a person who has arrived at union with God, for it is itself that very union. It consists in a certain touch of the divinity produced in the soul, and thus it is God Himself who is experienced and tasted there.[3] Although the touch of knowledge and delight that penetrates the substance of the soul is not manifest and clear, as in glory, it is so sublime and lofty that the devil is unable to meddle or produce anything similar (for there is no experience similar or comparable to it), or infuse a savor and delight like it. This knowledge savors of the divine essence and of eternal life, and the devil cannot counterfeit anything so lofty.

---

3. Although the general topic in this book deals with the purification of the spiritual faculties, John speaks here of experiences of actual union, substantial touches, proper to the state of transformation in God and to one already purified.

6. He could, nevertheless, ape that experience by presenting to the soul some very sensible feelings of grandeur and fulfillment, trying to persuade it that these are from God. But this attempt of the devil does not enter the substance of the soul and suddenly renew and fill it with love as does a divine touch. Some of these divine touches produced in the substance of the soul are so enriching that one of them would be sufficient not only to remove definitively all the imperfections that the soul would have been unable to eradicate throughout its entire life, but also to fill it with virtues and blessings from God.

7. These touches engender such sweetness and intimate delight in the soul that one of them would more than compensate for all the trials suffered in life, even though innumerable. Through these touches individuals become so courageous and so resolved to suffer many things for Christ that they find it a special suffering to observe that they do not suffer.

8. People are incapable of reaching this sublime knowledge through any comparison or imagining of their own, because it transcends what is naturally attainable. Thus God effects in the soul what it is incapable of acquiring. God usually grants these divine touches, which cause certain remembrances of Him, at times when the soul is least expecting or thinking of them. Sometimes they are produced suddenly through some remembrance, which may only concern some slight detail. They are so sensible that they sometimes cause not only the soul but also the body to tremble. Yet at other times with a sudden feeling of spiritual delight and refreshment, and without any trembling, they occur very tranquilly in the spirit.

9. Or again they may occur on uttering or hearing a word from Sacred Scripture or from some other source. These touches do not always have the same efficacy, nor are they always felt so forcefully, because they are often very weak. Yet no matter how weak they may be, one of these divine touches is worth more to the soul than numberless other thoughts and ideas about God's creatures and works.

Since this knowledge is imparted to the soul suddenly, without exercise of free will, individuals do not have to be concerned about desiring it or not. They should simply remain humble and resigned about it, for God will do His work at the time and in the manner He wishes.

10. I do not affirm that people should be negative about this knowledge as they should be with the other apprehensions, because this knowledge is an aspect of the union toward which we are directing the soul and which is the reason for our doctrine about the denudation and detachment from all other apprehensions. God's demands for granting such a grace are humility, suffering for love of Him, and resignation as to all recompense. God does not bestow these favors on a possessive soul, since He gives them out of a very special love for the recipient. For the individual receiving them is one who loves with great detachment. The Son of God meant this when He stated: *Qui autem diligit me, diligetur a Patre meo, et ego di-*

ligam eum et manifestabo ei meipsum (Those who love me will be loved by my Father, and I will love them and manifest Myself to them) [Jn 14:21]. This manifestation includes the knowledge and touches that God imparts to a person who has reached Him and truly loves Him. . . .

THE DARK NIGHT

BOOK ONE

Chapter Eight

[The beginning of the exposition of this dark night.]

1. This night, which as we say is contemplation, causes two kinds of darkness or purgation in spiritual persons according to the two parts of the soul, the sensory and the spiritual. Hence the one night of purgation will be sensory, by which the senses are purged and accommodated to the spirit; and the other night or purgation will be spiritual, by which the spirit is purged and denuded as well as accommodated and prepared for union with God through love.

The sensory night is common and happens to many. These are the beginners of whom we will treat first. The spiritual night is the lot of very few, of those who have been tried and are proficient, and of whom we will speak afterward.

2. The first purgation or night is bitter and terrible to the senses. But nothing can be compared to the second, for it is horrible and frightful to the spirit. Because the sensory night is first in order, we will speak of it now briefly; since it is a more common occurrence one finds more written on it. Then we will pass on to discuss more at length the spiritual night, for hardly anything has been said of it, in sermons or in writing; and even the experience of it is rare.[1]

3. Since the conduct of these beginners in the way of God is lowly and not too distant from love of pleasure and of self, as we explained, God desires to withdraw them from this base manner of loving and lead them on to a higher degree of divine love. And He desires to liberate them from the lowly exercise of the senses and of discursive meditation, by which they go in search of Him so inadequately and with so many difficulties, and lead them into the exercise of spirit, in which they become

---

1. In speaking again of the forms or levels of night, John follows the same basic division he made in *Ascent* 1, 1, 2: the night of the senses and that of the spirit. The first, which is common, is the lot of beginners as they pass into the stage of proficients; the second, which is rare, is the lot of proficients as they pass into the stage of the perfect. But as the commentary progresses it becomes clear that, because of the interdependence of sense and spirit, the one night or purification is not present without the other. In order of time, the effect is experienced predominantly first in the senses and then in the spirit.

capable of a communion with God that is more abundant and freer of imperfections. God does this after beginners have exercised themselves for a time in the way of virtue and have persevered in meditation and prayer. For it is through the delight and satisfaction they experience in prayer that they have become detached from worldly things and have gained some spiritual strength in God. This strength has helped them somewhat to restrain their appetites for creatures, and through it they will be able to suffer a little oppression and dryness without turning back. Consequently, it is at the time they are going about their spiritual exercises with delight and satisfaction, when in their opinion the sun of divine favor is shining most brightly on them, that God darkens all this light and closes the door and spring of the sweet spiritual water they were tasting as often and as long as they desired. For since they were weak and tender, no door was closed to them, as St. John says in the Book of Revelation [Rv 3:8]. God now leaves them in such darkness that they do not know which way to turn in their discursive imaginings. They cannot advance a step in meditation, as they used to, now that the interior sense faculties are engulfed in this night. He leaves them in such dryness that they not only fail to receive satisfaction and pleasure from their spiritual exercises and works, as they formerly did, but also find these exercises distasteful and bitter. As I said, when God sees that they have grown a little, He weans them from the sweet breast so that they might be strengthened, lays aside their swaddling bands, and puts them down from His arms that they may grow accustomed to walking by themselves. This change is a surprise to them because everything seems to be functioning in reverse.

4. This usually happens to recollected beginners sooner than to others since they are freer from occasions of backsliding and more quickly reform their appetites for worldly things. A reform of the appetites is the requirement for entering the happy night of the senses. Not much time ordinarily passes after the initial stages of their spiritual life before beginners start to enter this night of sense. And the majority of them do enter it because it is common to see them suffer these aridities.

5. We could adduce numerous passages from Sacred Scripture, for since this sensory purgation is so customary, we find a great many references to it throughout, especially in the psalms and the prophets. But I do not want to spend time citing them, because the prevalence of the experience of this night should be enough for those who are unable to find the scriptural references to it. . . .

BOOK TWO

Chapter Five

[Begins to explain how this dark contemplation is not only night for the soul but also affliction and torment.]

1. This dark night is an inflow of God into the soul that purges it of its habitual ignorances and imperfections, natural and spiritual, and which contemplatives call infused contemplation or mystical theology. Through this contemplation, God teaches the soul secretly and instructs it in the perfection of love without its doing anything or understanding how this happens.

Insofar as infused contemplation is loving wisdom of God, it produces two principal effects in the soul: It prepares the soul for the union with God through love by both purging and illumining it. Hence the same loving wisdom that purges and illumines the blessed spirits purges and illumines the soul here on earth.

2. Yet a doubt arises: Why, if it is a divine light (for it illumines souls and purges them of their ignorances), does one call it a dark night? In answer to this, there are two reasons why this divine wisdom is not only night and darkness for the soul, but also affliction and torment. First, because of the height of the divine wisdom, which exceeds the capacity of the soul. Second, because of the soul's baseness and impurity; and on this account the wisdom is painful, afflictive, and also dark for the soul.

3. To prove the first reason, we must presuppose a certain principle of the Philosopher: that the clearer and more obvious divine things are in themselves, the darker and more hidden they are to the soul naturally. The brighter the light the more the owl is blinded; and the more one looks at the brilliant sun, the more the sun darkens the faculty of sight, deprives it and overwhelms it in its weakness.[2]

Hence when the divine light of contemplation strikes souls not yet entirely illumined, it causes spiritual darkness, for it not only surpasses them but also deprives and darkens their act of understanding. This is why St. Dionysius and other mystical theologians call this infused contemplation a ray of darkness; that is, for the soul not yet illumined and purged. For this great supernatural light overwhelms the intellect and deprives it of its natural vigor.

David also said that clouds and darkness are near God and surround Him [Ps 18:12], not because this is true in itself but because it appears thus to our weak intellects, which in being unable to attain so bright a light are blinded and darkened. Hence, he immediately added: *Clouds passed before the great splendor of His presence* [Ps 18:12], that is, between God and our intellect. As a result, when God communicates this bright ray of His secret wisdom to the soul not yet transformed, He causes thick darkness in its intellect.

4. It is also evident that this dark contemplation is painful to the soul in these beginnings. Since this divine infused contemplation has many extremely good properties, and the still unpurged soul that receives it has many extreme miseries, and because two contraries cannot coexist in one subject, the soul must necessarily undergo affliction and suffering. Because of the purgation of its imperfections caused

---

2. Aristotle, *Metaphysics* 2, 1.

by this contemplation, the soul becomes a battlefield in which these two contraries combat one another. We will prove this by induction in the following way.

5. In regard to the first cause of one's affliction: Because the light and wisdom of this contemplation is very bright and pure, and the soul in which it shines is dark and impure, a person will be deeply afflicted on receiving it. When eyes are sickly, impure, and weak, they suffer pain if a bright light shines on them.

The soul, because of its impurity, suffers immensely at the time this divine light truly assails it. When this pure light strikes in order to expel all impurity, persons feel so unclean and wretched that it seems God is against them and they are against God.

Because it seems that God has rejected them, these souls suffer such pain and grief that when God tried Job in this way it proved one of the worst of Job's trials, as he says: *Why have you set me against you, and I am heavy and burdensome to myself?* [Jb 7:20]. Clearly beholding its impurity by means of this pure light, although in darkness, the soul understands distinctly that it is worthy neither of God nor of any creature. And what most grieves it is that it thinks it will never be worthy, and that there are no more blessings for it. This divine and dark light causes deep immersion of the mind in the knowledge and feeling of one's own miseries and evils; it brings all these miseries into relief so that the soul sees clearly that of itself it will never possess anything else. We can interpret that passage from David in this sense: *You have corrected people for their iniquity and have undone and consumed their souls, as a spider is eviscerated in its work* [Ps 39:12].

6. Souls suffer affliction in the second manner because of their natural, moral, and spiritual weakness. Since this divine contemplation assails them somewhat forcibly in order to subdue and strengthen their soul, they suffer so much in their weakness that they almost die, particularly at times when the light is more powerful. Both the sense and the spirit, as though under an immense and dark load, undergo such agony and pain that the soul would consider death a relief. The prophet Job, having experienced this, declared: *I do not want Him to commune with me with much strength that He might not overwhelm me with the weight of His greatness* [Jb 23:6].

7. Under the stress of this oppression and weight, individuals feel so far from all favor that they think, and so it is, that even that which previously upheld them has ended along with everything else, and that there is no one who will take pity on them. It is in this sense that Job also cried out: *Have pity on me, at least you my friends, for the hand of the Lord has touched me* [Jb 19:21].

How amazing and pitiful it is that the soul be so utterly weak and impure that the hand of God, though light and gentle, should feel so heavy and contrary. For the hand of God does not press down or weigh on the soul, but only touches it; and this mercifully, for God's aim is to grant it favors and not chastise it. . . .

Chapter Eleven

[The beginning of an explanation of verse 2 of the first stanza. Tells how the fruit of these dark straits is a vehement passion of divine love.]

1. In this second verse the soul refers to the fire of love that, like material fire acting on wood, penetrates it in this night of painful contemplation. Although this enkindling of love we are now discussing is in some way similar to that which occurs in the sensory part of the soul, it is as different from it in another way as is the soul from the body, or the spiritual part from the sensory part. For the enkindling of love occurs in the spirit and through it the soul in the midst of these dark conflicts feels vividly and keenly that it is being wounded by a strong divine love, and it has a certain feeling and foretaste of God. Yet it understands nothing in particular, for as we said the intellect is in darkness.

2. The spirit herein experiences an impassioned and intense love because this spiritual inflaming engenders the passion of love. Since this love is infused, it is more passive than active and thus generates in the soul a strong passion of love. This love is now beginning to possess something of union with God and thereby shares to a certain extent in its properties. These properties are actions of God more than of the soul, and they reside in it passively, although the soul does give its consent. But only the love of God, which is being united to the soul, imparts the heat, strength, temper, and passion of love, or fire, as the soul terms it here. The more the soul is equipped to receive the wound and union the more this love finds that all the soul's appetites are brought into subjection, alienated, incapacitated, and unable to be satisfied by any heavenly or earthly thing.

3. This happens very particularly in this dark purgation, as we said, since God so weans and recollects the appetites that they cannot find satisfaction in any of their objects. God proceeds thus so that by withdrawing the appetites from other objects and recollecting them in Himself, He may strengthen the soul and give it the capacity for this strong union of love, which He begins to accord by means of this purgation. In this union the soul will love God intensely with all its strength and all its sensory and spiritual appetites. Such love is impossible if these appetites are scattered by their satisfaction in other things. In order to receive the strength of this union of love, David proclaimed to God: *I will keep my strength for You* [Ps 59:10], that is, all the ability, appetites, and strength of my faculties, by not desiring to make use of them or find satisfaction in anything outside of You. . . .

SELECTED BIBLIOGRAPHY

TEXTS AND TRANSLATIONS

Vida y Obras de San Juan de la Cruz. Edited by Lucinio Ruano. 10th ed. Madrid, 1978.

The Collected Works of St. John of the Cross. Translated by Kieran Kavanaugh and Otilio Rodriguez. Washington, D.C.: Institute of Carmelite Studies, 1979.

The Complete Works of Saint John of the Cross. Translated by E. Allison Peers. 3 vols. London: Burns, Oates and Washbourne, 1934–35; Westminster, Md.: Newman, 1945.

John of the Cross: Selected Writings. Translated by Kieran Kavanaugh. The Classics of Western Spirituality. New York: Paulist; London, SPCK, 1987.

STUDIES

Baruzi, Jean. *Saint Jean de la Croix et le problème de l'expérience mystique.* Paris, 1924.

Dicken, E. W. Trueman. *The Crucible of Love.* New York: Sheed and Ward; London: Darton, Longman and Todd, 1963.

Maritain, Jacques. *Distinguish to Unite, or The Degrees of Knowledge.* Translated under the direction of Gerald B. Phelan. New York: Charles Scribner's Sons; London: Geoffrey Bles, 1959.

Morel, Georges. *Le sens de l'existence selon S. Jean de la Croix.* 3 vols. Paris, 1960–61.

Orcibal, Jean. *Saint Jean de la Croix et les mystiques rhéno-flamands.* Bruges, 1966.

Stein, Edith. *The Science of the Cross.* Translated by Hilda Graef. Chicago: Regnery; London: Burns and Oates, 1960.

Wojtyla, Karol. *Faith according to Saint John of the Cross.* Translated by Jordan Aumann. San Francisco: Ignatius Press, 1981.

Marie of the Incarnation

(1599–1672)

This seventeenth century Ursuline nun is, with Jonathan Edwards and Thomas Merton, one of our three representatives of Christian mysticism in the New World— somewhat paradoxically, because, though she lived and worked over thirty-two years in Quebec (where she is buried), spiritually she belongs entirely to the French seventeenth century. Born in 1599 in a middle-class family of Tours, she was married at age seventeen. The marriage, contracted out of obedience to her parents, failed to make her happy, but it gave her a son who would eventually bring her great religious consolation. After two years her husband died. Marie liquidated whatever was left of his declining silk business and, in 1621, agreed to manage her brother-in-law's household. His coach and transport commerce demanded much of his and of his wife's time away from home. Sharing the work of the servants, Marie deliberately exposed herself to their abuse, thus turning what could have been a comfortable position into an occasion for sacrifice and humiliation. In 1620 she experienced a mystical revelation which opened "the great door that gives access to the divine mercy." In 1625 she received the first of the great visions described in the report here reprinted. In 1631 she entered the newly established Ursuline novitiate of Tours. Her eleven year old son did not take the separation lightly and even incited his schoolmates to kidnap his mother from the convent. With the years he changed his views on religious vocation and, having first unsuccessfully attempted to enter the Jesuit order, joined the learned Benedictine Congregation of St. Maur. After her death he wrote his mother's biography based on her letters and her spiritual reports.

In 1639 Marie left with a young nun to start an Ursuline foundation in Quebec, after an emotional, definitive leavetaking from her son. Soon she became so involved in all the trials of the early colony that her letters constitute a significant source of historical information. From the parlor and the classroom of her convent she deeply influenced the religious life of the French as well as of the Indian population. After age forty she learned and mastered the three principal Indian languages: Algonquin, Iroquois, and Huron.

In 1633, while still in the Tours novitiate and at the request of her confessor, she wrote a report on her spiritual progress. This "relation" has survived only in the lengthy fragments incorporated in her son Dom Claude Martin's biography, together with one written in 1635. It appears to have contained a description of her spiritual progress during the early part of her life. Almost immediately after the mystical breakthrough, Marie seems to have experienced "intellectual" visions and a state of union. Throughout her report she uses the terminology of Teresa of Avila and John of the Cross. (For instance, in n. 48 the word "touches" directly translates *tocca* in the *Ascent of Mount Carmel.*) Not without reason Bossuet, in his *Instruction sur les états d'oraison,* called her "la Thérèse de nos jours et du Nouveau Monde."

In 1654, at the request of her Jesuit confessor and her son, she wrote another, more systematic account of her spiritual life. This text appears integrally in Claude Martin's 1677 biography, as well as in a manuscript copy of the original found in the Ursuline convent of Trois-Rivières (Quebec). In it Marie presents her spiritual life not as a mere succession of graces but as a process developing in clearly marked stages—an insight which she ascribes to divine illumination. The objective quality of this spiritual autobiography—in a letter to her son she calls it "toutes mes aventures"—strongly invites comparison with Teresa's *Life.* Though Marie lacks the liveliness, perhaps also the sharpness in distinguishing what had never been distinguished, her work displays the spiritual maturity of a report written by one who has completed all the stages of the spiritual process. (Teresa's great visions and her spiritual marriage followed long after the writing of her *Vida.*) At the same time, Marie's mysticism reveals a self-conscious quality which announces the end of an era. She has obviously learned all the concepts, knows what to expect, and how to classify it: the various kinds of visions, the spiritual betrothal and marriage.

Even the very deliberate search for suffering and humiliation suggests the arrival of the highly introspective and, for all its selflessness, very self-centered piety of the eighteenth and nineteenth centuries. Modern readers may find her tendency to measure love by the degree of self-influenced pain more than a little contrived. Yet they ought to remember that the various epochs of Christian mysticism have a style of their own, a style that heavily depends upon that of the surrounding culture. Marie's writings, though the work of a spiritually privileged person gifted with a discerning mind and, according to her editor, "the talent of a great writer," reflect some of that *preciosity* which Molière so effectively ridiculed. Thus she describes the dramatic situation of her personal life after the death of her husband only through the filter of almost cryptically chaste universalizations: "As soon as my bonds [of marriage] were broken and I had begun to taste the benefits of the Spirit and to know the vanity of things of this world, I felt myself called to religion [i.e., the Convent]. But there remained another bond [her son] which did not allow me [to follow this call] and which, according to my director, was, for the time being, willed by God." This is not the sort of prose that encourages a contemporary reader, however kindly disposed to the subject.

Yet this cultural distance vanishes the moment she begins her account of the great trinitarian visions (here reproduced) in the Sixth, Seventh, and Eighth States of Prayer. Between 1625 and 1631 Marie received three "intellectual" visions of the Trinity. The first, Marie herself points out, affected her understanding more than her will. Light and insight far beyond her powers of expression flooded her intelligence. She speaks of an "information" or "impression," indicating that a divine form was permanently imprinted upon her cognitive powers. The second vision, still "intellectual" in nature, had at the same time an overwhelmingly affective impact. She calls it "une impression amour-lumière" (as opposed to the "impression-lumière" of the first). Both visions follow a similar pattern. First an ecstatic view of the three divine Persons; then an intense concentration on the Word whereby the two other Persons recede into the background. In the third vision (reported in the Eighth State of Prayer), this priority of the Word makes place for a total possession of the soul by the three Persons of the Trinity. Though Marie does not attempt to define it herself, the terms used in her description suggest that it was as affectively charged as intellectually enlightening. Her soul is reaching a permanent state of union with God.

The final passage here reproduced (from the Thirteenth State of Prayer) concludes the *Relation.* It contains no visions at all, but a description of that permanent state of union that she had been experiencing in the years before her report. It is clearly meant to be a conclusion. In the pages preceding it she summarizes her passage, in later years, through the painful process of passive purgation, the final preparation for that uninterrupted peace which completes the mystical life. Her letters and later clarifications show her insight to have been correct. She appears to have remained as she was then until the end of her life. Precisely this completeness of the described process makes her report so unique in the history of mystical literature. A number of theological treatises (from Origen on) describe the stages of mystical progress, but here we possess a personal account of the completed experience.

Marie died in Quebec on April 30, 1672. Her son, Claude Martin, published her *Life* with the *Relation* of 1654 and fragments of that of 1633 in 1677. The only complete edition available remains that by Dom Albert Jamet, O.S.B.

Selections

THE RELATION OF 1654*

The Sixth State of Prayer

On the morning of Pentecost Monday [1625], while assisting at Mass in the chapel of the Feuillant Fathers—which was the place where I usually went to make my devotions and where our Lord had granted me His most signal favors—I was looking in the direction of the altar when all of a sudden my eyes were closed and my mind elevated and absorbed in a view of the most holy and august Trinity in a way I cannot explain. At once all the powers of my soul were suspended and felt the impression made upon them by this sacred mystery, an impression without form or figure, yet more clear and intelligible than any light. This impression begot in me the conviction that what my soul was experiencing was the truth, and this truth caused me to see in a flash the inner life which exists between the three Divine Persons: the love of the Father, who in contemplating Himself generates the Son, and this from all eternity unto all eternity. My soul received the impression of this truth in an ineffable manner which deprived me of all speech; it was engulfed in this light. Then it understood that the mutual love of the Father and the Son originates the Holy Spirit, which takes place by an immersion in each other's love without any prejudice to the distinction of the Persons. I received the impression that this origination is a spiration, but a spiration so elevated and so sublime that I have no terms for expressing it. While seeing the distinction [of Persons], I knew the unity of the essence of the three Divine Persons. And, although it would require many words to say it, in one moment, without any interval of time, I knew the unity [of the divine essence], the distinction [of the Persons], and the operations [which terminate] in the Persons and those [which terminate] outside Them. Nevertheless, in a certain spiritual manner I was enlightened by degrees in regard to the operations of the three Divine Persons [which terminate] outside Them. In this there was no intermingling, in any of these successive acts of enlightenment, of the things it was given me to understand; but all was presented with an unspeakable distinctness.

In the same impression [of this mystery] the most Holy Trinity revealed to my mind a knowledge of what it does through the medium of the supreme hierarchy of the angels; of the Cherubim, of the Seraphim, and of the Thrones, to whom it makes its holy will known without the medium of any created spirit. I distinctly learned the operations of each of the Divine Persons of the most august Trinity in each of

*From *The Autobiography of Venerable Marie of the Incarnation, O.S.U.: Mystic and Missionary,* trans. John J. Sullivan, S.J. (Chicago: Loyola University Press, 1964), 43–45, 56–60, 79–80, 178–82. Reprinted with permission of the publisher.

the choirs of this supreme hierarchy, and of the relations of each of the Persons to those choirs: that the eternal Father dwells among the Thrones, which signified for me the purity and the stability of His eternal thoughts; that the Word, through the splendor of His lights, communicates with the Cherubim; and that the Holy Spirit dwells among the Seraphim and replenishes them with His ardors; and finally, that the entire Trinity, in the unity of the divine essence, communicates with this supreme hierarchy, which in turn manifests the divine will to the other celestial spirits according to their ranks.

My soul was quite lost in these splendors, and it seemed that the Divine Majesty was pleased to illuminate it more and more regarding those things which creatures are impotent to express. I was also shown the subordination which the Divinity had fixed among the angels, so that some of them would be enlightened by others, according to their rank, but that when it so pleased God He enlightened them directly regarding His designs. He has done this also with some chosen souls in the world; and though I myself am filth and vileness, my soul has seen with certainty that it is of this number. And when my soul received this illumination it understood and experienced at the same time how it was created to the image of God: that the memory relates it to the eternal Father, the understanding to the Son, and the will to the Holy Spirit; and that, just as the most Holy Trinity is threefold in Person but one in essence, so also the soul is threefold in its powers but one in its substance.

This vision continued during the time of many Masses. Upon returning to myself I found myself on my knees just as I was when the vision began. . . .

The Seventh State of Prayer

Following upon my preceding state, one morning as I was at prayer God absorbed my spirit in Himself by an extraordinarily powerful attraction. I don't know what posture my body assumed at the time. Once again I was granted a vision of the most august Trinity, and its operations were manifested to me in a more elevated and distinct manner than formerly. The impression which I had of the Trinity the first time produced its principal effect in the understanding, and it seemed that the Divine Majesty granted it to me in order to enlighten me and dispose me for what He willed to do to me. But on this present occasion, although the understanding was enlightened and indeed more than on the previous one, it was primarily my will that was involved. For this new grace was granted entirely with a view to love; through love my soul found itself in a state of extreme familiarity with and fruition of the God of love.

Then, while I was engulfed in the presence of this most adorable Majesty, Father, Son, and Holy Spirit, in the acknowledgment and confession of my lowliness and in adoration of the Blessed Trinity, the Second Person of the Divine Word gave me to understand that He was truly the spouse of the faithful soul. I understood this truth with certainty, and the insight into it that was granted me was a proximate preparation for seeing it actualized in myself. At that moment this most adorable Person took possession of my soul and, embracing it with an inexplicable love, united it to Himself and took it for His bride. When I say that He embraced it, this of course was not after the manner of human embraces. Nothing which falls within the scope of the senses is like this divine operation, but it is necessary for me to express myself in terms of our earthly life, since we are composed of matter. This transpired by means of divine touches and of a mutual compenetration in such wise that, no longer being myself, I abided in Him through intimacy of love and of union, so that I was lost to myself and no longer aware of myself, having become Him by participation. Then, for short moments, I was aware of myself and beheld the eternal Father and the Holy Spirit, and then the unity of the divine existence. Being absorbed in the grandeur and in the love of the Word, I found myself impotent to render my homage to the Father and to the Holy Spirit, because the Word held my soul and all its powers captive in Himself, who was my Spouse and my Love, and who desired my soul entirely for Himself. . . .

I would have need of the powers of the Seraphim and of other blessed spirits to be able to narrate what transpired in this ecstasy and rapture of love which drew the understanding along with it and so made it incapable of regarding anything other than the treasures which it possessed in the sacred Person of the Eternal Word. It would be better to say that the powers of my soul, being engulfed and absorbed and reduced to the unity of the spirit, were all taken up with the Word, who, in the role of Spouse, granted to my soul great intimacy with Himself and the power to enjoy the dignity of bride. In this state the soul experiences that it is the Holy Spirit who moves it to treat as it does with the Word. It would be impossible for the creature, with all its limitations, to be so bold as to treat in this way with its God. And even if it were so forgetful of itself as to want to undertake to do so, it would not be in its power. Since these operations are entirely supernatural, the soul can only passively receive them and it would be impossible for it to distract itself from them or to apply itself to them merely more or less. The effects of these operations show the truth of this. And since the soul has been forestalled in this exalted grace and actually possesses it before perceiving its entry, the suddenness with which this happens shows that only a God of goodness and omnipotence could effect such an impression and operation.

The soul constantly experiences the presence of this gracious Being who has taken possession of her in the spiritual marriage and who inflames and consumes her with a fire so agreeable and pleasant that it is impossible to describe it. He causes her to chant a nuptial song in a manner which delights Him. Neither books nor study can teach the language of this song, which is entirely heavenly and divine. It owes its origin to the mutual embraces of the soul and this most adorable Word who by the kisses of His divine mouth fills her with His spirit and with His life. This nuptial song is the response of the soul to her well-beloved Spouse.

The spiritual marriage completely changes the state of the soul. Prior to this she was in a state of constant tendency toward and expectation of this exalted grace, which was shown her from afar inasmuch as she was made to experience the dispositions and preparations for receiving it. But now she no longer has such a tendency because she actually possesses Him whom she loves. Her being is entirely penetrated and possessed by Him. It is consumed by caresses and acts of love which cause it to expire in Him by suffering deaths the most sweet; moreover, these very deaths constitute the sweetness. I pause to consider whether I might be able to find any suitable comparisons with things of this world, but I can find none which would help me to describe the embraces of the Word and the soul. Although the soul knows that the Word is the great God, equal to the eternal Father, through whom all things have been made and subsist in being, still she embraces Him and speaks to Him face to face, knowing that she has been elevated to this dignity of having the Word for her Spouse and of being His bride and hence in a position to say to Him: "You are my other self, You are all mine. Come, my Spouse, let us be on with the affairs You have committed to me." The soul has no more desires, for she possesses her Beloved. She speaks to Him because He has spoken to her, but it is not by means of words. She performs her duties in order to seek His glory in and through all things, according to the lights He has given her, and to promote His reign as absolute Master of all hearts.

She redoubles her penances and spends herself in acts of charity for her neighbor, making herself all to all in order to gain them for her Beloved. Sometimes I would meet with a group of about twenty men, employees of my brother-in-law, in order to instruct them in what concerned their salvation. They gave me in an unconstrained and simple way an account of their actions, and they helped one another in the accusation of their faults whenever through forgetfulness anyone would leave something out. Occasionally I gathered them together in order to speak to them about God and teach them how they ought to observe His commandments. I would reprimand them very plainly, since these poor people were as submissive to me as children. I made those who had retired without saying their prayers get up again. They came to me for refuge in all their needs and especially in their sickness, as well as to have me restore good feelings between them and my brother-in-law whenever they displeased him. I had a strong urge to do all of that and to take care of them in their illnesses. Sometimes I had some lingering cases so that the place seemed like a hospital, with myself as infirmarian.

And in all these actions I had in mind that in doing them I was serving my Divine

Spouse. This lent agility to my body, so that doing these actions with this idea rendered them easy for me. In making the beds of the sick and of the well I was sometimes constrained, and indeed almost continually, to surrender myself to the interior touches which He who possessed my soul gave me to sustain me in the fatigue which I incurred for love of Him. I would prostrate myself on the ground and kiss it as an act of humility, judging that I was infinitely indebted to my Spouse for having given me the occasions for rendering Him some little services. In these lowly actions, in which I found a treasure, He continued and redoubled His caresses. I would hide myself then, for fear of meeting someone; and since the excess of His love in my soul was like a fire which stifled my breath, I spoke to him vocally in order to release this fire and was constrained to say to Him: "O my love, I can bear no more! Leave me to myself for a while, O my Beloved, for my weakness cannot bear the excess of Your love; or else take away my life, for Your love causes me to suffer more than a soul enclosed in the prison of this body can bear." I felt that He was pleased with my words, for it was His spirit which did not permit me to remain silent. . . .

The Eighth State of Prayer

One day, at the signal for the beginning of evening prayer, while I was kneeling at my place in choir, my soul was ravished by a sudden consolation. Then the three Persons of the most Holy Trinity manifested Themselves anew to me, together with the impression of these words of the most adorable Word Incarnate, *If anyone love Me, My Father will love him, and We will come to him and make Our abode with him.* This impression carried with it the effects of these divine words and the operations of the three Divine Persons in me in a higher degree than ever before; and these operations caused me to understand and experience these words by being penetrated by the reality which they signified. And the most Holy Trinity, in its unity, appropriated my soul to itself as a thing which was its own and which it had rendered capable of receiving its divine impression and the effects of its activity.

In this great abyss it was made known to me that I then received the greatest grace of all those given to me up till then: the communication of the three Divine Persons. In a manner more distinct and intelligible than by means of any words, I was enlightened as follows: "The first time that I manifested Myself to you it was in order to instruct your soul in this great mystery; the second time, it was in order that the Word might take your soul for His spouse; but this time the Father, the Son, and the Holy Spirit give and communicate Themselves in order to possess your soul entirely." Then the effect followed, and just as the three Divine Persons possessed me, I also possessed Them in a plentitude of participation of the treasures of the divine magnificence. The eternal Father was my Father, the most adorable Word was my Spouse, and the Holy Spirit was the one who by His operation acted in my soul and caused it to receive the divine impressions.

During this entire operation I saw myself as the nothingness which this great All had chosen to receive the effects of its great mercies. All I could say was, "O my great God! O most adorable Abyss! I am mere nothingness!" And then I heard this reply, "Even though you are mere nothingness, nevertheless you belong entirely to Me." This was repeated to me many times, in proportion to my abasements; and the more I abased myself, the more I saw myself exalted and my soul experienced caresses which could not be expressed in human language. Ah! Who could tell the greatness of the honor God does the soul which He has created to His image when it pleases Him to elevate it to His divine embraces? This is something so astonishing, in regard to the mere nothingness of the creature, that if such a soul were not sustained by the gentleness of the spirit of this same God and by His moderation, it would be reduced to the nothingness of annihilation. I am unable to express myself in any other way.

This whole marvelous impression and activity took place during the time of a half hour. I found myself [at the end of it] supported by my chair. I had sufficient liberty to take part in the chanting of Compline in choir, in spite of the divine emanations and embraces my soul had received and which had quite liquified it. . . .

The Thirteenth State of Prayer

. . . In proportion to the degree of God's purifying activity in the soul that He conducts along this spiritual way, He permits many exterior crosses to befall it in order that St. Paul's words may be verified from every aspect, *He has conformed them to the image of His Son.* And I repeat it, it is necessary to pass through great interior and exterior trials which would frighten the soul if it were permitted to see them before actually experiencing them, and would even cause it to quit everything in order to avoid having to bear them, if a secret power did not sustain it. For it seems that the waters of tribulation through which the soul has passed by means of so many spiritual circumcisions have extinguished the fire which consumed it so gently in the superior part of the soul when its powers were suspended and it enjoyed God in purity of spirit. In fact, the poor soul doesn't know where it is. It is enveloped in a spiritual cloud which has obscured its view and, so it seems to the soul, has taken away the portion which it possessed in its sovereign and unique Good, the adorable Word Incarnate. But finally the Word Incarnate takes pity on the soul by causing the cloud to evaporate and making it experience rather belatedly the import of this passage, *Behold, my conduit has been made into a copious brook and has almost become a sea.*

The soul possesses in larger measure than ever the goods of the adorable Word Incarnate and the Word Himself, who inundates and engulfs it in Himself in a manner worthy of His munificent largess. . . .

As regards the passage cited above, I now experience with a quite extraordinary clearness the ways of the adorable Word Incarnate, and I perceive with great clarity and certainty that He is love itself, that He is intimately united to my spirit and unites my spirit to His, and that *all His words are spirit and life* in me. Above all, my soul experiences that because it is intimately united with Him it is also intimately united with the eternal Father and with the Holy Spirit, and through this experience it perceives the truth of what our adorable Lord and Master said to His apostles during His last discourse with them and in His prayer to God His Father; thus, for example, it experiences the truth of His reply to Philip's request to see the Father—*Philip, he who sees Me sees the Father; how do you say, show us the Father? Do you not believe that I am in the Father and the Father in Me?*

This manner of union is very elevated and pure, for though I speak of the sacred Word Incarnate I don't mean to imply that I have an imaginative image of Him; for the soul experiences, in a spiritual purity and simplicity, that the Father and the Word Incarnate are only one with the adorable Spirit, although it by no means identifies their Persons. The soul attains to the divine operations through the Spirit of the adorable Word Incarnate. Now, by these motions, impressions, and operations this same Spirit causes me to speak at one time to the eternal Father and at another time to the Son and to Himself. Without any previous reflecting I find myself saying to the Father, "O Father, in the name of Thy well-beloved Son, I say this to You." And to the Son, "My well-beloved, my most dear Spouse, I ask of You that Your will be accomplished in me," and other things which this Spirit suggests to me. And I experience that it is the Holy Spirit who binds me to the Father and the Son.

Often I find myself saying to Him, "O Divine Spirit, direct me in the ways of my Divine Spouse." And I am constantly engaged in this converse with the Divine Persons, in a manner so delicate, simple, and deep that it defies expression. It is not an action; it is an atmosphere in the center of the soul wherein God abides, which is so pleasant that, as I've already said, I can't find words suitable for expressing myself. My glances at His adorable Majesty carry with them what this Spirit causes me to say to Him, and it is through Him that I speak. For I can say absolutely nothing in the language of the spirit, which is the language proper to this communication whereby His Divine Majesty wishes to honor my lowliness, except through His impulse. And since this impulse is extremely simple, how shall my tongue express what my spirit cannot distinguish because of its very great simplicity and purity and which becomes increasingly simple?

All the time of my spiritual exercises is passed in this way. Today these words of our Lord were imprinted on my spirit: *I am the vine and My Father is the husband-*

man. Every branch that does not bear fruit in Me He will cut off; and He will prune every branch that bears fruit so that it may bear more fruit. This passage clearly intimated to me the reasons for the diverse states of purgation which I've already described and also how important it is to be united to this divine vine, the adorable Word Incarnate, since no one can have life except he be engrafted in Him through the Holy Spirit. Then, too, the high point of the spiritual life and the consummation of the perfection of the saints consists in living only through Him, according to the text of St. Paul.

There is yet another disposition in which I find myself at times, one which derives from the one I spoke of in the last chapter. I find myself in it more often when I'm alone in my room, after I've returned from some exercise of rule in the chapel, especially after Holy Communion, more than at any other time. I experience an impression in my soul [on such occasions]. It's not that I really perceive an impression at the time, but I call it such in order to somehow express myself. It is something so elevated, so ravishing, so divine, so simple, and so far removed from what can be expressed in human language that all I can say is that during it I am in God, possessed by Him, and that He would soon consume me by the intensity and force of His love if I were not sustained by another impression which follows upon the former. This second impression doesn't cause the first to disappear but merely tempers its splendor, which is too great for one to bear in this present life. If it were not thus tempered by this second impression, which always has some reference to the adorable Word Incarnate, my Divine Spouse, I wouldn't be able to go on living, for my soul can live only in Him, in my fundamental state of love [for Him] day and night and at every moment.

The effects of this state are always an annihilation, along with a deep-seated knowledge that one is nothingness and weakness itself, a low estimate of oneself and of one's own activity, which is seen as always mixed with imperfection. And of this the soul has a real conviction, which serves to keep it profoundly humble, no matter how elevated it might be.

A further effect is a certain fear, without anxiety however, lest one be deceived in the ways of the spirit and mistake therein the false for the truth. This fear is useful for abnegation and the spirit of compunction. It is likewise conducive to peace, a peace which results from acquiescence in one's pains, sufferings, and crosses by receiving them from the hand of God as a chastisement inflicted by a good Father who lovingly corrects His child, which after its chastisement casts itself into His arms.

This state also begets a great patience with one's crosses and a whole-souled inclination towards peace and benignity with everyone—a gentle interior eagerness to be benevolent towards those by whom one has been offended and with whom one tactfully seeks contact in order to treat them as friends, whether by agreeable words or by rendering them certain services, or by meeting them with a friendly countenance, or in other ways capable of gaining their heart and showing them that one has nothing against them, while at the same time not seeming to take note of their offenses. . . . The faults and imperfections which a soul in this state commits result from forgetfulness and surprise, but these faults always come to nothing, for the purely natural man has lost his own power as a result of the divine operations.

This state also causes one to accept sufferings in a spirit of love for and union with the adorable Word Incarnate through loving communion with Him. It begets a great love of the vocation and state to which God calls the soul, as well as a disposition to do and undertake all through love for Him. It begets, too, an ever greater love for everything done and practiced in the Church of God, in which one sees only purity and holiness. Finally, it begets an all-embracing urge to permit oneself to be guided by those who hold the place of God and to submit one's own judgment to them.

I should mention here that the Spirit who has so lovingly guided me has always had in mind one same thing; it was always with a view to my living in the spirit of the Gospel that He has directed my soul in the practice of the virtues I've spoken about and of many others of which I've said nothing. From the very beginning my soul has felt a constant attraction towards that spirit and has aspired to a perfect possession of the spirit of Jesus Christ. And our Lord has granted me that degree of realization of my aspiration which He saw fit to give by means of His operations [in my soul] during the succession of states of prayer through which, in the excess of His great mercy, He has caused me to pass. Had I corresponded faithfully with those divine operations in my soul my progress in the way of perfection would have been quite different. But my infidelities give me reason to fear.

I beg the God of goodness, my adorable Spouse, to be pleased to drown them all in His precious blood and to have mercy on me. May He be eternally blessed, praised, and glorified by the saints, whom I beg to intercede for me before the divine justice.

SELECTED BIBLIOGRAPHY

TEXTS AND TRANSLATIONS

Ecrits spirituels et historiques. Edited by Albert Jamet. 4 vols. Paris and Quebec, 1929–39.

Correspondance. Edited by Guy-Marie Oury. 2 vols. Solesmes, 1971.

The Autobiography of Venerable Marie of the Incarnation, O.S.U.: Mystic and Missionary. [a translation of *La Relation de 1654*] Translated by John J. Sullivan, S.J. Chicago: Loyola University Press, 1964.

Marie of the Incarnation: The Relation of 1654. Translated by Irene Mahoney, O.S.U. Sources of American Spirituality. New York: Paulist, forthcoming.

STUDIES

Adriazola, Maria-Paul. "Vivre de l'Esprit de Jésus-Christ: Marie de l'Incarnation." Parts 1, 2. *Nova et Vetera* 53 (1978): 208–22; 291–308.

Bremond, Henri. *Histoire littéraire du sentiment religieux en France.* Vol. 6, *La conquête mystique: Marie de l'Incarnation; Turba Magna.* Paris, 1923. Reprint. Paris, 1967.

Jetté, Fernand, O.M.I. *The Spiritual Teaching of Mary of the Incarnation.* Translated by Mother M. Herman, O.S.U. New York: Sheed and Ward, 1963.

Michel, Robert, O.M.I. *Vivre dans l'Esprit: Marie de l'Incarnation.* Montreal, 1975.

Oury, Guy-Marie. *Marie de l'Incarnation, 1599–1672.* 2 vols. Quebec, Solesmes, and Tours, 1973.

Rétif, André. *Marie de l'Incarnation et la mission.* Tours, 1964.

Jeanne-Marie Guyon

(1648–1717)

No other spiritual movement presented in this collection has suffered more from misrepresentation and unfair polemics than what we have come to comprehend under the general, derogatory term "Quietism." Yet it started promisingly enough and to the end continued to enjoy some high ecclesiastical patronage. No one thought anything but good of the *Breve compendio intorno alla perfezione cristiana* written by the Italian Jesuit, Achille Gagliardi, under the inspiration of his penitent, Isabella Bellinzaga. Bérulle, Camus, Surin, and other luminaries of the French Church in the seventeenth century regarded it as a highly effective restatement of traditional, spiritual doctrine intended to meet the needs of the modern age. A famous spiritual director in Rome, Miguel de Molinos (b. 1628, near Saragossa) encountered an even more flattering reception with his *Spiritual Guide,* though his recommendations may have seemed a little one-sided to some. Only contemplative prayer leads to spiritual perfection, he taught. To attain it, the Christian should avoid active effort and concentrate entirely on inner quiet. When some critics (mostly Jesuits) objected, the Pope defended Molinos. Yet as rumors increased about the dangerous effect of his

theories on the morals of his penitents, the Holy Office impounded some 12,000 letters and had him arrested for doctrinal errors as well as for immoral conduct. Was Molinos guilty of the sixty-eight charges which he himself, practicing the non-resistance he preached, admitted in court? We shall never know until we gain access to the letters now held under sequester in the Vatican. Molinos spent nine years in a Roman jail, a model of piety and virtue, before dying there a saintly death. It is difficult to recognize the principles of the *Guide* (by then, duly "indexed") in the condemned propositions.

The Molinos affair was not the end of the movement, but merely its beginning. In France, Jeanne-Marie Guyon, the pious widow of an older cousin to whom family interests had sacrificed her, soon afterward began to spread similar theories in her *Moyen court et facile de faire oraison* (in English, translated as *Short Method of Prayer* [1685]). When questioned, she denied any influence of Molinos' doctrine. At first, the book enjoyed an enormous success not only among the devout, but even in the highest social circles — Madame de Maintenon attempted to convince King Louis XIV to live by its precepts. Yet soon it came under a cloud. Again, today's reader would be hard put to find anything more objectionable than a one-sided emphasis upon passive methods, and perhaps an oversimplification of the course of spiritual life. In the subsequent *Torrents spirituels* Jeanne Guyon partly removed the ambiguity by declaring that her message was not destined for all, but she added confusion by her explanations of the controversial concept of *quiet.* Did it consist in infused grace or in an acquired habit? The question would disturb few theologians today, but in the climate of the seventeenth century disputes about grace and free will, it assumed threatening proportions. Surely her "third state" of quiet appears totally to surpass a person's innate or acquired capacity. Nor can the reader fail to be struck by the similarity between Madame Guyon's theory and Saint Teresa's orthodox description of the upper mansions in *The Interior Castle.* Still we must admit that Jeanne's judgment did not always equal her extraordinary spiritual sensitivity. She tends both to generalize what should have remained restricted to the specifics of her own development, while at the same time, with most Quietists, she appears to consider her movement as that of a spiritual elite under her guidance. Much also has been made of the fact that she was theologically "uneducated"—with doubtful justification, considering the surpassing influence she exercised on some of the leading theologians of her age, such as Fénelon. One wonders whether she and her writings

may not have served as a scapegoat for various things some highly placed ecclesiastics (Bossuet and the Bishop of Paris among them) did not like. One of them was that an "uneducated" woman should presume to divulge principles of spiritual theology. There can be little doubt that the polemics against her writings were at least in part inspired by an almost universal prejudice against women who would assume any spiritual role higher than the one of obeying their spiritual director (a problem of which Teresa already dared to complain and of which Marie of the Incarnation presents a less blatant, but still disquieting instance). At least the general drift of Jeanne's doctrine appears sound enough.

In presenting spiritual life as a process in stages of increasing detachment and surrender to divine Providence, she stayed within a tradition that runs from the Greek Fathers to the present age. In any case, the modern reader, all too much inclined toward an active approach to spiritual life, is not likely to be led astray by a perhaps exaggerated emphasis on spiritual passivity. Madame Guyon's lasting contribution may well lie in those who, under the influence, however indirect, of her movement, were capable of expressing its principles in more accurate terms and of integrating them with a more balanced vision. Among them, first place must go to the author of *The Divine Abandon*, Jean de Caussade, S.J. But most influential was her direct disciple, Fénelon, a man who succeeded in creating as much controversy as Jeanne herself had caused.

Selections

A SHORT METHOD OF PRAYER*

CHAPTER ONE
[ON THE IMPORTANCE OF PRAYER]

. . . Prayer is the key of perfection and of sovereign happiness; it is the efficacious means of getting rid of all vices and of acquiring all virtues; for the way to become perfect is to live in the presence of God. He tells us this himself: "Walk before me, and be perfect" (Gen 17:1). Prayer alone can bring you into His presence, and keep you there continually.

What we need, then, is an attitude of prayer, in which we can *constantly* abide, and out of which exterior occupations cannot draw us; a prayer which can be offered alike by princes, kings, prelates, magistrates, soldiers, children, artisans, labourers, women, and the sick. This prayer is not mental, but *of the heart*.

It is not a prayer of thought alone, because the mind of man is so limited that while it is occupied with one thing it cannot be thinking of another. But it is the PRAYER OF THE HEART, which cannot be interrupted by the occupations of the mind. Nothing can interrupt the prayer of the heart but unruly affections; and when once we have tasted of the love of God, it is impossible to find our delight in anything but Himself.

Nothing is easier than to have God and to live upon Him. He is more truly in us than we are in ourselves. He is more anxious to give Himself to us than we are to possess Him. All that we want is to know the way to seek Him, which is so easy and so natural that breathing itself is not more so.

Oh, you who imagine yourselves incapable of religious feeling, you may live in prayer and in God as easily and as continuously as you live by the air you breathe. Will you not, then, be inexcusable if you neglect to do it, after you have learned the way?

CHAPTER TWO
[ON THE FIRST DEGREE OF PRAYER]

There are two means by which we may be led into the higher forms of prayer. One is *Meditation*, the other is *Meditative Reading*. By meditative reading I mean the taking of some truths, either doctrinal or practical—the latter rather than the former—and reading them in this way: Take the truth which has presented itself to

---

*All selections in this chapter are from J. M. B. de la Mothe Guyon, *A Short Method of Prayer and Spiritual Torrents,* trans. A. W. Marston (London: Sampson Low, Marston, Low, and Searle, 1875), 3–10, 13–15, 18–20, 194–203.

you, and read two or three lines, seeking to enter into the full meaning of the words, and go on no further so long as you find satisfaction in them; leave the place only when it becomes insipid. After that, take another passage, and do the same, not reading more than half a page at once.

It is not so much from the amount read that we derive profit, as from the manner of reading. Those people who get through so much do not profit from it; the bees can only draw the juice from the flowers by resting on them, not by flying round them. Much reading is more for scholastic than for spiritual science; but in order to derive profit from spiritual books, we should read them in this way; and I am sure that this manner of reading accustoms us gradually to prayer, and gives us a deeper desire for it. The other way is *Meditation*, in which we should engage at a chosen time, and not in the hour given to reading. I think the way to enter into it is this: After having brought ourselves into the presence of God by a definite act of faith, we should read something substantial, not so much to reason upon it as to fix the attention, observing that the principal exercise should be the presence of God, and that the subject should rather fix the attention than exercise reason.

This *faith in the presence of God within our hearts* must lead us to enter within ourselves, collecting our thoughts, and preventing their wandering; this is an effectual way of getting rid of distracting thoughts, and of losing sight of outward things, in order to draw near to God, who can only be found in the secret place of our hearts, which is the *sancta sanctorum* in which He dwells.

He has promised that if any one keeps His commandments, He will come to him, and *make His abode* with him (Jn 14:23). St. Augustine reproaches himself for the time he lost through not having sought God at first in this way.

When, then, we are thus buried in ourselves, and deeply penetrated with the presence of God within us—when the senses are all drawn from the circumference to the centre, which, though it is not easily accomplished at first, becomes quite natural afterwards—when the soul is thus gathered up within itself and is sweetly occupied with the truth read, not in reasoning upon it but in feeding upon it and exciting the will by the affection rather than the understanding by consideration: the *affection* being thus touched must be suffered to *repose* sweetly and at peace, *swallowing* what it has tasted.

As a person who only masticated an excellent meal would not be nourished by it, although he would be sensible of its taste, unless he ceased this movement in order to swallow it; so when the affection is stirred, if we seek continually to stir it, we extinguish its fire and thus deprive the soul of its nourishment. We must swallow by a *loving repose* (full of respect and confidence) what we have masticated and tasted. This method is very necessary, and would advance the soul in a short time more than any other would do in several years.

But as I said that the direct and principal exercise should be the *sense of the presence of God*, we must most faithfully *recall the senses* when they wander.

This is a short and efficacious way of fighting with distractions, because those who endeavour directly to oppose them irritate and increase them, but by losing ourselves in the thought of a present God, and suffering our thoughts to be drawn to Him, we combat them indirectly and without thinking of them, but in an effectual manner. And here let me warn beginners not to run from one truth to another, from one subject to another, but to keep themselves to one so long as they feel a taste for it: this is the way to enter deeply into truths, to taste them, and to have them impressed upon us. I say it is difficult at first thus to retire within ourselves, because of the habits, which are natural to us, of being taken up with the outside; but when we are a little accustomed to it, it becomes exceedingly easy, both because we have formed the habit of it, and because God, who only desires to communicate Himself to us, sends us abundant grace and an experimental sense of His presence, which renders it easy. . . .

CHAPTER THREE
[ON "THE PRAYER OF SIMPLICITY"]

The second degree has been variously termed *Contemplation, The Prayer of Silence*, and *of repose*, while others again have called it the *Prayer of Simplicity*, and it is of this last term that I shall make use here, being more appropriate than that of *Contemplation*, which signifies a degree of prayer more advanced than that of which I speak.

After a time, as I have said, the soul becomes sensible of a facility in recognising the presence of God; it collects itself more easily; prayer becomes natural and pleasant; it knows that it leads to God; and it perceives the smell of His perfumes.

Then it must change its method, and observe carefully what I am about to say, without being astonished at its apparent implausibility.

First of all, when you bring yourself into the presence of God by faith, remain a short time in an attitude of respectful silence. If from the beginning, in making this act of faith, you are sensible of a little taste of the presence of God, remain as you are without troubling yourself on any subject, and keep that which has been given you, so long as it may remain.

If it leaves you, excite your will by means of some tender affection, and if you then find that your former state of peace has returned, remain in it. The first must be blown softly, and as soon as it is lighted, cease to blow it, or you will put it out. It is also necessary that you should go to God, not so much to obtain something from Him as to please Him and to do His will; for a servant who only serves his master in proportion to the recompense he receives is unworthy of any remuneration.

Go, then, to prayer, not only to enjoy God but to be as He wills: this will keep you equal in times of barrenness and in times of abundance, and you will not be dismayed by the repulses of God nor by His apparent indifference.

CHAPTER FIVE
[ON ABANDONMENT TO GOD]

I beg you, whoever you may be, who are desirous of giving yourselves to God, not to take yourselves back when once you are given to Him, and to remember that a thing once given away is no longer at your disposal. *Abandonment* is the key to the inner life: he who is thoroughly abandoned will soon be perfect.

You must, then, hold firmly to your abandonment, without listening to reason or to reflection. A great faith makes a great abandonment; you must trust wholly in God, against hope believing in hope (Rom 4:18). *Abandonment* is the casting off of all care of ourselves, to leave ourselves to be guided entirely by God.

All Christians are exhorted to abandonment, for it is said to all, "Take no thought for the morrow, for your Heavenly Father knows that you have need of all these things" (Matt 6:32, 34). "In all your ways acknowledge Him, and He shall direct your paths" (Prov 3:6). "Commit your works to the Lord, and your thoughts shall be established" (Prov 16:3). "Commit your way to the Lord; trust also in Him, and He shall bring it to pass" (Ps 37:5).

Abandonment, then, ought to be an utter leaving of ourselves, both outwardly and inwardly, in the hands of God, forgetting ourselves and thinking only of God. By this means the heart is kept always free and contented.

Practically it should be a continual loss of our own will in the will of God, a renunciation of all natural inclinations, however good they may appear, in order that we may be left free to choose only as God chooses: we should be indifferent to all things, whether temporal or spiritual, for the body or the soul; leaving the past in forgetfulness, the future to providence, and giving the present to God; contented with the present moment, which brings with it God's eternal will for us; attributing nothing which happens to us to the creature, but seeing all things in God, and regarding them as coming infallibly from His hand, with the exception only of our own sin.

Leave yourselves, then, to be guided by God as He will, whether as regards the inner or the outward life.

SPIRITUAL TORRENTS

CHAPTER NINE
[ON THE HIGHEST DEGREE OF THE PASSIVE WAY OF FAITH]

All that has taken place up to this point has been in the individual capacity of the creature; but here the creature is taken out of his own capacity to receive an infinite capacity in God Himself. And as the torrent, when it enters the sea, loses its own being in such a way that it retains nothing of it, and takes that of the sea, or rather is taken out of itself to be lost in the sea; so this soul loses the human in order that it may lose itself in the divine, which becomes its being and its subsistence, not essentially, but mystically. Then this torrent possesses all the treasures of the sea, and is as glorious as it was formerly poor and miserable.

It is in the tomb that the soul begins to resume life, and the light enters insensibly. Then it can be truly said that "The people which sat in darkness saw great light; and to them which sat in the region and shadow of death light is sprung up" (Matt 4:16). There is a beautiful figure of this resurrection in Ezekiel (chap. 37), where the dry bones gradually assume life: and then there is that other passage, "The hour is coming, and now is, when the dead shall hear the voice of the Son of God; and they that hear shall live" (John 5:25). O you who are coming out of the sepulchre! you feel within yourselves a germ of life springing up little by little: you are quite astonished to find a secret strength taking possession of you: your ashes are reanimated: you feel yourselves to be in a new country. The poor soul, which only expected to remain at rest in its grave, receives an agreeable surprise. It does not know what to think: it supposes that the sun must have shed upon it a few scattered rays through some opening or chink, whose brightness will only last for a moment. It is still more astonished when it feels this secret vigour permeating its entire being, and finds that it gradually receives a new life, to lose it no more for ever, unless it be by the most flagrant unfaithfulness.

But this new life is not like the former one: it is a *life in God*. It is a perfect life. The soul *lives no longer* and works no longer of itself, but *God* lives, acts, and operates in it (Gal 2:20); and this goes on increasing, so that it becomes perfect with God's perfection, rich with God's riches, and loving with God's love.

The soul sees now that whatever it owned formerly had been in its own possession: now it no longer possesses, but is possessed: it only takes a new life in order to lose it in God; or rather it only lives with the life of God; and as He is the principle of life, the soul can want nothing. What a gain it has made by all its losses! It has lost the created for the Creator, the nothing for the All in all. All things are given to it, not in itself, but in God; not to be possessed by itself, but to be possessed by God.

Its riches are immense, for they are God Himself. It feels its capacity increasing day by day to immensity: every virtue is restored to it, but in God.

It must be remarked, that as it was only despoiled by degrees, so it is only enriched and vivified by degrees. The more it loses itself in God, the greater its capacity becomes; just as the more the torrent loses itself in the sea, the more it is enlarged, having no other limits than those of the sea: it participates in all its properties. The soul becomes strong and firm: it has lost all means, but it has found the end. This divine life becomes quite natural to it. As it no longer feels itself, sees itself, or knows itself, so it no longer sees or understands or distinguishes anything of God as distinct or outside of itself. It is no longer conscious of love, or light, or knowledge; it only knows that God is, and that it no longer lives except in God. All devotion is action, and all action is devotion: all is the same; the soul is indifferent to all, for all is equally God. Formerly it was necessary to exercise virtue in order to perform virtuous works; here all distinction of action is taken away, the actions having no virtue in themselves, but all being God, the meanest action equally with the greatest, provided it is in the order of God and at His time: for all that might be of the natural choice, and not in this order, would have another effect, leading the soul out of God by unfaithfulness. Not that it would be brought out of its degree or its loss, but out of the divine plan, which makes all things one and all things God. So the soul is *indifferent* as to whether it be in one state or another, in one place or another: all is the same to it, and it lets itself be carried along naturally. It ceases to think, to wish, or to choose for itself; but remains content, without care or anxiety, no longer distinguishing its inner life to speak of it. Indeed it may be said not to possess one: it is no longer in itself; it is all in God. It is not necessary for it to shut itself up within itself; it does not hope to find anything there, and does not seek for it. If a person were altogether penetrated with the sea, having sea within and without, above and below, on every side, he would not prefer one place to another, all being the same to him. So the soul does not trouble itself to seek anything or to do anything; that is, of itself, by itself, or for itself. It remains as it is. But what does it do? Nothing— always nothing. It does what it is made to do, it suffers what it is made to suffer. Its peace is unchangeable, but always natural. It has, as it were, passed into a state of nature; and yet how different from those altogether without God!

The difference is that it is compelled to action by God without being conscious of it, whereas formerly it was nature that acted. It seems to itself to do neither right nor wrong, but it lives satisfied, peaceful, doing what it is made to do in a steady and resolute manner.

God alone is its guide; for at the time of its loss, it lost its own will. And if you were to ask what are its desires, it could not tell. It can choose for itself no longer: all desire is taken away, because, having found its centre, the heart loses all natural inclination, tendency, and activity, in the same way as it loses all repugnance and contrariety. The torrent has no longer either a declivity or a movement: it is in repose, and at its end.

But with what satisfaction is this soul satisfied? With the satisfaction of God, immense, general, without knowing or understanding what it is that satisfies it; for here all sentiments, tastes, views, particular opinions, however delicate they may be, are taken from it: that certain vague, indefinable something, which formerly occupied without occupying it, is gone, and nothing remains to it. But this insensibility is very different to that of death, burial, and decay. That was a deprivation of life, a distaste, a separation, the powerlessness of the dying united with the insensibility of the dead; but this is an *elevation* above all these things, which does not remove them, but renders them useless. A dead man is deprived of all the functions of life by the powerlessness of death; but if he were to be raised gloriously, he would be full of life, without having the power to preserve it by means of the senses: and being placed above all means by virtue of his germ of immortality, he would no longer feel that which animated him, although he would know himself to be alive.

In this degree God cannot be tasted, seen, or felt, being no longer distinct from ourselves, but one with us. The soul has neither inclination nor taste for anything: in the period of death and burial it experienced this, but in a very different manner. Then it arose from distaste and powerlessness, but now it is the effect of *plenitude* and *abundance;* just as if a person could live on air, he would be full without feeling his plenitude, or knowing in what way he had been satisfied; he would not be empty and unable to eat or to taste, but free from all necessity of eating by reason of his satisfaction, without knowing how the air, entering by all his pores, had penetrated equally at all parts.

The soul here is in God, as in the air which is natural to it, and it is no more sensible of its fulness than we are of the air we breathe. Yet it is full, and nothing is wanting to it; therefore all its desires are taken from it. Its peace is great, but not as it was before. Formerly it was an inanimate peace, a certain sepulture, from which there sometimes escaped exhalations which troubled it. When it was reduced to ashes, it was at peace; but it was a barren peace, like that of a corpse, which would be at peace in the midst of the wildest storms of the sea: it would not feel them, and would not be troubled by them, its state of death rendering it insensible. But here the soul is raised, as it were, to a mountaintop, from which it sees the waves rolling and tossing, without fearing their attacks; or rather it is at the bottom of the sea, where there is always tranquillity, even while the surface is agitated. The senses may suffer their sorrows, but at the centre there is always the same calm tranquillity, because He who possesses it is immutable.

This, of course, supposes the faithfulness of the soul; for in whatever state it may be, it is possible for it to recede and fall back into itself. But here the soul progresses infinitely in God; and it is possible for it to advance incessantly; just as, if the sea had no bottom, any one falling into it would sink to infinitude, and going down to greater and greater depths of the ocean, would discover more and more of its beauties and treasures. It is even thus with the soul whose home is in God.

But what must it do in order to be faithful to God? Nothing, and less than nothing. It must simply suffer itself to be possessed, acted upon, and moved without resistance, remaining in the state which is natural to it, waiting for what every moment may bring to it, and receiving it from Him, without either adding to or taking from it; letting itself be led at all times and to any place, regardless of sight or reason, and without thinking of either; letting itself go naturally into all things, without considering what would be best or most plausible; remaining in the state of evenness and stability in which God has placed it, without being troubled to do anything; but leaving to God the care of providing its opportunities, and of doing all for it; not making definite acts of abandonment, but simply resting in the state of abandonment in which it already is, and which is natural to it.

SELECTED BIBLIOGRAPHY

TEXTS AND TRANSLATIONS

Oeuvres. Edited by J.-P. Dutoit. 40 vols. Paris [Lausanne], 1790.

Selections from the Autobiography of Madame Guyon. Translated by Thomas T. Allen. New Canaan, Conn.: Keats, 1980.

A Short Method of Prayer and Spiritual Torrents. Translated by A. W. Marston. London: Sampson Low, 1875.

Union with God. Edited by Gene Edwards. Gardiner, Maine: Christian Books, 1981.

STUDIES

Armogathe, J. R. *Le quiétisme.* Paris, 1973.

Cognet, Louis. "La spiritualité de Mme Guyon." *XVIIe siècle,* n. 12–14 (1952): 269–75.

Knox, Ronald. *Enthusiasm*, chapters 11–13. Oxford: Clarendon; New York: Oxford University Press, 1950. Reprint. Westminster, Md.: Christian Classics, 1983.

Mallet-Joris, Françoise. *Jeanne Guyon*. Paris, 1978.

Upham, T. C. *Life, Religious Opinions, and Experiences of Madame de la Mothe Guyon*. London, 1848, 1894.

François de Lamothe-Fénelon

(1651–1715)

The spiritual history of the Bishop of Cambrai, François de Salignac de Lamothe-Fénelon, is inextricably intertwined with that of Madame Guyon. She was the instrument of his "conversion"; he remained her champion during her troubles with the French hierarchy, and his interpretation of her theories led to his condemnation and practical disgrace. The culturally refined ecclesiastic taught at St. Cyr, the aristocratic school run by the King's favorite, Madame de Maintenon, and served as instructor of the Dauphin. His meeting and spiritual connection with Jeanne Guyon eventually cost him both positions, exposed him to a great deal of undeserved abuse by his former mentor, Bishop Bossuet, and finally led to a papal condemnation of his *Maximes des saints*. The "Quietist" training had taught him to accept all of those trials without abandoning his ideal or even his loyalty to his "spiritual mother," later his religious pupil.

It would be overly simplistic to present the two spiritual friends as being simply the double head of the one Quietist movement. "Quietism" never possessed a unified doctrine, for the simple reason that it never existed as a clearly defined movement. What Fénelon taught was not merely more theologically grounded than Jeanne Guyon's purely ascetic, mystical doctrine. His theology of pure love, though rooted in the same attitude of surrender, differed also in essence. In his *Explication sur les maximes des saints* he attempted to synthesize the basic principles of his spiritual theology while at the same time interpreting in a sense favorable to his and Guyon's theories the thirty-four articles issued by the committee set up by Bossuet to investigate her teaching. Throughout, the *Maximes* bear the mark of controversy. The open collision with the imperious, irascible Bossuet resulted in Innocent XI's condemnation of the work.

Fénelon links the doctrine of "quiet" contemplation to older French theories of pure love, especially that of Francis de Sales. Yet the final product is very much his own. Discursive meditation may assist those who have not attained perfect love, but those who have abandoned all "concupiscent" love of God and all hope of future benefits, in favor of totally selfless love, can express themselves only in acts of perfect simplicity. Fénelon attempts to reinterpret all of spiritual life by means of the distinction between the two loves. Hope marks the beginning stage of purgation. Charity itself belongs to the level of illumination. Only perfect love, expressed in an attitude of total indifference with respect to the vicissitudes of life, leads to union. Here alone the soul acquires that holy passivity which enables it to leave all initiative to the divine impulse of grace. Fénelon combines his spiritual theology with a somewhat hazardous psychology, dividing the higher soul from the lower one. He thus brings in yet another mystical tradition, according to which God remains in constant communication with the *fundus animae*, whatever may occur in the areas of will and intelligence. The development toward pure love, then, consists in the gradual surrender of all active control over one's spiritual life.

It is hard to find a single position in the *Maximes* that remains without precedent in the orthodox Christian tradition. The definition of "pure love" may be found in St. Bernard's *De diligendo Deo* and reappeared in various forms in the French School and, most prominently, in Saint Francis de Sales' *Treatise of Divine Love* as well as the work it inspired, Bishop Jean-Pierre Camus' *Défense du pur amour*. Nevertheless, the spiritual climate of Fénelon's work differs and, all questions of fairness aside, one understands how his demanding theory would discourage the fainthearted and offend those who recognize no higher authority in spiritual life than the words of Scripture and Councils. The air of Fénelon's spiritual universe is as thin as it is pure. His thought tends to drive all spiritual aspirants immediately up the mountain peaks of perfection. Some might rightfully object to being expelled from their own, more modest, spiritual niche. Others might be deluded into estimating themselves more spiritually advanced than they are. Fénelon's problem stems, at least in part, from having allowed the controversy with Bossuet to force complex issues into the inappropriate format of condensed dogmatic theses. His personal mode of thinking, so much subtler and richer in nuances, reveals itself more authentically in the letters of guidance which that most sensitive director and elegant stylist wrote to hundreds of spiritual sons and daughters.

Selections

THE MAXIMS OF THE SAINTS*

1. OF THE LOVE OF GOD

Of the love of God, there are various kinds. At least, there are various feelings which go under that name.

First, There is what may be called mercenary or selfish love; that is, that love of God which originates in a sole regard to our own happiness. Those who love God with no other love than this love Him just as the miser his money, and the voluptuous man his pleasures; attaching no value to God except as a means to an end; and that end is the gratification of themselves. Such love, if it can be called by that name, is unworthy of God. He does not ask it; He will not receive it. In the language of St. Francis de Sales, "it is sacrilegious and impious."

Second, Another kind of love does not exclude a regard to our own happiness as a motive of love, but requires this motive to be subordinate to a much higher one, namely, *that of a regard to God's glory.* It is a mixed state, in which we regard ourselves and God at the same time. This love is not necessarily selfish and wrong. On the contrary, when the two objects of it, God and ourselves, are relatively in the right position, that is to say, when we love God as He ought to be loved, and love ourselves no more than we ought to be loved, it is a love which, in being properly subordinated, is unselfish and is right.

2. OF PURE LOVE

I. Of the subjects of this mixed love all are not equally advanced.

II. MIXED LOVE becomes PURE LOVE when the love of self is relatively, though not absolutely, lost in a regard to the will of God. This is always the case when the two objects are loved in their due proportion. So that pure love is mixed love *when it is combined rightly.*

III. Pure love is not inconsistent with mixed love, but is mixed love carried to its true result. When this result is attained the motive of God's glory so expands itself, and so fills the mind, that the other motive, that of our own happiness, becomes so small and so recedes from our inward notice, as to be *practically* annihilated. It is then that God becomes what He ever ought to be—the centre of the soul, to which all its affections tend; the great moral Sun of the soul, from which all its light and

*From Archbishop Fenelon, *The Maxims of the Saints* (London: H. R. Allenson, n.d.), 9–20, 40–45, 51–52, 54–57.

all its warmth proceed. It is then that a man thinks no more of himself. He has become the man of a "single eye." His own happiness, and all that regards himself, is entirely lost sight of in his simple and fixed look to God's will and God's glory.

IV. We lay ourselves at His feet. Self is known no more; not because it is wrong to regard and to desire our own good, but because the object of desire is withdrawn from our notice. When the sun shines, the stars disappear. When God is in the soul, who can think of himself? So that we love God, and God alone; and all other things IN and FOR God.

3. OF PROGRESS

In the early periods of religious experience, motives which have a regard to our personal happiness are more prominent and effective than at later periods; *nor are they to be condemned.* It is proper, in addressing even religious men, to appeal to the fear of death, to the impending judgments of God, to the terrors of hell and the joys of heaven. Such appeals are recognised in the Holy Scriptures, and are in accordance with the view and feelings of good men in all ages of the world. The motives involved in them are powerful aids to beginners in religion; assisting, as they do, very much in repressing the passions, and in strengthening the practical virtues.

We should not think lightly, therefore, of the grace of God, as manifested in that inferior form of religion which stops short of the more glorious and perfected form of pure love. We are to follow God's grace, and not to go before it. To the higher state of PURE LOVE we are to advance step by step; watching carefully God's inward and outward providence; and receiving increased grace by improving the grace we have, till the dawning light becomes the perfect day.

4. OF PERFECT LOVE

He who is in the state of pure or perfect love has all the moral and Christian virtues in himself. If temperance, forbearance, chastity, truth, kindness, forgiveness, justice may be regarded as virtues, there can be no doubt that they are all included in holy love. That is to say, the principle of love will not fail to develop itself in each of these forms. St. Augustine remarks that love is the foundation, source, or principle of all the virtues. This view is sustained also by St. Francis de Sales and by Thomas Aquinas.

The state of pure love does not exclude the mental state which is called *Christian hope.* Hope in the Christian, when we analyze it into its elements, may be described as the desire of being united with God in heaven, accompanied with the expectation or belief of being so.

5. OF SANCTIFICATION

Souls that, by being perfected in love, are truly the subjects of sanctification do not cease, nevertheless, to grow in grace. It may not be easy to specify and describe the degrees of sanctification; but there seem to be at least two modifications of experience after persons have reached this state.

1. The first may be described as the state of *holy resignation*. Such a soul thinks more frequently than it will, at a subsequent period, of its own happiness.

2. The second state is that of *holy indifference*. Such a soul absolutely ceases either to desire or to will, except in cooperation with the Divine leading. Its desires for itself, as it has greater light, are more completely and permanently merged in the one higher and more absorbing desire of God's glory, and the fulfilment of His will. In this state of experience, ceasing to do what we shall be likely to do, and what we may very properly do in a lower state, we no longer desire our own salvation merely as an eternal deliverance, or merely as involving the greatest amount of personal happiness; but we desire it chiefly as the fulfilment of God's pleasure, and as resulting in His glory, and because He Himself desires and wills that we should thus desire and will.

3. Holy indifference is not inactivity. It is the furthest possible from it. It is indifference to anything and everything out of God's will; but it is the highest life and activity to anything and everything in that will.

6. OF NON-DESIRE

One of the clearest and best-established maxims of holiness is that the holy soul, when arrived at the second state mentioned, ceases to have desires for anything out of the will of God.

The holy soul, when it is really in the state called the state of NON-DESIRE, may, nevertheless, desire everything in relation to the correction of its imperfections and weaknesses, its perseverance in its religious state, and its ultimate salvation, which it has reason to know from the Scriptures, or in any other way that God desires. It may also desire all temporal good, houses and lands, food and clothing, friends and books, and exemption from physical suffering, and anything else, so far and only so far as it has reason to think that such desire is coincident with the Divine desire. The holy soul not only desires particular things, sanctioned by the known will of God; but also the fulfilment of His will in all respects, unknown as well as known. Being in faith, it commits itself to God in darkness as well as in light. Its NON-DESIRE is simply its not desiring anything out of God.

7. OF GUIDANCE

In the history of inward experience, we not unfrequently find accounts of individuals whose inward life may properly be characterized as *extraordinary*. They represent themselves as having extraordinary communications;—dreams, visions, revelations. Without stopping to inquire whether these inward results arise from an excited and disordered state of the physical system or from God, the important remark to be made here is that these things, to whatever extent they may exist, *do not constitute holiness.*

The principle which is the life of common Christians in their common fixed state is the principle which originates and sustains the life of those who are truly *"the pure in heart,"* namely, the principle of *faith working by love,*—existing, however, in the case of those last mentioned, in a greatly increased degree. This is obviously the doctrine of St. John of the Cross, who teaches us that we must walk in the *night of faith;* that is to say, with night around us, which exists in consequence of our entire ignorance of what is before us, and with faith alone, faith in God, in His Word, and in His Providences, for the soul's guide.

Again, the persons who have, or are supposed to have, the visions and other remarkable states to which we have referred are sometimes disposed to make their own experience, imperfect as it obviously is, the guide of their life, considered as separate from and as above the written law. Great care should be taken against such an error as this. God's word is our true rule.

Nevertheless, there is no interpreter of the Divine Word like that of a holy heart; or, what is the same thing, of the Holy Spirit dwelling in the heart. If we give ourselves wholly to God, the Comforter will take up His abode with us and guide us into all that truth which will be necessary for us. Truly holy souls, therefore, continually looking to God for a proper understanding of His word, may confidently trust that He will guide them aright. A holy soul, in the exercise of its legitimate powers of interpretation, may deduce important views from the Word of God which would not otherwise be known; but it cannot add anything to it.

Again, God is the regulator of the affections, as well as of the outward actions. Sometimes the state which He inspires within us is that of holy love;—sometimes He inspires affections which have love and faith for their basis, but have a specific character and then appear under other names, such as humility, forgiveness, gratitude. But in all cases there is nothing holy except what is based upon the antecedent or "prevenient" grace of God. In all the universe, there is but one *legitimate Originator.* Man's business is that of *concurrence.* And this view is applicable to all the stages of Christian experience, from the lowest to the highest.

8. OF ABANDONMENT TO GOD

Writers often speak of *abandonment.* The term has a meaning somewhat specific. The soul in this state does not renounce everything, and thus become brutish in its indifference; but renounces everything *except God's will.*

Souls in the state of abandonment not only forsake outward things, but, what is still more important, *forsake themselves.*

Abandonment, or self-renunciation, is not the renunciation of faith or of love or of anything else, except *selfishness.*

The state of abandonment, or entire self-renunciation, is generally attended, and perhaps we may say carried out and perfected, by temptations more or less severe. We cannot well know whether we have renounced ourselves except by being tried on those very points to which our self-renunciation, either real or supposed, relates. One of the severest inward trials is that by which we are taken off from all inward sensible supports and are made to live and walk by faith alone. Pious and holy men who have been the subjects of inward crucifixion often refer to the trials which have been experienced by them. They sometimes speak of them as a sort of inward and terrible purgatory. "Only mad and wicked men," says Cardinal Bona, "will deny the existence of these remarkable experiences, attested as they are by men of the most venerable virtue, who speak only of what they have known in themselves."

Trials are not always of the same duration. The more cheerfully and faithfully we give ourselves to God, to be smitten in any and all of our idols, whenever and wherever He chooses, the shorter will be the work. God makes us to suffer no longer than He sees to be necessary for us.

We should not be premature in concluding that inward crucifixion is complete, and our abandonment to God is without any reservation whatever. The act of consecration, which is a sort of incipient step, may be sincere; but the reality of the consecration can be known only when God has applied the appropriate tests. The trial will show whether we are wholly the Lord's. Those who prematurely draw the conclusion that they are so expose themselves to great illusion and injury. . . .

26. OF HOLINESS

Our acceptance with God, when our hearts are wholly given to Him, does not depend upon our being in a particular state but simply upon our being in that state in which God in His providence requires us to be. The doctrine of holiness, therefore, while it recognises and requires, on its appropriate occasions, the prayer of contemplation or of contemplative silence, is not only not inconsistent with other forms of prayer but is not at all inconsistent with the practice of the ordinary acts, duties, and virtues of life. It would be a great mistake to suppose that a man who bears the Saviour's image is any the less on that account a good neighbour or a good citizen; that he can think less or work less when he is called to it; or that he is not characterized by the various virtues, appropriate to our present situation, of temperance, truth, forbearance, forgiveness, kindness, chastity, justice. There is a law, involved in the very nature of holiness, which requires it to adapt itself to every variety of situation.

27. OF THE DIVINITY

It is in accordance with the views of Dionysius the Areopagite to say that the holy soul, in its *contemplative* state, is occupied with the *pure* or spiritual *Divinity*. That is to say, it is occupied with God, in distinction from any *mere image of God,* such as could be addressed to the touch, the sight, or any of the senses.

And this is not all. It does not satisfy the desires of the soul in its contemplative state to occupy itself merely with the attributes of God; with His power, wisdom, goodness, and the like; but it rather seeks and unites itself with the *God* of the attributes. The attributes of God are not God Himself. The power of God is not an identical expression with the God of power; nor is the wisdom of God identical with the God of wisdom. The holy soul, in its contemplative state, loves to unite itself with God, considered as the *subject* of His attributes. It is not infinite wisdom, infinite power, or infinite goodness, considered separately from the existence of whom they can be predicated, which it loves and adores; but the *God* of infinite wisdom, power, and goodness.

28. OF CHRIST

Christ is "the way, and the truth, and the life." The grace which sanctifies as well as that which justifies, is by Him and through Him. He is the true and living way; and no man can gain the victory over sin, and be brought into union with God, without Christ. And when, in some mitigated sense, we may be said to have arrived at the end of the way by being brought home to the Divine fold and reinstated in the Divine image, it would be sad indeed if we should forget the Way Himself, as Christ is sometimes called. At every period of our progress, however advanced it may be, our life is derived from God through Him and for Him. The most advanced souls are those which are most possessed with the thoughts and the presence of Christ.

Any other view would be extremely pernicious. It would be to snatch from the faithful eternal life, which consists in knowing the only true God and Jesus Christ His Son, whom He has sent.

29. OF FAITH

The way of holiness is wonderful, but it is not miraculous. Those in it walk by simple faith alone. And perhaps there is nothing more remarkable nor wonderful in it than that a result so great should be produced by a principle so simple.

When persons have arrived at the state of DIVINE UNION, so that, in accordance with the prayer of the Saviour, they are made one with Christ in God, they no longer seem to put forth distinct inward acts, but their state appears to be characterized by a deep and Divine repose.

The continuous act is the act of faith, which brings into moral and religious union with the Divine nature; faith which, through the plenitude of Divine grace, is kept firm, unbroken.

The appearance of absolute continuity and unity in this blessed state is increased perhaps by the entire freedom of the mind from all eager, anxious, unquiet acts. The soul is not only at unity with itself in the respects which have been mentioned, but it has also a unity of *rest*.

This state of continuous faith and of consequent repose in God is sometimes denominated the *passive* state. The soul, at such times, ceases to originate acts which precede the grace of God. The decisions of its consecrated judgment are the voice of the Holy Spirit in the soul. But if it first listens passively, it is subsequently its business to yield an active and effective co-operation in the line of duty which they indicate. The more pliant and supple the soul is to the Divine suggestions, the more real and efficacious is its own action, though without any excited and troubled movement. The more a soul receives from God, the more it ought to restore to Him of what it has from Him. This ebbing and flowing, if one may so express it, this communication on the part of God and the correspondent action on the part of man, constitute the order of Grace on the one hand, and the action and fidelity of the creature on the other. . . .

35. OF QUIESCENCE

Some persons of great piety, in describing the highest religious state, have denominated it the *state of transformation*. But this can be regarded as only a synonymous expression for the state of PURE LOVE.

In the *transformed* state of the soul, as in the state of PURE LOVE, love is its life. In this principle of love all the affections of the soul, of whatever character, have their constituting or their controlling element. There can be no love without an object of love. As the principle of love, therefore, allies the soul with another, so from that other, which is God, all its power of movement proceeds. In itself it remains without preference for anything; and consequently is accessible and pliant to all the touches and guidances of grace, however slight they may be. It is like a spherical body placed upon a level and even surface, which is moved with equal ease in any direction. The soul in this state, having no preferences of itself, has but one principle of movement, namely, that which God gives it. In this state the soul can say with the Apostle Paul, *"I live; yet not I, but Christ lives in me."* . . .

40. OF UNION WITH GOD

The holy soul may be said to be united with God, without anything intervening or producing a separation, in three particulars.

First.—It is thus united *intellectually;*—that is to say, not by any idea which is based upon the senses, and which of course could give only a material image of God, but by an idea which is internal and spiritual in its origin and makes God known to us as a Being without form.

Second.—The soul is thus united to God, if we may so express it, *affectionately.* That is to say, when its affections are given to God, not indirectly through a self-interested motive, but simply because He is what He is. The soul is united to God in love without anything intervening when it loves Him for His own sake.

Third.—The soul is thus united to God PRACTICALLY;—and this is the case when it does the will of God, not by simply following a prescribed form, but from the constantly operative impulse of holy love.

41. OF INTIMATE UNION

We find in some devout writers on inward experience the phrase SPIRITUAL NUPTIALS. It is a favourite method with some of these writers to represent the union of the soul with God by the figure of the *bride and the bridegroom.* Similar expressions are found in the Scriptures.

We are not to suppose that such expressions mean anything more, in reality, than that intimate union which exists between God and the soul when the soul is in the state of pure love.

42. OF ESSENTIAL UNION

We find again other forms of expression which it is proper to notice. The union between God and the soul is sometimes described by them as an *"essential"* union, and sometimes as a "substantial" union, as if there were a union of essence, substance, or being, in the literal or physical sense. They mean to express nothing more than the fact of the union of pure love, with the additional idea that the union is firm and established; not subject to those breaks and inequalities, to that want of continuity and uniformity of love which characterize inferior degrees of experience.

43. OF TRUE KNOWLEDGE

It is the holy soul of which St. Paul may be understood especially to speak, where he says, *"As many as are led by the Spirit of God, they are the sons of God."* (Rom. viii. 14.)

Those who are in a state of simple faith, which can always be said of those who are in the state of pure love, are the "little ones" of the Scriptures, of whom we are told that God teaches them. "I thank you," says the Saviour, "O Father, Lord of heaven and earth, that you have hid these things from the wise and prudent and have revealed them unto babes." Such souls, taught as they are by the Spirit of God which dwells in them, possess a knowledge which the wisdom of the world could never impart. But such knowledge never renders them otherwise than respectful to religious teachers, docile to the instructions of the Church, and conformable in all things to the precepts of the Scriptures.

SELECTED BIBLIOGRAPHY

TEXTS AND TRANSLATIONS

Oeuvres complètes. 10 vols. Paris, 1848–52.

Correspondance. Edited by Jean Orcibal. 5 vols. Paris, 1972–76.

Maximes des saints. Edited by Albert Chérel. Paris, 1911.

Christian Perfection. Translated by Mildred W. Stillman. New York and London: Harper and Brothers, 1947. Reprint. Minneapolis: Bethany House, 1976.

Fénelon's Letters to Men and Women. Selected by Derek Stanford. Translated by H. L. Sidney Lear. Westminster, Md.: Newman, 1957.

Letters of Love and Counsel. Translated by John McEwen. New York: Harcourt, Brace and World, 1964.

The Maxims of the Saints. London: H. R. Allenson, n.d.

STUDIES

Bremond, Henri. *Apologie pour Fénelon.* Paris, 1910.
Carcassonne, Elie. *Fénelon: L'homme et l'oeuvre.* Paris, 1946.

Cognet, Louis. *Crépuscule des mystiques: Bossuet, Fénelon.* Tournai and Paris, 1958.

Knox, Ronald. *Enthusiasm*, chapters 11–13. Oxford: Clarendon; New York: Oxford University Press, 1950. Reprint. Westminster, Md.: Christian Classics, 1983.

Varillon, François. *Fénelon et le pur amour.* Paris, 1957.

William Law

(1686–1761)

No contemporary reader of *A Serious Call to a Devout and Holy Life* (1728) would have guessed that its author would go on to write a book such as *The Spirit of Love* (1752, 1754). The solidly Christian but somewhat moralistic tract written in a style that holds the middle between *Pilgrim's Progress* and Francis de Sales' *Introduction to the Devout Life* stands as far as possible from any kind of mystical "enthusiasm." *The Spirit of Love*, conceived under the impact of Jacob Boehme's theosophy and of French "Quietism," must have seemed an abrupt mystico-theological flight toward the opposite side of the spiritual horizon. Nevertheless, both works were unquestionably written by the same saintly priest of the Church of England. For us today, the moral seriousness of the earlier one affords a welcome support to the religious solidity of the latter. Even as that other eighteenth century divine, the New Englander Jonathan Edwards, with whom he shared so many insights across a doctrinal abyss, Law revealed his innermost, spiritual vision only after having built a protective wall of ascetical and moral precautions against mystical illusions.

In an epoch notorious for questionable compromises between Church and state, William Law stands out as one who conformed his life entirely to his Christian convictions. Begun in the spirit and practice of renunciation, it concluded with total spiritual sacrifice. He was ordained into that section of the Church of England that for theological reasons remained loyal to the Stuart monarchy and refused to pledge ecclesiastical allegiance to the Hannover dynasty. To do so meant effectively to abandon all hope of ever obtaining an ecclesiastical or academic appointment. Law gained a living as tutor and private chaplain of Edward Gibbon, father of the famous historian. The latter, a critic hard to please in matters religious, later wrote the following testimony about his parents' chaplain: "In our family he left the reputation of a worthy and pious man who believed all he professed and practiced all that he enjoined." During that period Law wrote *A Serious Call to a Devout and Holy Life*.

Feeling called to move beyond "the common life" of the devout Christian he had so convincingly presented in this work, in 1740, together with Edward Gibbon's sister, Hester, and a wealthy widow, he withdrew to a solitude of prayer, study, and celibacy in his native King's Cliffe in

Northhampshire. The life of contemplation he had set out to seek was, however, not to be one of leisure. They founded a school for poor girls and later added an almshouse and another school which consumed all but a small fraction of their income. During this period Law underwent a spiritual revolution. Thoroughly acquainted with the Christian mystics and endowed with the ecumenical mind characteristic of those who share the life of the Spirit, Law more and more removed himself from the prevailing polemics and doctrinal controversies that dominated the relations among the various Christian Churches. Law himself had actively been engaged in theological polemics with dissenters and deists. Though his endeavors in this direction did not end altogether, he nevertheless abandoned his trust in their ultimate efficacy:

> He lost faith in the use of the external historical evidences for Christianity, which at best reached the reason and left the heart unaffected. Even intellectual orthodoxy came to seem an affair not at the center of things, any more than correct ritual. What mattered was a change of heart, a new and regenerate holy life; and having reached this conclusion, he gave up arguing and addressed himself to testifying, persuading, converting.[1]

His new "illumination," if the term applies to an insight more gradual than abrupt,

owed much to the writings of the unorthodox German visionary Jacob Boehme, with whom he shared the conviction that religious revelation had not stopped with the end of the New Testament but continues even today. What a mistake it is, he writes, "to confine inspiration to particular times and occasions, to prophets and apostles and extraordinary messengers of God, and to call it enthusiasm when the common Christian looks and trusts to be continually led and inspired by the Spirit of God" (SL 402). The result of Law's "conversion" is a strange but inspiring book consisting of a long letter (first published separately) and three fictional, rather artificial dialogues, entitled *The Spirit of Love.*

Before discussing it we must acquaint the reader with the earlier *A Serious Call to a Devout and Holy Life.* Here the emphasis is entirely on the sacralization of the "common life," that is, the life of the Christian taken up by secular occupations. Already in the later Middle Ages a tendency had emerged to lead a the life of piety outside the established ecclesiastical and monastic structures. In *The Imitation of Christ*, the Brothers of the Common Life had brought it to classical expression. But long before, beghines, spiritual Franciscans, and other more or less orthodox movements had prepared the ground, and even mystical works such as Ruusbroec's *Spiritual Espousals* had laid solid spiritual foundations for it. The new piety broke with a tradition that had reserved true devotion to religious orders and had abandoned the laity to the rudimentary catechesis of an often ignorant clergy. The Reformation tended to extend those principles to the entire Church. There seems to exist a direct link between this universalization of piety and the eighteenth

1. Austin Warren, Introduction to *William Law: A Serious Call to a Devout and Holy Life; The Spirit of Love*, The Classics of Western Spirituality (New York: Paulist, 1978), 22. References to these two treatises of Law in our text will use the abbreviations SC and SL, followed by the page number.

century attempt to harmonize the Christian life with the life of reason. In the extreme case of Deism, formulated in such works as Tindal's *Christianity not Mysterious*, Christianity itself became equated with the life of reason. Law staunchly rejected the deist equation (as in his *Case of Reason and Natural Religion Fairly and Fully Stated* [1731]). Nevertheless, he himself considers it to be a necessary condition of piety in "the common life" that the mysteries of Christianity basically correspond to the principles of reason. He even writes: "But as the religion of the Gospel is only the refinement and exultation of our best faculties, as it only requires a life of the highest reason, as it only requires us to use this world as in reason it ought to be used, to live in such tempers as are the glory of intelligent beings, to walk in such wisdom as exalts our nature and to practice such piety as will raise us to God, who can think it grievous to live always in the spirit of such a religion?" (SC 93). Yet Law's conclusions remain at the opposite end of those of deist humanism. For him the idea of a common piety to which all human beings are called lies at the very root of his humanism. Far from rendering revelation redundant or superfluous, it posits the intrinsic need of nature itself of a revelation and redemption. As he asserts in his later work: "For a religion is not to be deemed natural because it has nothing to do with revelation; but then is it the one, true religion of nature when it has everything in it that our natural state stands in need of" (SL 453).

Paradoxically, it was the rational, humanist quality of religion that opened Law's spirituality to the theosophical theories of Jacob Boehme. For in theosophy he found a doctrine that provided a religious interpretation of cosmic developments. These influences have rendered *The Spirit of Love* a controversial book—even in our own time. Many who had become ardent disciples of his early work refused altogether to take the later one seriously. We must admit that Boehme's impact is as disconcerting as it is confusing. It betrays the presence of a gnostic or manichean dualism between matter and spirit: "Nature is at first only spiritual" (SL 366); "All the matter or materiality of this world is the effect of sin" (SL 369). Particularly obscure is Law's concept of nature: "Nature has all evil, and no evil in itself. Nature, as it comes forth from God, is darkness, without any evil of darkness in it; for it is not darkness without or separate from light . . ." (SL 477). In itself, nature, though clearly distinct from God, is the ground of all possible good. As it actually exists, however, in its present, fallen state, nature no longer reflects the divine light; it has acquired the negative qualities of opaqueness, coldness, and hardness. This nature characterizes the material world we know—"an extremity of want continually desiring, and an extremity of desire continually wanting" (SL 478). It appears strife-ridden, full of contradictions, and perpetually at war with itself. The difference between the positive and the negative state of nature lies in its being taken on the one hand as that which is not for its own self but for the sake of something else, and being taken on the other as if it were for its own self. The second state perverts the *desire* which is its very core and the means of its fulfillment, and turns it against itself. The perversion results, as for Boehme, from a fall in the very essence of being which precedes all historical human sin. The fall of Lucifer and the angels stands at the origin of the material nature which we know and which determined the entire course of creation. Redemption will return nature to spirit, from which it was derived in all eternity.

In all of this Law follows Boehme, "the illuminated instrument of God" (SL 375), and, indirectly, some earlier gnostic sources. If he had said no more, his presence in an anthology of Christian mysticism would have been hard to justify, for in its essence *gnosticism* is not Christian. But on the most crucial point he parts company with both Boehme and the gnostics. For the idea of *wrath* which follows from the contrariety of nature exists not within God but exclusively in fallen nature as a result of its aversion from God. Law so strongly holds that in God there can only be love that he rejects any theory of redemption whereby God demands "satisfaction" for the insult inflicted by sin—whether it be the Anselmian theory of equity between sin and punishment, or the forensic doctrine of an "imputed" righteousness of the Reformation—according to which "a supposed wrath in the mind of the Deity [must] be first atoned and satisfied" (SL 442).

Even the idea of a divine grace being super-imposed onto nature—whether extrinsically as in Luther and Calvin, or intrinsically as in later Scholasticism—Law repudiates. Nothing "supernatural" is added to nature, but nature itself becomes internally transformed. Law's position on this point presents more than a conclusion from theological premises. His entire vision of nature is inspired by an overwhelming sense of God's presence. Nature remains linked to God in its created origin and the divine presence constitutes its very essence. Any reference to "elevation of nature" or "addition of grace" inadequately expresses the restoration of nature to its primeval state. To redeem what is divine in origin means, as the Cappadocian Fathers knew, to return it to its original sanctity. The source then of Law's theology of redemption and atonement is a mystical vision of nature. That he expressed this vision in theosophical terminology may render it less accessible to the modern reader. Yet the fundamental insight remains Christian and antignostic. He could easily have dispensed with Boehme's theosophical cosmology as a vehicle for expressing it. That he did use a language that in many respects moved in a direction opposite to that of his own intention vividly illustrates how spiritual writers use images and concepts in a freely symbolic manner. Generally, religious symbols retain a greater distance between symbol and symbolized transcendence. But among them, those of mystical life stand out by the often disconcerting freedom their users take with respect to the original meaning of words and other symbols. The case of William Law shows the difficulties to which this may lead. It is all the more imperative for his readers to penetrate the screen of language and to seek the original experience that inspired him to use it. In doing so they will discover a surprisingly fresh rethinking of traditional theology in the light of new experience. Whether that experience was of the extraordinary kind to which the modern age has come to reserve the term "mystical," we do not claim to decide.

Selections

A SERIOUS CALL TO A DEVOUT AND HOLY LIFE*

CHAPTER ONE
CONCERNING THE NATURE AND EXTENT
OF CHRISTIAN DEVOTION

Devotion is neither private nor public prayer, but prayers whether private or public are particular parts or instances of devotion. Devotion signifies a life given or devoted to God.

He therefore is the devout man who lives no longer to his own will, or the way and spirit of the world, but to the sole will of God, who considers God in everything, who serves God in everything, who makes all the parts of his common life parts of piety by doing everything in the name of God and under such rules as are conformable to His glory.

We readily acknowledge that God alone is to be the rule and measure of our prayers, that in them we are to look wholly unto Him and act wholly for Him, that we are only to pray in such a manner for such things and such ends as are suitable to His glory.

Now let anyone but find out the reason why he is to be thus strictly pious in his prayers and he will find the same as strong a reason to be as strictly pious in all the other parts of his life. For there is not the least shadow of a reason why we should make God the rule and measure of our prayers, why we should then look wholly unto Him and pray according to His will, but what equally proves it necessary for us to look wholly unto God, and make Him the rule and measure of all the other actions of our life. For any ways of life, any employment of our talents, whether of our parts, our time, or money, that is not strictly according to the will of God, that is not for such ends as are suitable to His glory, are as great absurdities and failings as prayers that are not according to the will of God. For there is no other reason why our prayers should be according to the will of God, why they should have nothing in them but what is wise, and holy, and heavenly, there is no other reason for this but that our lives may be of the same nature, full of the same wisdom, holiness, and heavenly tempers that we may live unto God in the same spirit that we pray unto Him. Were it not our strict duty to live by reason, to devote all the actions of our lives to God, were it not absolutely necessary to walk before Him in wisdom and holiness and all heavenly conversation, doing everything in His name and for

*All selections in this chapter are from *William Law: A Serious Call to a Devout and Holy Life, and The Spirit of Love,* ed. P. G. Stanwood, The Classics of Western Spirituality (New York: Paulist, 1979), 47–48, 50–52, 385–89, 402–12. Reprinted with permission of the publisher.

His glory, there would be no excellency or wisdom in the most heavenly prayers. Nay, such prayers would be absurdities, they would be like prayers for wings when it was no part of our duty to fly.

As sure therefore as there is any wisdom in praying for the Spirit of God, so sure is it that we are to make that Spirit the rule of all our actions; as sure as it is our duty to look wholly unto God in our prayers, so sure is it that it is our duty to live wholly unto God in our lives. But we can no more be said to live unto God unless we live unto Him in all the ordinary actions of our life, unless He be the rule and measure of all our ways, than we can be said to pray unto God unless our prayer look wholly unto Him. So that unreasonable and absurd ways of life, whether in labor or diversion, whether they consume our time or our money, are like unreasonable and absurd prayers and are as truly an offence unto God.

'Tis for want of knowing, or at least considering this, that we see such a mixture of ridicule in the lives of many people. You see them strict as to some times and places of devotion, but when the service of the church is over, they are but like those that seldom or never come there. In their way of life, their manner of spending their time and money, in their cares and fears, in their pleasures and indulgences, in their labor and diversions, they are like the rest of the world. This makes the loose part of the world generally make a jest of those that are devout because they see their devotion goes no further than their prayers, and that when they are over they live no more unto God till the time of prayer returns again, but live by the same humour and fancy and in as full an enjoyment of all the follies of life as other people. This is the reason why they are the jest and scorn of careless and worldly people, not because they are really devoted to God, but because they appear to have no other devotion but that of occasional prayers. . . .

It is very observable that there is not one command in all the gospel for public worship; and perhaps it is a duty that is least insisted upon in scripture of any other. The frequent attendance at it is never so much as mentioned in all the New Testament. Whereas that religion or devotion which is to govern the ordinary actions of our life is to be found in almost every verse of scripture. Our blessed Savior and His Apostles are wholly taken up in doctrines that relate to common life. They call us to renounce the world and differ in every temper and way of life from the spirit and way of the world. To renounce all its goods, to fear none of its evils, to reject its joys, and have no value for its happiness. To be as newborn babes that are born into a new state of things, to live as pilgrims in spiritual watching, in holy fear, and heavenly aspiring after another life. To take up our daily cross, to deny ourselves, to profess the blessedness of mourning, to seek the blessedness of poverty of spirit. To forsake the pride and vanity of riches, to take no thought for the morrow, to live in the profoundest state of humility, to rejoice in worldly sufferings. To reject the lust of the flesh, the lust of the eyes, and the pride of life; to bear injuries, to forgive and bless our enemies, and to love mankind as God loveth them. To give up our whole hearts and affections to God, and strive to enter through the strait gate into a life of eternal glory.

This is the common devotion which our blessed Savior taught in order to make it the common life of all Christians. Is it not therefore exceeding strange that people should place so much piety in the attendance upon public worship, concerning which there is not one precept of our Lord's to be found, and yet neglect these common duties of our ordinary life which are commanded in every page of the gospel? I call these duties the devotion of our common life, because if they are to be practiced, they must be made parts of our common life; they can have no place anywhere else.

If contempt of the world and heavenly affection is a necessary temper of Christians, it is necessary that this temper appear in the whole course of their lives, in their manner of using the world, because it can have no place anywhere else.

If self-denial be a condition of salvation, all that would be saved must make it a part of their ordinary life. If humility be a Christian duty, then the common life of a Christian is to be a constant course of humility in all its kinds. If poverty of spirit be necessary, it must be the spirit and temper of every day of our lives. If we are to relieve the naked, the sick, and the prisoner, it must be the common charity of our lives, as far as we can render ourselves able to perform it. If we are to love our enemies, we must make our common life a visible exercise and demonstration of that love. If content and thankfulness, if the patient bearing of evil be duties to God, they are the duties of every day and in every circumstance of our life. If we are to be wise and holy as the newborn sons of God, we can not otherwise be so but by renouncing everything that is foolish and vain in every part of our common life. If we are to be in Christ new creatures, we must show that we are so by having new ways of living in the world. If we are to follow Christ, it must be in our common way of spending every day.

Thus it is in all the virtues and holy tempers of Christianity; they are not ours unless they be the virtues and tempers of our ordinary life. So that Christianity is so far from leaving us to live in the common ways of life, conforming to the folly of customs and gratifying the passions and tempers which the spirit of the world delights in, it is so far from indulging us in any of these things that all its virtues which it makes necessary to salvation are only so many ways of living above and contrary to the world in all the common actions of our life. If our common life is not a common course of humility, self-denial, renunciation of the world, poverty of spirit, and heavenly affection, we don't live the lives of Christians.

THE SPIRIT OF LOVE

PART THE FIRST
IN A LETTER TO A FRIEND

. . . The perfection of every life is no way possibly to be had but as every flower comes to its perfection, viz., from its own seed and root and the various degrees of transmutation which must be gone through before the flower is found. It is strictly thus with the perfection of the soul; all its properties of life must have their true natural birth and growth from one another. The first, as its seed and root, must have their natural change into a higher state; must, like the seed of the flower, pass through death into life and be blessed with the fire and light and spirit of Heaven in their passage to it, just as the seed passes through death into life, blessed by the fire and light and air of this world till it reaches its last perfection and becomes a beautiful, sweet-smelling flower. And to think that the soul can attain its perfection any other way than by the change and exaltation of its first properties changed and exalted till it comes to have its flower is a total ignorance of the nature of things. For as whatever dies cannot have a death particular to itself but the same death in the same way and for the same reasons that any other creature, whether animal or vegetable, ever did or can die, so every life and degree of life must come into its state and condition of life in the same way and for the same reasons as life and the perfection of life comes into every other living creature, whether in Heaven or on earth. Therefore, the Deists' religion or reason, which is to raise the soul to its true perfection, is so far from being the religion of nature that it is quite unnatural and declared to be so by every working in nature. For since reason can neither give life nor death to any one thing in nature, but everything lives or dies according to the working of its own properties, everything dead and alive gives forth a demonstration that nature asks no counsel of reason, nor stays to be directed by it. Hold it therefore for a certain truth that you can have no good come into your soul but only by the one way of a birth from above, from the entrance of the Deity into the properties of your own soulish life. Nature must be set right, its properties must enter into the process of a new birth, it must work to the production of light before the spirit of love can have a birth in it. For love is delight, and delight cannot arise in any creature till its nature is in a delightful state or is possessed of that in which it must rejoice. And this is the reason why God must become man; it is because a birth of the Deity must be found in the soul, giving to nature all that it wants, or the soul can never find itself in a delightful state and only working with the spirit of love. For whilst the soul has only its natural life, it can only be in such a state as nature without God is in; viz., a mere hunger, want, contrariety, and strife, for it knows not what. Hence is all that variety of blind, restless, contrary passions which govern and torment the life of fallen man. It is because all the properties of nature must work in blindness and be doing they know not what till the light of God is found in them. Hence also it is that that which is called the wisdom, the honor, the honesty, and the religion of the natural man often does as much hurt to himself and others as his pride, ambition, self-love, envy, or revenge, and are subject to the same humor and caprice; it is because nature is no better in one motion than in another, nor can be so, till something supernatural is come into it. We often charge men, both in church and state, with changing their principles; but the charge is too hasty for no man ever did, or can change his principles but by a birth from above. The natural, called in scripture the old man, is steadily the same in heart and spirit in everything he does, whatever variety of names may be given to his actions. For self can have no motion but what is selfish, which way soever it goes, or whatever it does, either in church or state. And be assured of this, that nature in every man, whether he be learned or unlearned, is this very self and can be nothing else till a birth of the Deity is brought forth in it. There is therefore no possibility of having the spirit of love or any divine goodness from any power of nature or working of reason. It can only be had in its own time and place; and its time and place is nowhere but where nature is overcome by a birth of the life of God in the properties of the soul. And thus you see the infallible truth and absolute necessity of Christian redemption; it is the most demonstrable thing in all nature. The Deity must become man, take a birth in the fallen nature, be united to it, become the life of it or the natural man must of all necessity be forever and ever in the hell of his own hunger, anguish, contrariety, and self-torment; and all for this plain reason, because nature is and can be nothing else but this variety of self-torment, till the Deity is manifested and dwelling in it.

And now, Sir, you see also the absolute necessity of the gospel doctrine of the cross, viz., of dying to self as the one only way to life in God. This cross, or dying to self, is the one morality that does man any good. Fancy as many rules as you will of modeling the moral behavior of man, they all do nothing because they leave nature still alive, and therefore can only help a man to a feigned, hypocritical art of concealing his own inward evil and seeming to be not under its power. And the reason why it must be so is plain; it is because nature is not possible to be reformed; it is immutable in its workings and must be always as it is and never any better or worse than its own untaught workings are. It can no more change from evil to good than darkness can work itself into light. The one work therefore of morality is the one doctrine of the cross, viz., to resist and deny nature, that a supernatural power to divine goodness may take possession of it and bring a new light into it.

In a word, there are in all the possibility of things but two states or forms of life;

the one is nature and the other is God manifested in nature; and as God and nature are both within you, so you have it in your power to live and work with which you will, but are under a necessity of doing either the one or the other. There is no standing still; life goes on and is always bringing forth its realities, which way soever it goeth. You have seen that the properties of nature are, and can be, nothing else in their own life but a restless hunger, disquiet, and blind strife for they know not what, till the property of light and love has got possession of them. Now when you see this, you see the true state of every natural man, whether he be Caesar or Cato, whether he gloriously murders others or only stabs himself; blind nature does all the work and must be the doer of it till the Christ of God is born in him. For the life of man can be nothing else but a hunger of covetousness, a rising up of pride, envy, and wrath, a medley of contrary passions, doing and undoing it knows not what because these workings are essential to the properties of nature; they must be always hungering and working one against another, striving to be above one another, and all this in blindness, till the light of God has helped them to one common good, in which they all willingly unite, rest and rejoice. In a word, goodness is only a sound and virtue a mere strife of natural passions till the spirit of love is the breath of everything that lives and moves in the heart. For love is the one only blessing and goodness and God of nature; and you have no true religion, are no worshipper of the one true God but in and by that spirit of love which is God Himself living and working in you.

But here I take off my pen and shall leave the remaining part of your objection to another opportunity.

THE SECOND PART

The First Dialogue

Eusebius. . . . What a mistake is it . . . to confine inspiration to particular times and occasions, to prophets and apostles and extraordinary messengers of God, and to call it enthusiasm when the common Christian looks and trusts to be continually led and inspired by the Spirit of God. For though all are not called to be prophets or apostles, yet all are called to be holy as He who has called them is holy, to be perfect as their heavenly Father is perfect, to be like-minded with Christ, to will only as God wills, to do all to His honor and glory, to renounce the spirit of this world, to have their conversation in heaven, to set their affections on things above, to love God with all their heart, soul, and spirit, and their neighbor as themselves.

Behold a work as great, as divine and supernatural as that of a prophet and an apostle. But to suppose that we ought and may always be in this spirit of holiness, and yet are not and ought not to be always moved and led by the breath and Spirit of God within us, is to suppose that there is a holiness and goodness which comes not from God, which is no better than supposing that there may be true prophets and apostles who have not their truth from God.

Now the holiness of the common Christian is not an occasional thing that begins and ends, or is only for such a time, or place, or action, but is the holiness of that which is always alive and stirring in us, namely, of our thoughts, wills, desires, and affections. If therefore these are always alive in us, always driving or governing our lives, if we can have no holiness or goodness but as this life of thought, will, and affection works in us, if we are all called to this inward holiness and goodness, then a perpetual, always-existing operation of the Spirit of God within us is absolutely necessary. For we cannot be inwardly led and governed by a spirit of goodness, but by being governed by the Spirit of God Himself. For the Spirit of God and the spirit of goodness are not two spirits, nor can we be said to have any more of the one than we have of the other.

Now if our thoughts, wills, and affections need only be now and then holy and good, then indeed the moving and breathing Spirit of God need only now and then govern us. But if our thoughts and affections are to be always holy and good, then the holy and good Spirit of God is to be always operating as a principle of life within us.

The scripture saith, "We are not sufficient of ourselves to think a good thought." If so, then we cannot be chargeable with not thinking and willing that which is good but upon this supposition, that there is always a supernatural power within us, ready and able to help us to the good which we cannot have from ourselves.

The difference then of a good and a bad man does not lie in this, that the one wills that which is good, and the other does not, but solely in this, that the one concurs with the living inspiring Spirit of God within him and the other resists it, and is and can be only chargeable with evil because he resists it.

Therefore whether you consider that which is good or bad in a man, they equally prove the perpetual indwelling and operation of the Spirit of God within us since we can only be bad by resisting, as we are good by yielding to the Spirit of God, both which equally suppose a perpetual operation of the Spirit of God within us.

How firmly our Established Church adheres to this doctrine of the necessity of the perpetual operation of the Holy Spirit as the one only source and possibility of any degree of divine light, wisdom, virtue, and goodness in the soul of man, how earnestly she wills and requires all her members to live in the most open profession of it and in the highest conformity to it may be seen by many such prayers as these in her common, ordinary, public service.

"O God, forasmuch as without Thee, we are not able to please Thee, grant that Thy Holy Spirit may in all things direct and rule our hearts." Again, "We pray Thee, that Thy grace may always prevent and follow us, and make us continually to be given to all good works." Again, "Grant to us, Lord, we beseech Thee, the spirit to think and do always such things as be rightful, that we, who cannot do anything that is good without Thee, may by Thee be enabled to live according to Thy will." Again, "Because the frailty of man without Thee cannot but fall, keep us ever, by thy help from all things hurtful, and lead us to all things profitable to our salvation," etc. Again, "O God, from whom all good things do come, grant to us Thy humble servants that by Thy holy inspiration we may think those things that be good, and by Thy merciful guiding may perform the same."[1] But now the true ground of all this doctrine of the necessity of the perpetual guidance and operation of the Holy Spirit lies in what has been said above of the necessity of a two-fold life in every intelligent creature, that is, to be good and happy. For if the creaturely life whilst alone or left to itself can only be want, misery, and distress, if it cannot possibly have any goodness or happiness in it till the life of God is in union with it as one life, then everything that you read in the scripture of the Spirit of God as the only principle of goodness opens itself to you as a most certain and blessed truth, about which you can have no doubt.

Theophilus. Let me only add, Eusebius, to what you have said, that from this absolute necessity of a two-fold life in every creature, that is, to be good and happy, we may in a still greater clearness see the certainty of that which we have so often spoken of at other times, namely, that the inspoken Word in Paradise, the Bruiser of the Serpent, the Seed of the Woman, the Immanuel, the Holy Jesus (for they all mean the same thing) is and was the only possible ground of salvation for fallen man. . . .

The whole mediatorial office of Christ, from His birth to His sitting down in power at the right hand of God, was only for this end, to help man to a life that was fallen into death and insensibility in Him. And therefore His mediatorial power was to manifest itself by way of a new birth. In the nature of the thing nothing else was to be done, and Christ had no other way to proceed, and that for this plain reason, because life was the thing that was lost, and life wherever it is must be raised by a birth, and every birth must and can only come from its own seed.

But if Christ was to raise a new life like His own in every man, then every man must have had, originally, in the inmost spirit of his life, a Seed of Christ, or Christ as a Seed of Heaven, lying there as in a state of insensibility or death, out of which

1. The quotations are verbatim passages from collects in the *Book of Common Prayer* (1662).

it could not arise but by the mediatorial power of Christ, who as a second Adam was to regenerate that birth of His own life, which was lost in all the natural sons of Adam the first.

But unless there was this Seed of Christ or spark of Heaven hidden in the soul, not the least beginning of man's salvation or of Christ's mediatorial office could be made. For what could begin to deny self if there was not something in man different from self? What could begin to have hope and faith and desire of a heavenly life if there was not something of Heaven hidden in his soul, and lying therein as in a state of inactivity and death till raised by the mediation of Christ into its first perfection of life, and set again in its true dominion over flesh and blood?

Eusebius. You have, Theophilus, sufficiently proved the certainty and necessity of this matter. But I should be glad if you knew how to help me to some more distinct idea and conception of it.

Theophilus. An idea is not the thing to be here sought for; it would rather hinder than help your true knowledge of it. But perhaps the following similitude may be of some use to you.

The Ten Commandments when written by God on tables of stone and given to man did not then first begin to belong to man; they had their existence in man, were born with him, they lay as a seed and power of goodness hidden in the form and make of his soul and altogether inseparable from it before they were shown to man on tables of stone. And when they were shown to man on tables of stone, they were only an outward imitation of that which was inwardly in man, though not legible because of that impurity of flesh and blood in which they were drowned and swallowed up. For the earthly nature, having overcome the divinity that was in man, it gave commandments of its own to man and required obedience to all the lusts of the flesh, the lust of the eyes, and the pride of life.

Hence it became necessary that God should give an outward knowledge of such commandments as were become inwardly unknown, unfelt, and, as it were, shut up in death in the soul.

But now, had not all that is in these commandments been really and antecedently in the soul as its own birth and nature, had they not still lain therein, and although totally suppressed yet in such a seed or remains as could be called forth into their first living state, in vain had the tables of stone been given to man; and all outward writing or teaching of the commandments had been as useless as so many instructions given to beasts or stones. If therefore you can conceive how all that is good and holy in the commandments lay hid as an unfelt, unactive power or seed of goodness till called into sensibility and stirring by laws written on tables of stone, this may help your manner of conceiving and believing how Christ as a Seed of Life or power of salvation lies in the soul as its unknown, hidden treasure till awakened and called forth into life by the mediatorial office and process of the holy Jesus.

Again, "Thou shalt love the Lord thy God with all thy heart, with all thy soul, and with all thy strength, and thy neighbor as thyself." Now these two precepts, given by the written word of God, are an absolute demonstration of the first original perfection of man and also a full and invincible proof that the same original perfection is not quite annihilated but lies in him as a hidden, suppressed seed of goodness capable of being raised up to its first perfection. For had not this divine unity, purity, and perfection of love toward God and man been man's first natural state of life, it could have nothing to do with his present state. For had any other nature, or measure, or kind of love began in the first birth of his life, he could only have been called to that. For no creature has or can have a call to be above, or act above its own nature. Therefore, as sure as man is called to this unity, purity, and perfection of love, so sure is it that it was at first his natural, heavenly state, and still has its seed, or remains within him as his only power and possibility of rising up to it again. And therefore, all that man is called to, every degree of a new and perfect life, every future exaltation and glory he is to have from the mediation of Christ, is a full proof that the same perfection was originally his natural state and is still in him in such a seed or remains of existence as to admit of a perfect renewal.

And thus it is that you are to conceive of the holy Jesus, or the *Word* of God, as the hidden treasure of every human soul, born as a seed of the *Word* in the birth of the soul, immured under flesh and blood till as a daystar it arises in our hearts and changes the son of an earthly Adam into a son of God.

And was not the *Word* and *Spirit* of God in us all, antecedent to any dispensation or written word of God as a real seed of life in the birth of our own life, we could have no more fitness for the gospel redemption than the animals of this world which have nothing of Heaven in them. And to call us to love God with all our hearts, to put on Christ, to walk according to the Spirit, if these things had not their real nature and root within us, would be as vain and useless as to make rules and orders how our eyes should smell and taste, or our ears should see.

Now this mystery of an inward life hidden in man as his most precious treasure, as the ground of all that can be great or good in him and hidden only since his fall, and which only can be opened and brought forth in its first glory by Him to whom all power in Heaven and on earth is given, is a truth to which almost everything in nature bears full witness. Look where you will, nothing appears or works outwardly in any creature or in any effect of nature but what is all done from its own inward invisible spirit, not a spirit brought into it, but its own inward spirit which is an inward invisible mystery till made known or brought forth by outward appearances.

The sea neither is nor can be moved and tossed by any other wind than that which hath its birth, and life, and strength in and from the sea itself as its own wind. The sun in the firmament gives growth to everything that grows in the earth, and life to everything that lives upon it, not by giving or imparting a life from without, but only by stirring up in everything its own growth and its own life which lay as in a seed or state of death till helped to come out of it by the sun, which as an emblem of the Redeemer of the spiritual world helps every earthly thing out of its own death into its own highest state of life.

That which we call our sensations, as seeing, hearing, feeling, tasting, and smelling, are not things brought into us from without, or given unto us by any external causes, but are only so many inborn, secret states of the soul which lie in their state of hiddenness till they are occasionally awakened and brought forth into sensibility by outward occurrences. And were they not antecedently in the soul as states and forms of its own life, no outward objects could bring the soul into a sensibility of them. For nothing can have or be in any state of sensation but that which it is and hath from itself, as its own birth. This is as certain as that a circle hath only its own roundness. . . .

Look now at what you will, whether it be animate, or inanimate: All that it is, or has, or can be, it is and has in and from itself, as its own inward state; and all outward things can do no more to it than the hand does to the instrument, make it show forth its own inward state, either of harmony or discord. . . .

If our inward state is the renewed life of Christ within us, then every thing and occasion, let it be what it will, only makes the same life to sound forth and show itself; then if one cheek is smitten, we meekly turn the other also. But if nature is alive and only under a religious cover, then every outward accident that shakes or disturbs this cover gives leave to that bad state, whether of grief, or wrath, or joy that lay hid within us to show forth itself.

But nothing at any time makes the least show or sound outwardly, but only that which lay ready within us for an outward birth, as occasion should offer.

What a miserable mistake is it therefore to place religious goodness in outward observances, in notions and opinions which good and bad men can equally receive and practice, and to treat the ready real power and operation of an inward life of God in the birth of our souls as fanaticism and enthusiasm, when not only the whole letter and spirit of scripture, but every operation in nature and creature demonstrates that the Kingdom of Heaven must be all within us, or it never can possibly belong to us. Goodness, piety, and holiness can only be ours, as thinking, willing, and desiring are ours, by being in us as a power of heaven in the birth and growth of our own life.

And now, Eusebius, how is the great controversy about religion and salvation shortened.

For since the one only work of Christ as your Redeemer is only this, to take from the earthly life of flesh and blood its usurped power and to raise the smothered spark of Heaven out of its state of death into a powerful governing life of the whole man, your one only work also under your Redeemer is fully known. And you have the utmost certainty what you are to do, where you are to seek, and in what you are to find your salvation. All that you have to do, or can do, is to oppose, resist, and, as far as you can, to renounce the evil tempers and workings of your own earthly nature. You are under the power of no other enemy, are held in no other captivity, and want no other deliverance but from the power of your own earthly self. This is the one murderer of the divine life within you. It is your own Cain that murders your own Abel. Now everything that your earthly nature does is under the influence of self-will, self-love, and self-seeking, whether it carries you to laudable or blamable practices, all is done in the nature and spirit of Cain and only helps you to such goodness as when Cain slew his brother. For every action and motion of self has the spirit of Antichrist and murders the divine life within you.

Judge not therefore of yourself by considering how many of those things you do which divines and moralists call virtue and goodness, nor how much you abstain from those things which they call sin and vice.

But daily and hourly, in every step that you take, see to the spirit that is within you whether it be Heaven or earth that guides you. And judge everything to be sin and Satan in which your earthly nature, own love, or self-seeking has any share of life in you; nor think that any goodness is brought to life in you but so far as it is an actual death to the pride, the vanity, the wrath, and selfish tempers of your fallen, earthly life.

Again, here you see where and how you are to seek your salvation, not in taking up your traveling staff, or crossing the seas to find out a new Luther or a new Calvin to clothe yourself with their opinions. No. The oracle is at home that always and only speaks the truth to you because nothing is your truth but that good and that evil which is yours within you. For salvation or damnation is no outward thing that is brought into you from without, but is only that which springs up within you as the birth and state of your own life. What you are in yourself, what is doing in yourself, is all that can be either your salvation or damnation. . . .

And thus also you have the fullest proof in what your salvation precisely consists. Not in any historic faith, or knowledge of anything absent or distant from you, not in any variety of restraints, rules, and methods of practicing virtues, not in any formality of opinion about faith and works, repentance, forgiveness of sins, or justification and sanctification, not in any truth or righteousness that you can have from yourself, from the best of men or books, but wholly and solely in the life of God, or Christ of God quickened and born again in you, or in other words in the restoration and perfect union of the first two-fold life in the humanity.

SELECTED BIBLIOGRAPHY

TEXTS

Complete Works. 18 vols. London, 1762. Reprinted by G. Moreton [G. B. Morgan]. 9 vols. Brockenhurst and Canterbury, 1892–93.

Selected Mystical Writings of William Law. Edited by Stephen Hobhouse. London: Daniel, 1938. Rev. ed. New York: Harper, 1948. Includes twenty-four interpretative "Studies."

A Serious Call to a Devout and Holy Life; The Spirit of Love. Edited by Paul G. Stanwood. The Classics of Western Spirituality. New York: Paulist; London: SPCK, 1978.

STUDIES

Hopkinson, Arthur W. *About William Law*. London: SPCK, 1948.

Spurgeon, Caroline F. E. "William Law and the Mystics." In vol. 9 of the *Cambridge History of English Literature*, 305–28. Cambridge, 1912.

Walker, A. Keith. *William Law: His Life and Thought*. London: SPCK, 1973.

Jonathan Edwards

(1703–1758)

Nothing has damaged Jonathan Edwards' spiritual reputation more than the sermon by which he earned his greatest fame among his contemporaries, "Sinners in the Hands of an Angry God." The tone of that and a few similar sermons has obscured the far more fundamental insight that inspired them, namely, that religion consists so much in affection "that without affection there is no true religion." Edwards' theology of affective knowledge in religion, complete with rules for discerning genuine religious affection from "natural" *enthusiasm,* ranks him among the leading masters of spiritual life in Christianity. But there is more than theory. The personal narrative of his own "awakening" to a life in God's presence provides us with one of the most convincing documents of mystical experience in our entire tradition. It alone would suffice to refute the preposterous claim once made by W. T. Stace that there are no Protestant mystics.

Jonathan Edwards was born on October 5, 1703, at East Windsor, Connecticut. His father, for sixty-four years pastor of the local Congregational church, provided Jonathan with enough instruction in languages to allow him to enter Yale College before his thirteenth birthday. Probably during his final year of college he read John Locke's *An Essay concerning Human Understanding* (1690). This interpretation of all knowledge on the basis of sensation would in due time exert a strong influence upon the development of Edwards' own theory of religious emotions.[1]

Eighteenth century intellectual life in New England still centered entirely around the Puritan faith. Most of the writing occurred in parsonages, and oratory consisted mainly of sermons. Colleges had as their primary function the training of the future clergy: Harvard, Yale, the College of New Jersey (now Princeton) all developed out of what were basically divinity schools. It was quite natural, then, that the young Edwards, after graduation and some private study of theology, would become a preacher. Still too young to hold a permanent pastoral position at age nineteen, Edwards briefly served as temporary minister of a small Presbyterian congregation in New York and then returned as a tutor to his Alma Mater. The direct exposure to the

---

1. Recent studies by Leon Howard and Norman Fiering have shown, however, that this reading was far from being the "decisive" event in Edwards' intellectual life which it appeared to earlier commentators (especially Perry Miller).

rowdy Yale undergraduates had a sobering
effect upon his early views of human nature. Reflecting upon the experience of his
first year he writes: "I have now abundant
reason to be convinced of the troublesome-
ness and vexation of the world, and that it
never will be another kind of world."
Those laboring in the same vineyard can
testify that this conclusion still stands
today. In 1726 the young tutor was called
to a less profane environment as pastor at
the same Northampton (Massachusetts)
parish where his famous maternal grand-
father, Solomon Stoddard, had served for
over half a century. During Edwards' ten-
ure there that sudden, intense religious revival known as the "Great Awakening"
profoundly stirred the New England
churches. He himself played a leading role
in the movement and it was in the course
of it (1761) that he delivered the notorious
sermon at the end of which the congregation's crying and weeping drowned out the
preacher's voice.

On this and a few other occasions Edwards may have exceeded his own standards, for in his *Treatise Concerning Religious Affections* (1746), written during the
subsequent Awakening controversy, he
roundly condemned those who "appeared
to have great religious affections, [but] did
not manifest a right temper of mind, and
run into many errors in the time of their affections, and the heat of their zeal." Despite
a strong opposition, however, which would
eventually force him to resign his Northampton parish, Edwards continued to defend the need for "affection" in faith. For
support of his position he somewhat surprisingly turned to the theories of the
sober-minded and staunchly anti-enthu-
siastic John Locke. In his *Essay* Locke had
argued that all ideas in the mind originate
in, or are derived from, *passively* received
sensations and reflections. Edwards regarded affections, which he defines as "the
more vigorous and sensible exercises of the
inclination and will of the soul," as belonging to that primary layer of simple, underived ideas on which our entire mental life
is based. They function as "the springs of
motion and action" which determine our
moral life. Indeed, for Edwards, who rejects
a theory of free will, the affections *are* the
will and inclination.

Now, if the empiricist foundation of Edwards' theory of affections may be traced to
Locke, the emphasis upon affection in
moral and religious life connects it with
Shaftesbury and Hutcheson. They denied
that moral perception may be derived as
the conclusion from a process of reasoning.
It rather consists in a quasi-aesthetic, direct
feeling or intuition of what is good and evil.
Early on, Edwards had drawn a parallel between this moral sense and the religious
one. In *Divine and Supernatural Light*
(1734) we read:

> As with God, so with the *good*. There
> is a twofold understanding or knowl-
> edge of Good that God has made the
> mind capable of. The first . . . is merely
> *speculative* or *notional*. . . . And the
> *other* is that which consists in a sense
> of the heart. As when there is a sense
> of the beauty, amiableness, or sweet-
> ness of a thing.

Thus Edwards distinguishes a purely theoretical knowledge of God from the "sense
of the heart." The distinction reminds us of
Pascal's *raison du coeur* and anticipates
Newman's *real* knowledge.

At first Edwards appears to have considered religious affections part of the natural, God-given structure of the mind itself. Even as a person is, without "supernatural" assistance, capable of some sense of good and evil, so are his natural affections capable of ascending to that supreme Object in which they find their ultimate fulfillment. Later he reversed his position. Even when directed toward a divine object, natural affections remain "unsanctified" and, as part of man's cognitive and volitive natural apparel, inadequate for establishing a true relation with God. Though there exists a natural "fitness" in the human heart for entering into such a relation, its disposition can provide no more than a foundation. The "true" religious affections, absent from fallen nature, exclusively result from God's special grace. Hence that aesthetic attraction which Shaftesbury had posited as the core of moral perceptiveness, and which Edwards had transferred to religious life, served merely as the soil into which God could plant religious affections. The process was to be reversed. Instead of an aesthetic *eros* propelling the soul to God, a divine sense of holiness had first to be infused if a person was to attain a genuine sense of God's beauty. Only "a supernatural sense" conveyed by God's special grace would enable a person to perceive those divine realities that "the natural man discerns nothing of." God's Spirit may influence man's natural disposition in "common grace," but such grace does not communicate God's proper nature as a new, indwelling principle of action.

Despite the insurmountable separation between the two kinds of affections, they display a genuine parallelism. In the religion of the Spirit also, the springs of action are the affections. "Religion in the hearts of the truly godly, is ever in exact proportion to the degree of affection."

For although to true religion there must indeed be something else besides affection; yet true religion consists so much in the affections, that there can be no true religion without them. He who has no religious affection is in a state of spiritual death, and is wholly destitute of the powerful, quickening, saving influences of the Spirit of God upon his heart.

How can Edwards exclude from fallen nature any "godly" activity, and yet consider *affections* (the mainsprings of *nature's* activity) the basis of a genuinely spiritual life? By defining the religious affections themselves as a new, infused sense, "entirely different in its nature and kind from anything that ever their minds were the subjects of before they were sanctified," Edwards adds a principle of consciousness conceived after Locke's *passively* formed sensations and affections but proceeding from a different, supernatural source. He calls it "a new foundation laid in the nature of the soul for a new kind of exercise of the same faculty of understanding." Epistemologically he justifies these religious affections as merely another, passively communicated *idea,* equal to such underived, simple ideas as sensations and reflections. Yet theologically the new *sense* is of an entirely different nature. For Edwards the nature and quality of a thing is determined by its origin. Precisely their supernatural origin essentially distinguishes divine affections from others, even though the same "faculty of understanding" elicits them:

Edwards is irredeemably 'supernaturalist' if we take this . . . term to mean that whatever human nature is and does from itself is qualitatively different from what it is and does from beyond itself or from the Spirit of God. And the difference is owing to the difference between natural and supernatural origins.[2]

Theologically Edwards identifies the infused spiritual sense with the spirit of *agapē* poured out in our hearts. This identification with supernatural love forced him to take a stand on the theories of love that had come to dominate the moral discussion of his time. Two positions divided the philosophical camp. The first, as Edwards saw it, held that all love arises from self-love, and hence "that it is impossible in the nature of things, for any man to have any love to God, or any other being, but that love to himself must be the foundation of it." Such a love could clearly not serve as the basis of the divine *agapē* which introduces into the soul an ability to love God for His own sake. Yet the opposite, "benevolist" position appeared equally inadequate. Hutcheson, Hume, and other contemporaries had argued that benevolent, disinterested love, far from being a self-deception, stands on a par with self-love. Such an altruistic moral sense, however, fell far short of a divine love whereby the regenerate Christian loves God *for what he is in Himself.* This remains entirely hidden as much to altruistic love as to self-love and becomes accessible only to the person whose heart God has changed so as to apprehend "a beauty, glory, and supreme good, in God's nature as it is in itself." Agapic love transcends altruism as well as self-love: while the latter loves another being because it *appears lovely to me,* the former loves only because of "some gift bestowed" which both renders God lovable and compels the regenerate to love Him independently of any pleasure he or she may derive from it. The taste for the beauty and loveliness of things divine originates in God's "special grace," and only after having been regenerated does the soul perceive the divine beauty. Despite its similarities, Edwards' position on divine love did not agree with that of the "pure love" theory of his contemporaries, the French Quietists. According to them, truly divine love *excludes* self-love to a point where a person becomes wholly indifferent to his or her personal salvation. Edwards deemed self-love as well as "benevolent" love to be supported, on the natural level, by common grace. But it played no decisive part in the functioning of the supernatural, infused love of the elect.[3] On this issue the Calvinist Edwards may have come closer to the traditional Catholic doctrine than Bishop Fénelon. Edwards continued to maintain, whether consistently or not, that the totally selfless infused love of God is built upon the foundation of natural love which becomes inevitably mixed with self-love.

What distinguishes Edwards from the extreme forms of Calvinism as well as from Quietism is his determination to maintain a divine operation on two levels of real-

2. Conrad Cherry, *The Theology of Jonathan Edwards* (New York: Doubleday, Anchor Books, 1966), 230.

3. On this entire question we have followed the excellent analysis of "The Permutations of Self-Love" in Norman Fiering, *Jonathan Edwards's Moral Thought in British Context* (Chapel Hill: University of North Carolina Press, 1981), 150–99.

ity—one, "supernatural" and thus granted only by special grace; the other, belonging to a human nature that despite the separation caused by original sin continues to undergo the divine impact and in its basic structure deserves to be called good insofar as it serves as a natural foundation for the supernatural. God, Edwards writes in his final work, *The Great Christian Doctrine of Original Sin Defended* (1758), originally implanted two kinds of principles: those that belong to human nature as such, and "those that were spiritual, holy, and divine." When Adam sinned the superior principles left him "as light ceases when the candle is withdrawn," and the interior principles, left to themselves, became "absolute masters of the heart." Thus the good servant became the bad master. But the basic structure, however distorted by sin, remains when by special grace the higher principles are restored.

Some readers may object to the austere predestination theory expressed in the theology of a special grace reserved to the elect. Others may find the emphasis on sin and punishment hard to take. But Edwards' wonderful theory of religious affections is not bound up with spiritual elitism or pessimism. To deny oneself its riches because of either of these Puritan characteristics is to miss some of the finest spiritual literature written on this side of the Ocean.

Selections

PERSONAL NARRATIVE*

The first instance that I remember of that sort of inward, sweet delight in God and divine things that I have lived much in since, was on reading those words, I Tim. i. 17. *Now unto the King eternal, immortal, invisible, the only wise God, be honor and glory for ever and ever, Amen.* As I read the words, there came into my soul, and was as it were diffused through it, a sense of the glory of the Divine Being; a new sense, quite different from any thing I ever experienced before. Never any words of scripture seemed to me as these words did. I thought with myself, how excellent a Being that was, and how happy I should be, if I might enjoy that God, and be rapt up to him in heaven, and be as it were swallowed up in him for ever! I kept saying, and as it were singing over these words of scripture to myself; and went to pray to God that I might enjoy him, and prayed in a manner quite different from what I used to do; with a new sort of affection. But it never came into my thought, that there was any thing spiritual, or of a saving nature in this.

From about that time, I began to have a new kind of apprehensions and ideas of Christ, and the work of redemption, and the glorious way of salvation by him. An inward, sweet sense of these things, at times, came into my heart; and my soul was led away in pleasant views and contemplations of them. And my mind was greatly engaged to spend my time in reading and meditating on Christ, on the beauty and excellency of his person, and the lovely way of salvation by free grace in him. I found no books so delightful to me, as those that treated of these subjects. Those words Cant. ii. I, used to be abundantly with me, *I am the Rose of Sharon, and the Lilly of the valleys.* The words seemed to me, sweetly to represent the loveliness and beauty of Jesus Christ. The whole book of Canticles used to be pleasant to me, and I used to be much in reading it, about that time; and found, from time to time, an inward sweetness, that would carry me away, in my contemplations. This I know not how to express otherwise, than by a calm, sweet abstraction of soul from all the concerns of this world; and sometimes a kind of vision, or fixed ideas and imaginations, of being alone in the mountains, or some solitary wilderness, far from all mankind, sweetly conversing with Christ, and wrapt and swallowed up in God. The sense I had of divine things, would often of a sudden kindle up, as it were, a sweet burning in my heart; an ardor of soul, that I know not how to express.

Not long after I first began to experience these things, I gave an account to my father of some things that had passed in my mind. I was pretty much affected by the discourse we had together; and when the discourse was ended, I walked abroad

---

*From *The Works of President Edwards,* ed. Samuel Austin, 8 vols. (Worcester, Mass., 1808–09), 1:34–44.

alone, in a solitary place in my father's pasture, for contemplation. And as I was walking there, and looking up on the sky and clouds, there came into my mind so sweet a sense of the glorious *majesty* and *grace* of God, that I know not how to express. I seemed to see them both in a sweet conjunction; majesty and meekness joined together; it was a sweet, and gentle, and holy majesty; and also a majestic meekness; an awful sweetness; a high, and great, and holy gentleness.

After this my sense of divine things gradually increased, and became more and more lively, and had more of that inward sweetness. The appearance of every thing was altered; there seemed to be, as it were, a calm, sweet cast, or appearance of divine glory, in almost every thing. God's excellency, his wisdom, his purity and love, seemed to appear in every thing; in the sun, moon, and stars; in the clouds, and blue sky; in the grass, flowers, trees; in the water, and all nature; which used greatly to fix my mind. I often used to sit and view the moon for continuance; and in the day, spent much time in viewing the clouds and sky, to behold the sweet glory of God in these things; in the mean time, singing forth, with a low voice my contemplations of the Creator and Redeemer. And scarce any thing, among all the works of nature, was so sweet to me as thunder and lightning; formerly, nothing had been so terrible to me. Before, I used to be uncommonly terrified with thunder, and to be struck with terror when I saw a thunder storm rising; but now, on the contrary, it rejoiced me. I felt God, so to speak, at the first appearance of a thunder storm; and used to take the opportunity, at such times, to fix myself in order to view the clouds, and see the lightnings play, and hear the majestic and awful voice of God's thunder, which oftentimes was exceedingly entertaining, leading me to sweet contemplations of my great and glorious God. While thus engaged, it always seemed natural to me to sing, or chant for my meditations; or, to speak my thoughts in soliloquies with a singing voice.

I felt then great satisfaction, as to my good state; but that did not content me. I had vehement longings of soul after God and Christ, and after more holiness, wherewith my heart seemed to be full, and ready to break; which often brought to my mind the words of the Psalmist, Psal. cxix. 28. *My soul breaketh for the longing it hath.* I often felt a mourning and lamenting in my heart, that I had not turned to God sooner, that I might have had more time to grow in grace. My mind was greatly fixed on divine things; almost perpetually in the contemplation of them. I spent most of my time in thinking of divine things, year after year; often walking alone in the woods, and solitary places, for meditation, soliloquy, and prayer, and converse with God; and it was always my manner, at such times, to sing forth my contemplations. I was almost constantly in ejaculatory prayer, wherever I was. Prayer seemed to be natural to me, as the breath by which the inward burnings of my heart had vent. The delights which I now felt in the things of religion, were of an exceeding different kind from those before mentioned, that I had when a boy; and what I then had no more notion of, than one born blind has of pleasant and beautiful colors. They were of a more inward, pure, soul animating and refreshing nature. Those former delights never reached the heart; and did not arise from any sight of the divine excellency of the things of God; or any taste of the soul satisfying and life-giving good there is in them.

My sense of divine things seemed gradually to increase, until I went to preach at Newyork, which was about a year and a half after they began; and while I was there, I felt them, very sensibly, in a much higher degree than I had done before. My longings after God and holiness, were much increased. Pure and humble, holy and heavenly Christianity, appeared exceeding amiable to me. I felt a burning desire to be in every thing a complete Christian; and conformed to the blessed image of Christ; and that I might live, in all things, according to the pure, sweet and blessed rules of the gospel. I had an eager thirsting after progress in these things; which put me upon pursuing and pressing after them. It was my continual strife day and night, and constant inquiry, how I should *be* more holy, and *live* more holily, and more becoming a child of God, and a disciple of Christ. I now sought an increase of grace and holiness, and a holy life, with much more earnestness, than ever I sought grace before I had it. I used to be continually examining myself, and studying and contriving for likely ways and means, how I should live holily, with far greater diligence and earnestness, than ever I pursued any thing in my life; but yet with too great a dependence on my own strength; which afterwards proved a great damage to me. My experience had not then taught me, as it has done since, my extreme feebleness and impotence, every manner of way; and the bottomless depths of secret corruption and deceit there was in my heart. However, I went on with my eager pursuit after more holiness, and conformity to Christ.

The heaven I desired was a heaven of holiness; to be with God, and to spend my eternity in divine love, and holy communion with Christ. My mind was very much taken up with contemplations on heaven, and the enjoyments there; and living there in perfect holiness, humility and love: And it used at that time to appear a great part of the happiness of heaven, that there the saints could express their love to Christ. It appeared to me a great clog and burden, that what I felt within, I could not express as I desired. The inward ardor of my soul, seemed to be hindered and pent up, and could not freely flame out as it would. I used often to think, how in heaven this principle should freely and fully vent and express itself. Heaven appeared exceedingly delightful, as a world of love; and that all happiness consisted in living in pure, humble, heavenly, divine love.

I remember the thoughts I used then to have of holiness; and said sometimes to myself, "I do certainly know that I love holiness, such as the gospel prescribes." It appeared to me, that there was nothing in it but what was ravishingly lovely; the highest beauty and amiableness . . . a *divine* beauty; far purer than any thing here upon earth; and that every thing else was like mire and defilement, in comparison of it.

Holiness, as I then wrote down some of my contemplations on it, appeared to me to be of a sweet, pleasant, charming, serene, calm nature; which brought an inexpressible purity, brightness, peacefulness and ravishment to the soul. In other words, that it made the soul like a field or garden of God, with all manner of pleasant flowers; all pleasant, delightful, and undisturbed; enjoying a sweet calm, and the gently vivifying beams of the sun. The soul of a true Christian, as I then wrote my meditations, appeared like such a little white flower as we see in the spring of the year; low and humble on the ground, opening its bosom to receive the pleasant beams of the sun's glory; rejoicing as it were in a calm rapture; diffusing around a sweet fragrancy; standing peacefully and lovingly, in the midst of other flowers round about; all in like manner opening their bosoms, to drink in the light of the sun. There was no part of creature holiness, that I had so great a sense of its loveliness, as humility, brokenness of heart and poverty of spirit; and there was nothing that I so earnestly longed for. My heart panted after this, to lie low before God, as in the dust; that I might be nothing, and that God might be ALL, that I might become as a little child.

While at Newyork, I was sometimes much affected with reflections of my past life, considering how late it was before I began to be truly religious; and how wickedly I had lived till then; and once so as to weep abundantly, and for a considerable time together.

On *January* 12, 1723. I made a solemn dedication of myself to God, and wrote it down; giving up myself, and all that I had to God; to be for the future, in no respect, my own; to act as one that had no right to himself, in any respect. And solemnly vowed, to take God for my whole portion and felicity; looking on nothing else, as any part of my happiness, nor acting as if it were; and his law for the constant rule of my obedience: engaging to fight, with all my might, against the world, the flesh, and the devil, to the end of my life. But I have reason to be infinitely humbled, when I consider, how much I have failed, of answering my obligation.

I had, then, abundance of sweet, religious conversation, in the family where I lived, with Mr. John Smith, and his pious mother. My heart was knit in affection, to those, in whom were appearances of true piety; and I could bear the thoughts of no other companions, but such as were holy, and the disciples of the blessed Jesus. I had great longings, for the advancement of Christ's kingdom in the world; and my secret prayer used to be, in great part, taken up in praying for it. If I heard the least hint, of any thing that happened, in any part of the world, that appeared, in some respect or other, to have a favourable aspect, on the interests of Christ's kingdom, my soul eagerly catched at it; and it would much animate and refresh me. I used to be eager to read public news-letters, mainly for that end; to see if I could not find some news, favourable to the interest of religion in the world.

I very frequently used to retire into a solitary place, on the banks of Hudson's River, at some distance from the city, for contemplation on divine things and secret converse with God; and had many sweet hours there. Sometimes Mr. Smith and I walked there together, to converse on the things of God; and our conversation used to turn much on the advancement of Christ's kingdom in the world, and the glorious things that God would accomplish for his church in the latter days. I had then, and at other times, the greatest delight in the holy scriptures, of any book whatsoever. Oftentimes in reading it, every word seemed to touch my heart. I felt a harmony between something in my heart, and those sweet and powerful words. I seemed often to see so much light exhibited by every sentence, and such a refreshing food communicated, that I could not get along in reading; often dwelling long on one sentence, to see the wonders contained in it; and yet almost every sentence seemed to be full of wonders.

I came away from Newyork in the month of April, 1723, and had a most bitter parting with Madam Smith and her son. My heart seemed to sink within me, at leaving the family and city, where I had enjoyed so many sweet and pleasant days. I went from New York to Wethersfield, by water; and as I sailed away, I kept sight of the city as long as I could. However, that night after this sorrowful parting, I was greatly comforted in God at Westchester, where we went ashore to lodge: and had a pleasant time of it all the voyage to Saybrook. It was sweet to me to think of meeting dear christians in heaven, where we should never part more. At Saybrook we went ashore to lodge on Saturday, and there kept the Sabbath; where I had a sweet and refreshing season, walking alone in the fields.

After I came home to Windsor, I remained much in a like frame of mind, as when at Newyork; only sometimes I felt my heart ready to sink, with the thoughts of my friends at Newyork. My support was in contemplations on the heavenly state; as I find in my Diary of May 1, 1723. It was a comfort to think of that state, where there is fulness of joy; where reigns heavenly, calm, and delightful love, without alloy; where there are continually the dearest expressions of this love; where is the enjoyment of the persons loved, without ever parting; where those persons who appear so lovely in this world, will really be inexpressibly more lovely, and full of love to us. And how sweetly will the mutual lovers join together, to sing the praises of God and the Lamb! How will it fill us with joy to think, that this enjoyment, these sweet exercises, will never cease, but will last to all eternity. . . . I continued much in the same frame, in the general, as when at Newyork, till I went to Newhaven, as Tutor of the College; particularly, once at Bolton, on a journey from Boston, while walking out alone in the fields. After I went to Newhaven, I sunk in religion; my mind being diverted from my eager pursuits after holiness, by some affairs, that greatly perplexed and distracted my thoughts.

In September, 1725, I was taken ill at Newhaven, and while endeavouring to go home to Windsor, was so ill at the North Village, that I could go no farther; where I lay sick, for about a quarter of a year. In this sickness, God was pleased to visit me again, with the sweet influences of his Spirit. My mind was greatly engaged there, on divine and pleasant contemplations, and longings of soul. I observed, that those who watched with me, would often be looking out wishfully for the morning; which brought to my mind those words of the Psalmist, and which my soul with delight made its own language, *My soul waiteth for the Lord, more than they that watch for the morning; I say, more than they that watch for the morning;* and when the light of day came in at the window, it refreshed my soul, from one morning to another. It seemed to be some image of the light of God's glory.

I remember, about that time, I used greatly to long for the conversion of some, that I was concerned with; I could gladly honour them, and with delight be a servant to them, and lie at their feet, if they were but truly holy. But some time after this, I was again greatly diverted with some temporal concerns, that exceedingly took up my thoughts, greatly to the wounding of my soul; and went on, through various exercises, that it would be tedious to relate, which gave me much more experience of my own heart, than I ever had before.

Since I came to this town,[1] I have often had sweet complacency in God, in views of his glorious perfections and the excellency of Jesus Christ. God has appeared to me a glorious and lovely Being, chiefly on account of his holiness. The holiness of God has always appeared to me the most lovely of all his attributes. The doctrines of God's absolute sovereignty, and free grace, in shewing mercy to whom he would shew mercy; and man's absolute dependence on the operations of God's Holy Spirit, have very often appeared to me as sweet and glorious doctrines. These doctrines have been much my delight. God's sovereignty has ever appeared to me, great part of his glory. It has often been my delight to approach God, and adore him as a sovereign God, and ask sovereign mercy of him.

I have loved the doctrines of the gospel; they have been to my soul like green pastures. The gospel has seemed to me the richest treasure; the treasure that I have most desired, and longed that it might dwell richly in me. The way of salvation by Christ has appeared, in a general way, glorious and excellent, most pleasant and most beautiful. It has often seemed to me, that it would in a great measure spoil heaven, to receive it in any other way. That text has often been affecting and delight-

---

1. Northampton, Massachusetts.

ful to me, Isa. xxxii. 2. *A man shall be an hiding place from the wind, and a covert from the tempest, &c.*

It has often appeared to me delightful, to be united to Christ; to have him for my head, and to be a member of his body; also to have Christ for my teacher and prophet. I very often think with sweetness, and longings, and pantings of soul, of being a little child, taking hold of Christ, to be led by him through the wilderness of this world. That text, Matth. xviii. 3, has often been sweet to me, *except ye be converted and become as little children, &c.* I love to think of coming to Christ, to receive salvation of him, poor in spirit, and quite empty of self, humbly exalting him alone; cut off entirely from my own root, in order to grow into, and out of Christ; to have God in Christ to be all in all; and to live by faith in the son of God, a life of humble, unfeigned confidence in him. That scripture has often been sweet to me, Psal. cxv. 1. *Not unto us, O Lord, not unto us, but unto thy name give glory, for thy mercy, and for thy truth's sake.* And those words of Christ, Luke x. 21. *In that hour Jesus rejoiced in spirit, and said, I thank thee, O Father, Lord of heaven and earth, that thou hast hid these things from the wise and prudent, and hast revealed them unto babes: Even so, Father, for so it seemed good in thy sight.* That sovereignty of God which Christ rejoiced in, seemed to me worthy of such joy; and that rejoicing seemed to shew the excellency of Christ, and of what spirit he was.

Sometimes, only mentioning a single word caused my heart to burn within me; or only seeing the name of Christ, or the name of some attribute of God. And God has appeared glorious to me, on account of the Trinity. It has made me have exalting thoughts of God, that he subsists in three persons; Father, Son and Holy Ghost. The sweetest joys and delights I have experienced, have not been those that have arisen from a hope of my own good estate; but in a direct view of the glorious things of the gospel. When I enjoy this sweetness, it seems to carry me above the thoughts of my own estate; it seems at such times a loss that I cannot bear, to take off my eye from the glorious, pleasant object I behold without me, to turn my eye in upon myself, and my own good estate.

My heart has been much on the advancement of Christ's kingdom in the world. The histories of the past advancement of Christ's kingdom have been sweet to me. When I have read histories of past ages, the pleasantest thing in all my reading has been, to read of the kingdom of Christ being promoted. And when I have expected, in my reading, to come to any such thing, I have rejoiced in the prospect, all the way as I read. And my mind has been much entertained and delighted with the scripture promises and prophecies, which relate to the future glorious advancement of Christ's kingdom upon earth.

I have sometimes had a sense of the excellent fulness of Christ, and his meetness and suitableness as a Saviour; whereby he has appeared to me, far above all, the chief of ten thousands. His blood and atonement have appeared sweet, and his righteousness sweet; which was always accompanied with ardency of spirit; and inward strugglings and breathings, and groanings that cannot be uttered, to be emptied of myself, and swallowed up in Christ.

Once, as I rode out into the woods for my health, in 1737, having alighted from my horse in a retired place, as my manner commonly has been, to walk for divine contemplation and prayer, I had a view that for me was extraordinary, of the glory of the Son of God, as Mediator between God and man, and his wonderful, great, full, pure and sweet grace and love, and meek and gentle condescension. This grace that appeared so calm and sweet, appeared also great above the heavens. The person of Christ appeared ineffably excellent with an excellency great enough to swallow up all thought and conception ... which continued as near as I can judge, about an hour; which kept me the greater part of the time in a flood of tears, and weeping aloud. I felt an ardency of soul to be, what I know not otherwise how to express, emptied and annihilated; to lie in the dust, and to be full of Christ alone; to love him with a holy and pure love; to trust in him; to live upon him; to serve and follow him; and to be perfectly sanctified and made pure, with a divine and heavenly purity. I have, several other times, had views very much of the same nature, and which have had the same effects.

I have many times had a sense of the glory of the third person in the Trinity, in his office of Sanctifier; in his holy operations, communicating divine light and life to the soul. God, in the communications of his Holy Spirit, has appeared as an infinite fountain of divine glory and sweetness; being full, and sufficient to fill and satisfy the soul; pouring forth itself in sweet communications; like the sun in its glory, sweetly and pleasantly diffusing light and life. And I have sometimes had an affecting sense of the excellency of the word of God, as a word of life; as the light of life; a sweet, excellent lifegiving word; accompanied with a thirsting after that word, that it might dwell richly in my heart.

A TREATISE CONCERNING RELIGIOUS AFFECTIONS*

PART THREE:
THE DISTINGUISHING SIGNS

The First Sign

1. On the one hand it must be observed, that not everything which in any respect appertains to spiritual affections, is new and entirely different from what natural

---

*From *Religious Affections,* ed. John E. Smith, vol. 2 of *The Works of Jonathan Edwards* (New Haven: Yale University Press, 1959), 208–10, 392–97. Reprinted with permission of the publisher.

men can conceive of, and do experience; some things are common to gracious affections with other affections; many circumstances, appendages and effects are common. Thus a saint's love to God has a great many things appertaining to it, which are common with a man's natural love to a near relation: love to God makes a man have desires of the honor of God, and a desire to please him; so does a natural man's love to his friend make him desire his honor, and desire to please him: love to God causes a man to delight in the thoughts of God, and to delight in the presence of God, and to desire conformity to God, and the enjoyment of God; and so it is with a man's love to his friend; and many other things might be mentioned which are common to both. But yet that idea which the saint has of the loveliness of God, and that sensation, and that kind of delight he has in that view, which is as it were the marrow and quintessence of his love, is peculiar, and entirely diverse from anything that a natural man has, or can have any notion of. And even in those things that seem to be common, there is something peculiar: both spiritual love and natural, cause desires after the object beloved; but they be not the same sort of desires; there is a sensation of soul in the spiritual desires of one that loves God, which is entirely different from all natural desires: both spiritual love and natural love are attended with delight in the object beloved; but the sensations of delight are not the same, but entirely and exceedingly diverse. Natural men may have conceptions of many things about spiritual affections; but there is something in them which is as it were the nucleus, or kernel of them, that they have no more conceptions of, than one born blind has of colors.

It may be clearly illustrated by this: we will suppose two men; one is born without the sense of tasting, the other has it; the latter loves honey and is greatly delighted in it because he knows the sweet taste of it; the other loves certain sounds and colors: the love of each has many things that appertain to it, which is common; it causes both to desire and delight in the object beloved, and causes grief when it is absent, etc.: but yet, that idea or sensation which he who knows the taste of honey, has of its excellency and sweetness, that is the foundation of his love, is entirely different from anything the other has or can have; and that delight which he has in honey, is wholly diverse from anything that the other can conceive of; though they both delight in their beloved objects. So both these persons may in some repects love the same object: the one may love a delicious kind of fruit, which is beautiful to the eye, and of a delicious taste; not only because he has seen its pleasant colors, but knows its sweet taste; the other, perfectly ignorant of this, loves it only for its beautiful colors: there are many things seen, in some respect, to be common to both; both love, both desire, and both delight; but the love, and desire, and delight of the one, is altogether diverse from that of the other. The difference between the love of a natural man and spiritual man is like to this; but only it must be observed, that in one respect it is vastly greater, viz. that the kinds of excellency which are perceived in spiritual objects, by these different kinds of persons, are in themselves vastly more diverse, than the different kinds of excellency perceived in delicious fruit, by a tasting and a tasteless man; and in another respect it may not be so great, viz. as the spiritual man may have a spiritual sense or taste, to perceive that divine and most peculiar excellency, but in small beginnings, and in a very imperfect degree.

2. On the other hand, it must be observed, that a natural man may have those religious apprehensions and affections, which may be in many respects very new and surprising to him, and what before he did not conceive of; and yet what he experiences be nothing like the exercises of a principle of new nature, or the sensations of a new spiritual sense: his affections may be very new, by extraordinarily moving natural principles, in a very new degree, and with a great many new circumstances, and a new cooperation of natural affections, and a new composition of ideas; this may be from some extraordinary powerful influence of Satan and some great delusion; but there is nothing but nature extraordinarily acted. As if a poor man, that had always dwelt in a cottage, and had never looked beyond the obscure village where he was born, should in a jest, be taken to a magnificent city and prince's court, and there arrayed in princely robes, and set in the throne, with the crown royal on his head, peers and nobles bowing before him, and should be made to believe that he was now a glorious monarch; the ideas he would have, and the affections he would experience, would in many respects be very new, and such as he had no imagination of before; but all is no more, than only extraordinarily raising and exciting natural principles, and newly exalting, varying and compounding such sort of ideas, as he has by nature; here is nothing like giving him a new sense.

Upon the whole, I think it is clearly manifest, that all truly gracious affections do arise from special and peculiar influences of the Spirit, working that sensible effect or sensation in the souls of the saints, which are entirely different from all that it is possible a natural man should experience, not only different in degree and circumstances, but different in its whole nature: so that a natural man not only cannot experience that which is individually the same, but can't experience anything but what is exceeding diverse, and immensely below it, in its kind; and that which the power of men or devils is not sufficient to produce the like of, or anything of the same nature. . . .

The Twelfth Sign

The reason why gracious affections have such a tendency and effect [to bear fruit in Christian practice], appears from many things that have already been observed, in the preceding parts of this discourse.

The reason of it appears from this, that gracious affections do arise from those operations and influences which are spiritual, and that the inward principle from whence they flow, is something divine, a communication of God, a participation of the divine nature, Christ living in the heart, the Holy Spirit dwelling there, in union with the faculties of the soul, as an internal vital principle, exerting his own proper nature, in the exercise of those faculties. This is sufficient to show us why true grace should have such activity, power and efficacy. No wonder that which is divine, is powerful and effectual; for it has omnipotence on its side. If God dwells in the heart, and be vitally united to it, he will shew that he is a God, by the efficacy of his operation. Christ is not in the heart of a saint, as in a sepulcher, or as a dead Saviour, that does nothing; but as in his temple, and as one that is alive from the dead. For in the heart where Christ savingly is, there he lives, and exerts himself after the power of that endless life, that he received at his resurrection. Thus every saint that is the subject of the benefit of Christ's sufferings, is made to know and experience the power of his resurrection. The spirit of Christ, which is the immediate spring of grace in the heart, is all life, all power, all act; "In demonstration of the Spirit, and of power" (II Cor. 2:4). "Our gospel came not unto you in word only, but also in power, and in the Holy Ghost" (I Thess. 1:5). "The kingdom of God is not in word, but in power" (I Cor. 4:20). Hence saving affections, though oftentimes they don't make so great a noise and show as others; yet have in them a secret solidity, life and strength, whereby they take hold of, and carry away the heart, leading it into a kind of captivity (II Cor. 10:5), gaining a full and steadfast determination of the will for God and holiness; "Thy people shall be willing in the day of thy power" (Ps. 110:3). And thus it is that holy affections have a governing power in the course of a man's life. A statue may look very much like a real man, and a beautiful man; yea it may have, in its appearance to the eye, the resemblance of a very lively, strong and active man; but yet an inward principle of life and strength is wanting; and therefore it does nothing, it brings nothing to pass, there is no action or operation to answer the shew. False discoveries and affections don't go deep enough, to reach and govern the spring of men's actions and practice. The seed in stony ground had not deepness of earth, and the root did not go deep enough to bring forth fruit. But gracious affections go to the very bottom of the heart, and take hold of the very inmost springs of life and activity. Herein chiefly appears the power of true godliness, viz. in its being effectual in practice. And the efficacy of godliness in this respect, is what the Apostle has respect to, when he speaks of the power of godliness (II Tim. 3:5), as is very plain; for he there is particularly declaring, how some professors of religion would notoriously fail in the practice of it; and then in the fifth verse observes, that in being thus of an unholy practice, they deny the power of godliness, though they have the form of it. Indeed the power of godliness is exerted in the first place within the soul, in the sensible, lively exercise of gracious affections there. Yet the principal evidence of this power of godliness, is in those exercises of holy affections that are practical, and in their being practical; in conquering the will, and conquering the lusts and corruptions of men, and carrying men on in the way of holiness, through all temptation, difficulty and opposition.

Again, the reason why gracious affections have their exercise and effect in Christian practice, appears from this (which has also been before observed) that the first objective ground of gracious affections, is the transcendently excellent and amiable nature of divine things, as they are in themselves, and not any conceived relation they bear to self, or self-interest. This shews why holy affections will cause men to be holy in their practice universally. What makes men partial in religion is, that they seek themselves, and not God, in their religion, and close with religion, not for its own excellent nature, but only to serve a turn. He that closes with religion only to serve a turn, will close with no more of it than he imagines serves that turn: but he that closes with religion for its own excellent and lovely nature closes with all that has that nature: he that embraces religion for its own sake, embraces the whole of religion. This also shows why gracious affections will cause men to practice religion perseveringly, and at all times. Religion may alter greatly in process of time, as to its consistence with men's private interest, in many respects; and therefore he that complies with it only from selfish views, is liable, in change of times, to forsake it: but the excellent nature of religion, as it is in itself, is invariable; it is always the same, at all times, and through all changes; it never alters in any respect.

The reason why gracious affections issue in holy practice, also further appears from the kind of excellency of divine things, that it has been observed is the foundation of all holy affection, viz. their moral excellency, or the beauty of their holiness. No wonder that a love to holiness, for holiness' sake, inclines persons to practice holiness, and to practice everything that is holy. Seeing holiness is the main thing that excites, draws and governs all gracious affections, no wonder that all such affections tend to holiness. That which men love, they desire to have and to be united to, and possessed of. That beauty which men delight in, they desire to be adorned with. Those acts which men delight in, they necessarily include to do.

And what has been observed of that divine teaching and leading of the Spirit of God, which there is in gracious affections, shows the reason of this tendency of such affections to an universally holy practice. For as has been observed, the Spirit of God in this his divine teaching and leading, gives the soul a natural relish of the sweetness of that which is holy, and of everything that is holy, so far as it comes in view, and excites a disrelish and disgust of everything that is unholy.

The same also appears from what has been observed of the nature of that spiritual knowledge, which is the foundation of all holy affection, as consisting in a sense and view of that excellency in divine things, which is supreme and transcendent. For hereby these things appear above all others, worthy to be chosen and adhered to. By the sight of the transcendent glory of Christ, true Christians see him worthy to be followed; and so are powerfully drawn after him: they see him worthy that they should forsake all for him: by the sight of that superlative amiableness, they are thoroughly disposed to be subject to him, and engaged to labor with earnestness and activity in his service, and made willing to go through all difficulties for his sake. And 'tis the discovery of this divine excellency of Christ, that makes 'em constant to him: for it makes a deep impression upon their minds, that they cannot forget him; and they will follow him whithersoever he goes, and it is in vain for any to endeavor to draw them away from him.

The reason of this practical tendency and issue of gracious affections, further appears, from what has been observed of such affections being attended with a thorough conviction of the judgment, of the reality and certainty of divine things. No wonder that they who were never thoroughly convinced that there is any reality in the things of religion, will never be at the labor and trouble of such an earnest, universal and persevering practice of religion, through all difficulties, self-denials and sufferings, in a dependence on that, which they are not convinced of. But on the other hand, they who are thoroughly convinced of the certain truth of those things, must needs be governed by them in their practice; for the things revealed in the Word of God are so great, and so infinitely more important, than all other things, that it is inconsistent with the human nature, that a man should fully believe the truth of them, and not be influenced by them above all things, in his practice.

Again, the reason of this expression and effect of holy affections in the practice, appears from what has been observed of a change of nature, accompanying such affections. Without a change of nature, men's practice will not be thoroughly changed. Till the tree be made good, the fruit will not be good. Men don't gather grapes of thorns, nor figs of thistles. The swine may be washed, and appear clean for a little while, but yet, without a change of nature, he will still wallow in the mire. Nature is a more powerful principle of action, than anything that opposes it: though it may be violently restrained for a while, it will finally overcome that which restrains it: 'tis like the stream of a river, it may be stopped a while with a dam, but if nothing be done to dry the fountain, it won't be stopped always; it will have a course, either in its old channel, or a new one. Nature is a thing more constant and permanent, than any of those things that are the foundation of carnal men's reformation and righteousness. When a natural man denies his lust, and lives a strict, religious life, and seems humble, painful and earnest in religion, 'tis not natural, 'tis all a force against nature; as when a stone is violently thrown upwards; but that force will be gradually spent; yet nature will remain in its full strength, and so prevails again, and the stone returns downwards. As long as corrupt nature is not mortified, but the principle left whole in a man, 'tis a vain thing to expect that it should not govern. But if the old nature be indeed mortified, and a new and heavenly nature infused; then may it well be expected, that men will walk in newness of life, and continue to do so to the end of their days.

The reason of this practical exercise and effect of holy affections, may also be partly seen, from what has been said of that spirit of humility which attends them. Humility is that wherein a spirit of obedience does much consist. A proud spirit is a rebellious spirit, but a humble spirit is a yieldable, subject, obediential spirit. We see among men, that the servant who is of a haughty spirit, is not apt in everything to be submissive and obedient to the will of his master; but it is otherwise with that servant who is of a lowly spirit.

And that lamblike, dovelike spirit, that has been spoken of, which accompanies all gracious affections, fulfills (as the Apostle observes, Rom. 13:8–10 and Gal. 5:14) all the duties of the second table of the law; wherein Christian practice does very much consist, and wherein the external practice of Christianity chiefly consists.

And the reason why gracious affections are attended with that strict, universal and constant obedience which has been spoken of, further appears, from what has been observed of that tenderness of spirit, which accompanies the affections of true saints, causing in them so quick and lively a sense of pain, through the presence of moral evil, and such a dread of the appearance of evil.

And one great reason why the Christian practice which flows from gracious affections, is universal, and constant, and persevering, appears from what has been observed of those affections themselves, from whence this practice flows, being universal and constant, in all kinds of holy exercises, and towards all objects, and in all circumstances, and at all seasons, in a beautiful symmetry and proportion.

And much of the reason why holy affections are expressed and manifested in such an earnestness, activity, and engagedness and perseverance in holy practice, as has been spoken of, appears from what has been observed, of the spiritual appetite and longing after further attainments in religion, which evermore attends true affection, and don't decay, but increases, as those affections increase.

Thus we see how the tendency of holy affections to such a Christian practice as has been explained, appears from each of those characteristics of holy affection, that have been before spoken of.

And this point may be further illustrated and confirmed, if it be considered, that the Holy Scriptures do abundantly place sincerity and soundness in religion, in making a full choice of God as our only Lord and portion, forsaking all for him, and in a full determination of the will for God and Christ, on counting the cost; in our hearts closing and complying with the religion of Jesus Christ, with all that belongs to it, embracing it with all its difficulties, as it were hating our dearest earthly enjoyments, and even our own lives, for Christ; giving up ourselves, with all that we have, wholly and forever, unto Christ, without keeping back anything or making any reserve; or in one word, in the great duty of self-denial for Christ; or in denying, i.e. as it were disowning and renouncing ourselves for him, making ourselves nothing that he may be all. See the texts to this purpose referred to in the margin.[1] Now surely having an heart to forsake all for Christ, tends to actually forsaking all for him, so far as there is occasion, and we have the trial. An having an heart to deny ourselves for Christ, tends to a denying ourselves in deed, when Christ and self-interest stand in competition. A giving up ourselves, with all that we have in our hearts, without making any reserve there, tends to our behaving ourselves universally as his, as subject to his will, and devoted to his ends. Our hearts entirely closing with the religion of Jesus, with all that belongs to it, and as attended with all its difficulties, upon a deliberate counting the cost, tends to an universal closing with the same in act and deed, and actually going through all the difficulties that we meet with in the way of religion, and so holding out with patience and perseverance.

---

1. Edwards here refers to forty passages from Scripture, including Matt 5:29–30; Luke 5:27–28; Acts 4:34–35; Rom 6:3–8; Phil 3:7–10; Ruth 1:6–16; Ps 16:5–6; and Jer 10:16.

SELECTED BIBLIOGRAPHY

TEXTS

The Works of Jonathan Edwards. Edited by Perry Miller, John E. Smith, *et al.* 7 vols. to date. New Haven and London: Yale University Press, 1957–.

Jonathan Edwards: Representative Selections. Edited by Clarence H. Faust and Thomas H. Johnson. Rev. ed. New York: Hill and Wang, 1962.

STUDIES

Cherry, Conrad. *The Theology of Jonathan Edwards: A Reappraisal.* Garden City, N.Y.: Doubleday, Anchor Books, 1966.

Fiering, Norman. *Jonathan Edwards's Moral Thought and Its British Context.* Chapel Hill: University of North Carolina Press, 1981.

Haroutunian, Joseph. "Jonathan Edwards: A Study in Godliness." *The Journal of Religion* 11 (1931): 400–419.

Hatch, Nathan O., Harry S, Stout, eds. *Jonathan Edwards and the American Experience.* New York: Oxford University Press, 1987.

Jenson, Robert W. *America's Theologian: A Recommendation of Jonathan Edwards.* New York: Oxford University Press, 1987.

Miller, Perry. *Jonathan Edwards.* New York: Meridian Books, 1959.

Thérèse of Lisieux

(1873–1897)

The short life of St. Thérèse was outwardly so uneventful that some of the nuns with whom she lived during the final nine years of her life were not aware of any particular virtue in her and wondered aloud what could possibly be said in praise of her on the obituary notices that were to be sent to other Carmelite houses after her death. If today no one doubts her genuine sanctity, many would nevertheless deny that she should be counted among the mystics. In explaining our choice of Thérèse for inclusion in this anthology, we will at the same time be making some fundamental points about the nature and compass of Christian mysticism.

Thérèse was born at Alençon in Normandy on January 2, 1873, the ninth and youngest child of Louis Martin and Zélie Guérin. Of the five children who lived beyond childhood, four became Carmelite nuns in the convent at Lisieux, the city to which the family moved after Zélie's death in August 1877. Years later, Thérèse wrote of her mother's death as ushering in a particularly sad and trying period of her life, one that lasted more than nine years and was marked by bouts of depression, scrupulosity, and what we would call a nervous breakdown, which occurred when she was only ten years old. Already during these years she had a strong desire to enter Carmel, perhaps at first largely in order to follow the path of her elder sister and "second mother," Pauline, but later out of a firm conviction that this was God's will for her. With dogged persistence she finally obtained special permission to join the community at Lisieux only three months beyond her fifteenth birthday. During her early years in the convent she was regularly assigned only the menial employments common to postulants, novices, and the newly professed, but at the age of twenty she was named to the important position of assistant to the novice mistress. The first signs of tuberculosis appeared in the summer of the following year, 1894. After this she became progressively weaker, although she continued her regular duties without any relaxation for nearly two years. By early July 1897, Thérèse had become so ill that she was moved to the convent infirmary, where she died on the evening of September 30. She was beatified by Pope Pius XI in 1923 and canonized only two years later, May 17, 1925.

If there is any "secret" to the holiness of this young saint, it lies in her complete conviction that it is not so much what we do that counts in God's eyes as rather the love with which we do it—or, more exactly, the love with which we allow God to love in and through ourselves.[1] From John of the Cross she took the verse that she used on her own Carmelite coat of arms, "Love is repaid by love alone," and from the New Testament she absorbed and lived out the teaching that this love must be extended in utterly practical ways to everyone, starting with those whom we find naturally least attractive: one must render them "all possible services," search out their virtues rather than their faults, and answer with a kind word when tempted to respond in a disagreeable manner. The simple, even naive way in which she describes all this in the three manuscripts which together comprise her autobiographical *Story of a Soul* has inspired countless readers throughout the world and once led Pope Pius X to call her "the greatest saint of modern times." Something more must be said, however, to explain why she is also rightly to be considered a mystic.

To begin, it is worth examining why some would deny her this title. The eminent Swiss theologian Hans Urs von Balthasar, in his long and generally positive study of her spirituality, states categorically that she never "crossed the threshold into what is known as mysticism."[2] He justifies

this claim on the basis that her life was free of the presence of or even the longing for extraordinary "mystical phenomena"; after all, he notes, Thérèse repeatedly said or wrote such things as "I have never longed for visions"; "I have no wish . . . to have ecstasies"; "I have never wished for extraordinary graces. That does not fit in with my little way."[3]

In this line of argumentation, we have a particularly clear instance of what we referred to in our General Introduction as the increasing subjectivization of the understanding of mysticism in recent centuries. For many writers today, mysticism has come to mean simply an extraordinary grace given to those who directly experience the divine presence. If this understanding is accepted, then one might have to agree with von Balthasar that Thérèse of Lisieux was no mystic. But one should also recall that in its original Christian usage, the word "mystical" referred to the objective but "hidden" *(mystikos)* reality of Christ in Scripture, in the sacraments, and in all of history.[4] An immediate, vivid, and at times overwhelmingly ecstatic consciousness of this real presence has indeed often been found in those who have dedicated themselves in a particularly single-hearted way to the following of the Gospel. But this kind of experience did not belong to the essence of the mystical as this was originally understood by writers like Origen, Gregory of Nyssa, and Maximus the Confessor. According to that more objective understanding, as Louis Bouyer ob-

---

1. Thérèse once wrote: "Ah! Lord, I know you don't command the impossible. You know better than I do my weakness and imperfection; You know very well that never would I be able to love my Sisters as You love them, unless *You*, O my Jesus, *loved them in me.*" (*Story of a Soul: The Autobiography of St. Thérèse of Lisieux,* trans. John Clarke, O.C.D., 2nd ed. [Washington, D.C.: Institute of Carmelite Studies, 1976], 221.)
2. Hans Urs von Balthasar, *Thérèse of Lisieux: The Story of a Mission,* trans. Donald Nicholl (New York: Sheed and Ward, 1954), 252.

3. *Ibid.,* 254.
4. Louis Bouyer, Cong. Orat., "Mysticism: An Essay on the History of the Word," in *Understanding Mysticism,* ed. Richard Woods, O.P. (Garden City, N.Y.: Doubleday, Image Books, 1980), 42–55.

serves in the concluding chapter of his long and excellent study *Mysterion,* "the main thing is to be fully convinced that Christ is living in us, and especially to act accordingly, not to experience more or less directly the feeling that this is indeed so."[5]

That Thérèse had this conviction to a preeminent degree seems evident from almost every page of her writings. Looking back over her life, she once said that she did not believe she had ever gone more than a few minutes without thinking about God. For her, unlike Teresa of Avila or Marie of the Incarnation, this conviction of God's reality was not accompanied by personal experiences of ecstasy, nor did her conviction inspire Augustinian or Eckhartian reflections on the trinity of the mind as an image of God or on that "spark in the soul" which entirely transcends the world of space and time. In these respects, Thérèse actually differs from *all* the other authors included in this anthology, for she offers neither personal descriptions of ecstatic experience nor theological articulation about the nature of God's presence to the soul. What she does offer is a detailed, unembarrassed account of her growing abandonment to God's love in pure faith and of the ways this manifested itself both in her prayer and in her relations with other persons, especially with those whose companionship she would otherwise have avoided: "Jesus is telling me that it is this Sister who must be loved, she must be prayed for even though her conduct would lead me to believe that she doesn't love me. . . . And it isn't enough to love; we must prove it."[6] Her own awareness of the heroically faithful if unspectacular ways in which she did prove her love allowed her to say less than a month before she died: "Ah! It is incredible how all my hopes have been fulfilled. When I used to read St. John of the Cross, I begged God to work out in me what he wrote . . . to consume me rapidly in Love, and I have been answered."[7] The frequent, loving invocations of the Father and Jesus in her writings, her willingness to suffer tormenting temptations against faith in the conviction that there is no greater joy "than that of suffering out of love for You," her fervent desire to take up all of humanity in her offering of herself to God, and her constant attempts to show her love for all, especially for the most contrary and neglected of the nuns with whom she lived: all of this allows us to see in her—in the original, objective sense of the term—a preeminent example of the "mysticism of love."

---

5. Louis Bouyer, *Mysterion: Du mystère à la mystique* (Paris, 1986), 348.

6. *Story of a Soul,* 225.

7. *St. Thérèse of Lisieux: Her Last Conversations,* trans. John Clarke, O.C.D. (Washington, D.C.: Institute of Carmelite Studies, 1977), 177.

Selections

STORY OF A SOUL*

CHAPTER TEN:
THE TRIAL OF FAITH

June, 1897

You have told me, my dear Mother,[1] of your desire that I finish *singing* with you *the Mercies of the Lord* (Ps 88:2). I began this sweet song with your dear daughter, Agnes of Jesus, who was the mother entrusted by God with guiding me in the days of my childhood. It was with her that I had to sing of the graces granted to the Blessed Virgin's *little flower* when she was in the springtime of her life. And it is with you that I am to sing of the happiness of this little flower now that the timid glimmerings of the dawn have given way to the burning heat of noon. Yes, dear Mother, I shall try to express, in answer to your wishes, the sentiments of my soul, my gratitude to God and to you, who represent Him visibly to me, for was it not into your maternal hands that I delivered myself entirely to Him? O Mother, do you not remember the day?[2] Yes, I know your heart could not forget it. As for me, I must await heaven because I cannot find here on earth words capable of expressing what took place in my heart on that beautiful day. . . .

O Mother, how different are the ways through which the Lord leads souls! In the life of the saints, we find many of them who didn't want to leave anything of themselves behind after their death, not the smallest souvenir, not the least bit of writing. On the contrary, there are others, like our holy Mother St. Teresa, who have enriched the Church with their lofty revelations, having no fears of revealing the secrets of the King in order to make Him more loved and known by souls. Which of these two types of saints is more pleasing to God? It seems to me, Mother, they are equally pleasing to Him, since all of them followed the inspiration of the Holy Spirit and since the Lord has said: *"Tell the just man ALL is well"* (Is 3:10). Yes, all is well when one seeks only the will of Jesus, and it is because of this that I, a poor little flower, obey Jesus when trying to please my beloved Mother.

You know, Mother, I have always wanted to be a saint. Alas! I have always noticed that when I compared myself to the saints, there is between them and me the

---

*From *Story of a Soul: The Autobiography of St. Thérèse of Lisieux,* trans. John Clarke, O.C.D., 2nd ed. (Washington, D.C.: Institute of Carmelite Studies, 1976), 205, 207–08, 210–14, 219–20, 224–26. Reprinted with permission of the publisher. Copyright © 1975, 1976, by Washington Province of Discalced Carmelites, ICS Publications, 2131 Lincoln Rd., N.E., Washington, D.C. 20002.

1. Thérèse is writing at the request of Mother Marie de Gonzague, elected prioress March 21, 1896, to succeed Thérèse's sister Pauline (Mother Agnes of Jesus).

2. The day of her profession, September 8, 1890.

same difference that exists between a mountain whose summit is lost in the clouds and the obscure grain of sand trampled underfoot by the passers-by. Instead of becoming discouraged, I said to myself: God cannot inspire unrealizable desires. I can, then, in spite of my littleness, aspire to holiness. It is impossible for me to grow up, and so I must bear with myself such as I am with all my imperfections. But I want to seek out a means of going to heaven by a little way, a way that is very straight, very short, and totally new.

We are living now in an age of inventions, and we no longer have to take the trouble of climbing stairs, for, in the homes of the rich, an elevator has replaced these very successfully. I wanted to find an elevator which would raise me to Jesus, for I am too small to climb the rough stairway of perfection. I searched, then, in the Scriptures for some sign of this elevator, the object of my desires, and I read these words coming from the mouth of Eternal Wisdom: *"Whoever is a LITTLE ONE, let him come to me"* (Prov 9:4). And so I succeeded. I felt I had found what I was looking for. But wanting to know, O my God, what You would do to *the very little one* who answered Your call, I continued my search and this is what I discovered: *"As one whom a mother caresses, so will I comfort you; you shall be carried at the breasts, and upon the knees they shall caress you"* (Is 66:13, 12). Ah! never did words more tender and more melodious come to give joy to my soul. The elevator which must raise me to heaven is Your arms, O Jesus! And for this I had no need to grow up, but rather I had to remain *little* and become this more and more.

O my God, You surpassed all my expectation. I want only to sing of Your Mercies. "You have taught me from my youth, O God, and until now I will declare Your wonderful works. And until old age and grey hairs, O God, forsake me not" (Ps 70:17–18). What will this old age be for me? It seems this could be right now, for two thousand years are not more in the Lord's eyes than are twenty years, than even a single day (Ps 89:4).

Ah! don't think, dear Mother, that your child wants to leave you; don't think she feels it is a greater grace to die at the dawn of the day rather than at its close. What she esteems and what she desires only is *to please* Jesus. Now that He seems to be approaching her in order to draw her into the place of His glory, your child is filled with joy. For a long time she has understood that God needs no one (much less her) to do good on earth. Pardon me, Mother, if I make you sad because I really want only to give you joy. Do you believe that though your prayers are really not heard on earth, though Jesus separates the child from its mother for a *few days*, that these prayers will be answered in heaven? . . .

Dear Mother, you know well that God has deigned to make me pass through many types of trials. I have suffered very much since I was on earth, but, if in my childhood I suffered with sadness, it is no longer in this way that I suffer. O Mother, you must know all the secrets of my soul in order not to smile when you read these lines, for is there a soul less tried than my own if one judges by appearances? Ah! if the trial I am suffering for a year now appeared to the eyes of anyone, what astonishment would be felt![3]

Dear Mother, you know about this trial; I am going to speak to you about it, however, for I consider it a great grace I received during your office as Prioress.

God granted me, last year, the consolation of observing the fast during Lent in all its rigor. Never had I felt so strong, and this strength remained with me until Easter. On Good Friday, however, Jesus wished to give me the hope of going to see Him soon in heaven. Oh! how sweet this memory really is! After remaining at the Tomb until midnight,[4] I returned to our cell, but I had scarcely laid my head upon the pillow when I felt something like a bubbling stream mounting to my lips. I didn't know what it was, but I thought that perhaps I was going to die and my soul was flooded with joy. However, as our lamp was extinguished, I told myself I would have to wait until the morning to be certain of my good fortune, for it seemed to me that it was blood I had coughed up. The morning was not long in coming; upon awakening, I thought immediately of the joyful thing that I had to learn, and so I went over to the window. I was able to see that I was not mistaken. Ah! my soul was filled with a great consolation; I was interiorly persuaded that Jesus, on the anniversary of His own death, wanted to have me hear His first call. *It was like a sweet and distant murmur which announced the Bridegroom's arrival.*[5]

It was with great fervor that I assisted at Prime and the Chapter of Pardons.[6] I was in a rush to see my turn come in order to be able, when asking pardon from you, to confide my hope and my happiness to you, dear Mother; however, I added that I was not suffering in the least (which was true) and I begged you, Mother, to give me nothing special. In fact, I had the consolation of spending Good Friday just as I desired. Never did Carmel's austerities appear so delightful to me; the hope of going to heaven soon transported me with joy. When the evening of that blessed day arrived, I had to go to my rest; but just as on the preceding night, good Jesus gave me the same sign that my entrance into eternal life was not far off.

At this time I was enjoying such a living faith, such a clear *faith,* that the thought of heaven made up all my happiness, and I was unable to believe there were really impious people who had no faith. I believed they were actually speaking against their own inner convictions when they denied the existence of heaven, that beautiful

---

3. Her temptation against faith, which lasted from Easter, 1896.
4. The Altar of Reposition. The Carmelite nuns remained all night in prayer before the Blessed Sacrament.
5. *The Imitation of Christ* 3, 47.
6. On Good Friday, the prioress customarily gave the community an exhortation to greater charity; then each begged pardon from her Sisters.

heaven where God Himself wanted to be their Eternal Reward. During those very joyful days of the Easter season, Jesus made me feel that there were really souls who have no faith, and who, through the abuse of grace, lost this precious treasure, the source of the only real and pure joys. He permitted my soul to be invaded by the thickest darkness, and that the thought of heaven, up until then so sweet to me, be no longer anything but the cause of struggle and torment. This trial was to last not a few days or a few weeks, it was not to be extinguished until the hour set by God Himself, and this hour has not yet come. I would like to be able to express what I feel, but alas! I believe this is impossible. One would have to travel through this dark tunnel to understand its darkness. I will try to explain it by a comparison.

I imagine I was born in a country which is covered in thick fog. I never had the experience of contemplating the joyful appearance of nature flooded and transformed by the brilliance of the sun. It is true that from childhood I have heard people speak of these marvels, and I know the country in which I am living is not really my true fatherland, and there is another I must long for without ceasing. This is not simply a story invented by someone living in the sad country where I am, but it is a reality, for the King of the Fatherland of the bright sun actually came and lived for thirty-three years in the land of darkness. Alas! the darkness did not understand that this Divine King was the Light of the world (Jn 1:5, 9).

Your child, however, O Lord, has understood Your divine light, and she begs pardon for her brothers. She is resigned to eat the bread of sorrow as long as You desire it; she does not wish to rise up from this table filled with bitterness at which poor sinners are eating until the day set by You. Can she not say in her name and in the name of her brothers, *"Have pity on us, O Lord, for we are poor sinners!"* (Lk 18:13) Oh! Lord, send us away justified. May all those who were not enlightened by the bright flame of faith one day see it shine. O Jesus! if it is needful that the table soiled by them be purified by a soul who loves You, then I desire to eat this bread of trial at this table until it pleases You to bring me into Your bright Kingdom. The only grace I ask of You is that I never offend You!

What I am writing, dear Mother, has no continuity; my little story which resembled a fairy-tale is all of a sudden changed into a prayer, and I don't know what interest you could possibly have in reading all these confused and poorly expressed ideas. Well, dear Mother, I am not writing to produce a literary work, but only through obedience, and if I cause you any boredom, then at least you will see that your little child has given proof of her good will. I am going to continue my little comparison where I left off.

I was saying that the certainty of going away one day far from the sad and dark country had been given me from the day of my childhood. I did not believe this only because I heard it from persons much more knowledgeable than I, but I felt in the bottom of my heart real longings for this most beautiful country. Just as the genius of Christopher Columbus gave him a presentiment of a new world when nobody had even thought of such a thing; so also I felt that another land would one day serve me as a permanent dwelling place. Then suddenly the fog which surrounds me becomes more dense; it penetrates my soul and envelops it in such a way that it is impossible to discover within it the sweet image of my Fatherland; everything has disappeared! When I want to rest my heart fatigued by the darkness which surrounds it by the memory of the luminous country after which I aspire, my torment redoubles; it seems to me that the darkness, borrowing the voice of sinners, says mockingly to me: "You are dreaming about the light, about a fatherland embalmed in the sweetest perfumes; you are dreaming about the *eternal* possession of the Creator of all these marvels; you believe that one day you will walk out of this fog which surrounds you! Advance, advance; rejoice in death which will give you not what you hope for but a night still more profound, the night of nothingness."

Dear Mother, the image I wanted to give you of the darkness that obscures my soul is as imperfect as a sketch is to the model; however, I don't want to write any longer about it; I fear I might blaspheme; I fear even that I have already said too much.

Ah! may Jesus pardon me if I have caused Him any pain, but He knows very well that while I do not have *the joy of faith,* I am trying to carry out its works at least. I believe I have made more acts of faith in this past year than all through my whole life. At each new occasion of combat, when my enemy provokes me, I conduct myself bravely. Knowing it is cowardly to enter into a duel, I turn my back on my adversary without deigning to look him in the face; but I run towards my Jesus. I tell Him I am ready to shed my blood to the last drop to profess my faith in the existence of *heaven.* I tell Him, too, I am happy not to enjoy this beautiful heaven on this earth so that He will open it for all eternity to poor unbelievers. Also, in spite of this trial which has taken away *all my joy,* I can nevertheless cry out: *"You have given me DELIGHT, O Lord, in ALL your doings"* (Ps 91:5). For is there a *joy* greater than that of suffering out of love for You? The more interior the suffering is and the less apparent to the eyes of creatures, the more it rejoices You, O my God! But if my suffering was really unknown to You, which is impossible, I would still be happy to have it, if through it I could prevent or make reparation for one single sin against *faith.*

My dear Mother, I may perhaps appear to you to be exaggerating my trial. In fact, if you are judging according to the sentiments I express in my little poems composed this year, I must appear to you as a soul filled with consolations and one for whom the veil of faith is almost torn aside; and yet it is no longer a veil for me, it is a wall which reaches right up to the heavens and covers the starry firmament. When I sing of the happiness of heaven and of the eternal possession of God, I feel no joy in this, for I sing simply what I WANT TO BELIEVE. It is true that at times a very small ray of the sun comes to illumine my darkness, and then the trial ceases for *an instant,* but afterwards the memory of this ray, instead of causing me joy, makes my darkness even more dense.

Never have I felt before this, dear Mother, how sweet and merciful the Lord really is, for He did not send me this trial until the moment I was capable of bearing it. A little earlier I believe it would have plunged me into a state of discouragement. Now it is taking away everything that could be a natural satisfaction in my desire for heaven. Dear Mother, it seems to me now that nothing could prevent me from flying away, for I no longer have any great desires, except that of loving to the point of dying of love. . . .

This year, dear Mother, God has given me the grace to understand what charity is; I understood it before, it is true, but in an imperfect way. I had never fathomed the meaning of these words of Jesus: *"The second commandment is LIKE the first: You shall love your neighbor as yourself"* (Mt 22:39). I applied myself especially to *loving God,* and it is in loving Him that I understood my love was not to be expressed only in words, for: *"It is not those who say: 'Lord, Lord!' who will enter the kingdom of heaven, but those who do the will of my Father in heaven"* (Mt 7:21). Jesus has revealed this will several times or I should say on almost every page of His Gospel. But at the Last Supper, when He knew the hearts of His disciples were burning with a more ardent love for Him who had just given Himself to them in the unspeakable mystery of His Eucharist, this sweet Savior wished to give them *a new commandment.* He said to them with inexpressible tenderness: *"A new commandment I give you, that you love one another: THAT AS I HAVE LOVED YOU, YOU ALSO LOVE ONE ANOTHER. By this will all men know that you are my disciples,* if you have love for one another" (Jn 13:34–35).

How did Jesus love His disciples and why did He love them? Ah! it was not their natural qualities which could have attracted Him since there was between Him and them an infinite distance. He was knowledge, Eternal Wisdom, while they were poor ignorant fishermen filled with earthly thoughts. And still Jesus called them his *friends, His brothers* (Jn 15:15). He desires to see them reign with Him in the kingdom of His Father, and to open that kingdom to them He wills to die on the cross, for He said: *"Greater love than this no man has than that he lay down his life for his friends"* (Jn 15:13).

Dear Mother, when meditating upon these words of Jesus, I understood how imperfect was my love for my Sisters. I saw I didn't love them as God loves them. Ah! I understand now that charity consists in bearing with the faults of others, in not being surprised at their weakness, in being edified by the smallest acts of virtue we see them practice. But I understood above all that charity must not remain hidden in the bottom of the heart. Jesus has said: *"No one lights a lamp and puts it under a bushel basket, but upon the lamp-stand, so as to give light to ALL in the house"* (Mt 5:15). It seems to me that this lamp represents charity, which must enlighten and rejoice not only those who are dearest to us but *"All who are in the house"* without distinction.

When the Lord commanded His people to love their neighbor as themselves (Lev 19:18), He had not as yet come upon the earth. Knowing the extent to which each one loved himself, He was not able to ask of His creatures a greater love than this for one's neighbor. But when Jesus gave His Apostles a new commandment, HIS OWN COMMANDMENT (Jn 15:12), as He calls it later on, it is no longer a question of loving one's neighbor as oneself but of loving him as *He, Jesus, has loved him,* and will love him to the consummation of the ages. . . .

The Lord, in the Gospel, explains in what *His new commandment* consists. He says in St. Matthew: *"You have heard that it was said, 'You shall love your neighbor and hate your enemy.' But I say to you, love your enemies . . . pray for those who persecute you"* (Mt 5:43–44). No doubt, we don't have any enemies in Carmel, but there are feelings. One feels attracted to this Sister, whereas with regard to another one would make a long detour in order to avoid meeting her. And so, without even knowing it, she becomes the subject of persecution. Well, Jesus is telling me that it is this Sister who must be loved, she must be prayed for even though her conduct would lead me to believe that she doesn't love me: *"If you love those who love you, what reward will you have? For even sinners love those who love them"* (Lk 6:32). . . . And it isn't enough to love; we must prove it. We are naturally happy to offer a gift to a friend; we love especially to give surprises; however, this is not charity, for sinners do this too. Here is what Jesus teaches me also: *"Give to EVERYONE who asks of you, and from HIM WHO TAKES AWAY your goods, ask no return"* (Lk 6:30). Giving to all those who *ask* is less sweet than offering oneself by the movement of one's own heart; again, when they ask for something politely, it doesn't cost so much to give, but if, unfortunately, they don't use very delicate words, the soul is immediately up in arms if she is not well founded in charity. She finds a thousand reasons to refuse what is asked of her, and it is only after having convinced the asker of her tactlessness that she will finally give what is asked, and then only *as a favor;* or else she will render a light service which could have been done in one-twentieth of the time that was spent in setting forth her imaginary rights.

Although it is difficult to give to one who asks, it is even more so *to allow one to take what belongs to you, without asking it back.* O Mother, I say it is difficult; I should have said that this *seems* difficult, for *the yoke of the Lord is sweet and light* (Mt 11:30). When one accepts it, one feels its sweetness immediately, and cries out with the Psalmist: *"I have run the way of your commandments when you enlarged my heart"* (Ps 118:32). It is only charity which can expand my heart. O Jesus, since this sweet flame consumes it, I run with joy in the way of *Your NEW commandment.* I want to run in it until that blessed day when, joining the virginal procession, I shall be able to follow You in the heavenly courts, singing Your *NEW canticle* (Rev 14:3) which must be *Love.*

SELECTED BIBLIOGRAPHY

TEXTS AND TRANSLATIONS

Correspondance génerale. 2 vols. Paris, 1972–73.

Derniers entretiens avec ses soeurs. 2 vols. Paris, 1971.

Histoire d'une âme: Manuscrits autobiographiques. Paris, 1972.

St. Thérèse of Lisieux: General Correspondence. Translated by John Clarke, O.C.D. 2 vols. Washington, D.C.: Institute of Carmelite Studies, 1982 and 1988.

St. Thérèse of Lisieux: Her Last Conversations. Translated by John Clarke, O.C.D. Washington, D.C.: Institute of Carmelite Studies, 1977.

Story of a Soul: The Autobiography of St. Thérèse of Lisieux. Translated by John Clarke, O.C.D. 2nd ed. Washington, D.C.: Institute of Carmelite Studies, 1976.

STUDIES

Balthasar, Hans Urs von. *Thérèse of Lisieux: The Story of a Mission.* Translated by Donald Nicholl. London and New York: Sheed and Ward, 1954.

Combes, André. *Introduction à la spiritualité de ste Thérèse.* Paris, 1948.

Gaucher, Guy. *Histoire d'une vie: Thérèse Martin (1873–1897).* Paris, 1982.

Görres, Ida Friederike. *The Hidden Face: A Study of St. Thérèse of Lisieux.* Translated by Richard and Clara Winston. New York: Pantheon, 1959.

Rohrbach, Peter Thomas. *The Search for St. Thérèse.* Garden City, N.Y.: Doubleday, 1961.

Ulanov, Barry. *The Making of a Modern Saint: A Biographical Study of Thérèse of Lisieux.* Garden City, N.Y.: Doubleday, 1966.

Thomas Merton

(1915–1968)

"On the last day of January 1915, under the sign of the Water Bearer, in a year of a great war, and down in the shadow of some French mountains on the borders of Spain, I came into the world." Thus begins *The Seven Storey Mountain,* the autobiographical work which set Thomas Merton on the way to becoming the most widely read monk in the history of Christianity. Published only four years after Merton's first monastic profession, this book recounts his journey to religious and Christian conversion over the first three decades of his life. The continual rearrangement of his early life as he traveled about with his artist father after his mother's early death; the unhappiness of his years at a boarding school in France and the frank secularity of his life as a student at Cambridge University; the wholesome effect of his transfer to Columbia University and the lifelong friendships he formed there with professors and students alike; the profound influence of works by Christian authors, both ancient and modern; the impact of the simple, unaffected piety of worshippers at Corpus Christi Church in Manhattan; his reception into the Roman Catholic Church on November 16, 1938; and the retreat he made at the Trappist Abbey of Gethsemani dur-

ing Holy Week of 1941—these were among the most important episodes and turning points in Merton's life up to the time of his acceptance into that monastic community eight months after his first visit there.

In the monastery, and quite to Merton's surprise, the abbot encouraged him to cultivate his gift for writing. As a result, over the years he published numerous books and articles, including collections of his poetry, reflections on contemplative prayer and the mysteries of the Christian faith, studies of Christian mystics and Zen masters, essays of protest against social injustices, and entries from the journals that he kept with meticulous care throughout his life. Important responsibilities within the monastery were also entrusted to him: in 1951 he was placed in charge of the young monks studying for priestly ordination, and four years later he was given the still more responsible position of Master of Choir Novices, an office he held for ten years until, in 1965, he became the first American Trappist monk ever to obtain permission to live as a hermit. It was while living in his hermitage on the monastic property in the late 1960s that he received and was allowed to accept an invitation to address a meeting of Catholic religious in Bangkok, and it was while attending that conference that he suffered accidental death by electrocution on December 10, 1968, twenty-seven years to the day after his entrance into the monastery.

Those who knew Merton best often remarked on his many-faceted personality and the coruscating, dialectical nature of his intellect, which eluded facile pigeonholing. In his later years, he even sharply distanced himself from the world-renouncing, rather narrowminded young man who, in his early thirties, had published the account of his conversion to Catholicism and his eventual embracing of monastic life. But however much Merton may have changed during the years he lived as a monk, there were also some definite constants in his monastic life. Several of these are prominent in the selections we have chosen for this anthology. First, there was his quest for solitude. On one level, it was this search which led him to seek and finally obtain permission to live as a hermit. As our first selection emphasizes, however, the physical solitude of the hermit was not the most important kind for Merton: "The truest solitude . . . is an abyss opening up in the center of your own soul." For him, as for Meister Eckhart and so many of the mystical writers of earlier centuries, the real challenge of Christian existence was that of stripping off one's false, outer self and so attaining that deeper, truer self where one might meet God in utter openness and simplicity. The ruthless honesty of his journal entries, none of which did he ever want destroyed even though he knew that parts of them would scandalize some readers, is perhaps the clearest manifestation of his attempt to face up to this challenge.

Intimately related to this theme of soli-

tude is that of contemplation, a term which figures in the titles of some of his most important works *(Seeds of Contemplation; New Seeds of Contemplation; Contemplative Prayer)* and which is equally prominent in many of his other writings. Our second selection presents some of his more mature reflections on this subject. Merton was instinctively drawn to the tradition of apophatic mysticism. Like Gregory of Nyssa, he singles out the sixth beatitude— "Blessed are the pure of heart, for they shall see God"—as pointing the way to a vision of God in "clear darkness," apart from all the concepts and images with which we usually try to apprehend God. And like Eckhart, he insists that God will grant this gift only if we properly dispose ourselves to receive it "by resting in the heart of our own poverty, keeping our soul as far as possible empty of desires for all the things that please or preoccupy our nature, no matter how pure or sublime they may be in themselves."

For some years, Merton felt that this dark contemplation was normally possible only for those who, like himself, remained sequestered from the busyness of everyday secular life. In his early writings, he also at times had some very harsh things to say about non-Christian ways of prayer and meditation. On both these points he gradually came to modify his views. There may be, he finally concluded, many "masked" or "hidden" contemplatives living "in the world" and performing all sorts of apparently mundane activities and yet truly walking with God in a particularly pure way precisely because they are not attracting anyone's attention and not even worrying about whether or not they are gifted with that obscure sense of God's presence that is characteristic of a genuine mystical life.[1] Moreover, during the late 1950s and on into the 1960s he became more and more convinced that true contemplatives are to be found not just within Christianity but also in all the great religions of the world. His deep love of the writings of the Sufi mystics is particularly evident in the letters he wrote to the Pakistani scholar Abdul Aziz,[2] while his interest in and familiarity with Tibetan and Zen Buddhism led to mutually enriching meetings with the Dalai Lama, Daisetz Suzuki, and other major representatives of these traditions.

---

1. On this point, see Thomas Merton, "The Inner Experience: Kinds of Contemplation (IV)," *Cistercian Studies* 18 (1983): 289–300.

2. Merton's letters to Abdul Aziz may be found in *The Hidden Ground of Love: The Letters of Thomas Merton on Religious Experience and Social Concerns,* ed. William H. Shannon (New York: Farrar, Straus, and Giroux, 1985), 43–67.

Some of his later interest in Oriental writers may be glimpsed in the reference to the Zen master Basho in our final selection, but that selection even more significantly reveals Merton's abiding love for the world of nature as a privileged place for the encounter with God. He did indeed come to believe that this encounter may take place in urban settings as well, but till the end of his life he was at his most lyrical in writing of those times "when we are alone on a starlit night; when by chance we see the migrating birds in autumn descending on a grove of junipers to rest and eat ... or when, like the Japanese poet Basho, we hear an old frog land in a quiet pond with a solitary splash." For Thomas Merton, it was above all at such times that one might attain "a glimpse of the cosmic dance," where "the Lord plays and diverts Himself in the garden of His creation."

Selections

SEEDS OF CONTEMPLATION*

CHAPTER SIX

Solitude

The truest solitude is not something outside you, not an absence of men or of sound around you: it is an abyss opening up in the center of your own soul.

And this abyss of interior solitude is created by a hunger that will never be satisfied with any created thing.

The only way to find solitude is by hunger and thirst and sorrow and poverty and desire, and the man who has found solitude is empty, as if he had been emptied by death.

He has advanced beyond all horizons. There are no directions left in which to travel. And this is a country whose center is everywhere and whose circumference is nowhere. You do not find it by travelling but by standing still.

Yet it is in this loneliness that the deepest activities begin. It is here that you discover act without motion, labor that is profound repose, vision in obscurity, and, beyond all desire, a fulfillment whose limits extend to infinity.

Although it is true that this solitude is everywhere, there is a mechanism for finding it that has some reference to actual space, to geography, to physical isolation from the towns and the cities of men.

There should be at least a room, or some corner where no one will find you and disturb you or notice you. You should be able to untether yourself from the world and set yourself free, loosing all the fine strings and strands of tension that bind you, by sight, by sound, by thought, to the presence of other men.

Once you have found such a place, be content with it, and do not be disturbed if a good reason takes you out of it. Love it, and return to it as soon as you can, and do not be too quick to change it for another. . . .

Keep your eyes clean and your ears quiet and your mind serene. Breathe God's air. Work, if you can, under His sky.

But if you have to live in a city and work among machines and ride in the subways and eat in a place where the radio makes you deaf with spurious news and where the food destroys your life and the sentiments of those around you poison your heart with boredom, do not be upset, but accept it as the love of God and as a seed of

---

*From Thomas Merton, *Seeds of Contemplation* (Norfolk, Conn.: New Directions, 1949), 59–61. Reprinted with permission of New Directions Publishing Corp., New York, and Anthony Clarke Books, Wheathampstead, Hertfordshire, England. Copyright 1949 by Our Lady of Gethsemani Abbey.

solitude planted in your soul, and be glad of this suffering: for it will keep you alive to the next opportunity to escape from them and be alone in the healing silence of recollection and in the untroubled presence of God.

And yet remember, if you seek escape for its own sake and run away from the world only because it is (as it must be) intensely unpleasant, you will not find peace and you will not find solitude. If you seek solitude merely because it is what you prefer, you will never escape from the world and its selfishness; you will never have the interior freedom that will keep you really alone.

NEW SEEDS OF CONTEMPLATION*

CHAPTER THIRTY-ONE

The Gift of Understanding

Contemplation, by which we know and love God as He is in Himself, apprehending Him in a deep and vital experience which is beyond the reach of any natural understanding, is the reason for our creation by God. And although it is absolutely above our nature, St. Thomas teaches that it is our proper element because it is the fulfillment of deep capacities in us that God has willed should never be fulfilled in any other way. All those who reach the end for which they were created will therefore be contemplatives in heaven: but many are also destined to enter this supernatural element and breathe this new atmosphere while they are still on earth.

Since contemplation has been planned for us by God as our true and proper element, the first taste of it strikes us at once as utterly new and yet strangely familiar.

Although you had an entirely different notion of what it would be like (since no book can give an adequate idea of contemplation except to those who have experienced it), it turns out to be just what you seem to have known all along that it ought to be.

The utter simplicity and obviousness of the infused light which contemplation pours into our soul suddenly awakens us to a new level of awareness. We enter a region which we had never even suspected, and yet it is this new world which seems familiar and obvious. The old world of our senses is now the one that seems to us strange, remote and unbelievable—until the intense light of contemplation leaves us and we fall back to our own level.

*From Thomas Merton, *New Seeds of Contemplation* (Norfolk, Conn., and New York: New Directions, 1961), 225–32, 296–97. Reprinted with permission of New Directions Publishing Corp., New York, and Anthony Clarke Books, Wheathampstead, Hertfordshire, England, Copyright © 1961 by the Abbey of Gethsemani, Inc.

Compared with the pure and peaceful comprehension of love in which the contemplative is permitted to see the truth not so much by seeing it as being absorbed into it, ordinary ways of seeing and knowing are full of blindness and labor and uncertainty.

The sharpest of natural experiences is like sleep, compared with the awakening which is contemplation. The keenest and surest natural certitude is a dream compared to this serene comprehension.

Our souls rise up from our earth like Jacob waking from his dream and exclaiming: "Truly God is in this place and I knew it not"! God Himself becomes the only reality, in Whom all other reality takes its proper place—and falls into insignificance.

Although this light is absolutely above our nature, it now seems to us "normal" and "natural" to see, as we now see, without seeing, to possess clarity in darkness, to have pure certitude without any shred of discursive evidence, to be filled with an experience that transcends experience and to enter with serene confidence into depths that leave us utterly inarticulate.

"O the depth of the riches of the wisdom and knowledge of God!"

A door opens in the center of our being and we seem to fall through it into immense depths which, although they are infinite, are all accessible to us; all eternity seems to have become ours in this one placid and breathless contact.

God touches us with a touch that is emptiness and empties us. He moves us with a simplicity that simplifies us. All variety, all complexity, all paradox, all multiplicity cease. Our mind swims in the air of an understanding, a reality that is dark and serene and includes in itself everything. Nothing more is desired. Nothing more is wanting. Our only sorrow, if sorrow be possible at all, is the awareness that we ourselves still live outside of God.

For already a supernatural instinct teaches us that the function of this abyss of freedom that has opened out within our own midst, is to draw us utterly out of our own selfhood and into its own immensity of liberty and joy.

You seem to be the same person and you are the same person that you have always been: in fact you are more yourself than you have ever been before. You have only just begun to exist. You feel as if you were at last fully born. All that went before was a mistake, a fumbling preparation for birth. Now you have come out into your element. And yet now you have become nothing. You have sunk to the center of your own poverty, and there you have felt the doors fly open into infinite freedom, into a wealth which is perfect because none of it is yours and yet it all belongs to you.

And now you are free to go in and out of infinity.

It is useless to think of fathoming the depths of wide-open darkness that have yawned inside you, full of liberty and exultation.

They are not a place, not an extent, they are a huge, smooth activity. These depths, they are Love. And in the midst of you they form a wide, impregnable country.

There is nothing that can penetrate into the heart of that peace. Nothing from the outside can get in. There is even a whole sphere of your own activity that is excluded from that beautiful airy night. The five senses, the imagination, the discoursing mind, the hunger of desire do not belong in that starless sky.

And you, while you are free to come and go, yet as soon as you attempt to make words or thoughts about it you are excluded—you go back into your exterior in order to talk.

Yet you find that you can rest in this darkness and this unfathomable peace without trouble and without anxiety, even when the imagination and the mind remain in some way active outside the doors of it.

They may stand and chatter in the porch, as long as they are idle, waiting for the will their queen to return, upon whose orders they depend.

But it is better for them to be silent. However, you now know that this does not depend on you. It is a gift that comes to you from the bosom of that serene darkness and depends entirely on the decision of Love.

Within the simplicity of this armed and walled and undivided interior peace is an infinite unction which, as soon as it is grasped, loses its savor. You must not try to reach out and possess it altogether. You must not touch it, or try to seize it. You must not try to make it sweeter or try to keep it from wasting away. . . .

The situation of the soul in contemplation is something like the situation of Adam and Eve in Paradise. Everything is yours, but on one infinitely important condition: that it is all *given.*

There is nothing that you can claim, nothing that you can demand, nothing that you can *take.* And as soon as you try to take something as if it were your own—you lose your Eden. The angel with the flaming sword stands armed against all selfhood that is small and particular, against the "I" that can say "I want . . . " "I need . . . " "I demand. . . . " No individual enters Paradise, only the integrity of the *Person.*

Only the greatest humility can give us the instinctive delicacy and caution that will prevent us from reaching out for pleasures and satisfactions that we can understand and savor in this darkness. The moment we demand anything for ourselves or even trust in any action of our own to procure a deeper intensification of this pure and serene rest in God, we defile and dissipate the perfect gift that He desires to communicate to us in the silence and repose of our own powers.

If there is one thing we must do it is this: we must realize to the very depths of our being that this is a pure gift of God which no desire, no effort and no heroism of ours can do anything to deserve or obtain. There is nothing we can do directly either to procure it or to preserve it or to increase it. Our own activity is for the most part an obstacle to the infusion of this peaceful and pacifying light, with the exception that God may demand certain acts and works of us by charity or obedience, and maintain us in deep experimental union with Him through them all, by His own good pleasure, not by any fidelity of ours.

At best we can dispose ourselves for the reception of this great gift by resting in the heart of our own poverty, keeping our soul as far as possible empty of desires for all the things that please and preoccupy our nature, no matter how pure or sublime they may be in themselves.

And when God reveals Himself to us in contemplation we must accept Him as He comes to us, in His own obscurity, in His own silence, not interrupting Him with arguments or words, conceptions or activities that belong to the level of our own tedious and labored existence.

We must respond to God's gifts gladly and freely with thanksgiving, happiness and joy: but in contemplation we thank Him less by words than by the serene happiness of silent acceptance. "Be empty and see that I am God." It is our emptiness in the presence of the abyss of His reality, our silence in the presence of His infinitely rich silence, our joy in the bosom of the serene darkness in which His light holds us absorbed, it is all this that praises Him. It is this that causes love of God and wonder and adoration to swim up into us like tidal waves out of the depths of that peace, and break upon the shores of our consciousness in a vast, hushed surf of inarticulate praise, praise and glory!

This clear darkness of God is the purity of heart Christ spoke of in the sixth Beatitude, *Beati mundo corde, quoniam ipsi Deum videbunt.* And this purity of heart brings at least a momentary deliverance from images and concepts, from the forms and shadows of all the things men desire with their human appetites. It brings deliverance even from the feeble and delusive analogies we ordinarily use to arrive at God—not that it denies them, for they are true as far as they go, but it makes them temporarily useless by fulfilling them all in the sure grasp of a deep and penetrating experience.

In the vivid darkness of God within us there sometimes come deep movements of love that deliver us entirely, for a moment, from our old burden of selfishness, and number us among those little children of whom is the Kingdom of Heaven.

And when God allows us to fall back into our own confusion of desires and judgments and temptations, we carry a scar over the place where that joy exulted for a moment in our hearts.

The scar burns us. The sore wound aches within us, and we remember that we have fallen back into what we are not, and are not yet allowed to remain where God would have us belong. We long for the place He has destined for us and weep with desire for the time when this pure poverty will catch us and hold us in its liberty and never let us go, when we will never fall back from the Paradise of the simple and the little children into the forum of prudence where the wise of this world go up and down in sorrow and set their traps for a happiness that cannot exist.

This is the gift of understanding: we pass out of ourselves into the joy of emptiness, of nothingness, in which there are no longer any particular objects of knowledge but only God's truth without limit, without defect, without stain. This clean light, which tastes of Paradise, is beyond all pride, beyond comment, beyond proprietorship, beyond solitude. It is in all, and for all. It is the true light that shines in everyone, in "every man coming into this world." It is the light of Christ, "Who stands in the midst of us and we know Him not."

CHAPTER THIRTY-NINE

The General Dance

. . . What is serious to men is often very trivial in the sight of God. What in God might appear to us as "play" is perhaps what He Himself takes most seriously. At any rate the Lord plays and diverts Himself in the garden of His creation, and if we could let go of our own obsession with what we think is the meaning of it all, we might be able to hear His call and follow Him in His mysterious, cosmic dance. We do not have to go very far to catch echoes of that game, and of that dancing. When we are alone on a starlit night; when by chance we see the migrating birds in autumn descending on a grove of junipers to rest and eat; when we see children in a moment when they are really children; when we know love in our own hearts; or when, like the Japanese poet Bashō we hear an old frog land in a quiet pond with a solitary splash—at such times the awakening, the turning inside out of all values, the "newness," the emptiness and the purity of vision that make themselves evident, provide a glimpse of the cosmic dance.

For the world and time are the dance of the Lord in emptiness. The silence of the spheres is the music of a wedding feast. The more we persist in misunderstanding the phenomena of life, the more we analyze them out into strange finalities and complex purposes of our own, the more we involve ourselves in sadness, absurdity and despair. But it does not matter much, because no despair of ours can alter the reality of things, or stain the joy of the cosmic dance which is always there. Indeed, we are in the midst of it, and it is in the midst of us, for it beats in our very blood, whether we want it to or not.

Yet the fact remains that we are invited to forget ourselves on purpose, cast our awful solemnity to the winds and join in the general dance.

SELECTED BIBLIOGRAPHY

TEXTS

Contemplative Prayer. New York: Herder and Herder; London: Darton, Longmans and Todd, 1969.

New Seeds of Contemplation. New York: New Directions, 1962; London: Burns and Oates, 1964.

Seeds of Contemplation. New York: New Directions, 1949; London: Burns and Oates, 1957.

The Seven Storey Mountain. New York: Harcourt, Brace and Company, 1948; London: Sheldon, 1978.

A Thomas Merton Reader. Edited by Thomas P. McDonnell. Rev. ed. Garden City, N.Y.: Doubleday, Image Books, 1974.

STUDIES

Breit, Marquita E., and Robert E. Daggy. *Thomas Merton: A Comprehensive Bibliography.* New York and London: Garland, 1986.

Furlong, Monica. *Merton: A Biography.* San Francisco: Harper and Row; London: Collins, 1980.

Hart, Patrick, ed. *Thomas Merton, Monk: A Monastic Tribute.* New York: Sheed and Ward, 1974.

Kramer, Victor A. *Thomas Merton.* Twayne's United States Authors Series. Boston: Twayne, 1984.

Mott, Michael. *The Seven Mountains of Thomas Merton.* Boston: Houghton Mifflin, 1984.

Padovano, Anthony T. *The Human Journey—Thomas Merton: Symbol of a Century.* Garden City, N.Y.: Doubleday, 1982.

Teahan, John F. "A Dark and Empty Way: Thomas Merton and the Apophatic Tradition." *The Journal of Religion* 58 (1978): 263–87.

Henri Le Saux (Abhishiktananda)

(1910–1973)

Like so many of the Christian mystics of earlier centuries, Henri Le Saux drew extensively on sources outside his own Judeo-Christian tradition. For him, however, these were not primarily the Western sources of Platonic or Neoplatonic philosophy but rather the advaitic ("non-dualistic") doctrine of the Indian Upanishads. More exactly, it was not advaitic doctrine but advaitic *experience* which gave special impetus to Le Saux's sometimes anguished attempts to live out what he called the drama of "the coexistence of the Upanishads and the Gospel . . . within the same heart."[1] He was himself the first to admit that much of what he wrote was provisional, a first, groping attempt to articulate a Christian approach to advaitic experience, but he was equally certain of his calling to reveal something of India's potentially rich contribution to the Christian mystical tradition. In our day, when so much is being written about dialogue among the world's great religious traditions, it seems fitting to conclude our anthology with selections from one of the most important pioneers in this endeavor.

Born in Brittany on August 30, 1910, Henri Le Saux expressed at an early age the desire to become a priest and so entered the local minor seminary at the age of ten. Later, at the major seminary in Rennes, his superiors found him to be so promising a student that they wished to send him on to Rome for theological studies. Feeling called to the monastic life, Le Saux instead joined the Benedictine community at the Abbey of St. Anne in Kergonan. He made his solemn profession and was ordained to the priesthood in 1935 and for several years served in the monastery as a professor of Church history and later of patristics. But even before making his solemn vows and being ordained, the young monk had felt a desire to go to India and live there a strictly contemplative form of life. As the desire persisted, his abbot gave him permission in 1945 to initiate inquiries as to how it could be fulfilled. Having learned through a magazine article of the life that Fr. Jules Monchanin

---

1. Henri Le Saux, Letter to Fr. J. Lemarié, quoted by Odette Baumer-Despeigne, "The Spiritual Journey of Henri Le Saux—Abhishiktananda," *Cistercian Studies* 18 (1983): 317.

was already leading in India, Le Saux entered into correspondence with him and eventually joined him in South India toward the end of 1948.[2]

Together the two priests founded a Christian ashram along the banks of the Kavery River in Tamil Nadu. Le Saux called the ashram Shantivanam ("forest of peace") and soon took for himself the name Abhishiktananda ("bliss of the anointed one"). Shortly after arriving in India, Le Saux also accompanied Monchanin on a visit to the sacred mountain of Arunachala to meet the Indian sage Sri Ramana Maharshi. So profoundly impressed was Le Saux by this meeting and by the contemplative spirit of the place that even after Sri Ramana's death in 1950 he often returned to Arunachala to live as a Christian hermit in one or another of the caves on the mountain. It was here that his first great spiritual breakthrough occurred, described by him years later in the following words: "Step by step I descended into what seemed to me to be successive depths of my true self—my being, my awareness of being, and my joy in being. Finally nothing was left but he himself, the Only One, infinitely alone, Being, Awareness, and Bliss, Saccidananda. In the heart of Saccidananda I had returned to my source."[3]

After Monchanin's death in 1957, Le Saux became less and less interested in the

Shantivanam ashram and began spending more and more time in the northern part of the country in and near the Himalayas. Finally, in 1968 he entrusted the ashram to an English monk, Dom Bede Griffiths, and began living as a wandering *sannyasi*. During these years of the late 1960s and early 1970s, Abhishiktananda was at times actively engaged in helping the Catholic Church in India adapt the directives of the Second Vatican Council to its own particular situation, but at other times he lived in complete solitude in the heart of the Himalayas. Although he maintained a regular correspondence with several relatives and friends back in France and continued to publish some articles and books, he also had a keen sense of the inadequacy of his words. As he once wrote in a letter to his sister: "Why am I writing again? What I have to communicate is passed on with difficulty through words and not at all through books. People are on the lookout for ideas, and I should like to make them feel that what they need is to keep silence. The Spirit only makes himself heard by those who humbly abide in silence."[4]

On July 14, 1973, Abhishiktananda was stricken by a severe heart attack as he was about to board a bus in the city of Rishikesh. Both in his letters and in the journal entries that he wrote during the following months, it is clear that this occurrence was for him the vehicle of a great spiritual awakening, a renewal of life. Upon recovering his power of speech after the attack, his first words were: "It is beautiful, I cannot tell you how beautiful it is! Simply to open

2. Jules Monchanin was a priest of the archdiocese of Lyons who left France in 1939 in order to found in India an ashram dedicated to the contemplative life. The best introduction to Monchanin in English is *In Quest of the Absolute: The Life and Works of Jules Monchanin*, ed. J. G. Weber (Kalamazoo, Mich.: Cistercian Pubs., 1977).

3. Abhishiktananda, *Saccidananda: A Christian Approach to Advaitic Experience*, rev. ed. (Delhi: ISPCK, 1984), 172.

4. Quoted by Odette Baumer-Despeigne, "The Spiritual Journey of Henri Le Saux—Abhishiktananda," 326.

one's eyes on where one is!" And a month later he wrote to a friend: "Of the two weeks spent in bed I recall nothing but intense joy. It was a tremendous surprise but also a unique experience, this awakening to the Real in the unity of the Spirit."[5] Abhishiktananda died several months later, on December 7, 1973, and was buried in the cemetery of the Divine Word Fathers at Dolda.

Our selections from the writings of Abhishiktananda are taken from the fourteenth and fifteenth chapters of what is generally considered his most important work, *Saccidananda,* originally published in Paris in 1965 under the title *Sagesse hindoue, mystique chrétienne.* His familiarity with the Fathers of the Church and their mysticism of the image—a familiarity dating from his professorial years at Kergonan—is evident in these selections, but just as evident is his sense of the danger of becoming trapped by theological concepts and so missing what he calls "the momentous secret" of the Christian revelation: "If I am the image of God, this is true not only because I can discover in myself some analogies to the divine processions; it is true primarily because the Son reveals himself in me and lives in me, because the divine generation and the divine life are operative in me to my very depths."[6] He goes on to say that in India this image of God in the depths of the human heart has been given the name *Saccidananda,* a compound form composed of the Sanskrit terms *sat* ("being"), *cit* ("awareness"), and *ananda* ("bliss"). For Abhishiktananda, this ancient word signifies both the innermost mystery of God as

such and also the mystery of the divine presence in the depths of our own being. As he explains it, in these depths we may come to an awareness *(cit)* that our own being and existence *(sat)* is taken up into the simplicity and absoluteness of pure Being, and when this pure self-awareness has been sufficiently realized, "it is as if the whole being were flooded with an inexpressible sense of compassion, peace, joy and fullness, the *ananda* of Hindu tradition."[7]

Abhishiktananda admits, however, that this experience as transmitted by Hindu tradition may give the impression of being essentially monistic and static if it is considered in the light of the Christian experience of the Trinity. The special contribution of the latter experience is the revelation that being is essentially "being-with," communion, the mutual communication of love; that self-awareness comes to be only when there is mutual giving and receiving; and that supreme felicity cannot be a solitary bliss, since it is the fruit of love and therefore arises only in communication.

Elsewhere in his major work, Abhishiktananda correlates the three Persons of the Trinity with the three elements in the Sanskrit term: in *sat* is revealed the Father, the absolute source of being; in *cit* is disclosed the Son, the Father's self-knowledge; and in *ananda* is manifested the Spirit of love, who is endless fullness and bliss. Within the confines of this anthology it is not possible to reproduce his full discussion of these correlations and of the ways in which the term *Saccidananda* can help one meditate on the central mystery of the Christian faith. We hope that our selections from the

5. *Ibid.,* 328.
6. Abhishiktananda, *Saccidananda,* 165.
7. *Ibid.,* 170.

writings of this mystic will lead the reader to study his works at greater length. But even further reading will not, of itself, enable one to grasp the essential point which Abhishiktananda makes throughout his writings, a point in which he stands in agreement with the apophatic mystics of all times and places:

> As long as God—or the Mystery—is led back to the name that a group of humans give to Him or to the notion of Him fashioned by them, as long as His unnameableness is still a concept, an idea—the apophatism of theology—it is quite difficult for the be-liever . . . to recognize everywhere the total mystery of this Presence. Only when the soul has undergone the experience that the Name beyond all names can be pronounced only in the silence of the Spirit, does it become capable of that total openness which permits one to perceive the mystery in its sign.[8]

For Henri Le Saux, Abhishiktananda, India's gift to the Church is precisely this call to the profoundest depth of silence.

---

8. Henri Le Saux, *The Eyes of Light* (Denville, N.J.: Dimension Books, 1983), 43.

Selections

SACCIDANANDA*

Chapter Fourteen

THE IMAGE OF GOD

The heavens were not made in God's image, nor was the sun, nor the stars. You alone are a copy of the Being who is above all thought, a similitude of the incorruptible Beauty, and a reflection of the true Light. As you gaze at the Light, you are transformed into it, for its brightness shines in you, reflected in your purity . . . He who has cleansed the eye of his soul beholds in his own beauty the image of the divine nature . . . He deserves to be called blessed, because in gazing at his own beauty he beholds therein the very Pattern . . .

By scouring our spirit through the teaching of the virtues, God polishes the stone and gives it a brilliant finish, that is to say, he forms in us the image of Virtue itself, namely Christ, in whose image we have been created and which we have to become once more.

Gregory of Nyssa

Man is made in the image of God. This is one of the basic teachings of Holy Scripture, contained in the very first chapter of Genesis. Though in the first place it conveys a message about man himself and is intended to make him aware of his preeminent place in creation, it also teaches him something about God. If man is really made in the image of God, then it will be through knowing himself as he most truly is that he will be enabled to discover at least something of the mystery of him whose image he is. The beauty of his body and the nobility of his mind are ultimately nothing but reflections of the uncreated Beauty and Light. His faculties, his organs, even the shape of his body, are all in some sort an ikon of the Creator; and because of this, man is well advised to look at himself, and then in the silence of adoration to contemplate and wonder at the divine image in himself. But valuable as is such contemplation, man is far more truly called to enter into the deepest recesses of his soul and there to find the image of his God; for there in his depths he will discern at the same time his own mystery and that of his Creator and Father.

The theme of the Image was a great inspiration to the Doctors of the early Church. In particular, Gregory of Nyssa found it an effective instrument in christianizing the

*From Abhishiktananda, *Saccidananda: A Christian Approach to Advaitic Experience,* rev. ed. (Delhi, I.S.P.C.K., 1984), 163–77. Reprinted with permission of the Abhishiktananda Society, Delhi.

intuitions of Plotinus. Even today the theology of the Eastern Church is very much aware of it and derives much enlightenment from it.

Even apart from the biblical revelation this truth had already been glimpsed by man through reason and spiritual intuition, and philosophers made use of it in Greece as well as in India. However the human intelligence could not truly understand and assimilate the mystery of the Image, so long as the Spirit had not directly disclosed it to men. In India the Image was no more than a fleeting reflection of the divine, with no real stability, like a ray of light which is destined to be re-absorbed ultimately in the source from which it came. In Greece it was an idea, *eidos,* belonging only to the world of concepts. Furthermore, man misused the knowledge that had been given him and, as Paul says, too often made his own representations of God out of ideas conceived in his mind and idols fashioned by his hands. He lacked the good sense and humility to stand in silence before the mystery, open to the Spirit and simply attending to the reflection of the divine glory which was presented to him in his heart, his mind, his body and even in natural objects and natural forces.

Furthermore there could be no final truth in these partial reflections which man glimpsed in the mirror of creation. However glorious they seemed at first to be, they soon ran the risk of becoming deceptive symbols, quite incapable of leading him to the Real itself. Indeed, what real sense could there be in speaking of the 'image' of the One who is essentially above all form? Further, unless one is to misrepresent the true nature of God, God's 'image' can only be God himself. If anything else is taken as God's image, then his true nature is obscured and lost—and that is idolatry in either a crude or a subtle form. On the other hand, if man really discovers God at the centre of his own being, at the centre of all beings, then automatically there is no more any image, it simply vanishes. For there is no place to be found, either in man himself or anywhere else, where he can preserve his own individuality or the reality of creation, once they are seen in the light of the divine glory.

The Eternal Image

The words of Genesis, and equally the intuitions of the sages, could only be understood fully by the human mind when the Spirit had let man into the secret that the true Image of God is only to be found in the bosom of God himself. Only the divine consubstantial Word, who proceeds from the Father in unity of majesty and holiness, is the one who reflects the glory of God and bears the very stamp of his nature (Heb. 1:3).

It is in this eternal Image, and indeed as the image of this Image, that man has been created. This is rightly understood only by those who have learnt from the

Spirit the secret that they are 'born of God' (John 1:13, etc.). Man is not an image of the divine located in some inconceivable manner outside God. His existence springs from the very heart of the Trinitarian mystery. In the eternal Word he is a true word of God. In the eternal Image he is a genuine image of God. In God's Holy One he is himself holy. In God's Glory he is glorious, a living song of praise to God, a true *doxo-logy*. In the mutual presence to each other of the Father and the Son he is himself present to the Father's presence in him.

St Augustine made full use of his vast intellect in his attempt to discern in man's higher faculties a resemblance and analogy to the threefold relationship which constitutes the Trinity, and thus paved the way to the further refinements of scholasticism on which Latin theology still depends. Yet this whole enterprise seems somewhat lacking in boldness. It moves more or less within the limits of the Old Testament vision of God as a distant God, whose image, even in oneself, is not to be contemplated except in a mirror which is somehow 'external' to the Reality reflected in it. Its viewpoint does not seem to have fully integrated the momentous secret that Jesus revealed to his disciples. If I am the image of God, this is true, not only because I can discover in myself some analogies to the divine processions; it is true primarily because the Son reveals himself in me and lives in me, because the divine generation and the divine life are operative in me to my very depths.

Creation's call to exist is included within the procession of the Son. The call to be could not have come about either within the mystery of the Father, the unoriginate Origin, the absolute Beginning, or within the mystery of the Spirit, the absolute Finality, the ultimate Consummation of Being. Only in the mystery of the Second Person could the manifestation of the divine mercy be located. The entire Trinity is certainly present in the mystery of the Son, yet it is as the Image of the Father that the Son manifests the glory of the Trinity. It is also as the image of the Father within the Son, the eternal Image, that man reflects the same glory. Only in the Son does he realize his calling to be 'in the image and likeness of God'.

This is why it was the Son who became incarnate. It is in Christ, the incarnate Word, that the world has its being, so that all creation is a Christophany. By virtue of being a Christophany, and for no other reason, the world and all that it contains is a Theophany, a manifestation of God. This it is within the eternal manifestation of the glory which the Son possessed before the world was (John 17:5).

All of us who have been called in Christ pre-exist in an ineffable manner from all eternity in the Person of the Son (Eph. 1:4). Our call is to share in his own glory at its very source in the heart of God. Creation is not a supplement, an afterthought, something as it were added on to God after the Trinity had come to perfect expression in the procession of the Spirit. There is but one indivisible and unique divine act of trinitarian expansion in which Christ—and with him the whole universe, his plērōma—comes to be.

The Father is the original source of the image of God which man is in the Son, a source which reveals itself in the innermost heart of this image. There too the Spirit also is revealed, not as source but as perfection and fulfilment of the image. In fact the Spirit makes himself known everywhere as an irresistible call to the final perfection of all creation in the unity of God. His grace is the mighty 'indrawing' of the Breath of God which sweeps through all things from the beginning of the world to the *eschaton,* gathering up everything in heaven and earth. In the Spirit is finally consummated the mystery of God. In him the mystery of the Whole Christ, Christ in himself and in all creation, is fulfilled and consummated. The Spirit is also the Kingdom, according to the ancient patristic interpretation of the Lord's Prayer. The Spirit fills all things (Wisdom 1:7)—fills all with himself, for he is the *Self* of God, his ultimate interiority and truth. Beyond the Spirit there is nothing. He is the Fullness which fills all things, so that God may be all in all (1 Cor. 15:28). Thus it is in the Spirit that Christ—the total Christ including the Church, his Spouse and his plērōma—is the one and only eternal Image of the splendour and glory of God.

The Intuition of Saccidananda

This image of God in the depths of the human heart has been given in India the name of *Saccidananda.*

The expression 'Saccidananda' seems to have arisen spontaneously from the heart of India's seers, when they tried to find some way of referring to the mystery which they intuited beyond the range of thought. The welcome given to this term in the tradition undoubtedly proves its affinity with the Hindu soul. It is another sign that in India the Spirit is waiting for the Christian to claim his inheritance in this tradition, in order to throw open for him the door of his most secret abode.

The origins of the Sanskrit term 'Saccidananda' are very ancient. Even in the Upanishads primitive forms of it are found, and for many hundreds of years it has been accepted in the spiritual vocabulary of India as one of the best symbols for the innermost mystery of God himself, so far at least as man is capable of stammering about it. But equally it signifies the mystery of the divine presence in the innermost sanctuary of man's being. God's presence to himself and his presence to me—these two mysteries cannot be separated, as the presence is at the same time twofold and also unique, as Indian sages have well understood. God is the soul's guest; or rather, he is the one who makes himself present in me, so that I may be at home with him.

Indeed, in the last resort, his presence in me or to me is nothing else than his own presence to himself.

*   *   *

In my own depth, beyond all perceiving, all thought, all consciousness of distinction, there is the fundamental intuition of my being, which is so pure that it cannot be adequately described. It is precisely here that I meet God, in the mystery at once of my own being and of his. This in fact is the *sat* on which the Upanishadic seers made their meditations. In the last resort, what can I say of myself except that 'I am', as we are powerfully reminded by the experience which came to Ramana Maharshi as a youth? Just so, all that I can truly say of God is simply that 'He is'. This is what was revealed to Moses at Horeb, and it was also realized intuitively by the rishis:

> It is only by saying 'He is'
> that one may reach him! (*Katha Up.* 6, 12).

'He is'—nothing more can be said of him. He simply is, because he is. When my consciousness is pure enough to give a perfect reflection, then pure being, *sat,* mysteriously and inexorably reveals itself in me in its utter simplicity; indeed, it not merely discloses itself to me, but it also takes me up into its own simplicity and absoluteness. It makes me realize that my very being and existence is nothing other than its own being and existence. And yet this *sat,* for all that it is the deepest reality of every creature, remains infinitely beyond any of them. Nothing can hold it. It is for ever beyond the reach of any attempt to define it, or to think or speak of it. In its very immanence it is infinitely transcendent.

Sat is also *satyam,* truth, because being and the true are identical. Truth is the unveiling (cp. Greek *a-letheia*) of Being, of the Real, both in itself and in me. It is in the *sat* that I myself also am real and true, real with its reality and true with its truth, for what can subsist apart from it? No truth or reality can be outside it.

I am, and I can know that I am. This is the whole mystery of the human consciousness, the *cit* of Hindu tradition. Indeed, from the beginning nature contained within itself the potentiality of this self-awareness, which acted as a hidden force in promoting the development of the cosmic process. Finally in man the universe attained to self-awareness, the presence of the self to itself, in which alone *sat* becomes luminous and resplendent (if one may put it so) within itself. This does not mean that *sat* knows itself, in the ordinary sense of the word. Neither Plotinus nor the

Upanishadic seers would allow us to assert this; but one cannot deny that there exists a mystery of 'superknowledge', of pure awareness of self ('a simple intuition with regard to Itself,' as Plotinus says), of nothing-but-*cit*. This is the self-manifestation of *sat* in the most inward centre of the spirit, which as it reveals itself ever more clearly, becomes ever more impossible to grasp, even further beyond the power of the tongue to describe or the mind to comprehend.

In the mirror of pure awareness of myself I discover the mystery of *cit* in itself, that is, the non-reflective presence of the self to itself, the light that depends on no source, but shines with its own radiance and by its shining makes all things luminous:

> There the sun shines not, nor the moon, nor the stars . . .
> It shines itself, and after it all else shines,
> all things become luminous in its light
> *(Mundaka Up. 2,2,10).*

It is pure awareness, maintaining itself with no object to support or assist it. It is like a crystal which always reflects itself alone. It is the source and point of emergence of all consciousness, and at the same time the fullness and ultimate goal of all knowledge.

The Taittiriya Upanishad, instead of *cit,* prefers the term *jnana* (wisdom, *gnosis*):

> He who knows Brahman as truth *(satyam),* wisdom *(jnana)* and infinitude *(anantam),* hidden in the cave *(guha)* of the heart, in the highest heaven, attains all desires (2, 1).

The term 'wisdom' will certainly seem more meaningful than *cit* to those whose minds are formed in the Greek or Hebrew traditions. But it is well not to be beguiled by its superficial connotations, but rather to press on to the core of its transcendent meanings.

The awareness that shines in my depth is not anything that I might call my own, and treat as a personal possession. For that would immediately re-introduce a dualism, and that would be the end of that pure and ineffable awareness. Who could possibly 'possess' being, *sat?* Who could 'possess' the inward self-manifestation of *sat,* which is *cit,* the presence of *sat* to itself? Being, *sat,* simply is; it does not 'have' anything, and it cannot be 'had' by anything whatever. *Sat* and *cit,* being and awareness of being, cannot be 'other' to each other; their relationship is irreducibly non-dual, an *advaita. Cit,* the awareness that I am, which I reach in my innermost depth, is not an attribute of *sat;* it actually is itself *sat.* In Being's presence to itself, I am present to myself, aware of myself; there I am, and I am aware that I am.

Essential Bliss

For St. Gregory of Nyssa the yardstick of man's blessedness is the extent of his resemblance to God. Bliss is to gain access to the Original through beholding the image in the mirror of a pure heart.

So also for India's seers, bliss is to arrive at the final secret of the self, at the very point where man returns again to his Source and there discovers his own ultimate truth. When indeed pure self-awareness has been sufficiently realized, it is as if the whole being were flooded with an inexpressible sense of completion, peace, joy and fullness, the *ananda* of Hindu tradition. Every desire and every need find their satisfaction—indeed, they are both fulfilled and transcended. At that point a man forgets his existential anguish, his terror of not-being, the source of all his anxiety and fears. All inner disharmony is quieted in the transcendent unity of being and of being aware of being.

It is a wholeness which at the same time is infinity—*ananda* which is *an-anta* (endless), according to the expression which preceded that of *saccidananda.* Bliss and fullness indeed cannot but be infinite. That alone is true joy and peace, complete felicity, which cannot be impaired by the passage of time and is in itself without end. When I awake to the Real in the depth of my self-awareness, all limits, all death, time itself, are for ever transcended. I am for ever established in my own centre, in the very centre of all things, in the *ananda* of *cit* and *sat,* in the perfect bliss of Being and of Being's awareness of itself.

It is equally impossible to say of *ananda,* the infinite bliss which wells up at the very source of my being, that it is 'mine', as it is to say this of being *(sat)* or of the awareness of being *(cit).* That would again involve a duality, and would immediately cause the bliss to vanish. *Ananda* is, if possible, even further beyond the grasp of either sense or thought than are *sat* and *cit.* I may know that it is present; but if I try to look at it, it has already disappeared. It slips quietly away from anyone who tries to approach it. The mind only recognizes it when it is gone. Yet that which it leaves behind at the moment of vanishing, is like an all-pervasive yet indescribable perfume, a flavour which takes away the taste of everything else. Only by going beyond everything that I can call my own, can I taste—though it is not I that taste it—the savour of my ultimate depth. This is the bliss of simple being; and I am this very bliss, this *ananda,* since I *am.* Bliss is not something that I might grasp hold of to make it mine. If I try to make it mine, I destroy its infinite character. I should only succeed in seizing a limited happiness, measured by my capacity to feel and think.

Ananda itself, the ultimate expression of *cit* and of *sat,* is beyond all measure. It draws me irresistibly into its own infinitude, to my own deepest centre, to the very heart of Being and of Being's Presence to itself. . . .

* * *

In my own innermost centre, in the most secret mirror of my heart, I tried to discover the image of him whose I am, of him who lives and reigns in the infinite space *(akasa)* of my heart. But the reflected image gradually grew faint, and soon it was swallowed up in the radiance of its Original. Step by step I descended into what seemed to me to be successive depths of my true self—my being, my awareness of being, and my joy in being. Finally nothing was left but he himself, the Only One, infinitely alone, Being, Awareness and Bliss, Saccidananda. In the heart of Saccidananda I had returned to my Source.

'Tat tvam asi,' 'You are That!' were the last words I heard before I fell asleep in the slumber of Being, before I 'laid me down and slept . . . ' (Psalm 3:5).

> He gazed at the image
> in himself;
> but the image vanished
> in the Self;
> nothing remained of my gazing—
> only That which was gazed at . . .

Chapter Fifteen

AT THE HEART OF THE TRINITY

The night is far spent and the day is at hand
It is time for you to wake from sleep. (Rom 13:12, 11)

I am going to awaken him. (John 11:11)

Awake, you who are sleeping,
and rise from the dead;
and Christ will give you light. (Eph. 5:14)

The experience of Saccidananda which has been transmitted by Hindu tradition is undoubtedly one of the loftiest peaks of spirituality to which man can aspire.

When however it is considered in the light of Christian experience of the Trinity, it may give the impression of being essentially monistic and of terminating in unbroken silence. This would also appear to be the case with the OM, or *pranava,* which is its perfect symbol.[1]

When all man's faculties are stilled and even thought ceases, he passes into a kind of death, of which the sign is the silent fourth part of OM, where every conceivable sound is left behind. But what appears in human eyes to be the stillness of death is not a real death. Even if in a sense it is a void, it is also a fullness. However, within this silent immobility it may be difficult to recognize the presence of Life; and for the Christian, God has revealed himself in the Bible as 'the living God'—first in the Old Testament showing himself as ceaselessly concerned with man and in communication with him, and then in Jesus laying bare his inner mystery as an infinite overflow and exchange of life and love. In contrast OM is 'enstatic', and seems to draw all things into an eternal silence and stillness that is for ever shut in upon itself.

Paschal Awakening

But Being is essentially a call to life; in its inward stillness it is a surging energy!

When the Christian awakes from the advaitic experience and from the apparent sleep in which all consciousness of himself had faded away in the overwhelming awareness of Saccidananda, he finds himself contemplating Saccidananda as if from within, and at the same time rediscovers himself and all things. Hitherto he had tried to penetrate the mystery of being, awareness and bliss as from outside, but the mystery withstood him like an adamantine wall. He was caught in a dilemma: either he clung to an impossible dualism, imagining himself as an 'other'; or, when he experienced the incomprehensible but inevitable non-duality, his individual self vanished and was lost in an apparent fusion of identity. This meant that he could only sink into a profound sleep, *susupti,*[2] in which he was no longer conscious of anything whatever: 'I laid me down and slept ... ' *(ego dormivi et soporatus sum . . .),* according to the mysterious vision of the Psalmist (3:5).

However the Psalmist also prophesied an awakening from this slumber, from all

---

1. The syllable OM has come down to us from the most ancient Vedic times. It is India's supreme mantra, the most sacred sound of all. According to Indian ideas, it is composed of three—or rather, four—elements, united in a single sound, the fourth and last element being pure silence. In origin it must have been regarded as the simplest possible sound, composed of the vowel A combined with U to make O, and prolonged with a nasal after-sound, M. Since OM comes near to the utmost limit of what can be uttered or heard, it is better fitted than any other sound to express the bankruptcy of word and thought when the mind is directly presented with the ineffable mystery of God.

2. *Susupti*—profound or dreamless sleep, "when, asleep, one desires no desire and sees no dream, [having become] unified, a mere mass of cognition" *(Mandukya Up.* 5).

slumber: ' . . . and (I) rose up again, for the Lord sustained me' *(et exsurrexi quia Dominus suscepit me).*

Only the Lord in fact is capable of raising man from this slumber. This he does through his Word, which calls nothingness to be (Rom 4:17) and the dead to live (John 5:25; 11:43), in that mighty 'shaking' which marks the birth of the new creation. This awakening however takes place in the very heart of Saccidananda which is its source. Then the heavens behind which God had hitherto seemed to hide himself, the veil of emptiness and unknowing which enveloped the man who had direct experience of the Absolute, these at last are torn wide open (Mark 1:10; Luke 3:21)—as happened at the Lord's baptism, again at his transfiguration, and finally and for ever in the glory of his ascension.

The Lord's chosen one then advances from depth to depth, to inner centre after inner centre, in the mystery of Being, in the mystery of his being himself, for in this unfathomable abyss there is no last level. Gregory of Nyssa refers to this drawing of the soul ever onwards as *'epektasis',* and says that it will continue without end through an eternity of ages: 'He who ascends never stops, as he passes from one beginning to another, in an endless series of beginnings.' But it is a real progress from inwardness to inwardness to which he is called. From the bosom of Being itself he will contemplate Being and Truth, Wisdom and the Word, beholding what he *is* with an ineffable *awareness* of being in the *bliss* of the Spirit, *sat-cit-ananda.*

The 'cave of the heart' in which he now dwells is the Son's own abode. It is as a son himself that he receives in the Son an entirely new gift of pure grace—the Christian experience of Saccidananda. In the rising again of the Risen Lord he awakes to himself and recovers himself. With the Lord's own life he lives and in his bliss he shares.

This overwhelming awareness is unlike anything he could even imagine before the great sleep had enveloped him and carried him off into its depths. The sleep itself was a necessary precondition of his awakening and was pregnant with great promises, like the sleep of Adam from which Eve came into being, and like Christ's sleep on the Cross from which the Church was born—both signs of the Father's own mystery in which Being awoke to itself.

Now that the Christian jnani has penetrated to the heart of Saccidananda and experiences his 'connaturality' with God,[3] the Spirit of Wisdom makes known to him his last secrets. He now knows—

that Being, *sat,* opens itself at its very source to give birth eternally to the Son,

---

3. According to Thomas Aquinas (*Summa Theol.* II-II, 45, 2), it is through some kind of connaturality that man's spirit judges the things of God when he is moved by the Spirit of Wisdom, *non solum discens sed patiens divina,* "not only learning the things of God, but feeling, experiencing them," in the words of Dionysius the Areopagite (*Divine Names* 2).

and in him to countless creatures, each of which in its own way will for ever manifest and celebrate the infinite love and mercy of God;

that being is essentially 'being-with', communion, koinonia, the free gift of the self and the mutual communication of love;

that self-awareness, *cit,* only comes to be when there is mutual giving and receiving, for the *I* only awakes to itself in a *Thou;*

that the supreme and ultimate felicity, *ananda,* is fullness and perfect fulfilment, only because it is the fruit of love, for being *is* love. There cannot be a solitary bliss, any more than there can be solitary being or solitary self-awareness. There is no joy, as there is no being, except in communication, in giving and receiving.

All this is not merely a matter of knowledge to the jnani; he lives by it, he lives it, he is it. In the heart of Saccidananda there is no divisiveness, nothing withheld or concealed from the whole.

However, while abiding in the heart of Saccidananda, the jnani has not been swallowed up 'like a drop of water in the ocean', to quote a much overworked simile. The richness of Saccidananda consists precisely in the communication of its richness; its glory is the communication of glory. This glory is given to each one and also given by each one. This very fact of receiving and giving is what constitutes each of God's chosen ones as a personal centre within the one centre of Saccidananda, and enables him to recognize himself within the boundless ocean of Being, Awareness and Bliss. He knows himself as one who receives from the Father in the Son, and from the Son in the Spirit, both in eternity and in each moment of time; and again, both in eternity and in each moment of time, he is the one who in return gives himself to all, and thereby in the Spirit returns to the Father.

The jnani is the acceptance of the gift of God—the God who in his infinite freedom has drawn him out of nothingness, and in his infinite mercy has rescued him from sin and death. In accepting God's gift of being and forgiveness, he in his turn is the gift of himself to God, pure availability to his Lord. In every fibre of his being and to the very core of his being he is all communion—communion with the Father, the Son and the Spirit, communion with each of God's creatures. At the same time, in the distinction which allows him to have communion with the only Son, he is the son who hears the loving address: 'You are my beloved child.' In the distinction through which he has communion with his fellow-men, he represents the entire world in its longing to see the face of the Lord, and represents the whole Church, the koinonia of love, which in him aspires to its final perfection and fullness at the Parousia. In the distinction which brings him in the Son face to face with the Father, he rests silently in the bosom of the Father in the non-duality of the Spirit.

SELECTED BIBLIOGRAPHY

TEXTS AND TRANSLATIONS

Some of the works listed below were written in English by Abhishiktananda himself (e.g., *Prayer* and *The Further Shore*). In other cases, he was directly involved in the translation from French into English (e.g., *Saccidananda*). The publishers do not give the name of the English translator in the case of books published posthumously (e.g., *The Eyes of Light*).

Ermites du saccidananda. Tournai and Paris, 1957. Co-authored with Jules Monchanin.

La montée au fond du coeur: Le journal intime du moine chrétien-sannyasi hindou, 1948–1973. Edited by R. Panikkar. Paris, 1986.

Sagesse hindoue, mystique chrétienne: Du Vedanta à la Trinité. Paris, 1965.

Souvenirs d'Arunachala. Paris, 1978.

Les yeux de lumière. Paris, 1979.

The Eyes of Light. Denville, N.J.: Dimension Books, 1983.

The Further Shore. Rev. ed. Delhi: I.S.P.C.K., 1984.

Prayer. Rev. ed. Philadelphia: Westminster, 1972.

Saccidananda: A Christian Approach to Advaitic Experience. Rev. ed. Delhi: I.S.P.C.K., 1984.

The Secret of Arunachala. Delhi: I.S.P.C.K., 1979.

STUDIES

Baumer-Despeigne, Odette. "The Spiritual Journey of Henri Le Saux-Abhishiktananda." *Cistercian Studies* 18 (1983): 310–29.

Davy, Marie-Madeleine. *Henri Le Saux, Swami Abhishiktananda: Le passeur entre deux rives.* Paris, 1981.

INDEX

Abel, 367
Abhishiktananda. *See* Henri Le Saux
Abraham, 41
Absolute, the (a divine appellative), 10, 78, 429
Abyss (a divine appellative), 247, 319
Acts, Book of, 68, 130, 390n.1
Adam, 70, 364, 411, 429
Aelred, Letter on (spiritual) Friendship, 15
agape, 47, 372
Alacoque, Margaret Mary. *See* Margaret Mary Alacoque
Albert the Great; Comm. on Mt. 5:3, 162
All (a divine appellative), 319, 332, 379
Alumbrados, 272
Alvarez, Balthasar, 254, 273
amor. *See* love
Anchorite/Anchoress. *See* p. 211
Andrew of Crete, Hom. 7, 199
Anselm, 352
Anthropomorphite monks, 28
Anti-Christ, 367
Apocalypse of John. See *Revelation*
Apophatic mysticism, 9, 46, 77, 136, 225, 405, 417; theology of, 153. *See* also, 194–210, 415–431
Arian heresy, 28, 45
Aristotle, 160n.2; *Metaphysics,* 305; *The Topics,* 167n.3, 171
Artificer (a divine appellative), 109
Ascetic(ism), 12, 14, 71, 96, 97, 99, 102. *See also* 162–164, 173, 225, 298–299. *See also* 304, 338, 350, 358, 360

Augustine, 5, 11–13, 59–76, 101, 119, 157, 272, 329, 341, 422; *Christian Doctrine,* 169n.8; *City of God,* 60; *Confessions,* 59, 60–61, 64–66, 167; *The Literal Meaning of Genesis,* 61, 71–75, 212; *On the Trinity* (De Trinitate), 11, 60–61, 67–71; *True Religion,* 169
Augustinian order, 173, 271, 394
Awareness (a divine appellative), 416, 427, 430

Balthasar, Hans Urs von, 28, 44, 58, 88, 90, 100, 393, 402
Barlaam, the Calabrian monk, 194, 206, 208
Bartholomew, the apostle, 84
Basho, Zenmaster, 406
Basil the Great, 45
Beatitudes, the, 405, 412; Gregory of Nyssa's Sermon on, 46, 50–54
Beatrijs of Nazareth, 20
Beauty (a divine appellative), 60, 66, 114, 134, 199, 420; Divine, 52
Beghines, 20, 351
Beginning, absolute (a divine appellative), 422
Being (a divine appellative), 11, 12, 54, 55, 57, 68, 78, 81, 135, 138, 152, 265, 269, 316, 347, 381, 416, 417, 424, 426–7, 428, 430; as-such, 152; divine, 142, 376; Mystery of, 429
Beloved (a divine appellative), 134, 281, 317–18
Benedictine order, 309